Development and Management of Counseling Programs and Guidance Services

Development and Management of Counseling Programs and Guidance Services

ROBERT L. GIBSON
Indiana University

MARIANNE H. MITCHELL
Indiana University

ROBERT E. HIGGINS
University of Toledo

MACMILLAN PUBLISHING CO., INC.
New York
COLLIER MACMILLAN PUBLISHERS
London

Printed in the United States of America

Macmillan Publishing Co., Inc.
866 Third Avenue, New York, New York 10022

Collier Macmillan Canada, Inc.

Library of Congress Cataloging in Publication Data

Gibson, Robert L.
Development and management of counseling programs and guidance services.

Includes index.
1. Personnel service in education. 2. Counseling.
I. Mitchell, Marianne. II. Higgins, Robert E.
III. Title.
LB1027.5.G457 1983 371.4 82-8998
ISBN 0-02-341770-6 AACR2

Printing: 5678 Year: 0

ISBN 0-02-341770-6

Dedicated to our good friend and distinguished educator

Dr. Douglas M. McIntosh, CBE, LLD, FRSE, FEIS

Former Principal, Moray House College of Education, Edinburgh, Scotland

and

Former Director of Education, Fife Co., Scotland

Preface

The effectiveness of school counseling and guidance programs and institution and agency programs as well is determined in large measure by three factors: (1) accurate environmental and target population needs assessment; (2) appropriate planning to serve the identified needs; and (3) effective program leadership and management. With these factors in mind, this book has been designed to give the reader an introduction to the development, management, and leadership of programs of counseling and guidance in both school and nonschool settings. We believe the approaches to program development suggested in this text provide a means of developing guidance programs that are more responsive to current needs.

Attention is also given to the differing nature of guidance programs at the various educational levels and the resulting implications for program development. The reader will also find many practical suggestions and illustrations for his/her use in developing and implementing effective programs of counseling and guidance in a variety of settings.

This text can be useful to both the beginning counselor, seeking to understand how she or he can contribute to the more effective development and operation of his or her program, and experienced directors or program managers who may profit from new concepts and practices. In addition, school administrators and teachers should find this publication helpful in understanding how effective counseling and guidance programs are developed and what their respective contributions and roles may be.

Acknowledgments

The authors wish to express appreciation to the many publishing companies and their authors for permission to quote from their published works.

In addition, we wish to thank the many educational institutions and associations and their personnel who have provided us with illustrations, case studies, organizational charts, and other materials. We also acknowledge the many practicing counselors and our own graduate students, whose helpful suggestions have been incorporated into this publication. We are especially grateful for the help received from our graduate assistants par excellence, Ms. Patricia McClain and Ms. Lynn Krebs, Indiana University, and Ms. Judith Brissette, University of Toledo. We benefited from the constructive reviews of Dr. Richard R. Stevic, State University of New York at Buffalo, and Dr. Dean L. Hummel, Virginia Polytechnic Institute, Blacksburg, Virginia. Finally, our appreciation to Macmillan Publishing Company and particularly to our editor, Mr. Lloyd C. Chilton, for his wise counsel.

Contents

Development and Management of Counseling Programs and Guidance Services

CHAPTER 1

Introduction

Introduction

This book is concerned with programs of counseling and guidance. It is specifically concerned with how such programs are developed and organized, managed and led, and evaluated. Although a major emphasis in the book is on schools, since this is the most popular setting for programs of counseling and guidance, considerable attention is also given to the application of materials and the functioning of programs in nonschool settings. We frequently refer to programs in school settings as programs of counseling and guidance, whereas in agency settings we discuss counseling programs. These tend to be the traditional labels for programs in these respective settings with the difference being that a "guidance" program refers to a series of general services of which counseling is the "core" or "ultimate" service, whereas a counseling program indicates an emphasis on counseling as the specialized service provided. "Counselors" are the trained professionals who staff these programs and because of the nature of services provided, counseling is appropriately designated as one of the "helping professions."

The Helping Professions

In any examination of a profession and the development of the programs of that profession, it is desirable initially to examine some basis or foundation from which such professional programs emanate. Since this book focuses on the development, management, and leadership of counseling programs, we begin by responding to the questions—What is the profession of counseling? and What is its basis of service to humankind?

In examining counseling as a profession we, therefore, begin with counseling as a helping profession; a concept that forms the basis for the role and function of the counselor in today's society. A "helping" profession may be described as one whose members are especially trained and licensed or certificated to perform a unique and needed service for the fellow human beings of their society. Helping professionals *serve;* they are recognized by the society as the sole professional providers of the unique and needed services. The helping professions include medicine, law, dentistry, education, psychology, and social work. Each of these professions has the roots of its development and existence in the nature of humankind and the nature of society, past and present. It is on these bases that services are determined and programs for providing these services are developed. The paragraphs that follow briefly review some of the basic concepts of humankind and society as a basis for the helping professions in general and the profession of counseling in particular.

Conceptions of Humankind and the Helping Professions

In the instance of the helping professions, including counseling, it is appropriate to begin with the very foundation of their existence—namely, the human client. This client has certain distinguishing characteristics that provide a basis for the profession of counseling and the institutions and agencies through which this profession contributes its special knowledge and skills to the development of peoples and societies. Although any attempt to characterize such a versatile and ever-changing species as the human being is fraught with peril, we have and do possess certain stable yet unique traits that set us apart from other living species. In the main these are what we might term the "privileges" of the human race. They provide not only the basis or focus of our "being" but for our "doing" as well. They also suggest roles that human beings can play in helping their fellow human beings. These distinguishing characteristics include the following.

- Humans are among the weakest species at birth. We are born *without* genetically imprinted behaviors possessed by many forms of life. Young animal life in the forests and jungles of the world can survive without adult help; young human life cannot. Our early survival—for years—is dependent solely on the attention, care, and affection of others. The human need for love and care and the degree to which it is provided becomes a critical basis for the lifelong adjustment or lack of it for the individual.
- Humankind has the greatest potential for growth and development of all the species. The brain itself triples in physical size, and multiplies even more in capacity. This brainpower, coupled with a surplus of energy (over all other species) gives us almost limitless possibilities. The realization of human potential does not, however, rest with the individual alone, but is dependent on many environmental variables *and* assistance in recognizing and developing one's potential.
- Humankind has the highest level of communication skills—skills that enable us to express our thoughts in detail to many others—skills to teach our language to others—even animal species at certain levels—skills which enable us to record—to send and receive. These dual capacities, sending and receiving, in both word *and* gesture, form the bases for human relationships skills and for love and affection, which in turn forms the primary stimulus for the human race! This ability to relate to others thus becomes the core of a happy, well-adjusted life.
- The human species exhibits a wider range of differences than any other. These differences not only clearly distinguish each human from every other human but also multiply the potential of the society and stimulate the advance-

ment of civilizations. The concept of individual differences provides the rationale for client analysis in the helping professions.

- The human species manipulates and is manipulated by his or her environment; thus the behavior of the human being cannot be adequately understood apart from the environmental context within which it occurs. Thus, environmental analysis is becoming increasingly important to the professional counselor.
- Humankind is the only living organism that captures the time stream. We can recall the past, act in the present, and plan for the future. This gives humans the capability for building on their past experiences, avoiding past mistakes, anticipating the future, and planning for the development of their potential.
- Humankind has the ability to reason and to gain insight. These twin factors enable us to make reasoned choices among alternatives and to change. This aptitude for planned individual change is significant in the important arenas of individual development and social adjustment (relationships with one's peers). Our ability to understand ourselves and act rationally also contributes to the maturing process.

From images of the human species, McCully (1969) drew inferences for counseling and other helping relationships as follows.

> 1. All men at birth possess the potential for the distinguishing characteristics of the human species; and 2. the environmental conditions the individual experiences from birth on may either nourish or suppress their realization. (pp. 134, 135)

In light of these premises it is appropriate to suggest at even this early point in our discussions that a fundamental basis for counseling program development must be rooted in our understanding of the characteristics of all our clientele, including their needs, plus an understanding of the environment that shapes their characteristics and needs.

It is also important to recognize the role of societal needs and expectancies in the development and functioning of a profession. The brief historical review that introduces the next section of this chapter indicates the influences of societal events on the shaping of professions.

Societal Needs and the Helping Professions

Down through the ages the needs and values of societies have been reflected in the institutions that served them and the occupations they supported. In the early tribal societies, preparation for life centered largely around learning the techniques for survival—hunting, fishing, the art of war, the providing of shelter and clothing. These activities were essential to the perpetuation of their societies. Later, as tribes merged to become empires or states, societal institutions were altered to meet the needs of their societies. For example, in the ninth century the Emperor Charlemagne felt the need to identify and educate the manpower talent of his empire as a means of protecting and advancing his rule. The institution of education was altered accordingly. Eight hundred years later, Great Britain, plagued with many problems arising from crime and delinquency, responded by making provisions under the so-called poor laws for apprenticeship training for children from "bad" homes. The institutions of law and education responded.

In the nineteenth-century United States, our embryonic society viewed the role of the school as one of providing instruction in the three R's—"readin', ritin' and 'rithmetic," with school "years" of three to six months with due consideration given to the seasons for harvesting, hunting, and planting. Later, as our society began to require more of its citizens, school years were lengthened, curricula was broadened, and specialization was introduced.

Over the centuries human life has been highly valued in all the Western societies. As a result, medicine has been of paramount importance and the physician has had a high and prominent status in the society.

In recent generations, however, the increased complexity of modern societies has made it, so at least it would appear, increasingly difficult for the traditional institutions and professions to respond quickly and relevantly to the needs of society. One effort to respond on the part of the helping professions such as medicine and law, for example, has been a proliferation of specialists who seek to develop greater expertise and to give more professional attention to some of the critical societal needs within the realm of their professional responsibility. Society is well aware of the advancements the medical profession has made since the turn of the century in the treatment and cure of such life-threatening diseases as pneumonia, tuberculosis, poliomyelitis, and, more recently, cancer. Today, the cancer researcher and specialist is at the forefront of medicine's continued attack on this disease.

Although specialists have developed within the traditional helping professions, another outcome of the changing concerns and needs of societies has been the emergence of professional helpers as specialists in other professions. Especially appropriate to our discussions have been the emergence and development of the community mental health movement, a hybrid of the professions of medicine and psychology; the counseling psychology movement, an area of specialization in the profession of psychology; and the school counseling movement, an area of specialization in the profession of education.

Societal Characteristics and the Counseling Mission

Counseling is basically a social process; that is, it is dependent on a social interaction between the counselor and his or her client. Beyond that, it is also shaped by the social characteristics and social problems of the culture. We must assume, therefore, that counselors and the programs of counseling and guidance they represent will more effectively cope with the challenges of their clientele if the cultural influences and structures of the society are recognized. This recognition enables the development of program foundations that promise greater relevancy for all whom they serve.

The Characteristics of a Culture

We are born into a culture, a culture that has been made by our ancestors. This culture includes both the material objects that have been developed for our use and the meanings that they have for us. It further includes the attitudes and values that we exhibit and the institutions we create to preserve them. It is also evident that we have not only been born into this culture but that we are shaped by it as well. This "shaping" is encouraged by the "rules" of the society, including our laws and both formal and informal rewards and punishments.

This culture in which we live and develop determines our coping styles, language, child rearing and family expectancy patterns, prejudices, beliefs, and traditions. Based on this cultural environment, our personal hierarchy of values will also include concepts of education, worthwhile educational goals, views of teachers and other educators, plus viewpoints on student expectancies at the different education levels, all of which influence individuals as they pursue their formal education.

What are some cultural characteristics of the United States that are germane to the development of the helping profession of counseling? Schmidt (1977) suggested three characteristics of United States culture that are conducive to the development of counseling as a professionally practiced act of helping as follows.

1. A pervasive inclination, perhaps a social compulsion, to experiment and innovate; to try new and different methods of solving problems and initiating change. In a climate of innovation, many traditions and institutions may be notably shortlived, with the new and different often being preferred to the old and familiar in fashions, recreation, education, business, and social behavior. Such a pervasive commitment to change would seem to create a need for educational or helping efforts to enable individuals to understand and cope with the uncertainty and anxiety which accompany it.
2. A high degree of physical mobility together with an emphasis on individual achievement. Census data indicate that Americans are highly mobile but the pattern is generally observed to be one of movement of individuals or immediate families rather than extended families or entire communities as in traditional nomadic cultures. Reasons for moving are diverse but of some prominence is the search for means or opportunities for improving oneself (e.g., education, jobs) or for finding more desirable or hospitable environments. Two concomitants of this type of mobility which are of relevance to professional counseling are first, the reduced importance of the family as a source of support and assistance, and second, the increase in the importance of self-reliance and the valuing of self-improvement as a basis for attaining rewards and achieving identity.

> 3. A high level of economic development, leading to a condition of material abundance and a high standard of living. The interdependence of high production and high consumption tended to result in an elevated standard of living. The industrial economy also instigated much physical mobility. More recently, as the economy began shifting from an industrial to a service emphasis, marketing and advertising efforts were adapted to persuading people to need and use the growing array of services. These economic factors seem to interact with previously noted cultural characteristics relevant to professional counseling. In a culture having a self-improvement emphasis, some of the increased time and energy available from a reduced work-week would likely be given to the self as an object of concern. Questions of goals, purposes, values, identity, and happiness would conceivably arise. (p. 20)

Although individuals who grow up in a culture will have some understandings of others who develop in the same culture, attempts to study the American culture and its impact on the individual are complicated by the fact that the United States, perhaps more than any other nation, is a society of subcultures. This is not to suggest that there is no American culture; nor would we deny that the mingling of cultures can lead to the diminishing of their characteristics. The fact is, however, that subcultures are still significant influences on the life-styles of countless thousands of Americans and these influences cannot be denied or ignored by agencies or institutions that seek to serve them. Nor can counselors ignore the conflicts that often confront individuals who are, in a sense, living in one culture and being educated or working in another. In these many instances counselors are witnesses to failures of individuals to find adequate substitutes for the value system of an old culture resulting in what might be called a psychological impasse. Under such circumstances counselors can no longer function at their optimum levels. Certainly, in recent generations, we have been made painfully aware of the inadequacies of our American educational and social system in providing adequate developmental and acculturation opportunities for many of our black, Chicano, Puerto Rican, Chinese, and other youths from minority cultures.

Because of the impact of formal education on the individual, and also in recognition of the fact that more counselors are employed in schools than in any other setting, we should note that educational systems are developed to preserve and advance the cultures they serve. The influence of the culture on the school, as on the individual, is most significant. For example, the attitudes, values, and needs of a culture will be reflected in who goes to school, when they go, where they go, what is taught, by whom, and how. It will also be reflected in how schools are developed, maintained, and operated. Further, the school will also reflect in its curricula those knowledges, skills, and values that are believed to be significant to members of the culture. In most cultures, there will be a core of knowledge that is considered important to all members of the society. Such a core is traditionally composed of an educational content—i.e., language arts, social studies, and sciences; and a moral content—i.e., right from wrong, appropriate and inappropriate behavior, beautiful and ugly. Beyond these provisions for a core or basic education, specialities are provided. The "special" educational programs also reflect the unique or special educational requirements believed to be needed or desirable in the society.

In most cultures, children, adolescents, and to a limited degree, young adults, are the students. They attend schools that are usually conveniently located for the population they are designed to serve (although in some areas busing has altered this) and are staffed by adults who are viewed as specially prepared by their own previous education and/or experiences to serve in schools as teachers.

Because schools become a part of the "tradition" of a culture, they, like most traditions, are strongly resistant to revolutionary change. When educational changes do take place, they are usually gradual and reflect changing needs as perceived by the society they serve. Moreover, when new models for educational change have been conceived "by educators for educators," they have often failed to gain popular cultural acceptance, or do so only after long periods of time. Instant dramatic educational changes, which are often temporary, appear to occur only during emergencies that threaten the culture.

It is, however, possible that cultural and related educational change will greatly accelerate in the future. Rapid technological developments, the impact of television as a means of instant communication, the influences of heretofore "unlistened-to" minorities or subcultures, a new and louder voice for our younger and older citizens, and governmental efforts to make the society more rapidly responsive to the needs of both majority and minority groups all promise to alter both the origin and rate of educational change. Counseling programs in schools, then, must be alert to both traditional expectancies and indicators for change. Since at least a third of the young adult's life has been spent in school, counseling programs in nonschool settings must also be sensitive to the impact of school experiences and schooling characteristics on their clientele.

Societal Characteristics and Social Problems

The cultural characteristics of a society include the behavior expectancies that are an outgrowth of the values of the society. These behavioral expectancies are usually reinforced by the society through a system of direct or indirect rewards and punishments that seek to encourage the desired behavior and discourage, alter, or treat the undesired behavior. In this way "norms" for acceptable behavior that are compatible with the expectancies of the society are communicated and contrasted with "abnormal" or unaccepted behavior. The behavioral problems of a society may be viewed as major threats to a society and the well-being of its members. They may also be viewed as an index of the degree to which individuals are unable to adapt to the expectancies of their society. In either instance, there are implications for counselors and the counseling mission in a society.

Since the major social problems that currently confront our society are well recognized, a simple review will suffice to remind us that some of the most persistent of these problems are the following:

- crime and delinquency
- substance abuse, alcohol and drugs
- school problems, including vandalism and violence in schools
- divorce and other family problems
- psychological disorders that disable or handicap many from functioning adequately
- persistent unemployment and poverty for many.

In slightly more detail, crime and delinquency, as a pervasive social problem, continues to increase. The involvement of youth in crime is particularly disturbing as data indicate that more than one half of all serious crimes in the United States are committed by youths aged ten to seventeen. Further, over one million young people are seen in our juvenile courts in a year and a majority of delinquents commit their first offenses prior to the age of ten. In fact, since 1960, juvenile crime has risen twice as fast as that of adults. Violent crimes also continue to rise. In 1978 the murder rate was 10.1 per 100,000 population, and was double this average in cities with populations of over 250,000. Reported rapes averaged 30.8 per 100,000; aggravated assault 256, burglary 1,424 and larceny-theft, 2,744, all per 100,000 population. The potential for counselors and counseling programs in prevention and rehabilitation in this social problem arena alone is mind-boggling.

Substance abuse is a serious problem at all levels and all ages in the American society. These abuses, reflecting the insecurity of contemporary life, range from aspirin to tranquilizers, to alcohol, marijuana, and hard drugs. The age of these abusers appears to be dropping rapidly and it is now estimated that over 80 per cent of students in the United States have used some form of these substances. Substance use is not limited to any socioeconomic, racial, or age group. The available statistics emphasize the extent of the problem: "Approximately 60% to 90% of the young people are using alcohol, 40% to 60% tobacco (with a million new teenage smokers yearly), 6% to 40% marijuana, 5% to 15% LSD, and 3% to 17% heroin" (Cornacchia, Bentel and Smith, 1973, as seen in George and Cristiani, p. 238). The use and abuse of drugs is a primary concern of both communities and schools, and counselors must be informed and prepared to intervene in drug and alcohol problems, including assistance to family members of alcoholics and drug addicts.

Various national polls have consistently noted the concerns of Americans for their schools and their serious problems. For example,

- According to the 1977 FBI reports, 700,000 teachers were assaulted in U.S. schools. Many assaults were not reported.
- It is estimated that the average cost of vandalism to an average metropolitan school district is approximately $100,000

a year. The cost of vandalism reaches over $600,000,000 a year in the United States.

- More than half of all school dropouts have average or above average intelligence, but are underachievers.
- It has been estimated that in New York City alone, every day over 200,000 children are truant.
- In one state approximately 50,000 students, including about 10,000 first graders, failed to earn promotion. It cost the state approximately $36,000,000 to have these students repeat that grade. Had it been possible to reduce the first grade failure rate by 50 per cent, a savings of more than $17,000,000 would have resulted, which is enough money to construct and equip 1,000 new classrooms or to pay for 4,000 new classroom teachers. (*Status of Guidance and Counseling in the Nation's Schools*, 1976, p. 46)

It is clear that within the school environment itself the seeds of failure, frustration and anger, delinquency, and crime are sown and cultivated. The challenge to school counselors to deal with these staggering problems on their "home grounds" is all too frequently unmet. As numerous studies have concluded, the best school counseling programs are more frequently than not located in those schools that need them least and vice versa.

Rapid changes in society have resulted in new patterns of family living. In the United States one out of every five families moves each year. In Florida alone, for example, from October to April each year, approximately 41,000 migrant children enroll in school. One of every three mothers in the nation is working and in one of every five families the mother is not home when the children return from school (*The Status of Counseling and Guidance in the Nation's Schools*, 1976, p. 45).

The impact of divorce on children can be devastating, and as George and Cristiani note (1981) an estimated one million children are affected each year by divorce. The authors go on to note that

> the effects of divorce on the child depends on many factors: the child's age, self-concept, emotional maturity, sensitivity, and ability to cope. The relationship and communication between the child and the parents also greatly affect the child's adjustment process. Regardless of the child's coping skills, the child needs to openly

> vent all feelings related to the divorce. A skillful counselor can greatly contribute to the child's emotional and psychological adjustment. (p. 237)

Despite numerous agencies that are concerned with the problems of mental health, emotional disturbance continues to be an acute problem in both schools and society. The 1978 Report of the President's Commission on Mental Health indicated that at least 15 per cent of the people in the United States require some form of professional mental health treatment. In every school it is estimated that between 10 to 15 per cent of the children suffer emotional disorders which are serious enough to warrant professional attention. In some areas 25 per cent represents a more realistic figure. Only 30 per cent of all children referred to outside community agencies can be seen because of long waiting lists. Of those children who are seen only 20 per cent can continue beyond the initial stage of treatment (*The Status of Counseling and Guidance in the Nation's Schools,* 1976, p. 46).

Inflation and its handmaiden, poverty, continue to be national problems. In 1978, the U.S. Department of Commerce (1979) estimated that approximately 24.5 million people lived below the poverty level. The impact of poverty on minorities and families maintained by women continued to be significantly higher than the national average, and three-fifths of all poor persons resided within metropolitan areas. Among all these populations the unemployment rate is particularly high among out-of-school teenagers. The relationships between teenage unemployment and teenage criminal activities are clear and pose implications for school counseling and career guidance programs, employment counseling, and job placement efforts by government employment counselors and other community agencies.

The Counseling Mission and the Development of Counseling Programs

MENTAL HEALTH AND THE COMMUNITY SETTING FOR COUNSELING

It is not uncommon to hear references to a "sick society," but it is difficult to find researched or published criteria by which such a determination can be made. In fact, such references may be technically inaccurate, for as Ewalt (1958) has pointed out, "A social environment or culture may be conducive either to sickness or health, but the quality produced is characteristic only of a person; therefore, it is improper to speak of a 'sick society' or a 'sick community.' " The community does represent a collection of people, however—a group, and like any group of people, the community can undergo anxiety, depression, elation, and so forth. These feelings can be reflected in community actions to "protect" themselves or to ameliorate the perceived causes of undesired feeling and/or in the general attitudes of the populace. Too, like any group, the community is driven closer together and becomes more cohesive in times of crises or perceived danger or in times of great achievements or recognition. From this viewpoint, communities utilize in a very real sense the same behavior patterns as individuals.

A determination of community factors that significantly influence the emotional well-being or mental health of its citizens is made even more difficult by the absence of a generally accepted simple, specific definition of mental health. Jahoda (1958) concluded, after a thorough search of the literature, that the most effective resolution of the definitional problem was to identify the criteria by which mental health could be adjudged. A similar approach could be effectively employed by specialists to gain an understanding of the psychological climate provided by a school or community.

Of the various types of criteria that could be utilized for the study of a community's psychological influence on its population, two appear to have special significance for community-based counselors. One of these is based on objective census-related data; the other is based on a more subjective determination of the psychological climate provided each of its inhabitants by the community as a whole. The objective criteria by which a community's emotional well-being may be evaluated are the published statistics citing the prevalence within a community of clinically adjudged psychological disorders, drug and alcohol abuse, juvenile delinquency and crime, family break-ups, criminal abuse and neglect of children, minority group prejudice, and racial disorders. Importantly included in such an analysis would be the availability of facilities and specialists to provide preventive and remedial aid and the philosophy upon which such assistance is based, although an objective determination of the latter may be more difficult to obtain.

The second and more subjective approach that counseling personnel could utilize for the determination of a community's psychological climate involves the application of criteria recommended for the evaluation of an individual's mental health. In essence, it requires a determination of the degree to which optimal mental health is facilitated. Based on this criterion, this type of study would require an analysis of the interpersonal environments to determine, for example, the extent to which:

a. The development of one's positive self-attitude is fostered.
b. Each individual is given the opportunity to become what he has the potential to become.
c. Respect for all individuals is demonstrated and encouraged.
d. Each is enabled to maintain his individuality while remaining a part of his society.
e. Each is helped to find meaning and purpose in life.
f. Each is helped to develop the ability to take life as it comes and master it. (Jahoda, 1958, pp. 23–64)

In any event, the nature or characteristics of an environment are influenced to a considerable degree by the typical characteristics of the inhabitants of that environment. In other words, the mental health of a community is the "sum total" of the mental health of its members.

Mental Health and the Educational Setting for Counseling

Schools may be seen as social institutions in which individuals are associated in a variety of ways. Although the major association may be viewed as the teacher-pupil association, there are obviously a variety of other relationships, both formal and informal that result from the educational setting and the student will in many instances view association with peers as the major association. As Robertson notes (1977), "every school is a miniature social system, with its own social structure, system of statuses and roles, subcultures, values and traditions, and rituals and ceremonies. Each school, classroom, and clique is an interacting social unit. The study of what actually goes on inside the school has been an important focus of sociological research."

The school, then, is a social institution whose members participate in social activities, assume or are assigned social roles, and, in general, behave and function in a way within the system that is expected or approved by the members. Further, the school may be studied as a distinct social institution with characteristics that distinguish it and set it apart, such as a definite population, a clearly defined structure, a network of anticipated social relationships within this structure, and its own unique personality or culture. By studying the social system of the school, we can gain insight into and understanding of the sources and qualities of the various influences on the mental health and behavior of all those who are involved with the school in one way or another.

The major characteristics of this system are observable in the social structure of the school and the classroom and in the teacher-pupil relationship. Goslin (1965) notes that the structural characteristics of the school can be organized under two principle headings: (1) "those aspects of the system that are concerned with relationships among members of the student body and (2) those that pertain to relations among faculty members and between teachers and administrators." In the former instance, for example, the particular modes of grouping students for instructional purposes will often have social implications. A case in point is the controversial practice of ability groupings. Such groupings tend to identify the academic "elites" as well as those from the other side of the academic tracks. Consistent groupings promote social friendships, activities, and significant roles from the membership of this elite group. Another example is the degree to which the school will encourage and provide for various co-curricular or socially oriented activities for its student membership and the influence of these activities on social relationships among students. Even the traditional structuring of the student body by classes (senior, junior, sophomore, freshman) creates a status hierarchy within the institution. It is apparent that school practices may either reinforce existing differences between students or create a more common culture by establishing situations in which contact is encouraged between students of varying backgrounds and abilities.

The student is not the only member of the school society that is influenced by its social structure. The teacher is also a participant in this social system that extends beyond the classroom. This system results from the formal organizational structure of the school, plus a network of informal relationships established by the teacher during his or her day-to-day interaction with the other workers in the school setting. The system of social relationships between teachers and between teachers and administrators obviously has an impact on the classroom itself.

Many educational sociologists have pointed out the existence of distinct classroom social systems. Experienced teachers can describe the social organization within their classrooms—how various subgroups function or fail to function and the roles which members of the group represent in those classrooms.

The understanding and management of the ever-shifting classroom social system is one of importance for those teachers, guidance counselors, and administrators who are concerned with student development from both a social and educational viewpoint. Within the classroom, the two-person group composed of the teacher and student can also be a most significant influence on social relationships, roles, and functions. The roles that both teacher and student perceive for themselves and each other have implications for the behavior and learning of the individual student and the behavior and teaching technique of the individual teacher. It is important, therefore, that the classroom teacher be alert to the nature, quality, and implications of his or her interactions with students; that she or he give due attention to the human element as well as to the academic element in his or her daily planning; and that she or he view the school counselor as a human resource consultant available and able to assist him or her in this planning.

Mental Health and Noneducational Settings for Counseling

Although the community as a population unit and the school as a societal institution provide the settings for community mental health agencies and school counseling and guidance programs respectively, we briefly examine programs that provide counseling services organized in a variety of other settings. These settings are as follows.

Employment Counseling. Counseling was specifically provided for by the U.S. Employment Security Offices by the G.I. Bill of 1944, which emphasized providing job counseling for returning veterans of World War II. The focus of employment counselors is to provide appropriate job placement of their clientele. In this process the employment counselor may assist clients to develop attitudes, identify their abilities, and adjust to personal problems that are influencing their employment. Employment counselors may also administer and interpret standardized tests, particularly the Government Aptitude Classification Test (GATB). In defining the role of the employment counselor, the National Employment Counselors Association suggested that

> to carry out employment counseling responsibilities effectively, employment counselors must develop the following basic competencies.
>
> *Relationship Skills*
> The ability to establish a trusting, open, and useful relationship with each counselee, accurately interpreting feelings as well as verbal and nonverbal expressions, and conveying to the applicant this understanding and whatever pertinent information and assistance are needed.
>
> *Individual and Group Assessment Skills*
> The ability to provide ongoing assessment in individual and group settings involving the appraisal and measurement of the counselee's needs, characteristics, potentialities, individual differences, and self-appraisal.
>
> *Group Counseling*
> The ability to apply basic principles of group dynamics and leadership roles in a continuous and meaningful manner to assist group members to understand their problems and take positive steps toward resolving them.
>
> *Development and Use of Career-related Information*
> The ability to develop and use educational, occupational, and labor market information to assist counselees in making decisions and formulating occupational plans.
>
> *Occupational Plan Development and Implementation*
> The ability to assist the counselee in developing and implementing a suitable employability plan that helps move the job-

seeker from current status through any needed employability-improvement services, including training and related supportive services, into a suitable job.

Placement Skills
The ability to ascertain and to communicate understanding of employers' personnel needs, to make effective job development contacts, and to assist the counselee in the presentation of qualifications in relation to the employer's needs.

Community Relations Skills
The ability, based on extensive knowledge of the important service delivery systems in the community, to assist counselees in obtaining the services needed.

Work Load Management and Intraoffice Relationships Skills
The ability to coordinate the various aspects of the total counseling program in the employing agency, resulting in a continuous and meaningful sequence of services to counselees, agency staff, and the community.

Professional Development Skills
The ability, based on interest in furthering professional development, to engage in activities that promote such development individually and within the profession, and to demonstrate by example the standards and performance expected of a professional employment counselor (National Employment Counselors Association, 1975). (pp. 152–153)

Marriage and Family Counseling. For generations such popular songs as "Always" have extolled the virtues and promise of everlasting love once one's "true love" was discovered. However, in recent years, we have noted an increasing number of songs such as "Pass on By" and "Slipping Around" that suggest considerable deviations from the older theme. As the previously cited statistical data regarding divorces indicate, modern marriage vows might more appropriately read "until death or divorce us do part." The surfacing, if not increasing evidence, of the extent of marital problems in recent generations has led to the rapid development of a speciality area in counseling focusing on marriage and its related problems. The rapid growth of the American Association of Family and Marriage Counselors, a professional organization for these specialists, is further testimony to the growth of this field. Marriage and family counselors may come from such diverse professional backgrounds as psychiatry, psychology, law, and the ministry. As Bockus (1980) notes "The field of marital therapy appears to be in a state of teeming and productive disarray." Counselors specializing in marriage and family relations may generally be found in a variety of counseling and agency settings, including private practice. Counseling in this area obviously is concerned with both the husband and wife and their interactions. However, this does not mean that the individual marriage partner is neglected and, in some instances, the emphasis may be placed on the individual and the concern for the relationship is temporarily abandoned. Marriage counseling and marriage counselors do not seek the preservation of the marriage as an automatic outcome. As with any counseling, the client must be free to make his or her own personal decisions with the counselor assisting him or her or assisting each of the marriage partners to think through and arrive at an appropriate decision. Although the title of marriage and family counselor may suggest formally wedded couples only, other couples involved in intimate relationships may also seek their assistance.

Corrections Counseling. Counselors who work in correctional settings are typically utilized in institutions provided separately for either juveniles or adults. In these categories further separations are usually made on the basis of sex and severity of crime or rehabilitation potential; i.e., maximum security prisons, work-release farms, and so forth. Moos (1975) identifies six correctional programs as follows:

1. *The therapeutic community program.* Inmates in these programs are seen as active and involved in spending their time constructively. They express their feelings freely and are encouraged to be independent, in preparation for their release.
2. *The relationship-oriented program.* The primary emphasis in this program is on the relationship dimensions of involvement and support and on the system maintenance dimensions of order and organization and clarity. Staff control is played down.
3. *The action-oriented program.* This is a prerelease program in which participants are expected to take leadership, are strongly encouraged to be independent, assume responsibility, and engage in making specific plans for their departure from the institution and return to normal participation in society.

4. *The insight-oriented program.* This type of program seeks to assist inmate participation in gaining insight into their behavior and its consequences.
5. *The control-oriented program.* Control-oriented programs are most likely to be a part of correctional institutions. As the term implies, these and similar custodial programs find the clients in a controlled environment.
6. *The disturbed behavior program.* The disturbed behavior program is designed to assist the rehabilitation of those inmates whose behavior indicates severe psychological disturbance, the treatment of which must precede any further rehabilitation efforts.

Pastoral Counseling. From the standpoint of sheer numbers and geographic coverage, pastoral counseling provides a significant mental health resource. Not only are the clergy generally available to listen to the concerns and personal problems of their parishioners, but they are frequently the first source to which people in trouble turn (Gibson and Mitchell, 1981). In recognition of the mental health function of the clergy, many theological training programs now include courses in general counseling, related psychology, and pastoral counseling. Special programs have also been developed in clinical pastoral education for theology students and clergymen who desire further training. Although many of these specialized programs are comparatively short-term, others provide intensive training in clinical settings. Additionally, clergy are increasingly enrolling in regular preparation programs in counselor education.

Armed Services Counselors. The armed services provide counseling for both the mental health and career development concerns of its members. These services are provided by trained counselors who are usually, but not always, members of the armed services. The counselor's functions include organizing and interpreting the military and civilian experience-education backgrounds of service personnel and relating these data to service career opportunities. The counselor also seeks to help service personnel clearly understand the steps necessary to achieve their maximum career potential. Service counselors also aid in the transition and placement of service personnel from military to civilian careers.

Summary and Implications

The helping profession of counseling is based on the nature of humankind and the culture that surrounds the individual. Counseling programs in both school and nonschool settings must therefore reflect and be responsive to the basic traits of their clients and the needs of the society they serve. Counseling programs must be planned in such a way as to reflect this responsiveness. If the counseling program is to be truly responsive, it must understand the cultural backgrounds of its client population and the implications of these backgrounds for their growth, development, and concerns. Programs must also respond to the social structures of the school and/or community and to the roles and relationships within these structures and their implications for the individual's growth and development. The psychological environment of the home, school, and community is influential in the development and functioning of school counseling and guidance programs. The implications of these cultural, social, and psychological perspectives cannot be overlooked if counseling programs are to achieve and maintain relevance. To see and serve the needs of a wide range of clients, counseling programs in today's society function in a variety of settings representing differing specializations within the profession. Chapter 2 discusses the personnel for these programs in various settings.

CHAPTER 2

The Personnel for Counseling Programs

Introduction: The Professional Team

Teamwork is a popular American concept that appears to have been originally and still is prevalently associated with athletic teams. Coaches and sportswriters consistently extol the virtues of the cooperative enterprise known as teamwork. Even though individual stars are clearly identifiable in most team sports, they are always quick to acknowledge the contributions of their teammates to their stardom and the interdependence that each member of the team has on the others in the pursuit of their mutual goals. This harmonious working together to accomplish a mutual goal is also noticeable in such cooperative endeavors as musical groups, surgical teams, army tank crews, and aircraft crews. One could almost conclude that we have become a nation of "teams" as recent generations have seen the concept of teamwork expanded to encompass many organizations as well as institutional and agency settings. It is no longer uncommon, for example, to hear industrial leaders talk about the labor-management team or the school principal to commend his or her educational team or a community agency to refer to its psychological team.

Regardless of the fact that the terminology may be overworked at times, we must accept the concept of teamwork as an important one if we are to efficiently and effectively bring all the potential resources of the psychological community to bear on behalf of its clients. In advocating a "team" concept we note the following.

- Teams are composed of individuals who are bound together in the pursuit of a common goal. This pursuit is enhanced by their functioning together as a unit. Teams are most effective when members of the team learn mutually complementary roles in order that duplication, overlapping, and competitive activities may be minimized.
- Working together, sharing knowledge and teamwork, when feasible, permits each (team member) to use his or her unique talents while determining who will perform the shared talents (Geoffrey and Mulliken, 1980).
- There is no single "best" team system or pattern of team organization; rather, many variations may be anticipated, since a team presumes the best available combination of personnel for the task at hand. For example, some teams may include both community and school personnel, faculty and student representatives, and/or professionals and paraprofessionals.
- The counselor, as well as other professional helpers, may have a variety of roles and may be a member of a variety of "teams" within a specific setting. We recognize that the number and variety of these roles will vary from setting to setting, as on some teams, for example, the counselor will be expected to function as a leader, whereas on others, he or she will function as a follower. Like the skilled magician or juggler, she or he must be adept in "wearing the hat" most appropriate to the immediate activity in which she or he is engaged.

The Professional Helping Team for Schools

The school counseling program is an integral part—an important "team" in the total educational enterprise. Whereas this very fact is one of the potential strengths of the program, since by implication everyone is thus involved, it is also at the same time, a complicating factor. If, in fact, everyone is involved, then roles and relationships must be clarified to the point that each recognizes not only his or her own role and function but also that of colleagues in the total counseling and educational effort. Thus, whereas the team concept for schools has long suggested that the school counselor, teacher, administrator, and other personnel specialists must work together to accomplish the objectives of the school counseling and guidance program, one of the perennial problems which countless studies have enumerated has been the failure to clearly define, in both theory and practice, roles and relationships in such programs.

Another contributing factor that must be taken into consideration is the continuous call for educational change and innovation which threatens to obliterate many of the traditional structures and roles within education. Thus, at a time when many counselors are still trying to clearly identify their roles and relationships within the educational framework as viewed traditionally, changes are taking place that may very well make this attempt an example of "too little, too late." Therefore, rather than attempt to specify roles in terms of job descriptions, it is more appropriate to examine the special contribution each member of the "team" may be reasonably expected to make.

Figure 2–1 depicts the "base" (school or system), major responsibility, and relationships among those specialists who comprise the professional helping team for schools.

The School Counselor's Special Contributions

The school counselor is obviously the central figure on the educational guidance team, for she or he is the specialist who brings unique knowledge and skills to the program without which it could not function. More specifically, the counselor is frequently the only professional in the school setting prepared to offer individual and group counseling to students, parents, and teachers. The counselor also possesses special knowledge in the area of educational and career development, and understands appraisal techniques that will enable him or her to identify pupil characteristics and relate these to their development and adjustment, future planning and placement needs.

In addition to these traditional skills and knowledge, school counselors have, in recent years, played increasingly significant

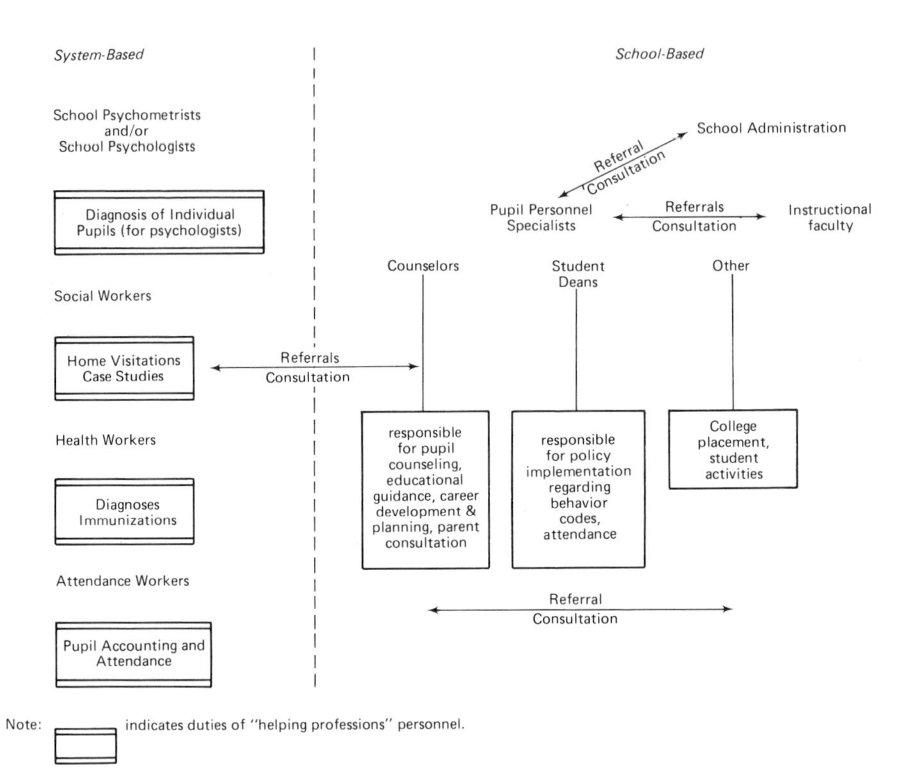

FIGURE 2–1. Professional Roles, Relationships and Responsibilities of Helping Professionals.

roles as consultants to other adults both within and without the educational setting who are also concerned with the pupil's well-being and development. Counselors will recognize that on many occasions they will be more effective when working through and with other significant adults in the individual pupil's life, such as parents, other educators, ministers, and youth workers. This consultation involvement with parents, teachers, and other adults is receiving greater attention as "writers within the counseling profession indicate that all school counselors must conceptualize pupils not as isolated individuals but as members of systems; i.e., family systems (Blocher, 1974a), learning systems (Blocher, 1974b, 1977), and community systems (Goodyear, 1976; Lewis and Lewis, 1977)." (Young, 1979, p. 247)

> Several reasons can also be stated for the school counselor's choosing to use the school setting for increased involvement and counseling with family systems. First, many personality theories support the idea that family environment and child-rearing practices influence the developing individual. Second, there has been increased acceptance of the school's becoming more involved with the home environment. Third, schools are established by society to maximize the potential effectiveness of its children and youth—and the counselor, as a part of the school must accept this responsibility. Fourth, logic dictates that more information about the family can be obtained from first-hand observation of the family, rather than reports by the children. Fifth, efficient and proficient referrals of individuals and families by school counselors to community agencies maximize the assistance available and enhance the professionalism of school counselors. Finally, increased responsibilities of the school counselor necessitate that all counseling strategies be the most effective possible. (Young, 1979, p. 248)

In the "learning systems," counselors should also more actively pursue their consulting roles with school administrators and classroom teachers in broad areas of student needs and concerns, such as course offerings, work-study programs, positive school and classroom environment, meaningful activities, and student representation in school affairs. In the broadening of their professional educational consultation responsibility,

> counselors should also work closely together with curricular specialists to assist one another when curricular or guidance and counseling objectives are hindered or subverted by school structure and organization. Further, counselors and curricular specialists should develop strategies and tactics in concern to overcome obstacles and rigidities in school structure and organization impeding legitimate outcomes for students. In so doing, counselors and curricular specialists realize that structural and organizational improvements in schools may frequently bring about desired student behaviors just as validly as curricular or guidance measures. (Aubrey, 1979, p. 161)

In community systems school counselors must frequently anticipate a role as career consultants. In this capacity the counselor will plan for the integration of school and community career development resources to ensure their efficient and effective utilization. This suggests that counselors assume a major role in the school's career education program. To this end, school counselors will need to consider the following recommendations.

> a. Involve business, labor, community representatives, and parents in the development of career education programs as teachers and resource people.
> b. Introduce occupational coping skills seminars to assist students in the transition from school to work, e.g., job seeking, interviewing, resumé preparation, and self-analysis leading to self-improvement.
> c. Sponsor or teach career exploratory courses throughout the school year as a part of the total guidance program. (Ryan and Sutton, 1978, p. 269)

The effective school counselor in the last decades of the twentieth century must also be able to assess social and psychological characteristics and relate these to educational developments and individual adjustments; be able to identify and recognize the influences of cultures and subcultures on their members; and be prepared to function as a human resources developer and agent of change in the educational-community setting. Podemski and Childers (1980) recommend that

> To establish more response by schools, school counselors, as a result of their professional training, experiences and organizational placement in schools, are in a position to harness forces that can stimulate the change process and thereby make school systems better learning environments. At a time when counselors and other educators feel greater pressure for accountability than ever before, the counselor is in a unique organizational position to serve as an institutional change agent. In the change agent role, the counselor is concerned with organizational development as well as the shaping and reformulation of the school's curriculum, program, and the organization itself to meet more effectively the needs of students, parents, and the community. (p. 173)

As the counseling and guidance specialist on the guidance team, the school counselor *must* also function as the guidance team leader. The development of the school guidance program, while involving other educational professionals, must, by virtue of the special knowledges and skills required, be directed by a trained, professional, and certified school counselor. The school counselor's responsibilities as a program leader are discussed in greater detail in Chapter 5.

Counselors often have difficulty distinguishing themselves from other helping professionals because their specialized skills and knowledge are not unique to counseling. As Pate (1980) notes

> Our knowledge and skills are shared by psychologists, educators, social workers, and other helping professionals. While we cannot claim that counseling has a unique knowledge base, counselors' interpretation of their knowledge and skills into service is an important aspect of our claim to professional status and suggests a place for counselors in a psychological society. (p. 521)

Pate goes on to suggest that

> a. Counselors must continue to emphasize the developmental nature of counseling. Our unique contributions are the assistance we give counselees to realize their potential better and our interventions to remove institutional barriers to that realization.
> b. Counselors should continue to recognize education as important to their profession, just as they so recognize the field of psychology. Much of what counselors do for counselees is education or reeducation. We teach counselees to use their resources and to develop new resources.
> c. Certainly counselors can take pride in the profession's historical ties with vocational counseling. Although we should not be content to equate counseling with career counseling, we should remind our publics that we have a long record of commitment to career counseling. (p. 522)

Other Pupil Personnel Workers

Most comprehensive programs of pupil personnel services in schools will include other professionals whose training and anticipated role may share some similarities to that of the school counselor. These include school psychologists, psychometrists, psychiatrists, and social workers, as well as the personnel whose training is more distinctive, such as the school nurse, physician, dentist, and dental hygienist. Each of these professional specialists also has unique contributions to make to the achievement of the school's objectives. However, if each specialist is to make a meaningful contribution, she or he must have some recognition of the roles and specialities of other pupil personnel workers, as well as a recognition of the expectancies normally assigned to him or her. We now briefly examine the special competencies of the more popular of these other pupil personnel workers.

School Psychologist. The school psychologist is an important and integral member of the pupil personnel team. In most school settings, the traditional responsibility of the school psychologist is to diagnose and study individual children, who are usually experiencing problems in their educational or personal development. In this role, the school psychologist evaluates various aspects of a child's experiences and behavior that are relevant to an understanding of the child's school difficulties and achievements. For this role the school psychologist is trained in the use of psychological tests and also is prepared to engage in individual or group therapy with disturbed children. The psychologist may also aid teachers and parents in understanding the implications of a child's behavior. Although the school psychologist has often been thought of primarily as a problem diagnostician, there has been an increased effort in recent years to consider other options. For example, Granowsky and Davis (1974) suggested that the school psychologist has an option for three different roles: (1) the diagnostic approach, (2) the community-centered approach, and (3) the administration approach. Based on a rapidly changing society, the authors suggest that psychologists examine their role definitions and select the one that is most appropriate for their particular school. The traditional diagnostic role employs (1) diagnostic testing and reporting; (2) designing educational strategies for pupils and teachers; and (3) evaluating these strategies. Such an approach involves behavioral approaches and classroom intervention and service.

A second role model would be that of the community-based school psychologist. Such a person would operate from a mental health center, be administratively independent of the schools, and act as a consultant to the school staff. Granowsky and Davis state that this model allows (1) the school psychologist to place his or her allegiance with the child rather than the school; (2) direct and more intense contact with the parents; (3) expanded resources utilizing the total mental health center staff; and (4) dual therapy emphasizing educational remediation plus individual growth. The psychologist would, in addition, provide the school with traditional services.

The third role model views the school psychologist as a part of the central administration. The psychologist (1) facilitates the group process and interchange among the professional staff; (2) identifies high priority problems; and (3) organizes an effective team of psychological specialists. The authors believe that the school psychologist in this role would be proactive rather than reactive.

Based on his or her skill in diagnosis, the school psychologist can assist the school counselor and other pupil personnel workers in gaining a better understanding of individual students and their problems. The school psychologist can also serve as a resource person for case studies and as a source for referral for certain categories of disturbed pupils.

The School Psychometrist. The school psychometrist is a pupil personnel worker whose training, background, and job functions are in many instances so similar to the school psychologist that little besides their job titles distinguishes them. However, the school psychometrist is often more limited in training and, as a result, is also more restricted in the kinds of activities in which she or he engages in the school. The major emphasis in the training of psychometrists and on their job performances is usually in the area of psychological measurement. In some school settings, the major contribution of the psychometrist to the school pupil personnel and guidance program may be in the organization and administration of the school's standardized testing program.

The School Social Worker. The role and function of the school social worker, like those of the school counselor, have evolved and broadened from its beginnings in the early 1900s, and have been influenced in their development by compulsory education laws, new knowledge about individual differences among children, and a recognition of the impact of education and the school on school-aged youth. Today, the school social worker works to eliminate the social-emotional influences that handicap the student's formal education. To this end, the social worker actively works with the family, school, and community, and seeks the involvement and cooperation of parents in facilitating the development of their children. This may involve interpreting to the family their child's behavior as the school views it and, in turn, receiving information regarding the child's behavior at home. The end goal is to have the parents participate positively in the school-child-parent relationship. The school social worker also functions in a liaison role between the school and community, and is particularly interested in eliminating the community causes of school problems rather than treating the results. In working with the family, school, and community, the social worker seeks to identify and eliminate the base causes of problems. Primary services of the social worker include case studies, group work, and consultation. In the school setting, the social worker is a valuable "Team" member who can make a significant contribution to the in-depth understanding of an individual student's problems through case studies and who also provides significant linkages between the school, home, and community.

School Medical Personnel. Most school systems employ medical personnel on at least a part-time basis. These personnel consist typically of the school physician, school dentist, school nurse, school dental hygienist, and school psychiatrist. These personnel can contribute to achieving a better understanding of the pupils' physical or clinical problems. The school counselor can, in turn, give to these personnel a better understanding of the causative factors of the student's physical and mental well-being. Medical personnel can also contribute to increased counselor understanding of pupil adjustment needs through in-service case studies and consultation.

The potential interrelationships between school health services and school guidance services was noted in the publication *Suggested School Health Policies,* prepared by the National Committee on School Health Policies of the National Education Association and the American Medical Association in 1966. This publication suggested four important aspects of the school health service: health appraisal, health counseling and interpretation, emergency care for injury and sudden illness, and communicable disease—prevention and control. Among the techniques suggested were: continuous observation, particularly by teachers; screening tests; psychological and social evaluation; and health records. The publication also suggested the importance of interpreting pupil health needs to parents, pupils, and teachers. It was also recommended that health personnel be aware of the influences of the teacher and other educators on the emotional and social environment of the pupil. Thus, these commonly expressed concerns of both school counselors and school medical personnel indicate their natural allegiance in the development of cooperative programs for the development and adjustment of the individual.

Other Pupil Personnel Assignments. In addition to the previously described professionals who, by nature of their training and certification, are specially prepared for their contribution to pupil adjustment and development, others, by virtue of their assignment, are also often members of the pupil personnel team. These individuals most frequently have the titles of attendance worker, dean, director of student activities, and placement director.

Attendance Worker. The attendance worker is probably the oldest "traditional" pupil personnel worker. Although most schools no longer label this individual "truant officer" (a few schools have even labeled this person "attendance counselor"), the basic responsibility of this individual is still in pupil accounting. The emphasis in pupil accounting, however, has gradually changed from threats and punishment to encouragement and remediation. In this role, the attendance officer and the counselor can each provide valuable information and consultation to each other. As an example, it is particularly important that the attendance officer and counselor coordinate their efforts in seeking solutions to the perennial dropout problem, identifying its causes, consulting with parents of dropouts, and encouraging the reentry of dropouts into school.

Student Deans. Whereas student deans have been more traditionally associated with college student personnel services, some high schools and junior colleges often employ pupil personnel workers designated as deans of students, deans of boys and girls, or deans of men and women in addition to school counselors. The function of these individuals has often appeared to be one of administering student facilities, activities, and regulations. As a result, they are frequently viewed more as administrators than personnel workers. Student deans have also been frequently cast in the role of the disciplinary agents for the school. In this role, their potential contribution to the school guidance program is discounted by many who contend that guidance and discipline are a poor "mix." (Many also contend that guidance and discipline are interrelated.) A number of programs utilize the title of "dean" for their counselors, and traditional "deans" in other programs are trained counselors.

Student Activities Director. The director of student activities, as the title implies, is primarily responsible for the administering of the student activity programs within the school. In this capacity she or he may regulate and coordinate student group activities, identify and plan for needed activities, and assess or evaluate the individual activities and the activity program in general. Through cooperation with the school counselor, students may be assisted in participating in activities that will promote their growth and adjustment, serve their interests, and develop their special abilities. At the same time, coordination of guidance activities with other student and school activities can be facilitated.

Placement Directors. Placement directors are most likely to be found in large secondary schools and institutions of higher education, where their role is primarily on part-time and/or full-time career placement. In addition, at the secondary school level, placement personnel will also be frequently concerned with the placement of students in posthigh school educational institutions. The increased emphasis of career guidance in the 1970s resulted in a corresponding emphasis on, and an increase in the number of, placement specialists in high schools. Cooperation with the school counselor and school psychologist will enable those responsible for pupil placement more effectively to *coordinate* pupil interest, abilities, and experiences with placement opportunities and needs. A few schools also have college counselors or placement specialists whose major function is to facilitate the placement of interested and qualified students in a college of their choice.

The School Administrator

As indicated earlier in this chapter, the guidance team for schools consists not only of the professional counseling staff and other trained pupil personnel workers but also the school administrator. The school administrator, who may be a superintendent of schools, junior college president, or building principal, is justified in expecting the staff of the school counseling and guidance program to contribute to the achievement of the institution's objectives. The administrator must also recognize that this contribution will be severely handicapped if she or he fails to realize his or her important responsibilities in the success of this program.

The school administrator represents the educational leadership both in the community and in the specific educational institution as well. In this capacity, it is the administrator's responsibility to give open and recognized support for the school counseling and guidance program. The administrator should also provide advice and direction on budget expectations, physical facilities, ancillary professional and service personnel, and policy guidelines. The school administrator is also responsible for indicating to the school counseling and guidance personnel those counseling and guidance activities which she or he views as mandatory or desirable in facilitating the goal attainment of the total educational program. In most settings, the administrator will have the primary responsibility for communicating program characteristics, achievements, and needs to school boards and others within the educational system and to the tax-supporting public.

The Classroom Teacher

With the exception of the home, pupils spend a far greater portion of their crucial developmental years in school than in any other type of institution. During these years, pupils obviously spend a far greater portion of their in-school time with the classroom teacher than with any other professional educational personnel. The teacher-pupil relationship is the central, or key, activity in the educational endeavor. It is therefore obvious that other activities in the educational setting which are concerned with the pupils' development, adjustment, and total growth must, of necessity, involve those who work closest with them and, as might be anticipated, usually know them best. This means that the classroom teacher is an indispensable member of the guidance team.

The classroom teacher at every educational level has the opportunity to fulfill his or her important role in the school guidance program through functioning in the following ways.

As a Listener-Adviser. Mary had been increasingly distracted from her schoolwork and in a rather absent-minded manner she had been inattentive in class for more than a week. This was unlike the vivacious, energetic, and capable student Miss Jones had observed Mary to be in the first few weeks of class. Miss Jones decided that at the first opportunity she would examine Mary's record and consult with her school counselor prior to initiating any discussions with Mary. Miss Jones is an example of a guidance-oriented teacher who is alert to the needs of her students and aware of the valuable assistance that the school counselor may be able to provide in helping her meet these needs. Miss Jones and her fellow teachers at every educational level have countless opportunities to advise, consult, or just act as receptive adult listeners to students and their problems, concerns, decisions, achievements, and failures. This, then, is a primary role and function of the classroom teacher. This role of a listener-adviser does not suggest that the classroom teacher is a counselor in the professional sense (for counseling is a complex, special skill which requires specialized training), but does recognize that she or he is in the front line of the school counseling program.

As a Referral Agent. If, in our previous situation, it became apparent that Mary's difficulties were too complex for Miss Jones to handle, a guidance-minded teacher like Miss Jones very likely would discuss with Mary the possibility and advantages of talking with Mr. Haseley, the school counselor. In this capacity, Miss Jones would illustrate the important function of the classroom teacher serving in a referral role in the school guidance program. It is obviously impossible for the school counselor in his or her limited contacts with the total student population to be personally aware of all or even a small portion of students who may be in need of counseling assistance. Therefore, the alert classroom teacher in his or her role as a referral agent can ensure that students with significant problems will not go unnoticed and uncounseled.

As a Human Relationship Facilitator. When Johnny entered Miss Jones's class this morning, another pupil in the class spoke a cheery hello to which Johnny replied, "Shut your damn mouth." Johnny then proceeded to shove his way rudely through a group of girls who were standing near his desk. Coming to his desk, Johnny noticed some books of another student on his seat. He kicked them onto the floor saying, "They aren't mine! What the hell are they doing here?" The classroom provides an interesting setting for the study of human relationships. In recent years we have come to recognize the importance of the classroom setting for the development of human relationship skills in the individual student. The classroom teacher then, as the normally recognized leader of the classroom group, has another important role—i.e., that of a human relationship facilitator and developer. This means, first of all, that the teacher reflects and demonstrates good human relationships before and with her or his students. It also means that the classroom teacher plans and directs group interactions which promise positive human relationship experiences for each individual participant. Further, many students will need individual tutoring in developing and mastering these skills, just as in any other type of learning. In the case just cited for example, the ever-alert Miss Jones might illustrate, demonstrate, or explain to Johnny, while in conference, how his behavior affects others, and together they might plan a strategy for improving his relationships with his fellow students. Even though the teacher is the focus of human relationship development activities in the school, the school counselor should be viewed and used as the human relationship consultant in the educational setting.

As a Career Educator. Another important role and function of the classroom teacher, which is emphasized by the national career education movement, is the planned contribution in every subject-matter class for the pupils' overall career and related educational development. In this role the teacher has the opportunity to provide a data base from which pupils will make their eventual career decisions and to understand the relationships between education and career planning. Indeed, at every educational level, the teacher has the opportunity to provide for career-oriented experiences that are appropriate to the levels of readiness of their students. The classroom teacher must also provide the student with the opportunity to examine and develop various career-oriented skills and examine roles that may have career applications for him or her in the future. The school's program of career guidance must be centered in the classroom and integrated into the ongoing and total educational program of the institution. Since the total development of the individual is vital, the career aspects of this development cannot be separated from the whole.

For the classroom teacher's important role as a career and educational developer, the school counselor can again function as an expert consultant. The counselor can also assist the classroom teacher in securing appropriate educational and occupational development materials and can take responsibility for planning special activities that are related to the ongoing classroom experiences of the student.

Whereas the preceding paragraphs have described the overall role and function of the classroom teacher as a guidance program implementer and as an important contributor to the school guidance team, the classroom of the guidance-minded teacher offers the most natural, consistent, and effective setting for providing pupils with developmental guidance. We, therefore, encourage teachers to seek preparation for their important role on the school guidance team.

Paraprofessionals

In recent years education has witnessed an increase in the utilization of individuals who are not by training or experience classified as professional educators. These individuals, who have been labeled most commonly as paraprofessionals or educational aides, have served in a variety of capacities, such as providing clerical assistance to classroom teachers, supervisory assistance to classroom teachers, supervisory assistance to study groups, tutorial assistance to younger and often "slow" learners, and various service activities, i.e., cafeteria and transportation. Although the coming of the paraprofessional has not been without attending controversies, the economic and facilitative advantages appear to be slowly winning over the opposition that still exists to their employment.

The utilization and related controversies of the employment of paraprofessionals in school guidance and counseling programs has closely paralleled that of other areas of education. However, a study by the Guidance Committee of the North Central Association of Colleges and Secondary Schools (1972) seems to indicate both acceptance and an increased utilization of paraprofessionals in school guidance programs.

In view of the increased acceptance of the paraprofessional in the school guidance program, four major principles relevant to the role and function of paraprofessionals are examined in the paragraphs that follow.

a. Paraprofessionals are employed only when their utilization enables the professionals in the program to function more effectively. Most practicing counselors do not have to review the proliferation of articles in the professional journals to know that they are spending a disproportionate amount of their professional time and effort on clerical and other repetitive tasks which do not require their professional skills. The employment of paraprofessionals to relieve school counselors of such routine chores, is a popular and appropriate paraprofessional role. However, when the paraprofessional is viewed as an alternate to the employment of additional professional personnel with the assumption that she or he can handle certain professional duties, the guidance program suffers both in image and function, as well as in potential service. This suggests that paraprofessionals should only be employed in those activities which are commensurate with their training and experience.
b. Where employed, paraprofessionals should be provided with opportunities for both training and advancement. If the paraprofessional is an asset to school guidance and counseling programs, his or her contributions to the program can be further enhanced by a planned training program that seeks to provide the paraprofessional with additional appropriate knowledge and skills and to prepare him or her for increased program responsibility. The lat-

ter would also suggest the existence of career ladders that would enable the professional to anticipate and work toward advancement in the school system. In some instances, it may be possible for the paraprofessional to complete a counselor training program and thus move from the role of paraprofessional to professional.

Many community colleges around the country have developed human services training programs which focus on the preparation of paraprofessionals for work in psychological, social welfare, and educational agencies and institutions. A few community colleges have also initiated programs that are tailored to a given paraprofessional specialty. Zimpfer (1979) notes that a community college program will typically lead to an associate degree, which provides a sense of status and achievement to the student. The opportunities for job advancement are greater for this person than for the lesser-trained paraprofessional. Similarly, the opportunity for transfer into four-year and ultimately even into graduate training, if the student has the aptitude and the desire, is also afforded. Horizontal mobility is also an advantage of a community college program. Because of its breadth, the knowledge and skills acquired by the paraprofessional are often generalizable to a variety of settings. (Zimpfer, 1979, p. 18)

c. Individuals who are selected to work as paraprofessionals in school guidance programs should be carefully screened prior to their employment. As previously stated, school guidance program personnel should demonstrate positive human relationship techniques and understandings. This "modeling" cannot be limited to just the professional staff. Such nonprofessionals as the receptionist, student helpers, secretaries, and paraprofessionals will also be in contact with students and others served by the school guidance program. They, too, are important in the creation of models and perceptions by which others make judgments.
d. Paraprofessionals should function within the ethical guidelines of the professionals they are assisting. Those paraprofessionals who are associated with the school guidance program should be informed of, and expected to

function within, those ethical guidelines prescribed for their professional colleagues. This initially means that they must be informed of their guidelines and the resultant expectancies, and that adequate supervision must be provided to ensure their conformity to the guidelines. The objectives of the school guidance program could be thwarted if, for example, paraprofessionals inadvertantly broke rules of confidentiality or good human relationship practices.

The Professional Helping Team for Community Agencies

Mental Health Centers

The Community Mental Health Centers Act of 1963 and its subsequent amendments stimulated a nationwide development of community-based agencies that provided services for the prevention and treatment of mental health disorders. The act originally provided for five essential services: inpatient care, outpatient care, emergency services, partial hospitalization, and consultation and education. Later, additional services were provided including diagnostic services, rehabilitation services, precare and aftercare services, training, research, and evaluation. These services are available in mental health centers to all individuals who reside in the geographical area designated as the center's responsibility. The inability of individuals to pay for these services need not prevent them from being utilized. No minimum period of residence in the service area is required for treatment. Self-referral or referral by the family of clients is the most popular approach to the services of community mental health centers. Next in popularity are referrals from family physicians, the legal system, schools, and other community agencies.

The professional team for community mental health centers may include psychiatrists, psychologists, social workers, and other mental health personnel, including counselors and psychiatric nurses. In addition to the professional team, administrators and support personnel and even volunteer workers also work in many centers. The responsibilities of the professional staff is dictated by their professional training and background.

Other Social Service Agencies

Small Community-Based Social Service Agencies. During the past fifteen years, thousands of small, nonprofit, community-based social service agencies have been established. Community-based social-service agencies are those whose scope of operation is focused on the immediate community or on specific needs within a community and whose principal function is to meet a specific social or human-service need. These grass roots organizations are usually effective, because they are able to take risks, adjust to societal changes, and provide opportunities for people willing to engage in one-to-one relationships with clients.

The staffs of these agencies usually consist of a director, an assistant director or project coordinator, a secretary (usually part-time), and a volunteer support system. Volunteers perform highly specialized functions that require experience and skills as well as odd jobs that require no formal training (Clifton and Dahms, 1980, p. 2).

The services provided by these small community-based agencies may emphasize or include referral assistance; educational activities such as consumer skills, remedial education, and training for the handicapped; job placement and job training related to placement; and advocacy and outreach functions. The small social service agencies provide assistance to a wide range of individuals: elderly people who have limited financial resources, teenagers "on the run," veterans involved with drug abuse, family members coping with divorce, recently widowed individuals struggling to deal with their loss, and countless others (Clifton and Dahms: 1980, p. 8).

The "team" for these small agencies may consist of only one or two full-time professionals, frequently psychologists or sociologists, "backed up" by a variety of volunteers, and, in some settings, by part-time employees as well.

Service Agencies for the Aging. The "graying of America" has led to increased interest in and services for the aged. The largest network of agencies to serve our aging population are those agencies that were established under the 1973 amendments to the Older Americans Act. Approximately 600 agencies nationwide are operative under this act. Each agency is responsible for determining the needs of the elderly in its area and planning a strategy to meet these needs. Roles and activities for which counselors may be particularly well qualified are providing retirement counseling, assisting in adjustments to the deaths of spouses, and providing avocational and recreational guidance.

Aging agency "teams" are typically headed by the agency program administrator whose staff may include social workers, psychologists, counselors, nurses and nurses aides, and nonprofessional assistants, who are often volunteers.

Rehabilitation Counseling. Rehabilitation counselors work with disabled clients to assist them in overcoming deficits in their skills. In these efforts the counselor is seeking to bring physically, mentally, or emotionally disabled individuals back into the mainstream of society. For disabled adults, this includes entry into an appropriate career. The rehabilitation counselor's role is a complex one and may include providing for a broad range of psychological and career-oriented services, coordinated with other community agencies and consultation with families and employers or educators. Rehabilitation counselors may also work with special types of clients such as the deaf, blind, the mentally ill, or the physically handicapped. The majority of rehabilitation counselors work for government agencies or nonprofit organizations. In these settings, they often work in close cooperation with physicians and/or psychiatrists. With the implementation of Public Law 94-142, which provides for the integration of handicapped students into the mainstream of education, rehabilitation counselors may be increasingly employed by school systems or utilized as resource personnel to consult with school counselors in dealing with the particular problems that handicapped individuals face in the school setting.

Other Helping Agencies and Institutions

Counselors in both school and nonschool settings should be aware of the resources that are available to their clients in noncounseling settings. For example, many communities have established career centers that provide career information and guidance and related planning activities. Women's centers and minority centers also are sources of specialized career assistance. Local libraries often have excellent career informational materials. It is important that counseling program managers appraise themselves of all possible resource bases for their clients and establish channels for communication and cooperation in these bases.

Summary and Implications

In most professional settings the counselor is a team member. As a team member she or he has the responsibility to recognize and communicate his or her appropriate role and function and to recognize and encourage the contributions of other team members to the school or agency counseling program. In school settings the helping professional team is usually composed of school psychologists and/or psychometrists, school social workers, and medical personnel. Pupil personnel workers (such as student deans and attendance workers), school administrators, and the classroom teacher also have valuable roles and very important contributions to make in the school counseling program.

In community mental health centers, psychiatrists, psychologists, social workers, counselors, and nurses often comprise this agency team. They, too, must learn to function together and to recognize and respect each other's contributions to the total agency endeavor. Other community-based social service agencies, such as those serving small communities, the aged, or rehabilitation clients, also employ counselors and other helping professionals.

In all of these settings, the counselor has the opportunity to advance himself or herself and the counseling profession by exemplifying the human relationship skills that she or he is—in theory at least—supposed to possess, which includes functioning as an effective team member. Chapter 3 discusses the needs assessment approach to determining the priorities that counselors should address if their role and function is to be a relevant one.

CHAPTER 3

Needs Assessment: The Foundation for Program Development

Introduction

In the 1970s a heretofore rarely heard of word became, almost overnight, a key word in the vocabulary of educational leaders and, later, other public servants who depended on taxpayers' support. This popular, if sometimes threatening, word was *accountability*. The use of this term was an outgrowth of demands that education be held accountable for its actions—that some evidence of accomplishments and gains be provided in return for public support for education in the form of tax investments. The principal of accountability suggests that tax-supported efforts, including programs of counseling and guidance, both in and out of schools, must justify their existence through evidence of their accomplishments. Accountability also implies that the accomplishments of an institution or organization are relevant to the purposes for which the taxpayers or other payers established the agencies or organizations.

In establishing relevance and a basis for accountability, programs have increasingly and routinely begun with a process popularly labeled as "needs assessment." Kaufman and Harsh (1969) suggest that "A need 'is the discrepancy between what is and what should be.' It is a noun, i.e., a thing. As used here, a need is nothing more or nothing less than the documented gap or difference between *the results* we are currently achieving and *the results* we wish to achieve. It is a gap in ends, not means. A needs assessment is a formal collection of these gaps, the placing of the gaps in priority order, and selecting the gaps of highest priority for action and resolution. It is a formal process" (Kaufman and Harsh, 1969, p. 20).

As needs assessment forms a basis for accountability, it also ensures a greater degree of program relevancy. Since the outcomes of needs assessment suggest that this is what the data (much of it factual) tell us we should be doing, it is difficult for program planners to avoid doing the necessary, the relevant.

In recent generations one of the many consistent criticisms of counseling and guidance, especially in school settings, has been the loss of relevancy; the suggestion that programs are making provisions for needs that no longer exist and are ignoring the real needs of the populations they are designed to serve. Relevancy suggests that the objectives of each counseling program, whether it is school, institutional, or agency based, must be determined by the needs of the particular clientele that they exist to serve. Thus, for example, although a school or agency may have a counseling and guidance program that is similar to that of other schools or agencies, it may also have one that differs considerably from others. Each program must be specifically designed for the clientele it is designed to serve. It cannot be a model superimposed from without; rather, it must evolve from the needs existing within the population the program is designed to serve.

School and other counseling programs are not just "need" oriented. They are also reflective of the characteristics of their client population in a broader sense. The interests, abilities, backgrounds, experiences, achievements, and personalities of their program's target population determine program goals and activities. The fact that counseling programs must reflect client characteristics and needs if they are to remain relevant implies that the individual programs may, and probably should, differ in some details from year to year as the characteristics and needs of its student or other client body changes.

Assessment: The Tri-Part Concept

One concept for viewing and organizing the assessment phase of program development is one that presumes that the community, the institution (i.e., the school), and the target population are all influential in determining program direction. Such an approach recognizes the impact of the community on both the institution and the individual, the influence of the institution on programs and the individual, and interrelationships among community, institution, and individual, which create individual needs and influence how these needs can best be served by counseling and other human services programs within the community area.

COMMUNITY

The impact of environments on human functioning has been documented throughout history. The early explorers of America and other countries wrote about the "abundance" or scarcity of the land, wildlife, and so forth; their battles with the elements and sometimes other humans; and the natural resources available or lacking to meet their needs. Wartime diaries of soldiers have always been popular reading, and in recent years such publications as *One Day in the Life of Ivan Denisovich* (Solzhenitsyn, 1963) describing life in a Siberian work camp, have enjoyed wide readership. However, for a more exact and scientific study of environmental influences, we have to turn to those of sociologists and social psychologists, with special attention to their studies of the community as an entity. We are particularly interested with the influence of community characteristics on the agencies, institutions, and ongoing activities within the community. For example, as educational sociologists have noted, the school as a major community institution is subject to a variety of influences that reflect the characteristics of the supporting community. In this regard, the size and nature of the population of the community will influence the school and its programs in a variety of ways. Size alone will affect the ease and even sometimes the frequency of communication between the school and the community. In general, the larger the community, the more difficult it becomes for the school to "get its message across." Community concern in general and parental concern in particular with both schools and community-based agencies tend to increase as the size of community decreases. The distribution of the community's population across age, occupation, education, religion, and ethnic subgroups indicate characteristics of the community population that have a direct bearing on educational and public agencies and policies and programs.

Community mores or the mores of the various subcultures within a community are important in planning. They may be characterized by their own language, traditions, value systems, coping styles, concepts of education, and the pupils' social settings. These characteristics have implications for the strategies in which programs of counseling and guidance and other educational endeavors must engage if they are to secure and retain support, as well as serve the needs of the various ethnic groups in the community.

These characteristics also have implications for the staffing of school and other counseling programs. Where significant subcultures or minority groups exist within a community, counselors who are themselves members of subcultures or minorities may function directly or indirectly to bridge the communications and understanding gaps between the students from these groups and the school. The school counseling and guidance program must assume responsibility for the identification and characterization of the significant subcultures or minority groups in the school population and must further provide consulting services to assist faculty and staff in adapting the school educational program to meet their needs.

The economic characteristics of a community are among the more obvious influences on tax-supported activities. These characteristics will indicate the tax potential for educational and other purposes, the occupational level and educational aspirations which may be anticipated from students, the economic orientation of a community, and its future growth potential. The standard and cost of living in a community are often important in professional recruitment. The distribution of wealth and the resultant influences on social structures in a community can have residual effects on the school and on its activities.

The stability of the community's economy cannot be overlooked in any long-range educational planning. The state of development or depletion of the community's and surrounding area's natural resources can provide indications of economic trends. The combination of community priorities and community wealth are, in themselves, highly predictive of the expenditure one can anticipate for the community's educational and other tax efforts.

In community assessments we could define a community according to Sanders (1966) as a "territorially organized system coextensive with a settlement pattern in which (1) an effective communication network operates, (2) people share common facilities and services distributed within this settlement pattern, and (3) people develop a psychological identification with the 'locality symbol' (the name)." Another popular theorist in this field, Warren (1972), considers a community to be "that combination of social units and systems which perform the major social functions having locality relevance."

In a nonscientific sense a community may be a label for identifying a specific geographic area encompassing a recognized population.

Bloom (1977) notes that social scientists have developed the following four somewhat different approaches to studying the community.

The Community as a Place to Live

In this approach qualitative data are gathered to respond to such questions as "What kinds of people live in the area? What are the employment opportunities, the shopping facilities, the opportunities for recreation? What are the chief religious groupings, the general educational level, the housing pattern? What are the prevailing community attitudes and sentiments? What is family life like? How are newcomers received?" (p. 174).

The Community as a Demographic or Ecological Unit

In using this approach, the social scientist studies the spatial distribution of people, of occupations, and of activities and commonly makes use of subarea analyses of communities. By contrasting subareas, the social scientist can define neighborhood characteristics and can study the interrelationships of these characteristics. Having determined the basic elements of the community, at least from a demographic point of view, the researcher can identify how these elements change over time and can determine, for example, that an increasing proportion of the population of the central city are members of minority groups, or that crimes against property are substantially more common in certain areas of the community, or that certain forms of disruptive behavior occur with unusually high frequency in those sections of the city in which certain demographic characteristics prevail. This second approach to the study of the community, in contrast to the first approach, is highly quantitative in character. (p. 175)

The Community as a Way of Life

This is an ethnographic approach frequently used by anthropologists. It is highly subjective and usually requires extensive periods of residence in the community, fluency with the local language, and a high level of participation in community life. The spatial and demographic characteristics of the community are not separated out for study; rather, researchers using the ethnographic method seek to develop insight into the total culture. Because of the subjective nature of the approach, Sanders suggested that it "is as much a creative as a scientific act." (Bloom, 1977, p. 175); (Sanders, 1966, p. 18)

The Community as a Network of Social Relationships

In this approach the community is viewed as a social system. Patterns of social relationships and their groupings into larger and more complex social units are examined.

In addition to these four specific approaches, a fifth method utilizing a combination of these techniques could also be employed.

The Organization

It is not uncommon to hear statements such as "I've had a terrible day at the office, so just stay out of my way," or "if I don't get out of that school soon I'm going to go ape!" These and other similar statements simply suggest what many workers have recognized—that our work environment—our job—has a tremendous psychological impact on us. Moreover, in recent decades the impact of the organization on its members has been increasingly recognized and the assessment of organizations has become correspondingly popular. Organizational climate research has occupied a popular position in individual and organizational psychology and popular publications such as *Up the Organization* (Townsend, 1970) have caught the public's fancy. More recently, schools and other institutions have also given considerable attention to the interactions between the environment of the school or institution and the achievements, morale, or attitudes of their clientele.

Forehand and Gilmer (1964) defined organizational climate as a "set of characteristics that describe an organization and that (a) distinguish the organization from other organizations, (b) are relatively enduring over time, and (c) influence the behavior of people in the organization." From a counseling viewpoint, the climate or environment of the school as an organization is important from two interrelated influences. One is the impact that the school's environment has on the development, achievement, and overall mental health of the individual pupils—and also their teacher. The other is the influence of organizational characteristics on counseling program development.

Educational Environment and School Youth. From the long and complex history of human efforts to understand human behavior, a fundamental belief has emerged that suggests that human behavior is the result of the interactions of personal *and* environmental characteristics. For school-aged youth, no environment is more significant than their school environment. In this setting, youths of this age group spend a major portion of their waking hours, in both curricular and extracurricular pursuits, form their most significant peer relationships, interact with another set of significant adults (teachers), and at the same time are called upon to achieve, compete, often conform, and, eventually, to make crucial plans and decisions.

In this environment the foundations for self-discipline, humor and societal values, and attitudes toward self and others are established. Thus, the social-emotional atmosphere of the school and classroom is of vital importance and this environment may either facilitate, distract from, or inhibit learning and the total growth and development of the student. Within the school, the environment of the individual classroom is of vital importance and, as numerous studies have concluded, the teacher more than any other person, determines the environment of the classroom. Gazda and others (1977) pooled the findings of a number of studies and noted the following. (a) "The teacher's behavior largely determines the quality of emotionality in the classroom; (b) teacher-pupil relationships may affect pupils at deep psychological levels, and (c) the way a teacher behaves in interacting with students affects how students come to view others (social attitudes) and how they will treat others (human relations)" (p. 10). Recognizing the impact of the educational environment on school-aged youth, we must assume the importance of its assessment in any planning of counseling program development within school settings and in developing any "outside school" counseling program that may serve numerous school-aged youth.

Educational Characteristics and Program Development. The impact of educational characteristics of a school system on the component parts of that system, such as the school guidance program, are usually apparent to educators within that system. The more significant of these are categorized as "personnel" characteristics, "system" characteristics, and "material" characteristics. "Personnel" characteristics are reflected in school board personnel, the school administrators of the system, and the faculty and student body. "Systems" characteristics are reflected in the organizational structure and "channels" of an organization. "Material" characteristics include budget, facilities, and material resources.

Personnel Characteristics. Since boards of education tend to develop or approve policy, the composition of these boards is significant. In some situations unfortunately, boards of education may be viewed largely as tools of the political party in power. In other situations, boards of education may have members who are unsympathetic to education or who have particular biases that they seek to promulgate through board actions. The degree to which special interest groups are heard through boards of education may influence the development of special programs within schools. Board of education support and understanding is crucial to counseling program support. Knowing one's local board of education and how it functions is therefore important in counseling program development.

The support of school administrators and their concepts of counseling program role and function are both crucial to program development. In most elementary, junior or middle, and secondary schools the building principal is perhaps the most influential administrator in the system insofar as programs within his or her building are concerned. It is therefore important that direct communication between the counselor and school principal be established and maintained at all times. The characteristics of the school faculty can also have a bearing on program development. As discussed in Chapter 2, the faculty's understanding and support of a school counseling program is another crucial element. Factors such as the age, training, background, experience, and interests of the faculty can also be significant in determining directions for program development. The student population of the school—its background and characteristics—will also have a significant impact on program development and activities.

Systems Characteristics. The organizational structure of the school system can be an influence on program development and operation. An administrative structure that has an extensive network of channels and multiple decision points will restrict programs, the ability to expedite action, change, progress, and overall program development. Communication also tends to be stifled within such overstructured systems.

Another significant characteristic of the school organizational structure that must be considered is that of the curricula. Various curricular patterns and programs and the flexibility or rigidity that they imply for student educational planning are significant educational characteristics which, in turn, influence program planning.

Material Characteristics. Other significant characteristics of the educational system that should be considered are the budget, facilities, and other material resources.

The Target Population

Germane to the development of any program of counseling services, in any setting, is an understanding of the characteristics of the target population, including their needs which may be appropriately addressed by counseling. Although global information may be gleaned from such sources as census data, school reports, and reports of community agencies that provide meaningful indicators, more specific indices are needed. These can only be obtained by focusing on the target population.

The assessment of the target population may be approached

from two viewpoints. One viewpoint is data from the group for whom the services are intended (i.e., high school students, older adults, couples, and families), whereas the other is representative of those individuals who may have significant impressions of the target population, as, for example, in the case of school-age youth, parents, teachers, religious leaders, juvenile authorities, and youth employers. Typically, the assessors of target populations are seeking to characterize or profile the potential users of a specific program of counseling services, including their needs that such services may address. These characteristics usually include basic demographic data (age range, sexual distribution, educational background, parental background, sociopersonal data, and so forth), achievements, attitudes and values, and problems and concerns, including needs, both perceived and documented. The end result should be a reasonably accurate picture of the nature of the clientele to be served and the nature of their problems.

Assessment: The Process

Community Assessment

The process of collecting community data on some systematic basis has a long tradition in the United States. U.S. Census data have been collected every decade for nearly 200 years and this data base is being continually broadened to include economic and social information as well. Although the extensive data collection process engaged in by the U.S. Census Bureau is to be admired and the results should be utilized in many, if not most, community studies, it is far too demanding a process to repeat when undertaking a community needs assessment. There are, however, some proven and less complex approaches to community needs assessment. Some of the more popular of these are briefly described in the paragraphs that follow.

The Key Informant Approach. The key informant approach is a relatively simple and inexpensive survey technique that involves selected community leaders. These leaders can be utilized to provide an estimate of such concerns as youth needs and problems and/or community mental health needs and required services. This technique provides a broad picture of needs and services that are perceived as being important by the community as represented by its leadership. In implementing this technique a staff team may initially develop a list of community leaders identified as potential interviewees or contributors. This initial list may be used to generate additions, although we caution against involving too many individuals in carrying out this technique. Two main criteria for selecting a "key informant" should be the individual's knowledge of the community, its people and their needs, and the informant's importance for the viability of the counseling program's development.

Once the key informants are identified, information may be identified through a structured interview and/or questionnaire. A suggested interview guide format for key informant interviews, focusing on community mental health (suggested by Warheit, Bell, and Schwab, 1974) is provided in Figure 3–1.

Possible subjects to discuss with each person interviewed:

I. Community Problems (general)
- —in order of priority of importance
- —existing sources of help for each problem
- —unmet needs and problems, by groups
- —who gets most consistently left out of services?
- —which problems are not visible?

II. Mental Health Problems
- —a priority listing of seriousness (including prevalence)
- —existing sources of help for each problem
- —community attitudes toward use of public mental health services
- —groups that get most mental health services
- —groups that are most underserved

III. Attitudes toward the Community Mental Health Center (CMHC)
- —who gets to the Community Mental Health Center for help?
- —what other mental health resources do people in the community use? who uses them?
- —who does not/will not go to the CMHC and why?
- —which groups in need of mental health services get the least help? (Locate these as possible on a map of community).

FIGURE 3–1. Suggested Interview Guide Format for Key Informant Interviews. Demographic information and answers to closed-end questions on needs or on available or necessary services may also be appropriately collected. [Warheit, Bell, and Schwab, 1974]

The Community Forum Approach. The community forum approach is like an open town meeting, a gathering of members of the designated community. It is an especially useful technique for gaining citizen involvement in community mental health center assessment and evaluation activities. This approach is useful for proceeding from citizen participants in needs assessment to gathering a wide variety of views and attitudes related to community agencies or school counseling programs as well.

In utilizing this technique, it is usually desirable to identify a small cadre of community people who will help publicize and plan the actual forum. Because of the nature of this kind of meeting, it is important that it be as well planned as far in advance as possible. This includes determining and publicizing the purpose for the meeting, having the meeting itself chaired by a community person who is credible to most groups, and having this individual explain the purpose of the meeting, establish ground rules, and so forth. Follow-up and reporting are also important if the forum's momentum-generating capacity is not to be lost.

The Delphi Technique. The Delphi technique is another popular approach to conducting needs assessment. This approach systematically utilizes expert opinions as a basis for providing information about desirable educational or other agency goals. This technique, developed by the Rand Corporation, requires that educational goals and objectives be positively related to those factors that influence the quality of an individual's life. The Delphi process is as follows:

1. People are selected from the community who are believed to have useful information about schools, learning, and community life.
2. Individuals selected are organized into subgroups with each member being asked to write what they consider to be the important goals of education. These statements are collected and clustered under agreed upon descriptor names. (All statements are to be included.) The final list of clusters or goal statements are given to all the participants who rate their importance on a scale of 0–100.
3. In the next round all members of each subgroup repeat the same process except that they are now asked to iden-

tify factors that they believe produce a high quality of life in the community. The same clustering and prioritizing techniques are utilized.

4. At this point the subgroups are now requested to rate the goals of education in terms of their contributions to the quality of life factors. This furnishes an index of the relevance of educational goals to the hoped-for quality of life of individuals in the community.
5. Finally, the list of goal statements ranked for their importance to "the good life" is given back to the group who are then asked to indicate how well their schools are doing in progressing toward these goals.

Discrepancies noted between goal importance and perceived goal achievements may produce a numerical value of the needs related to improvement.

The Community Survey Technique. Although all the previously indicated techniques are, in a sense, a type of community survey, the process described at this point is perhaps the most popular approach to community needs assessment inasmuch as it involves a variety of techniques sampling a wide range of relevant data. This approach considers the full range of information available about a given community and then seeks to identify the most relevant of these data in view of the goals of the assessment. A data collection team is organized and a specific plan for the data collection is developed. This plan should specifically indicate the kinds of information needed, what data will provide this information, where the data are available, how it will be collected, who will collect it, and when. Figure 3–2 presents a sample data collection plan. Figure 3–3 presents a sample of a community survey checklist that may be a first step in collecting a broad range of community information. Figure 3–4 presents in chart form the flow of a sequence of activities for needs assessment and program planning.

The Nominal Group Approach. The nominal group approach is a structured workshop that minimizes face-to-face interaction among the participants in order to obtain the views of a wider range of participants. The structured approach of this workshop is designed to identify the widest possible range of strategic prob-

Type of Data	Source or Locale	How Collected	Who Collects	By When	Comments
I. Environment					
Population	Census-Courthouse	Personal visit with data collection form	Will Count	Oct. 10	
Geographic	State Survey-Box 811 State Capital	Letter of request	N. East	Oct. 15	
Economic	Major businesses and Chamber of Commerce Census	Personal data collection, visit, and interview	"Luckey" Bucks	Oct. 10	Mrs. Bradley will answer questions at C of C
Sociopersonal	Census	As indicated	Lotta Smiley	Oct. 20	
	Local Government Employment Office	Personal visit with data collection form as indicated	N. East	Oct. 20	
	Community Mental Health Center		N. East	Oct. 20	
	Law enforcement agencies—Courthouse	Personal visit and interview with data collection forms	N. East	Oct. 20	
	Churches		Will Count	Oct. 25	
	Civic Clubs		Will Count	Oct. 25	
	Family Services		Will Count	Oct. 25	
Political	Census	as indicated	Will Count	Oct. 10	May also want to interview local party heads.
Media	Local newspapers—offices of the *Snowdeep Herald*	Personal visit Review selected issues over a five-year period	Ima Reader	Oct. 10	Especially note front, editorial, and sports pages, plus educational column on Friday

Annual school report	Principal's office	Personal visit	Will Count	Nov. 8	
Annual departmental reports	Principal's office	Personal visit	Will Count	Nov. 8	
Miscellaneous school reports	Principal's office	Personal visit	Will Count	Nov. 8	
Board of Education minutes	Principal's office	Personal visit	Will Count	Nov. 8	
School paper *The Gaff & Gab*	Room 210, school	Personal visit and review of selected issues over a 5-year period	Ima Reader	Nov. 8	
School principal	Principal's office	Individual interview	Lotta Smiley	Nov. 8	
Teachers	(Use Room 102)	Individual interviews	"Luckey" Bucks N. East	Nov. 8 Nov. 8	
III. Target population					
Students	School	Questionnaires mailed to total sample	Will Count	Nov. 20	Time limit 45 minutes (one class period)
Teachers	School	Questionnaires to total sample	"Luckey" Bucks	Nov. 20	
Parents	Various addresses	Questionnaires mailed to representative sample	Ima Reader	Dec. 1	
Alumni	Various addresses		N. East	Dec. 1	
School leavers	Various addresses	Questionnaires mailed to representative sample	N. East	Dec. 1	
School administrators	County education offices	Questionnaire mailed to total sample	Lotta Smiley	Dec. 1	
Community leaders	Various addresses	Questionnaire mailed to representative sample	Lotta Smiley	Dec. 1	

FIGURE 3–2. Data Collection Plan for Counseling Program Development Snowdeep Senior High School.

(Data Collection)
for:

Community: ______________________
Survey Dates: ______________________
Survey Team: ______________________
____
____

______ 1. Census data
______ 2. News media analysis
______ 3. Board of Education (Minutes of) meetings
______ 4. Annual reports of schools
______ 5. County government data
______ 6. City government data
______ 7. Employment agencies
______ 8. Church board reports
______ 9. Chamber of Commerce data
______ 10. Geographic data
______ 11. Ecological-environmental data
______ 12. Other significant data (list sources)
____
____
____

Note: If data are not available, place notation "NA" in blank at left of item. Otherwise, when data are collected place a "√."

FIGURE 3–3. Community Survey Checklist.

lems and to aid in the development of alternative program plans. The workshop is made up of a small group of community people who share their views with respect to community needs, barriers to services, or needed programs in a highly structured group setting. The result is a broad listing of needs, barriers to desired programs, and a group rank ordering of priority goals to be achieved.

ORGANIZATIONAL ASSESSMENT

Whereas community assessment enables planners to more objectively determine those community characteristics and needs that influence counseling program development within school or

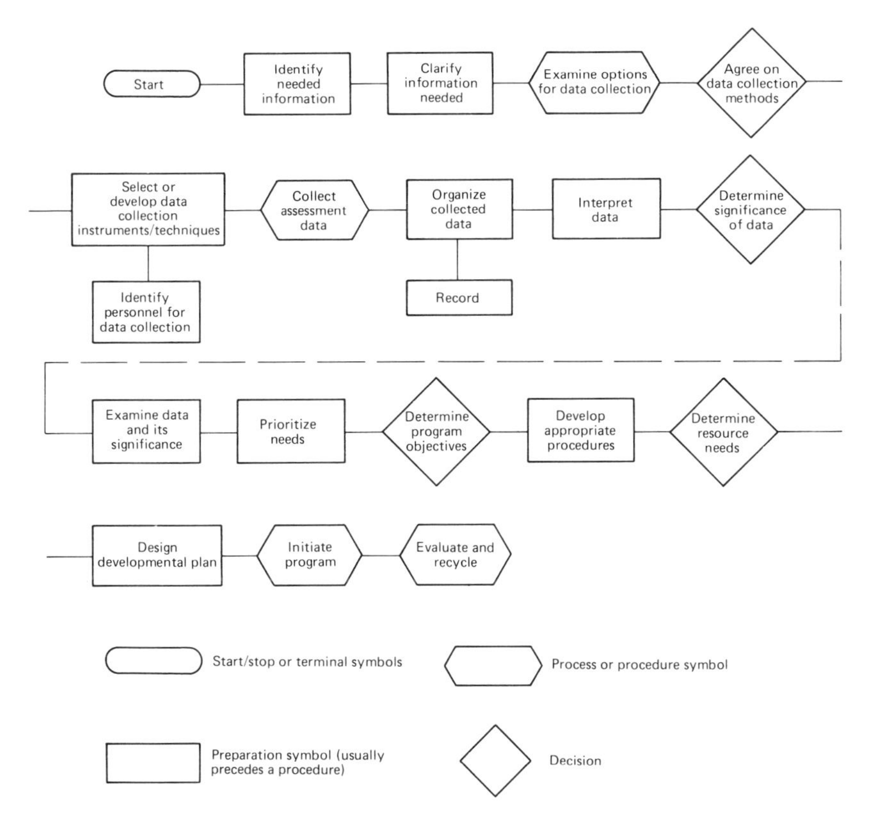

FIGURE 3–4. Example of a Sequence of Activities for Needs Assessment and Program Planning.

agency setting, the scope of the assessment must, as a second step, be narrowed to focus on the organization within which the counseling program functions—school, agency, hospital, industry—and in which a target population is served.

Organizational assessment itself is a popular and recognized activity. In schools particularly, assessment is probably most readily associated with accreditation procedures, as most schools seek the accreditation of their state department of public instruction and many seek a higher level of approval from their regional associations as well. These assessments, however, tend to emphasize an evaluation of the organization's functioning, which may, in the process, identify organizational needs, but do not as a rule function on the systematic identification of the needs of the target population the organization serves.

In needs assessment for program development, the process applied to the "parent" organization might be simply viewed as follows.

a. Identification of the significant characteristics of the organization

↓

b. Identification and/or development of procedures and instruments for collecting data regarding step (a).

↓

c. Determining who will collect the data (utilizing the procedures and instruments developed in the previous step and establishing time lines for the data collection.)

For counseling program development, the assessment of an organization should result in the identification of organizational characteristics and their impact on the delivery of counseling services to a target population. The identification of these characteristics includes assessment of some or all of the following.

Organizational Structure. What is the structure of the organization? Is it simple and recognizable by those within the structure? Does it facilitate program development, examination, and change? Is it an open structure with a free flow of communications? Does it enable units within the organization, as well as the organization as a whole, to readily and effectively meet their responsibilities, respond to their needs, and solve their problems? Are responsibilities for decision making, feedback, and evaluation recognized, accepted, and acted on?

Organizational Leadership. What are the positions of leadership in the organization? What are their responsibilities? How do the individuals function in these leadership roles? Does the leadership share decision making, planning, and so forth? Does the leadership both give and seek consultation from the membership of the organization, especially in meeting the needs of the population the organization is designed to serve?

Organizational Priorities. What are the priorities of the organization? How are they determined? Are they universally agreed upon and recognized within the organization? Are these priorities compatible with the mission of the counseling program? Are the priorities acted upon?

Organizational Resources. What are the resources available to the organization? To what degree are they adequate in view of the organization's mission and priorities? How are they distributed and utilized within the organization? Is there an identifiable trend in the availability of resources to the organization? Are the critical and unique resources needed for counseling program development available?

Organizational Policies. Are the policies of the organization stated in a format that is written and available or distributed? How are the policies of the organization determined? Are policies implemented in practice? Are subunits free to develop their own policy guidelines? Do the organizational policies facilitate or handicap in any way counseling program development and functioning?

Populations and Subpopulations. What is the general population that the organization is designed to serve? What are the characteristics of this population (i.e., distribution by age, sex, socioeconomic background, race, religion, careers and/or career planning, educational background, and so forth)? What are the identifiable accomplishments, attitudes, concerns, and needs of these populations?

Organizational Climate. What is the social climate of the organization? The social climates of various organizations and institutions have been described as supportive, controlling, structural, flexible, intellectual, artistic, or practical (Anastasi, 1976, p. 619). Does the climate encourage and/or discourage certain types of behaviors, activities, and program developments? Does the climate itself generate certain target population needs? Do different subpopulations perceive the organization's climate differently?

Particularly in schools there are two distinct populations: the professional faculty and staff and the student body who will be viewing the climate of the school from obviously differing perspectives. Faculty, for example, may view climate in terms of

Have the Following Been Procured?	Yes	No	Not Available	Comments
1. An organizational chart?				
2. Statements of institutional				
a) philosophy				
b) goals/objectives/priorities				
c) policies				
d) procedural guidelines				
3. Description of role and function of				
a) major subunits				
b) personnel				
4. Records and/or descriptors of institutional resources				
5. Reports of institutional functioning				
a) minutes of staff (i.e., faculty) meetings				
b) minutes of board of trustees or education meetings				
c) annual reports				
6. Review of significant institutional records (for example in schools, these would include attendance, academic achievements, standardized test results, curricular distributions, follow-up studies, school leavers, delinquency, rewards, and punishments, etc.)				
7. Other significant documents:				
______________________				
______________________				
______________________				

FIGURE 3–5. Procurement Checklist.

leadership and collegial support, individual autonomy and responsibility, recognition and rewards, rigidity or flexibility of the organization, how conflicts and issues are resolved (democratic versus autocratic), openness to change, and, usually to a lesser degree, the characteristics of the physical environment itself. For the school-age youth comprising a given student body, the school environment plays an important role in their adjustment at all ages, not only to school but to life itself. Factors such as satisfaction and adjustment to school in general, the classroom(s), and the classroom teacher are recognized in the development of such instruments as *The Quality of School Life Scale* (Houghton Mifflin,

1978). Another recognized important "environmental" influence on this group is their relationship with their peers.

Once the influential characteristics of an organization have been determined, a variety of data collection options may be considered. These include structured interviews, examination of existing records and relevant documents, questionnaires, checklists, and rating scales. Figure 3–5 is an example of a data-collection aid.

Such a checklist facilitates the identification and collection of important documents and lends organization to the effort that results from having it down in "black and white."

A second example of an instrument that might be used in organizational assessment is an "Organizational Trait Scale" (Figure 3–6). Such a scale could be distributed to both the administration and teaching faculty in a school, for example, or the "leadership" and "followership" of any organization for that matter, thus providing an opportunity, if desired, to compare and contrast views of the two groups.

In a school setting another technique, a simple structured interview, may be developed around the following questions.

1. Basic background data from interviewee (position in school, experience background here and previously, and other personal data that may lend depth to interpretation of the responses.)
2. What do you view as the major strengths of your school?
3. What are its major weaknesses?
4. What are the priority needs of your student population? (Both academic and nonacademic)
5. How well does this school recognize and respond to these needs?
6. How can this organization more effectively respond to these needs?
7. What role or/how can/ the school's counseling program contribute to meeting these needs?
8. Additional comments?

School-Community Readiness Assessment

An important influence on the development of school counseling and guidance programs is the readiness of the school and

The following is a list of organizational traits. You are asked to rate your organization on each of these traits by circling the appropriate number opposite the item. The number 5 is high or excellent, 3 is average, 1 is low or poor.

Trait	Scale				
1. Organizational structure is clear.	1	2	3	4	5
2. Organizational structure makes sense to me.	1	2	3	4	5
3. Organizational goals and priorities are clearly recognized.	1	2	3	4	5
4. Organizational goals and priorities are acted upon.	1	2	3	4	5
5. Organizational goals and priorities complement and are consistent with the goals and priorities of my own unit.	1	2	3	4	5
6. Policy guidelines are known and acted upon.	1	2	3	4	5
7. Democratic leadership.	1	2	3	4	5
8. Opportunity for input into decisions	1	2	3	4	5
9. Decisons are data based.	1	2	3	4	5
10. Communications are open.	1	2	3	4	5
11. Opportunities to experiment, innovate, change, etc.	1	2	3	4	5
12. Resources in general.	1	2	3	4	5
13. Resources for your program.	1	2	3	4	5
14. Reward system.	1	2	3	4	5
15. Organization is people-oriented (versus procedure oriented)	1	2	3	4	5
16. Professional staff (faculty) morale.	1	2	3	4	5
17. Student body (or other) morale.	1	2	3	4	5
18. Collaboration and cooperation (versus competition).	1	2	3	4	5
19. Opportunities for advancement.	1	2	3	4	5
20. I enjoy my job.	1	2	3	4	5
For Schools Especially					
21. Major needs of our students are recognized.	1	2	3	4	5
22. Major needs of our students are acted upon.	1	2	3	4	5
23. School counseling program is important.	1	2	3	4	5
24. School counseling program is effective.	1	2	3	4	5

FIGURE 3–6. Organizational Trait Scale.

the community to accept and implement such a program. In many instances educational personnel who have resided in the community and worked in the school system will be able to rather subjectively assess the probable receptivity of school and community to new or developing programs. This approach to readiness assessment has certain obvious limitations, however, if it is limited to a narrow representation of viewpoints (i.e., educational personnel only). Also, subjective descriptions do not identify specific positive or negative forces that may need to be considered in developing strategies for program development. Although most educators, including school counselors, are aware of factors that may influence the receptiveness or readiness of their school to accept new programs or significantly develop existing programs, there have been only limited efforts to organize these identifiable factors into a more objective approach.

We suggest that an alternate approach to subjective assessment or personal opinions may lie in the use of some objective technique, such as checklists and rating scales. Several authors of this text have been involved in research and experimental activities seeking to develop an appropriate program-readiness scale that might be used in school situations. An example of such an instrument, perhaps best labeled as a weighted checklist, is indicated in Figure 3–7.

This checklist presents twenty items with weighted values of 1 to 5 each, making possible a maximum of 250 points. Preliminary studies seem to suggest that these indicate the following levels of readiness:

226+	Outstanding possibilities for establishing a guidance program
201–225	Excellent
145–200	Average
121–144	Some difficulties
100–120	Many problems
Under 100	Nearly impossible

In addition, users of the instrument should be able to identify possible obstacles to, as well as possible support for, program development. A modified version of this instrument might be used for counseling programs in other settings.

Instruments such as the one depicted in Figure 3–7 could be presented to a cross section of community residents, including clergy, businesspeople, politicians, government figures, other youth workers, medical and legal personnel, educators, and parents. These citizens should be individuals who have resided within the school community area for a minimum of five years and who have an active interest in education in their community. This checklist is used for illustrative purposes only. Those who develop and use such checklists should employ them with caution and interpret the results as indications only and not as absolutes.

Factor	Weighted Value	×	Rated Value (1 to 5)	=	Item Score
1. Administrative support	5		_____		_____
2. Board of Education support	5		_____		_____
3. Budget	4		_____		_____
4. Community resources	2		_____		_____
5. Community spirit or pride	1		_____		_____
6. Community support for education	3		_____		_____
7. Counselor role and function (understanding of)	3		_____		_____
8. Educational accomplishments of school and community	2		_____		_____
9. Facilities	3		_____		_____
10. Parent support	2		_____		_____
11. Community perception (evaluation) of the school	3		_____		_____
12. Pupil support	1		_____		_____
13. Pupil-counselor ratio	2		_____		_____
14. Recreational program (community)	1		_____		_____
15. Secretarial service available to program	1		_____		_____
16. School "esprit de corps"	1		_____		_____
17. School referral resources	2		_____		_____
18. Teacher support	5		_____		_____
19. Political interference, absence of	2		_____		_____
20. School—Community communications	2		_____		_____
Total	50	×	5	=	250 points

(Formula: Weighted Value × Rated Value = Item Score)

All items in the above judged on a five point rating scale as follows:
Excellent = 5; Good = 4; Average = 3; Poor = 2; Very poor or non-existent = 1.

FIGURE 3–7. Readiness Factors in Initiating a School Guidance Program.

ASSESSING THE TARGET POPULATION

Developing a Plan. The needs assessment of the target population provides the critical data for determining program objectives. It is the key to a relevant program, a program that is meeting the real needs of clients. It is essential in any plan for accountability. This assessment most certainly should involve the target group—the potential clients or recipients of the counseling services. For school counseling program development, students are the target population to be surveyed. However, the additional surveying of their "significant others"—teachers and parents—can provide validating and insightful data that should be considered in any complete program of assessment.

As with all forms of assessment, planning must precede data collection. For example, to assess the needs of a student population the following procedural sequence might be planned.

a. Identify the primary population (students) and relevant subpopulations (teachers, parents) to be surveyed.
b. Specify the information desired from the participating populations.
c. Determine and design the appropriate data collection procedures and/or instruments.
d. Determine the sampling procedures to be utilized.
e. Establish a data-collection timetable and assign data-collection responsibilities.

An example of such a plan is illustrated in Figure 3–8. Examples of questionnaires for data collection from students, parents, and teachers are provided in Appendixes A, B, and C.

Utilizing Sampling Procedures. As noted in the plan illustrated in Figure 3–8, the total student population would be surveyed as would all the faculty and professional staff. However, a portion of the parents and community leaders would be involved through the use of random and/or representative sampling procedures, respectively. These and other sampling procedures are frequently desirable in needs assessments, when it would be impossible or inconvenient from a time, expense, or accessibility standpoint to use all of the individuals that constitute an identifiable population. An identifiable population is a group of people who share one or more characteristics in common. This sampling of populations is referred to as inferential statistics. Popular sampling techniques include the following.

1. Representative Sample—a sample that is representative or reflects all of the characteristics of the group which comprise the total population. This technique provides a

Primary Populations:
High School Students

Subpopulations to sample:
Parents
High School Professional Staff
Community Leaders

Information Desired	To Be Collected from	How Collected	Sample	By Whom	By When
Attitudes toward:		Questionnaire			
School	Students		All students	Dr. Bean	Nov. 1
Home	Parents		Random sample	Dr. Hart	Nov. 10
Community	Teachers and staff		All teachers	Dr. Gayle	Nov. 15
	community leaders		Representative Sample	Dr. Clifford	Nov. 15
Behaviors:		Questionnaire			
At home	Students		All students	Dr. Bean	Nov. 15
With peers	Parents		Random sample	Dr. Hart	Nov. 15
In special situations	Teachers and staff		All teachers	Dr. Gayle	Nov. 15
Generally	Community leaders		Representative sample	Dr. Clifford	Nov. 15
Emotions	Parents	Questionnaire	Representative sample	Dr. Hart	Nov. 25
	Teachers	Questionnaire	Representative sample	Dr. Gayle	Nov. 25
Interests:		Questionnaire			
Educational	Students		All students	Dr. Bean	Nov. 25
Career					
Recreational					
Social					
Hobbies					
Needs:		Questionnaire			
Problems and concerns	Students		All students	Dr. Bean	Nov. 25
	Parents		Random sample	Dr. Hart	Nov. 25
	Teachers and staff		All teachers	Dr. Gayle	Nov. 25
Values:	Students	Questionnaire	Representative sample	Dr. Clifford	Nov. 25
	Teachers	and Interview	Representative sample	Dr. Clifford	Nov. 25

FIGURE 3–8. Needs Assessment Plan for Brock High School.

miniature replica both qualitatively and quantitatively of the total group.

For example, in conducting a student survey in a high school with 4,000 students with distribution indicating—

800—12th graders of which 50 per cent are female
900—11th graders of which 60 per cent are female
1100—10th graders of which 40 per cent are female
1200—9th graders of which 45 per cent are female

A representative sample of 10 per cent would result in surveying

80—12th graders of which 40 per cent are female
90—11th graders of which 54 per cent are female
110—10th graders of which 44 per cent are female
120—9th graders of which 54 per cent are female

2. Random Sample—a sample that is picked in a manner which assures that every member of the group or population has an equal chance of being selected. For example, a 10 per cent random sample from 4,000 students might be drawn by placing all 4,000 names in a container and having someone blindfolded draw out 400 of the names. Another random method might arrange all the names alphabetically, then roll a dice and if, for example, the number six came up, the sample would begin with student number 6, then number 12, and so forth, until the desired number of students were selected.
3. Stratified (random) Sample—A sample that, although random, has been subdivided into some system of classification in order to get a more accurate representativeness of the total group. For example, in the high school of 4,000 students we might select randomly 10 per cent from each of the four grade levels represented in the school population.
4. Convenience Sample—A convenience or nonprobability sample is one that does not reflect the characteristics of a specific population, but rather, it is one selected primarily on the basis of its availability. For example, in our high school of 4,000, the school principal might decide that the only sample available for our survey would be those 318 students scheduled for a study hall sometime during the school day. (Obviously samples of convenience should be

avoided wherever possible because of their limited generalizability.)

In concluding this brief review of sampling approaches we might note some practical observations about sampling size as suggested by Best (1981).

1. The larger the sample, the smaller the magnitude of sampling error.
2. Survey-type studies probably should have larger samples than needed in experimental studies.
3. When sample groups are to be subdivided into smaller groups to be compared, the researcher initially should select large enough samples so that the subgroups are of adequate size for his or her purpose.
4. In mailed questionnaire studies, since the percentage of responses may be as low as 20 to 30 per cent, a larger initial sample mailing is indicated.
5. Subject availability and cost factors are legitimate considerations in determining appropriate sample size. (p. 14)

The Collection of "People" Data. In most needs assessment, data are examined from two basic sources. One valuable source can be precollected or nonpeople data such as reports and records, often originally collected for other purposes (i.e., course data, school reports) but that also provide useful information for needs assessment and later program planning. The other basic data needed are that which are "original" or unique to the needs of the assessment. These data must usually be generated through the participation of others and, as such, this "people" data collection involves some special considerations as follows.

1. Explain why the data are being collected, the nature of the information being sought, how it will be collected, and how it will be used. In other words, orient the potential participant to the study. His or her understanding will help the participant to respond as effectively as possible.
2. Convenience to the respondent is important. This means consideration of the time involved, simplicity of response, and the collection of useful but not superfluous data. Where appropriate, response deadlines may, be estab-

lished, but they should be sufficiently in advance so as not to risk those participating in the study.

3. There should be opportunities for respondents to comment or enlarge on their responses or add additional viewpoints beyond those solicited. These opportunities may be especially appropriate when data are collected through such limited response instruments as rating scales and checklists.
4. Consideration should be given in surveys to the use of some common items across all groups (i.e., parents, students, teachers, community leaders). The responses of different groups to similar items provide meaningful data for comparative validation and interpretation purposes.

Summary and Implications

It is important that counseling programs in any setting be relevant; that they be designed to meet the actual and priority needs of clientele. Further, these needs should be met in a manner that is both efficient and effective. The basis for designing relevant, efficient, and effective programs that can be accountable is a planned program of assessment. Such an assessment would ideally include the community, the organization, and the target population.

A variety of techniques and models is available to gather assessment data. Those which are determined to be most useful for a given situation should be incorporated into a data-collection plan. Such a plan is essential in ensuring that the needed data is collected as efficiently as possible. Typically a plan would indicate the types of data needed, likely sources, how it would be collected, by whom, and by what date.

Needs assessment is not an end in itself. The collection of data implies interpretation and application to the development of accountable and relevant counseling programs. Chapter 4 discusses such program development.

CHAPTER 4

Initiating and Developing School Programs of Counseling and Guidance

Introduction

In 1958 the National Defense Education Act was enacted by Congress and signed into law by President Eisenhower. Among the significant sections of this act were those providing support for the training of school counselors and the development of school counseling and guidance programs. As a result, guidance programs were rapidly initiated in many school systems in the period that followed. However, inadequate planning in too many instances led to mediocre programs, which accomplished little for education in general and the guidance movement in particular. These inadequately conceived and planned programs provided a basis for many of the popular criticisms of school counseling and guidance program effectiveness even today. Those programs that were and are successful (and there are many) were built around certain professionally recognized principles, were cognizant of the community and educational characteristics which influenced program development, and were carefully planned and systematically developed. This chapter discusses principles that are appropriate to program planning and development and the factors that influence the initiation and development of school counseling and guidance programs. Program reorganization and change are also discussed.

Utilizing Assessment Data for Program Development

The previous chapter discussed the collection of community, organizational, and target population data and, as noted in the summary of Chapter 3, data collection is not an end in itself. The eventual purpose of data collection is to ensure meaningful direction for program planning; to enhance relevance; to provide for program accountability.

The first step toward utilizing the collected data is the summarization and organization of the data into some sort of meaningful configurations or displays. It is important to keep in mind that a lot of useful information can often appear to overwhelm the potential users unless it is clearly and concisely presented. However, this does not mean "briefing" data to the point where accuracy of interpretation is threatened. In organizing the collected information, consideration should be given to the purposes for which the data were collected, who will be reviewing the data, and possible categories into which the data might be placed. The final outcome should result in ease and accuracy of interpretation.

Once the data have been summarized, the program planners are ready to proceed to interpretation. Here the importance of fairly discrete categories will be noticed, since each "category," cluster, or cell of data should be examined to determine its meaning for program development (or reorganization). At this point cross-item relationships may also be noted. Next, one must ask, What are the implications and significance that can, with reasonable validity, be attached to these interpretations? It is not until this step is completed that planners can proceed to identify program priorities.

Priority needs, once they are identified, should be listed and examined. In this examination questions that must be asked include: "Is this priority need a responsibility of the counseling program? If yes, have we secured or can we secure the resources and/or expertise to adequately respond? Will the possible outcomes be worth the effort and resources expended? Is there a reasonable chance that the need can be adequately responded to? and, most importantly, what priority should be given this need (i.e., highest, important, average, low)!" The outcome of this step should be a listing and ordering of potential program priorities, which should then be carefully examined and, if deemed advisa-

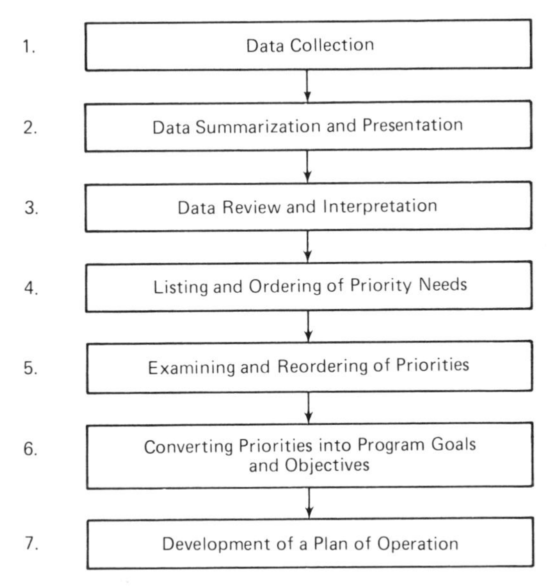

FIGURE 4–1. Sequence of Procedures for Utilizing Assessment Data.

ble, reordered into a final hierarchy. This final ordering then becomes the basis for program goals and objectives and the related procedural planning. Figure 4–1 presents the steps of this process.

Principles for Program Development

GUIDANCE IS A CONTINUOUS PROCESS

A longer living, more active adult population, multiple and midlife career changes, and changing society values are but a few of the many reasons given for suggesting that in the near future counseling may be viewed as a lifelong service. For optimal initial assistance to youth while in school, formalized school counseling and guidance services must be provided from childhood to early adulthood—from kindergarten through college. To defer the provision of such services until a student enters high school, as is too typically the case, is to deny the student vitally needed assistance during the crucial period when he or she is developing and solidifying the self and the social attitudes that will largely determine the course of his or her life. An abundance of evidence indicates that many of the critical problems of today's society such as crime and delinquency, substance abuse, poor human and societal relationships, (i.e., divorce, spouse and child abuse, social prejudice) have their beginnings in the individual's elementary school years. Similarly, to provide assistance only in times of crises—whether in childhood or adolescence—is to deny the individual the help that is vitally needed in mastering the developmental tasks dictated by our culture for one's developmental level. Thus, to be preventive and of maximum developmental value, counseling and guidance services must be continuous and an ongoing process.

The Guidance Process Is Carried Out Through Certain Specific Services or Acknowledged Responsibilities

To meet the student needs for which it is designed, the guidance process must be highly formalized, with its objectives specifically defined and the responsibilities of the personnel charged with its implementation clearly delineated. The objectives derived from a regular and planned program of needs assessment for a specific school will determine the kinds and extent of the program's activities; these activities will determine the specific responsibilities of the professional counseling personnel. Only through carefully structured programmatic approaches that specify objectives, functions, and responsibilities can the guidance process be adequately implemented and objectively evaluated.

The School Counseling and Guidance Program Is Relevant to Student Characteristics and Needs

The counseling and guidance objectives of a given school must be determined by the needs of the students of that school. Although a school may have a program similar to that of other schools, it may also have one that differs considerably from others. To function effectively, a guidance program must be specifically designed for the students the program is to serve. It cannot be a model superimposed from without; rather, it must evolve from the needs existing within. School guidance programs are not just "need" oriented; they are also reflective of the characteristics of their student population. The interests, abilities, backgrounds, experiences, achievements, and personalities of students determine the goals and activities of guidance programs. The fact that the guidance program must reflect student characteristics and needs if they are to remain relevant implies that the individual school guidance program may differ from year to year as the characteristics and needs of its student body changes.

School Guidance Programs Are Coordinated by, and Under the Leadership of, a Trained Guidance Counselor

An effective program of counseling and guidance requires not only specifically delineated services and responsibilities but expert leadership as well. The necessary leadership must be provided by a professional specialist who understands all aspects of the counseling and guidance program and who, by virtue of training and experience, can administer the program as initially conceived and modify it as needs demand.

This leadership of counseling and guidance programs by professional counselors should be evident at every level within the educational structure. In other words, school counselors in school counseling and guidance programs should work under a professional counselor's leadership. The professional counseling leadership of the various schools within a system should also function under professional counseling supervisory and leadership personnel from the system administrative level. All too often we find the latter principle violated once we move into the structure of the school system's superintendent's office, where sometimes it is erroneously assumed that school administrators can provide leadership for any and all of the specialized programs. Since many counselor education programs at the specialist and doctoral-degree level do, in fact, prepare professional counselors to function as systems directors or supervisors of guidance services, school systems should secure appropriately trained and experienced counseling personnel to lead their programs at all levels.

The School Counseling and Guidance Program Is Coordinated with, and Contributary to, the Curricular Program of the Institution.

For maximum benefit to both the student and the school, the counseling and guidance program must function as an integral part of the total school program. Such services and activities cannot be seen as supplementary to a school's program; they must become an integral part of it. However, if the school's counseling and guidance program is to function as an integral part of the total educational program, school counselors must understand those concepts and practices related to the term *curriculum*. As indicated, a school guidance program must be relevant to student characteristics and needs, which include those of significance to the development of an appropriate curriculum within the educational institution. It is the counselor's responsibility, therefore, to bring this "need" information and its implications to bear as one of his or her contributions to the educational program.

In this regard, the school counselor works for curricular opportunities which, in effect, emphasize individualized academic programs that accommodate student differences. The counselor seeks to help the curricula adjust to the student, rather than vice versa. Such adaptations further ensure program relevance and probable motivation.

It would also appear that the counselor's participation in educational program development would provide greater assurance of a human development and learner-centered curriculum, rather than a content- or subject-matter-centered curriculum. As a guide for assisting school counselors in identifying curriculum goals and relevant activities and outcomes, Shane, Shane, Gibson, and Munger presented the diagram that appears as Figure 4–2.

The School Guidance Program Is Coordinated with, and Related to, Community Services and Needs

The natural link that exists between the school and other institutions and agencies designed to serve youth must be strengthened and utilized. Failure of the school to communicate and cooperate with youth-oriented and/or mental health-based community agencies not only denies students the greater degree of assistance such cooperation would provide but also often actually inhibits the provision of help, since the independent actions of the school or the involved agency may negate the value of actions taken by the other. The school should take the responsibility for establishing a liaison with mental health clinics, juvenile courts, community youth centers, drug prevention and treat-

	CURRICULUM GOALS	NATURE OF LEARNING	THE CURRICULUM GUIDE	CURRICULUM ORGANIZATION
THE REACTIONARY POSITION	To develop a "meritocracy"; to provide a classical background for an elite.	An abstract process of mental discipline; intellectual training.	Formal course of study. Directive.	Subject-centered; compartmentalized content.
THE CONSERVATIVE POSITION	To teach the "fundamentals" (3R's); to develop mastery of content.	Instilling the "proper" response to the "right" stimulus. Behavioristic.	Specific study guides. Prescriptive.	Some correlation between or among subjects.
THE LIBERAL POSITION	To help all children develop their potentialities. To emphasize human development, and social competence.	Gestaltist and field theory oriented. Meaning, purpose, interest and motivation stressed.	Flexible; often suggestive and permissive within limits agreed on by cooperative planning.	Emphasis on flexible structure governed by professional judgment.
THE EXPERIMENTAL POSITION	Exploratory. Methodically concerned with experimentation to bring about changes and improvements in child and society.	Continuing probes into the nature of learning; no fixed commitment to a given theory.	Usually in a state of process or emergent development; also may be highly structured for experimental purposes.	Varied. Seeks to be functional in a given situation rather than set or performed.

FIGURE 4–2. A Guide to Curriculum Goals.

ment centers, and other special agencies designed to meet youth needs. Only when all mental health-oriented institutions and groups coordiante their efforts will their maximum potential be realized.

The School Counseling and Guidance Program Maintains the Degree of Flexibility Necessary to Adjust to Changing Needs and Opportunities

To assure as much as possible the attainment of the objectives that underlie its design, the counseling and guidance program in a school requires a cohesive, well-defined structure. However, that structure cannot be static and inflexible but must function in such a way as to be responsive to the changing characteristics of both the needs and opportunities of youth. As noted, guidance programs must recognize that the characteristics of the student population, including its assessed needs will change on a year-to-year basis and that these changes must also be reflected in program alterations.

The School Counseling and Guidance Program Is Developmental in Nature with Provisions Included for Ongoing Evaluation, Research Activities, and In-Service Training

Throughout their school years, children are going through a developmental process. Recognizing this process, educational programs are designed to reflect and provide for their developing educational needs. School counseling and guidance programs must also reflect a developmental approach. Such an approach is a positive one that seeks to contribute to the individual's growth as opposed to a remedial or correctional approach. If this program itself is to be truly developmental in nature, it must have provisions for evaluation within its design, and for continuous program growth; research to provide for new and more effective procedures; and in-service training to assure the continuous growth of administration, faculty, and guidance staff. In-service training, or staff development, is often overlooked in planning program development; however, once faculty and staff cease to grow and develop professionally, the programs within which they function will be seriously handicapped.

The School Counseling and Guidance Program Is Viewed as a Contributing Part of the Total Pupil Personnel Program of a Given Educational Institution

Chapter 2 emphasized the importance of the pupil personnel team. It was pointed out that this team includes other pupil personnel and social service workers as well as the school counseling and guidance staff. Program development will be handicapped if attempts are made to nurture its growth in isolation from other related services. One does not grow by duplicating or overlapping one's efforts with those of other professionals with similar objectives and related skills. To facilitate the utilization of helping professionals, a real need exists in many schools and school systems for clear statements of role and functions and concomitant delimitations of duties of the various pupil personnel workers in order to minimize the possibility of duplication of effort. Once this has been accomplished, the school counseling and guidance program, as well as the other pupil personnel programs, are, in effect, freed to concentrate on making the most meaningful contribution appropriate to their area of specialization.

Planning for Program Development

Needs assessments are not an end in themselves. Simply to know what is needed, even why it is needed and how it should be provided, is not enough. There must be some basis for the organizing and converting of ideas into action. This basis is provided by planning. Planning is not only collecting needed data, but also is the process of converting needs assessment data and prioritized needs into program goals and objectives; the identification of appropriate procedures to achieve the program's objectives; the allocation of personnel and other resources assigned to carry out the procedures; a timetable for the procedures and related evaluation and feedback cycles. In any efforts directed toward counseling program organization, development, or reorganization, planning can form a basis for the following.

Planning Forms the Basis for Action

Once a plan has been formulated, it enables those involved to do something with a purpose. Planning thus provides a basis for meaningful action, a discussion of alternatives, the reaching of consensus, and the development and implementation of procedures.

Planning Forms the Basis for Organization or Organizing

Planning provides a rationale or logical reason for doing what has to be done at a specific time. In a sense, planning is "getting it all together." It enables those effected to anticipate, to schedule, and to make commitments.

Planning Provides a Basis for Involvement

A plan enables individuals to see how and why they should contribute to the activities of an organization. It gives a reason for being involved as well as direction for that involvement.

Planning Provides a Basis for Assignments

Through planning, those involved know who is doing what, when, where, and how. Planning provides a basis for the delegating of responsibility, for the delineating of role and function, and for the prevention of overlapping and duplication. In a manner of speaking, it lends clarity and direction to one's job.

Planning Forms the Basis for the Evaluation of Program Progress

Since planning involves the establishment of dates, expectations, and anticipated outcomes, this timetable of activities provides recognizable hallmarks for program expectancies for which evaluation activities can be planned.

Planning Provides the Basis for Project Probabilities

As previously noted, planning objectively involves anticipating outcomes. These projections provide a basis for predicting and making future commitments.

Planning Provides the Basis for Decision Making

Planning provides a frame of reference within which decisions can be made based on logic and reason.

Planning Provides a Basis for Commitments

The formation of a plan provides a basis for commitment of resources including personnel and efforts. It provides a basis for budget requests and support, and it provides the opportunity for securing the public commitment of the institutional or agency leadership.

Planning Forms a Basis for Communication

A plan provides an opportunity to inform others both inside and outside the organization of what they may expect. It is an "advertising" or public relations opportunity as well.

In a discussion of planning (in higher education) Clark (1980) notes that

> Traditional planning systems dominate the field of education, from the development of national policy for school improvement to planning within individual institutions. Such systems posit several requisites for planning which include:
>
> a. *A keystone role for goals* in the planning process; a clear understanding of an organization's goals or mission is an a priori condition for rational planning. Tradition views organizations by definition as goal-achieving, goal-driven entities.
> b. *A sequential, rational process* that allows the planner and the organization to build upon preceding steps.
> c. *Fidelity in communication* across hierarchical levels in the organization and *adequate coupling* among planning process steps that (1) facilitate consensus about goals, (2) allow cumulative goal

building across organizational levels, and (3) provide for understanding of intentions so that these can be reflected in individual and sub-group actions.

d. *A comprehensive information base* on which the planning can proceed, including data on internal and external impact factors that will allow decision makers to assess alternative courses of action. (p. 2)

Clark (1980) further notes that a view of the planning process can be summarized conceptually, methodologically, and operationally as follows:

a. Conceptually, planning is not a "synthetic" management function but an essential part of the way in which individuals in organizations make sense of and create their organizational reality.
b. Methodologically or tactically, the attempt to fit organizations to a planning model is less useful than the assumption that an appropriate design for planning can be generated for and adapted to the planning efforts of every organization.
c. Operationally, all organizational participants should be considered to be active planners. Consequently, those individuals assigned formal administrative responsibilities for planning should view themselves less as managers, initiators, and monitors and more as stimulators, facilitators, and orchestrators. (p. 17)

Approaches to Program Development

Having recognized the need for planning, we now examine a few of the many possible models that might form a basis for program development.

The Systems Approach to Guidance Program Management

In recent generations, as business, industry, government agencies, and educational institutions have increased in their complexity, they have sought new and more effective models for program planning and management—for conceptualizing the problems of their programs and devising appropriate solutions.

The systems approach has been perhaps the most widely used of these new models, and such terms as *systems engineering, operations research, simulation* and *games, flowcharts,* and *behavioral objectives* have become identified with this method. The following material was taken from Burack and Torda. (1979, p. 42)

> Systems thinking means viewing the organization in terms of its larger environment and treating the organization both as a whole and as a set of intricately related parts. To some extent, we all think along these lines. But we generally fail to carry the analysis of the system very far.'
>
> . An organization never reaches a stable level of existence, no matter how well things are operating. The organization always exists in a larger environment such as neighborhood, region, or country and must adapt to social, economic, and political changes occurring at each level. (p. 42)
>
> All organizations must respond and adapt to ever-changing external and internal conditions. All organizations have an internal division of work tasks, which creates differing reactions to the needs or problems facing the overall system. This, in turn, creates unavoidable tensions among the parts. All organizations have interaction between external and internal circumstances, which may eventually bring about change in organizational goals, products, or services. (p. 42–43)
>
> To understand any system, then, it is necessary to take account of the range of influences that operate within and beyond system boundaries to determine the needs of the system as a whole and the differences among its parts. Most important, it is the reciprocal and multidirectional nature of these effects that must be understood. Actions that originate at any level or in any part of a system have repercussions elsewhere within it. This in turns means new consequences for the system. For example, the enforcement of equal opportunity legislation has forced a number of organizations to change their personnel practices. These effects have been felt throughout the organization but in widely different forms and degrees. (p. 43)
>
> Determining how it all hangs together is the essence of systems thinking. (p. 43)

Springer, writing in the *Saturday Review* (1967), describes the systems approach as "a rational method of using a given set of resources to produce a system capable of achieving a given set of objectives . . . (which promotes greater innovation because it produces continuous, dynamic modifications . . . (because) precision and attention to each step in the process is controlled and measured to produce that efficiency." The systems approach is based on scientific principles and, in practice, provides more specific and precise criteria for determining and identifying program goals and processes and measuring outcomes. A school counseling and guidance program planned, developed, and managed by a systems approach would probably exhibit the following characteristics.

1. Problem identification results from a needs assessment of the school community environment in which the program functions. Such an assessment is interdisciplinary in both approaches and inclusive factors (as previously noted in Chapter 1.)
2. Relevant program goals are identified for the system. These goals are slated in concrete, specific, and measurable terms. A priority hierarchy may also be specified. As Hosford and Ryan (1970) and others have pointed out, defining the outcome in behavioral (performance) terms is critical to the systems approach.
3. The achievement of these goals becomes the mission of the guidance team. A "team" is viewed as comprised of all those, whatever their discipline or commitment, who can contribute to goal attainment.
4. A model is designed to represent the anticipated system. Alternates are considered and carefully analyzed to identify the most promising approaches. This model identifies the various system components, human and machine, and suggests the ways in which they interact in achieving the program goals. All relevant variables are examined, and their possible effects are studied. These include purposes, people available, information, resources, methods, outputs, constraints, time limits, priorities, and possible prerequisites. The model is "global"—as broad and all encompassing as possible. Simulation techniques may be employed in the design and preparation of staff to function within the model or to evaluate its potential.
5. Control of, and communications among, the various com-

ponents become a prime responsibility of the program manager, in order to ensure a maximizing of the systems movement toward goal attainment.

6. Evaluation, alteration, and creation is an ongoing process within the system to ensure continued adjustments desirable in achieving maximum goal thrust. Systematic feedback is provided to ensure that input from the evaluation process goes into program improvement.

A flowchart model that reflects these characteristics was suggested by Hosford and Ryan (1970, p. 224) as indicated in Figure 4–3.

Planning, Programming, Budgeting System (PPBS)

The planning, programming, budgeting system (PPBS) is a management technique that seeks to allocate resources in a way which will maximize benefits with reasonable cost. Although the emphasis on this "system" may be declining, it is still a fairly popular approach of which program managers should be aware. The core of the PPBS is the program budget that facilitates planning and integrating program goals with budget allocation. PPBS procedures seek to provide guidelines for funding based on pro-

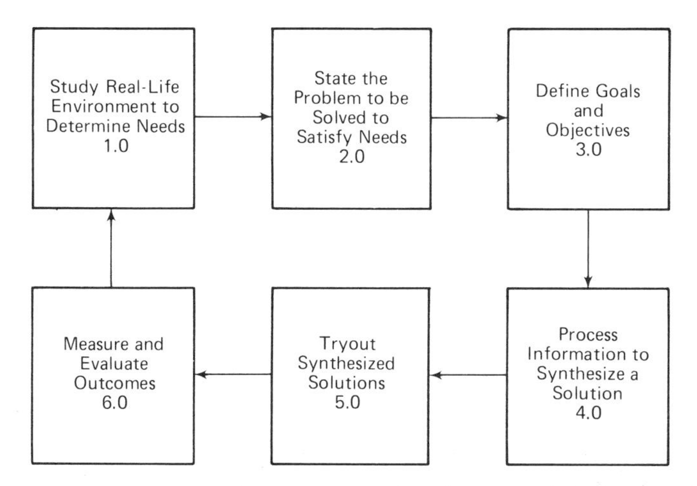

FIGURE 4–3. Process of Creating a Flowchart Model. [Adapted from Ryan, 1970].

gram needs, rather than extraneous factors. PPBS provides a structured approach for needs assessment, priority identification, goal formulation, procedure development, and evaluation. According to Kuhn, 1975

> It gathers detailed information about the existing state of affairs and scans the available alternative responses. It evaluates the costs and benefits—human and social as well as monetary—of each response, using explicit criteria.
>
> In its most complete form it includes estimates of upper and lower limits on both costs and benefits, and makes multiple estimates as they would appear under different sets of value judgments. With this information it is possible to identify an optimal choice, or at least to narrow the range to two or three potentially best ones. PPBS also includes steps for implementing a decision, in terms of both actions and finances. Fully implemented PPBS not only goes about a particular decision systematically, it also analyzes each activity of a department in combination with all of its other activities, in light of their separate and total effects. (p. 293)

Note Figure 4–4.

PPBS can be of significant help to management in bringing about organizational optimization. It can lead to an analysis of whether an organization is achieving service goals and of the relative costs and benefits of each component's contribution toward that goal. There are many levels of sophistication at which a program budget and an integrated planning system can be implemented, ranging from a highly quantified series of cost-benefit choices to a

I. NEEDS ASSESSMENT.
↓
II. SELECT PRIORITIES.
↓
III. DEFINE AND WRITE GOALS AND OBJECTIVES.
↓
IV. DEVELOP ACTIVITIES (PROGRAMS) TO MEET GOALS AND OBJECTIVES.
↓
V. EVALUATE RESULTS.

FIGURE 4–4. Sequential Phases of PPBS Applied to Counseling and Guidance.

> more loosely formalized structure. Much of the success in applying PPBS to a human service organization will depend on the funding patterns of the organization's different programs and whether they allow a sufficient amount of freedom for comparative assessment and integration. Also, and perhaps more importantly, the state of the human service technology is a vital factor. It must be of a sufficient level of development to permit the kind of critical and useful assessment needed to render a PPBS appropriate. Despite these potential problems, the general approach inherent in PPBS can provide management with the opportunity for organizational optimization. (Miringoff, 1980, p. 122)

Management by Objectives (MBO)

Management by Objectives (MBO) is a system in which management attempts to aim all significant activities in an organization toward the achievement of specified, agreed-upon objectives. MBO is designed to promote goal attainment, organizational clarity of action, and increased satisfaction on the part of organizational members who benefit in an environment of achievement. Although it is fairly standardized in the literature as to its general parameters, the point is often made that the application of MBO varies with the characteristics of the organization involved.

> According to Miringoff (1980), essentially MBO is summarized by the following characteristics.
>
> a. Makes objectives explicit; recognizes multiobjective situations.
> b. Identifies conflicting objectives; provides for participation management.
> c. Ensures a control mechanism providing for feedback and measurement of accomplishment.
> d. Fosters managerial acceptance of responsibility and evaluation of managers by results.
> e. Encompasses little formal administrative machinery. (p. 123)

The following (MBO) worksheet could be used for designing programs to deal with organizational concerns.

1. Describe project:
2. Identify target population:
3. Prepare goal statements:

4. Specify objective(s) within project:
5. Describe baseline data required:
6. Identify necessary programs or activities to accomplish(4):
7. Identify constraints or obstacles to be overcome:
8. Identify others who must participate or become involved to accomplish objectives:
9. Identify review periods for monitoring or feedback:
10. Identify persons involved in review:
11. Identify techniques for presentation and review. (Burgess, 1978)

Developmental Planning

If programs of counseling and guidance are presumed to attend to the developmental needs of pupils, planning for such programs might also be developmental, indicating immediate, intermediate, and long-range program goals. As a starting point, it may be appropriate to envision an ultimate, "utopian" program for the school setting for which it will be designed and, once having established these long-range goals, determine those priorities based on needs assessment that should be given immediate attention, those which may need attention within the next several years, and those which the program ultimately hopes to accomplish.

Programs should never reach the point where they function simply to maintain the status quo. In other words, counseling and guidance programs should at all times be developmental in some ways, for development implies continuous growth and improvement.

A developmental plan has a logical, sequential pattern of development and proceeds from a foundation that seems appropriate to subsequent development. As previously suggested, the appropriate foundation from which planning proceeds are needs and environmental assessments and their relationship to the resources at hand. As another example, it would seem desirable that some system for recording and storing pupil data be developed prior to the actual collection of that data. Once collected, the use of the data would follow. Thus the logical sequence would be planning—collecting—using.

Developmental planning also implies flexibility. This permits initial planning for program development to be limited to that which can be reasonably achieved. Programs that are overly ambitious in their design allow little room for alternate or unexpected opportunities. A part of flexibility in planning should be the identification of possible problems and alternate procedures for goal achievement.

Since developmental planning requires the continuous involvement of teachers and others, it must give a high priority to communication, coordination, and cooperation. Like the other components of program development, these activities should not be left to chance. It is important, for example, that there be a plan for communicating the development of the school guidance program to faculty members individually and in groups, as well as students, parents, and others.

Cooperative relations with other programs are also developed as the program itself is planned. Cooperation with other programs and individuals is important if the school guidance program is to anticipate the need for reciprocal cooperation. In communicating with the various groups and individuals who comprise the community educational family, different approaches must be utilized that recognize the uniqueness and differences of these individuals and groups. For example, techniques for communicating with parents would certainly be different in many ways than those that are effective with students. As noted, all too often in recent years guidance programs increasingly fail to communicate their "mission" clearly and effectively to others, resulting in many questioning the need for guidance programs in schools. Coordination and cooperation failures have also adversely affected the positive image that school guidance programs seek to portray.

An example of a planning calendar reflecting a developmental plan for initiating a school guidance program at Sycamore Knolls High School is provided in Figure 4–5 and Figure 4–6.

As noted in the developmental plan for Sycamore Knolls High School, high priorities have been given in the initial months to communications with, and involvement of, the school faculty. Individual faculty conferences have preceded small-group conferences, laying the groundwork for the program planning workshop that follows. It should also be noted that there are simultaneous efforts being made to assess pupil needs. Important community groups in Sycamore Knolls have also been communicated with. Thus, in the planning year only a very limited number of actual guidance activities are taking place.

These guidance activities might almost be classified as those

Month	Program Planning and Development	Pupil Appraisal	Individual Counseling	Occupational Educational Information	Group Guidance	Placement and Follow-Up	Other
Sept.	Individual Faculty Conferences		Faculty or student referrals				
Oct.	Small group faculty meetings; Discussions with P.T.A., Lion's Club, Rotary Club, Church Council	Small group meetings with students; Review of pupil records	Faculty or student referrals				
Nov.	Faculty workshop	State scholarship testing program Small group meetings with students	Faculty or student referrals				State Guidance conference
Dec.	Prepare 3-year plan	Small group meetings with students	Faculty or student referrals			Follow-up of classes (including leavers) of 1970, 1971, 1972	
Jan.	Faculty discussion, revise and finalize 3-year plan	Examine school record system	Faculty or student referrals				

Month	Program Planning and Development	Pupil Appraisal	Individual Counseling	Occupational Educational Information	Group Guidance	Placement and Follow-Up	Other
Feb.	Communicate plan to all concerned	Work with student-faculty committee to develop guidance record system	Faculty or student referrals				Staff applications for summer guidance workshops
Mar.		Initiate collection of additional pupil data for junior class	Faculty or student referrals			Job and College placement conferences with and for seniors	
April		Initiate collection of additional pupil data for junior class	Faculty or student referrals			Job and College placement conferences with and for seniors	APGA National meeting
May	Review of program development with faculty	Initiate collection of additional pupil data for junior class	Faculty or student referrals	Small-group schedule planning conferences for sophs and juniors		Job and College placement conferences with and for seniors	Evaluation and projection
June	Preparation of annual report; Revise planning for next year		Review of counseling cases of the year			Job and College placement conferences with and for seniors	

FIGURE 4–5. Organizational Plan for Developing the School Guidance Program at Sycamore Knolls High School.

Year II.	Program Development:	1. Continued and broadened scope of communication, coordination, and cooperation with all concerned with particular attention to minority groups in school and community.
		2. Human relationship development program will be planned in cooperation with student council and faculty committee and initiated.
		3. Visits to area industries, colleges, and occupational-educational agencies will be initiated.
		4. Small group-guidance (student problems) seminars will be conducted.
	Professional Development:	5. Dept. staff will take lead in organizing an area counselors association.
Year III.	Program Development:	1. Summer guidance and pupil development program will be planned and initiated.
		2. Occupational-educational information library will be organized.
		3. Student-guidance council will be organized.
		4. Orientation program will be planned for next year.
		5. Three-year evaluation with outside consultant will take place.
		6. One additional staff member will be added for next year (interviews this year).
	Professional Development:	7. A professional library and resource laboratory will be developed in the guidance offices.

FIGURE 4–6. Tentative Projected Plans for Years II and III.

for meeting emergency needs only. The bulk of the energies of the guidance staff are directed toward planning the most relevant program possible for the Sycamore Knolls High School. Although the staff has projected plans for the following years, it has been careful to label these plans as tentative, and the plans are stated in rather broad, general terms. The match between needs and resources will provide indications of additonal resources that may be needed or limitations which must be recognized in meeting a specific program need.

Following this step, the program planners may move to design specific procedures or activities for using their available resources to meet the identified needs. Plans for evaluation should be also incorporated into the development of each of the specific activities of the program. Once the procedures have been identified for meeting program objectives, specific responsibilities for their execution should be assigned and a procedural timetable developed. The program manager has the responsibility to ensure the overall scheduling of the various guidance activities in such a way that the program will be viewed as a cohesive, functioning whole.

Developing the Fundamental Activities of the School Counseling and Guidance Program

If we were to follow the development of the counseling and guidance program for Sycamore Knolls High School, we would note the emergence of certain fundamental activities. These activities might be those suggested under the traditional program or labels, such as child study or pupil appraisal, information service and career development, counseling, group guidance and placement, follow-up, and evaluation. (These are discussed more fully in the following chapters.) At this point, however, we are primarily concerned with their emergence in a pattern of program development.

As previously suggested, the first consideration in determining the activities of a program and the sequence in which they are to be developed is a determination of the priority needs to which the program should respond. Following a determination of these needs and their priorities, there must be an assessment of resources and capabilities, both material and human, available to the program in meeting these needs. Based on these assessments, the meaningful and logical specification of program procedures and attending evaluation procedures are possible.

Program Reorganization and Change

A variety of factors, including changing needs of the population that counseling programs are designed to serve, reductions in resources available, new federal or state legislative enactments, new professional theories and techniques, and significant societal/cultural changes, can result in the need to "remodel"—reorganize existing ongoing counseling programs. Since more school and agency programs are currently in existence than we can anticipate will be developed during the remainder of this century (barring federal legislation and massive funding mandating elementary school guidance programs), counselors will be more frequently involved in the reorganizing and changing of existing programs than in the initiating of new programs. Although the principles and practices are similar (i.e., environment and needs assessment base, determine program priorities and objectives, plan appropriate procedures), existing program "remodeling" is usually more difficult than new program initiation and development because we are not introducing something "new"; rather, we are changing something "old."

We accept change as an unvarying characteristic of society. Humankind in recent generations has come not only to accept change but also to expect it and, in many instances, even demand it. Even so, the rapidity, nature, and extent of change never cease to amaze us and frequently find us unprepared and often fearful of the consequences.

Thus, even though we recognize the inevitability and desirability of change, we often find the prospect of change, especially in our work or local environment, threatening. A statement by our "boss" that there's "going to be some changes made around here" will almost always be viewed, at least initially, as a threat . . . and we frequently hear individuals reminisce about the "good ole days" and yearning for a return to the past . . . suggestive that change is not for the better. In education, media and other citizen demands are frequently made for a return to the "3 Rs," and even to resources of bygone years as when some schools have, in recent years, readopted the old McGuffey readers with much local support and enthusiasm. We are suggesting that despite the favorable conditions for change in our society today, the counseling program manager should be cognizant of those factors that also inhibit change.

The school in particular, as one of the oldest institutions in our society, has over the years developed organizational structures, policies, and practices that have become traditional and ingrained in our society in general and in the educational profession in particular. These organizational structures, policies, and practices are usually less susceptible and more resistant to change than in some of the other institutions of society (e.g., economics and business, government, and the armed services) that are more responsive to public influence. Thus, the factors that inhibit educational change with which school counselors must anticipate coping are not infrequently within the educational structure itself.

Griffiths (1964) points out some of these inhibitors or conditions for change:

a. The major impetus for change in educational organizations must come from the outside. In a study of elementary school principals it was noted that those who scored relatively higher on organizational change were not aggressive leaders as such, but administrators who tended to make changes in the organization to please outsiders and supervisors or to comply with suggestions of subordinates. Griffiths also hypothesized that the changes made in response to insiders were concerned with clarification of rules and procedures whereas those made in response to outsiders were concerned with *new* rules and procedures.
b. The degree and duration of change is directly proportionate to the intensity of the stimulus from the outside. In this regard, it was noted, for example, that the rate of instructional innovation in New York State public schools more than doubled within fifteen months of the launch of the Soviet Sputnik and the public demands for relevant educational change.
c. Change in an institution is more probable when a new chief administrator comes from outside the system. Carlson (1961) noted in a study of school superintendents that those who were appointed from inside the system function in such a way so as to maintain the system, whereas those who were appointed from the outside tend to be more susceptible to change and innovation.
d. The more hierarchical the structure of an organization, the less is the possibility of change. Also, the more complicated route one must follow to bring about change, the less is the likelihood that one will pursue it to its conclusion. Masses of committees and subcommittees, assistant

administrators, reviewing bodies, and so forth preclude the possibility of rapid change. Under such conditions, recommendations for change have about as much opportunity to survive as the captive who ran the long gauntlet of the Indian tribe.

e. The more functional the system, the less is the likelihood for change. When there is harmony within an institution in which individuals "know their place" (role and function) and are relatively comfortable in that place, there is less likelihood for change. In effect, each member of the staff is saying to the other, "If you won't rock the boat, I won't." Thus, change is often viewed synonymously with upheaval, uncertainty, and even conflict.

f. Schools are usually more receptive to changes that come from the top down—not from the bottom up. Some administrators may not be overly receptive to drastic or dramatic changes emanating from the "lower end of the ladder." Although they move vigorously to implement their own ideas (and reputation for "really changing things" and "getting things done"), in practice at least, they are usually considerably less receptive to significant changes suggested by teachers, service personnel, or even worse (!) students.

Additionally, in our experiences, we have noted the following.

- Change is facilitated when it is accepted and openly supported by the "status" figures of the organization—individuals who have significant influence within the organization. On the other hand, if change appears to pose an actual or imagined threat to the present status or influence of these individuals, resistance will be immediate and intense.

  Change is also facilitated when it appears there will be "gains" for the system but no "lossess" or "losers." This suggests that a clear picture is presented of why the changes are desirable, what the changes will be, how they will effect the school or agency in general and "you" individually—what benefits "you" can expect, and so forth. A positive reputation of the "change agents" themselves is a help in stimulating confidence in the change.

- In schools, changes in counseling and guidance programs receive more support when it appears that their changes will be only minimally disrupting, if at all, to the other program components in the school. This puts a high premium on planning, communicating, and coordinating.
- The chances for successful program changes are also linked to the ratio of resources required to ensure success versus the resources likely to be available. We have on occasion noted competition in schools among too many departments seeking faculty support and involvement, and budget resources as well, to bring about changes in their respective programs. In these situations, the end result usually is that there is little if any change for anyone.

We must accept as factual that change is inevitable in programs of counseling and guidance in both school and nonschool settings and that such change is usually desirable and can be for the better. A consideration of suggestions from the business world could increase the chances of successful change. Woodcock and Francis (1979), for example, offer seven suggestions for helping change succeed.

> a. Visualize clearly what the change will look like when it has been accomplished.
> b. Take stock of the present situation so that you really understand what needs to be done.
> c. Make a realistic plan of action that will suit your needs and be manageable in your situation.
> d. Check progress and, if necessary, amend the plan in the light of your experience.
> e. Help everyone discover, in his/her own terms, what s/he needs to do as part of the process.
> f. Let people take risks as securely as possible and remember that sometimes innovations fail. New ventures need support, not obstruction.
> g. Think about the forces that are likely to resist change and those that are likely to prompt change. Try to minimize the resisting forces and maximize the driving forces. (pp. 20–21)

Kellogg and Burstiner (1979) suggest that critical factors in reorganizing successfully include the consideration of the following:

Speed

Anyone who has been through a reorganization knows that as soon as one person is aware of a coming change, information leaks and rumors fly. Small buzz sessions occur. Productivity drops. So speed is essential from the first move to the last. Once the machinery has been set in motion, each step should be taken according to a well-planned but nonetheless rapid timetable.

Timing

There is no good time for an organization change. It always seems to affect someone or some work at precisely the wrong moment, so it is quite useless to wait for a "right" moment. If you are within days of completing an important piece of work, however, it is probably desirable to finish it before undertaking major change, even though you feel that particular piece of work will not be affected at all. Organization change is upsetting. It is like a virus; its first effect on just about everyone is adverse.

Involvement

You will want to make it clear that many of your decisions stem from information supplied by the pros in the organization. In this sense they are already involved in the change. But you will also want to give each key person something active to do to help effect the change—some detailed planning, some materials to prepare, some piece of work needing special attention. Not only do you need this contribution, but it will help the employee to overcome whatever resistance to change that he or she feels.

More than this, you will want to clarify quickly the role each key individual will play in the new organization. Professionals, particularly able ones, have a way of becoming restless and seeking other employment whenever they feel left out or uncertain for even a short while.

Communication

As soon as individuals affected by a change know about it and agree to it, put that part of the new structure in writing for all employees. Elaborate in some detail on its functions, the reasons for any change, and the disposition of work displaced or to be phased out.

This will need to be supplemented by group meetings where you can explain more fully and personally why you are doing what you are doing and your hopes and plans for the new arrangement. These meetings will also give you the opportunity to answer the many questions employees may have. By all means, invite those who helped study the situation and made recommendations to take part in the presentation, to answer questions on which they are the experts, and to provide information in specialized areas.

Control of Work During Changeover

This can be critical. While admitting that there will be some productivity loss, as a new manager you want to avoid having the organization change mean a major set-back for the work for which you are responsible. During this period it is well worthwhile to list any major milestones scheduled for completion during, say, the next two months and negotiate these accomplishments. This may mean an interim appointment or two. Reviewing the status of each of these projects weekly pays off, even though organizationally you may be reaching below the usual reporting level and extending your work day. (pp. 77–78)

A Case Study: Developing a School Guidance Program for Warwick

The data presented in the following case study is representative of an actual community and its school system. The report that follows also presents the recommendations of the committee which conducted the study preliminary to the development of a guidance program in the school system. The community name and other identifying nomenclature has been altered, however, in order not to impede the continuing development of its school guidance programs.

Warwick, Indiana is a small rural community situated in Hamilton County along the west forks of the Bermuda River. Historically the community is one of the oldest in Indiana, having been established in 1820 as a county seat with the first stone building, the courthouse, which was built in 1822. Many of the current residents of Warwick can trace their ancestors to the original "five families" who did much to settle the community and promote its economic growth.

The town showed a steady, if not spectacular, growth, and in 1828 the first school was erected. However, from their first beginning, schools in Warwick have encountered economic difficulties. When Hamilton County was established in 1820, Section 5 of the enabling act directed the county agent to sell lots and to preserve 10 per cent of sales and 10 per cent of donations for the use of a county library. The sixteenth section of each congressional township was set aside as school lands, the proceeds from which were to be used to establish schools. Through congressional acts, the Ordinance of 1787 and the legislative enactment of 1816, provisions were made for the establishment of schools and for their financial support. However, the funds received from sale of school lands and from donations were too small; the lands were not cared for properly enough to produce the best price upon sale; and the accumulated funds were frequently dissipated or invested inadequately to produce a maximum of return. Another stumbling block was the fact that the population was small and scattered, making it almost impossible to assemble sufficient pupils at any one school site without having them travel long distances over inadequate roads and trails and without making them cross unbridged rivers and streams through wilderness where many wild animals still roamed.

The lack of qualified teachers was another stumbling block to the foundation of an adequate school system in the middle 1800s, and some of these teachers themselves were educated little above the common, or elementary, grades. During the Civil War (1861–65), all three male teachers left Warwick to serve in the Union Army. Because income from teaching in Warwick was inadequate to provide a living, the teacher had to supplement his wages by other means, such as farming, preaching, carpentry, or the like, as was common among teachers of small communities during the 1800s.

During the first quarter of the present century the community of Warwick in general, including its schools, experienced an economic boom that brought the community to its present population level of approximately 2,500 and saw the building of a new elementary school in 1907 and the first secondary school in 1909, which was later remodeled and enlarged in 1924. For the first time, Warwick was competitive with other surrounding school districts in the salaries it was able to offer its teachers. In fact, educational progress was so great in the period just prior to World War I, that Warwick claimed to have "the best little school system" in Indiana. However, this economic boom and subsequent development of education was short-lived and the community was particularly hard hit by the Depression. In the period from 1930 to 1933 schools were forced to operate on short terms (six months or less) due to lack of funds, and once again teachers in the system found it necessary to seek means of supplementing their income. Finally, in the 1940s the Warwick school district moved to consolidate with schools from three area townships for economic reasons. As a result, the current Warwick area school is housed in a building completed in 1954, which has all grades, kindergarten to twelfth.

The school system is administered by a superintendent and has principals for the elementary grades, junior high, and high school. The school board is made up of three trustees—one each from the surrounding townships, and three appointed by the Warwick Town Board, and one member-at-large appointed by the township trustees.

Warwick today has a population of approximately 2,500. Its government is a town board consisting of three members elected for four-year terms. The public roads coming into the town are U.S. 231, Indiana state roads, 64, 157, and 87, with I-70 forty-six miles to the north. Motor Freight Co. provides public freight with three lines from its Indianapolis terminal—eighty-eight miles to the east. Airlines are available through private and charter facilities at Paget—twenty-three miles to the west—and commercial facilities at Indianapolis.

Industries of the community include Warfield Shale, brick manufacturing; Warwick Woolen Co., rugs and blankets; Warwick Silo Co., concrete silos; Creek Manufacturing Co., lift jacks, door jacks, special hydraulic products; Black & Milan, Inc., farm equipment, and the Warwick Stables and Riding School. With these limited industries the income level is low and the opportunities for area employment is very limited.

There is a town library, the Carnegie Public Library, available to area residents. There are about 14,000 books presently housed in this library.

The medical personnel for the community consist of three doctors and two dentists. Hospital facilities are located at Paget, where a new building is being built. There is a daily and weekly newspaper that gives good coverage for Warwick and the surrounding area. Indiana Bell has the telephone system, and Western Union telegraph is available at Paget. There is an AM radio station at Warwick and at Bloomington. The fire department consists of a paid chief and sixteen volunteers. The police department has a chief and three officers operating with a radio-equipped patrol car. In addition, the Hamilton County's Sheriff's Department operates out of a new jail in Warwick, with two deputies and two radio-equipped patrol cars.

Warwick has a three-acre public park with a tennis court, two basketball courts, a softball diamond, and two shelter houses. It also contains a new swimming pool and a community building. Also available within driving distance are Shakamak State Park, McCormicks Creek State Park, and Monroe Reservoir.

The natives of Warwick are intensely loyal to their community and to the varied churches and clubs that are a part of community life. They display a conservative attitude toward the new and different. They often do, however, respond to the needs of their schools when these needs are specified by community and educational leaders.

Median family income in Warwick is low by comparison with other counties in the state and nation. In 1980, for example, the adjusted gross income for a Hamilton County family was $8,147.56 compared to the state average of $9,737.14. Chronic unemployment and the prevalence of unskilled labor are difficult problems in Hamilton County. A state survey suggested that a solution might result from a strong emphasis on vocational education.

Currently, Warwick's vocational education program is limited to beginning courses in agricultural production, home economics, business, and industrial arts. According to Mr. Thomas, Director of Vocational Education at Warwick High School, these offerings only scratch the surface of available offerings. He suggests that the changed occupational structures in the area point to a need for new vocational education course offerings to complement those available in existing curricula (i.e., a health occupation curriculum would provide trained personnel for meeting the health requirements of Warwick's large old-age population; trade, industrial, and technical education courses would lead to a growing pool of skilled workers, thus assisting needed growth). He further recommended that present vocational education programs be expanded within existing facilities to provide secondary, postsecondary, and adult education to the town residents.

The Warwick comprehensive school has a total enrollment of 1,390 students, distributed as follows: 812 in the elementary division, grades one through six; 329 in the junior high division, grades seven through nine; and 249 in the high school division, grades ten through twelve. A total of 47 faculty staff the educational program of the school.

The curricula of Warwick High School prepares students in six areas: academic, scientific, commercial, home economics, agriculture, and industrial. The academic and scientific students are well prepared for college with four years of English and math, as well as advanced science. The commercial curriculum prepares students for jobs in the community; however, there are few business courses. In conjunction with the business department, a work-study program has been initiated with local businesses. Students work from two to four hours per day without pay, depending on their class schedules and the available work. The agriculture curriculum is limited to students who live in rural areas because they must have a project. All terminal students are prepared in general education and specific-skill courses. Experience has shown, however, that many of the prescribed courses are beyond the intellectual capacity of a large population and are alien to interests and irrelevant to life-style.

The greatest curriculum need may be for remedial courses in English and mathematics, since at present there are no courses especially designed for those students with basic education deficiencies.

Various standardized tests would indicate that the general ability levels of the Warwick students are about average compared with other communities of similar size and characteristics. One recently administered intelligence scale suggested that 23 per cent of the student population were above average in their academic potential, 61 per cent were average, and 16 per cent were below average. However, the dropout rate is one of the highest in the area, and only approximately 10 per cent of each graduating class over the past five-year period has enrolled in colleges, universities, or other post-high school educational opportunities. The faculty of the school may present a study in contrasts. Approximately 25 per cent of the faculty are teachers with less than three years' experience, trained only at the bachelor's degree level. At the other extreme, 34 per cent of the faculty have over twenty years teaching experience, and many of these have accumulated most of that experience in the Warwick school system. All of the system's administrative staff, with the exception of the school superintendent, have come up through the Warwick system. The superintendent was hired two years ago from an out-of-state school system with the challenge to "make the Warwick school system first-rate." One of his first moves was to appoint a committee to study the feasibility of initiating a guidance program for the Warwick school system. This committee has studied the community and identified much of the data presented up to this point. They have also administered a readiness factor survey to sixteen residents of the community. They were chosen at random and included four parents, three members of the school staff, three business people, two ministers, one doctor, and three students. Each individual participated cooperatively. The average score was 132.1, which could indicate that there will be several difficulties when initiating the guidance program. The following table lists a detailed report of this survey.

Readiness Factors in Initiating a School Guidance Program in Warwick, Indiana

Factor	Average	Weighted Value
1. Administrative Support	3.0	5
2. Board of Education Support	3.0	5
3. Budget	2.3	4
4. Community Resources	2.6	2
5. Community Spirit	2.8	1
6. Community Support	2.9	3
7. Counselor Role and Function	2.9	4
8. Educational Accomplishments of School and Community	2.8	2
9. Facilities	2.3	3
10. Parent Support	2.4	1
11. Previous Guidance Program Development	2.6	2
12. Pupil Support	3.2	1
13. Pupil-Counselor Ratio	3.1	2
14. Recreational Program (Community)	2.1	1
15. Secretarial Service	1.9	2
16. School "Esprit de Corps"	2.9	1
17. School Referral Resources	2.6	2
18. Teacher Support	2.9	5
19. Trained Personnel	2.3	2
20. Unique Characteristics of School or Community	2.0	1

Suggested Exercise. Before you proceed to read the actual report prepared by the guidance planning committee, how would you respond to the following questions?

1. What are some of the significant community characteristics that would be considered in guidance program development?
2. What are some of the significant educational characteristics that should be considered in guidance program development?
3. How would you proceed at this point, and what recommendations would you make regarding the initiation and development of a guidance program for Warwick?

THE RECOMMENDED GUIDANCE PROGRAM

We (the Planning Committee) believe that the entire focus in developing a guidance program must be to fit it to the needs of the Warwick school system and the youth it educates.

The specific guidance services that the planning committee sees as necessary will be those needed and utilized by almost all good guidance programs. Certainly within the scope of what is outlined here will be a cognizance of the varying emphasis needed to stress the uniqueness of the Warwick student population and the Warwick school system.

The majority of this report will be concentrated on meeting the immediate goals as envisioned in a program for the next academic year; however, we will also anticipate intermediate and long-range goals. This latter element is perhaps the most nebulous and the hardest to put into concrete terms; for Warwick, while basically stagnate at this time, may be a totally different community within five or ten years because of a possible influx of people from Bloomington or Indianapolis seeking the quieter elements of rural life.

The program will be geared for grades seven through twelve, with the greatest emphasis on the secondary school program. We are not initiating junior high or elementary guidance programs because it is not deemed feasible at this time, due to the general climate in the community and budgetary limitations. Many of our guidance services will spill over (in a very limited sense) into the elementary school, because the single school building houses all educational divisions.

Individual Analysis

A number of texts define individual analysis as the process of collecting, organizing, synthesizing, and interpreting relevant information of varied types about pupils for the purpose of gaining a better understanding of the individuals with which it is concerned. The process is most important from the standpoint of the faculty and curriculum planning, and for the pupil's self-understanding.

Organization of the individual analysis service must follow an assessment of what needs to be known about pupils, selection of the instruments and procedures for collecting this information, and the development of a system for recording the information and making it available.

The assessment process can be conducted through faculty meetings, and one of the high school counselors can be responsible for acquiring the information desired from the elementary level. It is feasible that the medical personnel serving the school, a part-time physician, a nurse, and a school psychologist (on a visiting basis from Vigo County) should also be a part of this assessment procedure. Committees in each of the educational divisions will decide upon the data-collecting instruments to be used at appropriate grade levels. In this step, the counselor's primary task will be to serve as advisor, to provide samples of various instruments, and to coordinate their efforts. The counselor will not be responsible for administering these instruments, recording the results, or for the filing system used. Rather, his or her job will be that of information, interpretation, and integration of the instruments used. The committees will also be responsible for determining and utilizing a record-keeping system, and in this case, the counselor will demonstrate and show samples of multicard and cumulative card systems, their advantages, their disadvantages, and their use.

Referral forms, anecdotal records, and interviews can and should be used at all grade levels. We do not mean to imply that each child will have information about him or her at every grade level; we do mean, however, that the guidance personnel should supervise the development of the pupil-analysis instruments and forms that best suit the needs of the Warwick School system. The guidance personnel should then instruct those who will be using them as to their proper usage; they should also integrate and interpret the results in either individual sessions with the persons involved or through in-service training sessions. Above all, the counselor should be aware of the responsibility to use this information with faculty, parents, and students to better the understanding and development of the pupils.

The Information Service

It is recommended that the information services be reactive to the educational, vocational, and personal-social needs of agencies. It is most important to have information that students need, as well as to have the information and materials needed by the teaching faculty and guidance staff.

Educational information should include information on trade schools, technical institutions, colleges, universities, and any other educational opportunities available after high school. Brochures and pamphlets on many state and out-of-state institutions should be available and attractively displayed. The department should investigate the inexpensive kits that help students evaluate and contrast their own needs and situation with the type of school that is best suited to them. Warwick's proximity to several universities provides opportunities to visit college campuses. Warwick's students should be provided with a wide range of experiences (through field trips, guest speakers, films, etc.) that will give them the ability to focus on the types of education they wish to pursue, instead of having them "fall into" school or a job on a hit-or-miss basis. The low economic level of Warwick will certainly be a determining factor in whether advanced schooling is available (from a practical and personal standpoint) to these students. The counselor will need to be aware of every possible source of monetary support for them. Federal and state loans, scholarships, student aid, and available student jobs must be an integral part of the counselor's knowledge and resources.

Since two-thirds of the students either fail to graduate or don't continue their education, occupational information and career guidance must be emphasized. A work-study program started by one of the vocational teachers last year is already successful in preparing students for jobs. Since there is no major industry in Warwick, information about other areas of employment must be provided. To this end an extensive file of loose-bound materials—pamphlets, brochures, etc.—should be readily available to students. Maximum use of occupational slides should be made, both in individual counseling and through interest-creating demonstrations made by classroom teachers in the school's various departments. A filing system of occupations by subject matter seems more advantageous than a central location system because it provides opportunity for the students to make use of materials under the direction of the classroom teacher who possesses expertise in the field.

It is recommended that field trips, guest speakers from representative industries, and films be a part of the local school program. Although there is an existing "closeness" in the community, the personal-social information service can be of great importance to parents and to students. The personal-social information activities should strive to assist pupils in their social development and in the acquisition of human relationship skills.

Although the community is small and rural, it would be a fallacy to think that the needs of the students do not coincide with the current issues found in large communities. Programs utilizing school, community, and area resources should be encouraged to deal with the issues of sexuality, drugs, mental hygiene, family problems, and premarital concerns. These should be specific parts of the school program and should be related to community life. In a coordinated effort, the counselor must make wise use of local and area lawyers, law enforcement officials, judges, political leaders, clergymen, medical personnel, parents, and university personnel to meet the needs in this regard.

Films, filmstrips, books, pamphlets, and brochures should be purchased for the guidance department and various other departments of the school; in addition to these, the counselor should be on the alert for the many publications of insurance companies, health organizations, and federal and state departments that would be helpful. A coordinated effort on the part of the librarian and the guidance department is recommended to make these items readily available and used.

Warwick's counseling program should make full use of the

agencies in the surrounding area where additional services can be obtained for the students. The Warwick counselor must determine the need in a particular situation, the type of service required, the available services in the area, and how to help students use these services. Those who are available for service include local physicians and nurses, the school psychologist who works at the school one day every two weeks (she is needed more often than this), the speech and hearing therapist, the special education teachers, lawyers, clergymen, law enforcement officials, and the welfare agency. Additional services should include child guidance clinics, marriage counseling centers, family aid society, and mental health facilities. (For the most part these are available in Indianapolis and through several state universities.) Financial assistance is available through the school (their funds and the school lunch program), through local business people and service and professional organizations. Vocational assistance can be obtained from the state employment agency, vocational rehabilitation center, and service and professional organizations.

We would stress that the counselor must be aware of the organizations where help is available and must communicate these services to the students and their parents. The counselor must attempt to coordinate the available programs through a community- and school-based service-information committee composed of both school and community leaders. In this manner, the services could be utilized to their fullest capacity. The counselor could most effectively acquaint parents and students with the new and different services that are available; the counselor could also reassure them in a supportive role.

We recommend that the counselor assume the responsibility of assessing these resources and organizing them in such a way that they are used. This calls for an interweaving of presentations in classes, in activity periods, through publicity in the school, and in the local newspapers. The counselor, furthermore, needs continuous feedback on how the services are being used and how they can be improved.

The Counseling Service

The counseling service can be described as the keystone or the heart of the guidance program. The counselors at Warwick should spend a considerable amount of time in the consultant role because of the problems to be faced and the limited personnel. But if they are highly trained and are specialized in the skills of counseling, the counseling service will be, as it should be, the core of the guidance program. The focal point on which the service is based is the counselor as a person. There will be no program unless the counselors have understanding, warmth, humanness, and other essential traits that are associated with effective counselors. (Personnel will be handled in another section of this project, but needless to say, the counselor's personal qualities, specialized training, abilities—in fact, the very person of the counselor—are all quite essential to the effective functioning of the guidance program.)

The basic categories in which the counseling service will be offered are those conferences initiated by the counselors, those referred by other persons, and those who are self-referred. The major responsibility of the counselor should be to assist an individual through the counseling relationship to utilize his or her own resources and environmental opportunities in the process of self-understanding, planning, decision making, and coping with problems relative to developmental needs and to vocational and educational planning.

It is essential that several conditions exist if students are to utilize the counseling service. First of all, they have to know where to come and how to make use of the service. They need to know that the counseling office is a place where anyone can go and receive a friendly reception, regardless of who he is or what his problem is. They need to know that some counselor will always be there to serve them. Since there will be two counselors, one should be in or near the office at all times during the school day in order to be available for emergency or walk-in situations. It is important that students be able to make appointments, see a counselor, and/or secure information easily and without undue delay or frustrations.

All conferences and advising of students cannot or need not be done by the school counselors, however. Much can be done by other school personnel, such as the administrators, teachers, doctor, nurse, etc. Thus, it becomes a recommended function of the counselor to inform the faculty of the resources of their office and of referral and other procedures for their utilization. (The counseling service will probably be best received by the newer and younger members and will be most threatening to the older members of the faculty, since Warwick's faculty is split between both of these types.)

A faculty committee consisting of interested persons is recommended at the elementary and the junior high levels to identify those students in need of assistance and to secure counseling for them.

The Consultant Service

In addition to the counseling service, the counselor should act as a consultant. In this situation he or she is not assisting a pupil directly but is assisting others in methods of dealing with children. The counselor should plan to work with faculty members, administrators, parents, and other interested persons in the community. He or she should consult in the areas of pupil analysis, counseling techniques, learning behavior, career information, and other related items of interest to the persons involved. For example, the counselor can be involved as a consultant with faculty members on many different occasions. He or she should assist teachers with specific pupils through interpreting test material and by providing background information and insight as to how best to help the student. The counselor can be of special value to the administrators on behavior problems. (But it is not recommended that he or she handle discipline.)

The counselor can be an effective aid to willing and concerned parents about how to best provide a home climate conducive to learning and to meeting the needs of their children. In this role the counselor acts as a consultant on how to meet these goals most effectively. However, because of the rural setting, economic problems, and lack of school interest, the counselors at Warwick will generally have difficulty working with the parents. The counselor will need to spend time on the more serious home problems with the parents in their settings, since a social worker will not be available. The counselors must make effective use of group techniques by bringing parents together and by breaking down the fear and the resistance to the school and its setting. The administrators, nurse, and physician can be of valuable assistance with these home situations also.

The counselor can act as a consultant to the community agencies that are formed for the purpose of providing for the needs of Warwick's children and young adults. All these community agencies need a direct channel of communication to the school, and vice versa. The counselor helps to fulfill this role. He or she can also provide ideas and show the community agencies what the needs are and how best to meet them.

The counselor's chief concern will be the child in school, but he or she will also be concerned with and will be active in efforts to improve counseling and other services by competent people for the parents and for other adults in the community. The counselor should seek the establishment of necessary community services and should work in close cooperation with them.

Group Guidance Service

Group guidance strengthens the guidance program by augmenting the other basic services. One main advantage of group guidance is the time element—the counselor uses time to his or her advantage as he or she serves several students simultaneously; also, group work gives the students the opportunities for mutual sharing and for exploration of problems and concerns. The group guidance service would have two functions in our recommended program.

Group counseling can be effectively used to allow the students to explore personal and social problems in the security of a peer group. Group work would also be useful in vocational exploration. By grouping students with similar vocational aspirations, the counselor could utilize films, speakers, trips, and discussion periods to explore the particular field of interest. It is important to note that group counseling would not be a substitute for individual counseling.) Group counseling would be useful in discussion of dating, sex, marriage, the responsibilities of adulthood, and drugs.

Group counseling should also include parent and community involvement. This would enable the adults to better understand the concerns of the high school students, and vice versa.

These group activities should give the counselor valuable insights into the concerns of the students and adults of the Warwick

School System, helping him or her to assess and meet the needs of the students, school, and community.

Placement Service

Effective placement should result in the satisfactory adjustment of the individual to the next situation, whether it be in school or on the job. In organizing the placement service in Warwick, pupils critically need placement assistance in both the curricular program and the job market.

One area of importance is that of career placement. We are concerned with the identification of those skills, aptitudes, abilities, and interests that the students possess. It is a team approach in which the teacher, the administrator, the counselor, and the community agencies (e.g., Indiana State Employment Office, the Chamber of Commerce) play an important role in our service. Programs such as VIEW (Vital Information for Education and Work), in addition to the administration of interest inventories, will enable us to identify pupils' needs and abilities. The outcome of the survey of the community is that although the school will not be able to develop a formalized and centralized placement bureau because of the scarcity of resources, it is imperative that there be career placement if the guidance program is to fulfill its role in this respect.

One immediate goal should be to organize a committee whose functions are to direct the placement activities of the school. Perhaps the members might desire to expand in certain areas, such as part-time work, work-experience programs, or college placement. Wherever possible, the committee members should investigate employers and employment conditions. A long-range objective is to provide a work-experience program (which we consider a valuable experience for the pupils in Warwick, since most are not bound for college). The work-experience program has exploratory values, provides desirable work habits involving practical experience in assuming responsibility, and affords the students the opportunity to discover themselves.

The other important area in placement has an educational character. Initiated early in high school, it would assist the pupil in selecting the program best suited to his or her needs and to his or her vocational and educational goals. Gathering over a period of time information regarding the students' abilities, emotional stability, socioeconomic background, educational achievement, interests, and aspirations in a cumulative folder will help the school be more effective in the vocational, as well as the educational, area. Complete familiarity is needed with both the pupils and the educational programs available.

Follow-up Service

In an attempt to measure the outcome of the guidance program, we recommend a follow-up service. The dropout and the graduate are among the major evaluators of the school and, at the same time, being products of the school, serve as a major source of evaluation of the school by others. A follow-up of the dropout has many possibilities and can be one of the more fruitful types of research for a school.

The follow-up service objectives are of assistance in improving the curricula, stimulating better teaching, and improving the guidance services. In order to achieve these goals we recommend a variety of methods, such as conferences with pupils, teachers, and community leaders; check lists; interviews; and questionnaires. The information will help students, teachers, and counselors. The following information will be collected through this service: (1) Factors determining mobility among students; (2) identification of facilities used by former students to obtain employment; (3) discovering the weakness and strengths of the vocational and educational guidance program; (4) determining the reasons students leave before graduation and the characteristics of potential dropouts; (5) evaluation of counseling services; (6) evaluation of curricular needs of students and the necessity for change in course content; (7) ascertaining the need for parent counseling; (8) determining the degree of realism of occupational choice made in high school; (9) gathering occupational information; (10) preparing the counselor for counseling tasks; (11) discovering the success of teenage marriages that occurred while the students were in school or after the students dropped out to get married.

Through the follow-up service, then, the school will gather

the necessary information to aid the student, the teacher, the administrator, the counselor, and the community.

GOALS, PROCEDURES, AND ACTIVITIES

Objectives for the First Year. The plan developed for Warwick High School is intended to provide meaningful activities for the guidance program. Some of these objectives will encompass previous programs; others will be initiated for the first time; and still others are ultimate goals.

1. Establish a relationship with faculty members, administrators, and other service personnel.
2. Establish familiarity with school programs, calendar, curricula, etc.
3. Establish familiarity with and appraise school facilities and resources.
4. Acquaint school personnel with the guidance program.
5. Establish relationship with pupils, parents, and community.
6. Acquaint pupils, parents, and community with the guidance program.
7. Establish needs and priorities for the guidance program.
8. Establish orientation program for the incoming freshmen.
9. Develop and organize a system of pupil records and data.
10. Develop and organize a system of educational, personal, social, and occupational information.
11. Establish military-service information committee.
12. Initiate placement service with area employers.
13. Initiate referral service with local personnel, area services, and Indiana University.
14. Develop testing program, including tests locally normed.
15. Initiate guidance information and counseling groups.
16. Develop individual counseling service.
17. Initiate community counseling aides program.
18. Develop in-service programs for elementary personnel.
19. Develop in-service programs for secondary personnel.
20. Initiate follow-up service.

21. Evaluate guidance program with the faculty, pupils, and community.
22. Develop and revise guidance program for following years.
23. Develop work-study program.

Intermediate Goals

1. Secure one full-time counselor for junior high school.
2. Orient new personnel to the guidance program.
3. Expand curriculum offerings.
4. Expand guidance information service.
5. Acquire additional guidance resources.
6. Revise needs of the school, pupils, and community.
7. Expand placement service for pupils.
8. Develop further the community counseling aides program.
9. Secure one full-time elementary counselor to serve the elementary school.
10. Expand elementary guidance program.
11. Evaluate the guidance program.
12. Expand work-study program.

Ultimate Goals

1. Secure enough guidance personnel to have a 200 : 1 ratio at all levels.
2. Secure enough secretarial and auxiliary help to serve additional personnel.
3. Expand all services to the level at which they are self-sustaining and self-administering.
4. Secure auxiliary personnel, services, and resources for Hamilton County needs.
5. Secure a full-time director of guidance.
6. Continue flexible programs that meet the needs of Hamilton County as their needs change and grow.

Organization and Administration

August. *Activities.* Develop orientation program for incoming freshmen; evaluate present pupil records system; develop and organize information service; organize and schedule school guidance programs; become familiar with community and resources; become familiar with school and resources; evaluate forms to be used, such as referral, rating scales, questionnaires, etc.; meet with all guidance personnel to coordinate program and schedules; orient secretary to her duties; learn administrative procedures regarding transcripts and transfer students; meet with freshmen to work out schedule problems; register transfer students; order any materials needed.

September. *Activities.* Meet with parents about student problems; form relationships with faculty and additional personnel; relate guidance program to staff and pupils; initiate counseling service; ascertain needs through faculty, pupils, and community; meet with juniors about PSAT; meet with college-bound seniors; develop and organize a pupil records system; decide on the types of forms that are most needed; meet with administration to explain guidance programs; test freshmen for general differential aptitude; give "How to Study" course to freshmen; send out grade deficiency reports on all students.

October. *Activities.* Initiate group guidance service; work out schedule problems; begin in-service training for aides; give Lorge Thorndike IQ to seventh and tenth grades; begin in-service sessions for faculty; initiate referral service for pupils; do individual counseling; finish pupil records system and explain to faculty; expand information service; give PSAT/NMSQT test to juniors; attend meeting for changes in college admission requirements (College Admissions Congress).

November. *Activities.* Continue enlarging group guidance and counseling service; hold a career night; begin college applications; check on continuing candidate Hoosier Scholars; continue program for in-service sessions for faculty; initiate elementary in-service training; coordinate program with other special school services; devise with faculty the testing program to be used; create home visitation program; give achievement test to the freshmen.

December. *Activities.* Notify State Scholarship continuing candidates; initiate placement service with area employers for second semester; check on financial aid for college-bound; expand referral service for pupils; continue with training and program for community counseling aides; have personal-social information service, including groups and individual counseling; requisition materials for second semester; do test norming and interpretation; counsel students for second semester enrollment.

January. *Activities.* Set up group minicourses on sex, marriage, drugs, etc.; start placement service; organize testing program for end of first semester; hold group sessions for potential midyear dropouts; do semester evaluation with all guidance personnel; conduct personal conferences with all faculty members; give Armed Forces Aptitude Test to seniors.

February. *Activities.* Continue elementary in-service training; update pupil records from first semester; develop occupational information for regular classes; have testing program and records for all new students; organize resources for use in family planning and marriage, etc.

March. *Activities.* Develop post-high school educational materials for regular classes; set up career night for next school year; hold registration instruction for SAT; conduct second semester classroom programs on family, marriage, etc.; expand available referral resources; meet with community counseling aides; do individual counseling; continue home visitation program; do testing program for eighth grade; conduct rehabilitation counseling to provide money for college.

April. *Activities.* Develop placement service for summer and post-high school employment; conduct meetings with area employers; update pupil records and information service; decide on evaluation forms with faculty; conduct scheduling for next year; do recreation planning with school and community for the summer; do achievement testing; college entrance exams (SAT test); do eighth grade enrollment for next year; give Iowa Tests of Basic Skills to seventh and eighth grades.

May. *Activities.* Conduct group sessions for potential dropouts for next year; make final survey of all pupil records; make evaluation of needs and resources for following year in elementary schools; do placement for following year; complete scheduling for following year; interpret and share evaluation of form results; do follow-up information for following year; evaluate total guidance program with community agents, faculty, and pupils; meet with all guidance personnel; develop community counseling aides program for summer; terminate groups; send records and files to post-high school institutions where needed; conduct surveys of future occupational and educational intentions; requisition supplies for next school year.

Special Subreport Guidance Personnel and the Warwick Educational System

Introduction. Guidance services constitute an integral part of the educational program. These services should be under the professional direction and coordination of qualified and highly skilled leaders. Also, for the guidance program to complement the other educational endeavors, it must be well organized and coordinated with other educational programs within both the school and the community. This section will attempt to outline a practical, efficient way of selecting and organizing the guidance personnel for Warwick. Due to the proximity of the junior high grades and their usage of the facilities and programs, the guidance personnel are also available to them.

Personnel

The guidance counselor is identified most often as the person responsible for the guidance program in most schools. However, while the counselor does indeed provide many of the guidance services available for students, the counselor alone cannot provide all of the services necessary for a complete guidance program. A comprehensive guidance program requires a team effort. In essence, every person involved with education can contribute to the total guidance effort and is, therefore, part of the guidance team.

The personnel of Warwick can be divided into four categories: administrators, instructors, specialists, and auxiliary helpers. The staff from each of these areas can perform duties in their special areas that assist the guidance program.

ROLES

In specifying the type of role the personnel in each area assumes, two major elements must be considered, namely the personal traits necessary for the position and the function each position performs in relation to guidance.

Administrators. The administrators should have the following personal traits: they should be knowledgeable in broad general areas; possess good administrative techniques; be personable and approachable; be responsive to group and individual needs; be decisive, dependable, organized, communicative, and nonjudgmental.

The administrator should be responsible for the following: assessing guidance needs in relation to the entire educational effort; planning the guidance program around innovative ideas; making final decisions concerning the guidance program; initiating the guidance program and coordinating it with other programs; hiring qualified personnel for the guidance program; defining personnel roles in relation to the guidance program; obtaining and assembling resources, materials, finances, and facilities; supervising guidance activities; supporting the guidance program and mediating conflicts; evaluating the effectiveness of the program through meaningful research; reassessing needs and revising and expanding the guidance program; establishing policy guidelines for the personnel and program.

Instructors. The instructors should possess the following personal traits: they should be knowledgeable in human development, education, and their subject area(s); be personable and approachable; be responsive to students' needs; be skilled at facilitating learning and social and personal development; be innovative in the classroom; be accepting of each student; be dependable, democratic, open-minded, and communicative.

In addition, the instructor should be responsible for providing the following guidance services in the classroom: recognizing and dealing with emotions in the classroom, facilitating social and personal development, teaching study skills, exploring educational and occupational opportunities, providing opportunities for success, and identifying special needs of students. She or he is also responsible for consulting with guidance specialists, referring individuals to guidance specialists, and meeting with students and parents individually.

Specialists (Counselors). The specialists should possess the following personal traits: they should be knowledgeable in human development, education, guidance theory and techniques; be personable and approachable; be responsive to individual needs and concerns of students, parents, and staff; be empathetic, understanding, and accepting; be innovative and creative; be dependable, patient, trustworthy, communicative, and nonjudgmental.

The specialists should be responsible for the following functions: planning the guidance program around innovative ideas; promoting good public relations with staff and community; providing the majority of guidance services for the school, i.e., providing individual appraisal; counseling individuals and groups; consulting teachers and parents; providing educational, vocational, and personal information; directing educational, vocational, and personal placement; directing follow-up studies of dropouts and graduates; designing research studies which contribute to the field of knowledge.

Auxiliary Helpers. The auxiliary helpers should possess the following personal traits: they should be skilled in their special area(s); be dependable and capable; be conscientious and personable.

Our auxiliary helpers should be responsible for providing a comfortable and pleasant environment for learning and for activities, for aiding those responsible for learning and for school activities, and for performing necessary and functional tasks in their special area(s).

Selection of Guidance Personnel. The selection of well-qualified personnel for Warwick School System is an important aspect of the total guidance program. Of particular concern is the selection of outstanding guidance counselors. The following criteria should be considered in selecting a guidance counselor.

1. Educational credentials
   a. bachelor's degree; major in education or behavioral sciences preferred
   b. master's degree in counseling and guidance with wide background in behavioral sciences and education
   c. transcript with better-than-average grades desirable

   d. good recommendations from professors and/or former employer(s)
2. Professional status
   a. state certification in counseling and guidance
   b. teaching experience at same level as counseling position may be helpful
   c. counseling experience desirable
   d. good recommendations from employers and colleagues
3. Personal attributes
   a. personal traits desirable for counselor as described earlier
   b. an understanding of the needs and concerns of a rural school and community
   c. a genuine interest in young people
   d. supportive of school system—its goals and functions
4. Other considerations
   a. sex: even ratio desirable
   b. community member
   c. age: young or middle-aged desirable

Organization

The organizational structure of the guidance program is essential if the personnel are to coordinate their efforts. The team approach seems to us to be the most efficient way of providing the basic services to the Warwick system. Although the administrator (the director of guidance) is responsible for the basic organization of the guidance program, each member of the team must be responsible for his or her allocated duties if the program is to run smoothly and efficiently.

The organizational structure for the proposed guidance program for Warwick schools is a combined centralized-decentralized system. A central guidance team will serve the entire school system, while satellite teams will serve the individual school sections. Two outside groups have distinctive roles—one, as a referral-consultant and two as an advisory-study team. These groups work directly with the central guidance team. A third group of community volunteers work with the satellite teams. (See Figure 4–7.)

The Central Guidance Team serves in an administrative ca-

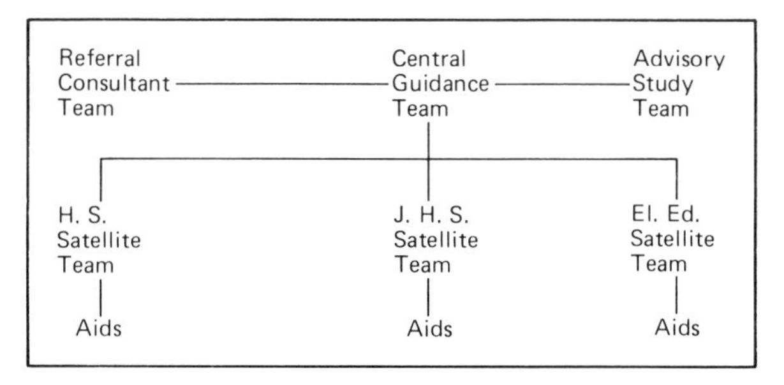

FIGURE 4–7. Organizational Structure of Proposed Guidance Teams.

pacity. The director of guidance has the major responsibility of supervising and coordinating the guidance activities. The team also provides special services not available in the individual school sections, such as intensive medical care, attendance regulation, and testing. The central guidance team is also responsible for making referrals to outside agencies. The team works directly with the advisory-study team and acts upon its suggestions. (See Figure 4–8.)

The Referral-Consultant Team serves the school system indirectly by providing special services that are not available in the school system. The specialists in this group can also help the school personnel in meeting the special needs of students by serving as consultants.

The Advisory-Study Team functions as a catalyst for program development and change. Since the members of the team represent all those involved in the guidance program, this group is best

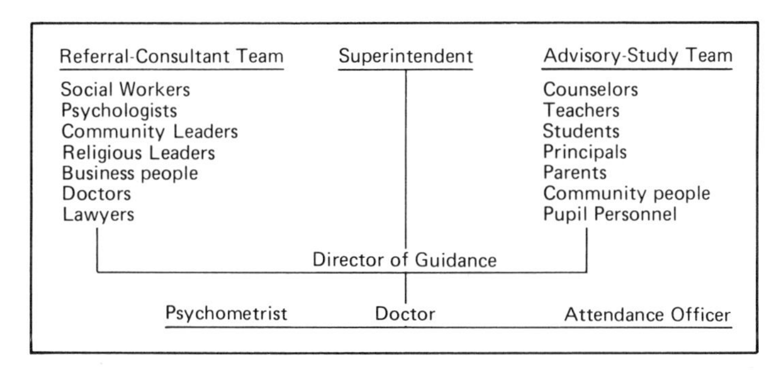

FIGURE 4–8. Central Guidance Team.

able to ensure that the guidance program is relevant to the needs of those it serves. Because of the nature of this group, it is desirable that representatives of certain interest groups—namely, the teachers, students, parents, and community people—rotate membership regularly.

The Satellite Team is directly responsible for providing the students with the majority of services offered by the guidance program.

End of Case Study

Following this review of the committee's reports and recommendations for initiating and developing a guidance program in the Warwick Comprehensive School, discuss why you agree or disagree with the report, its strengths and weaknesses, and any significant alterations or additions you would suggest.

Summary and Implications

The collection of community, organizational, and client population characteristics provides a basis for determining priority client needs and how those needs may best be met. These needs in turn lead to the identification of program goals and objectives and related program planning. This planning takes place within a framework of guiding principles. A variety of approaches or models is available as guidelines for program development. Four of the more popular ones are: systems approach; planning, programming, budgeting system; management by objectives; and developmental planning.

Regardless of how effective a program may be in meeting the needs of its client population, the inevitability of changes in influencing characteristics and client needs must be anticipated. This implies that program reorganization and change is inevitable. Successful change, however, does not just happen; it too has to be planned for and possible problems and/or resistance should be considered in such planning. Successful program planning and development is dependent on successful program management and leadership if it is to achieve its potential. Suggestions for management and leadership are offered in Chapter 5.

CHAPTER 5

Program Leadership and Management

Introduction

The successful development and continuous improvement of counseling and guidance programs are dependent in any setting on professional leadership and effective management. This assumes that an individual who accepts appointment to such a position recognizes and is amenable to the expected responsibilities of a program leader and is hopefully skillful in administering and managing them. Program leadership is also enhanced by certain personal characteristics—those traits in practice that distinguish a "leader" from a "director" or an "administrator." These traits, as well as the responsibilities of program leadership and the activities involved in exercising this leadership, are discussed in the paragraphs that follow. (These qualities represent the ideal and few will exhibit all of the characteristics identified. This does not mean, however, that they are not goals worthy of a leader's pursuit.)

Program Leadership

WHAT IS LEADERSHIP?

Webster (1976) offers a variety of definitions of a leader, including "a person who by force of example, talents, or qualities of leadership plays a directing role, wields commanding influence, or has a following in any sphere of activity or thought." Perhaps the most common view of leadership is that reflected traditionally in the political or military structures of many nations which see the leader as a director. This model has also been popular in educational and other organizations. However, in educational circles in recent generations there has been an influx of influences from the disciplines of psychology, sociology, anthropology, and other fields engaged in the study of roles, group dynamics, and human relationships. These influences have contributed to trends from the "director-directing" view to the "democratic-leading" view of educational leadership. Thus, the concept of a program administrator-leader as one who directs is not only inadequate but, from the point of view of our current democratic values, is no longer possible for maximum program achievements for any appreciable period of time. Perhaps equally important is the fact that of all the personnel within the school or agency setting, counselors should be most adept at the practice and facilitation of human relationships. It should, therefore, be anticipated that the leader of such a program will exemplify the best of democratic-leadership qualities in the management and development of counseling and guidance programs.

Characteristics of a Program Leader

Although no one single characteristic or set of characteristics identifies leadership potential, some can at least provide us with clues. Having recognized the importance of leadership to program development and management, we now examine some of these characteristics that may tend to identify individuals with leadership potential.

One Who Has Been Successful in Past Professional Endeavors. An obvious clue to leadership is one's past professional accomplishments. We can note almost daily leadership choices that are made on the basis of this criterion alone: the company that promotes a young executive because she or he has a reputation for "getting things done," . . . the elected governor of a state who has previously been a successful mayor and local politician, or the new head football coach who was hired because he has never had a losing season. If an individual's past accomplishments include those in a leadership capacity, we can have even more confidence in his or her potential. Program development also demands leadership that is not content with maintaining the "status quo," that will not tolerate failure. A leader must have confidence in his or her ability to do the job and to inspire confidence in others. A program leader must also be one who is capable of helping others to succeed. All of these needs suggest one who has experienced past successes.

One Who Is "Extra" Competent and Knowledgeable in His or Her Field. Leadership requires that one be a respected member of his or her profession. This respect is usually earned through one's demonstrated knowledge and competency in his or her field. Program leadership potential is further enhanced when the leader, by virtue of his or her "extra" knowledge and superior professional skills, is capable of contributing to the professional growth of his or her staff. In practice, a counseling and guidance program leader is one who not only has management and development skills but who is also a superior counselor, an astute appraiser of individual traits, and an expert practitioner of human relationship skills in both individual and group situations.

One Who Is an "Idea" Person. A leader must not only be adept at identifying and utilizing the good ideas of his or her colleagues (and giving them credit for them), but must also contribute worthwhile ideas of his or her own. A leader should be resourceful and imaginative. She or he accepts and contributes to promising innovations, and takes the initiative in searching out, through examination of the literature, promising practices and research findings that may be applied to his or her own situation. In the school setting, the counseling program leader is constantly receptive to the ideas of others—teachers, parents, pupils, administrative staff—and ready to implement those that appear usable; for the leader recognizes that neither she nor her staff can possibly have all the answers.

One Who Is a Professional and Ethical Individual. A program leader must also be respected as representing the highest ideals of his or her profession. The leader is committed to the profession and demonstrates this commitment by the manner in which she or he meets professional obligations, observes the ethics and standards of the profession, and supports and contributes to the development of the profession. The characteristics of the professional counselor are discussed at greater length on page 149 of this chapter.

The Leader Assumes Responsibility and Makes Decisions. Leadership imposes responsibility and decision making. As the one in charge, the program leader must accept the final responsibility for the successes and failures of the program and for making many decisions that effect its development. Program leaders are among those who indicate a willingness to accept responsibility and make decisions—a willingness to act. Although they will utilize democratic procedures in decision making and will delegate responsibilities where appropriate, leaders will never forfeit the responsibilities that accompany program leadership.

One Who Creates an Atmosphere Conducive to Professional Accomplishment. Educators constantly and justifiably stress the necessity of providing a school and classroom atmosphere that is conducive to learning. Industrial managers recognize and seek to provide a work environment that stimulates employee productivity. In both school and nonschool settings, the counseling program leader also recognizes the desirability of establishing a working atmosphere that is conducive to professional achievements. The leader seeks to accentuate the strengths of colleagues, encourages, and motivates. The leader believes in and utilizes the democratic process, and supports the interests of staff members. In short, a program leader in any setting tries to establish those conditions that promote staff esprit de corps.

A Leader Is Insightful. The ability to gain and communicate insights has always been one of the characteristics of a skilled counselor. A counseling program leader should also exhibit this skill, but in a broader setting than the counseling relationship. First, a leader continuously demonstrates insights in relations with others. Secondly, she or he demonstrates program insights that enable him or her to recognize and order program and task priorities, characterize and overcome difficulties, and perceive needed program changes. A leader will also demonstrate insights into problems confronting the program and their solutions.

She or He Is Likable. Although history is replete with many examples of leaders who would not appear to be likable, and not all likable people have leadership potential, the ability to get along with and be enjoyed by others is a trait that strengthens leadership. Certainly, the history of the United States suggests that our culture is most responsive to those who were popular—likable—as well as effective leaders, such as Presidents F. D. and "Teddy" Roosevelt and John Kennedy, General Robert E. Lee, and Mayor Fiorello La Guardia. The very nature of counseling and the potential characteristics it demands of counselors—i.e., warmth, acceptance, attending behaviors, and so forth—suggest traits that makes one likable to his or her fellow human beings, and therefore, are doubly appropriate for the counseling program leader.

A Leader Is an Organizer. Most educational leadership studies indicate that leaders are organizers (Halpui, 1966, p. 81). They have high initiation of structure provided by a plan that is carried out through specified and clearly recognized procedures. Meeting deadlines and high standards of performance are expected of a leader. The leader's attitudes and policies that promote structure are made clear to those involved. Most individuals prefer working in well-organized organizations. They recognize that good organization increases the potential of their efforts; poor organization will be a detractor.

What Program Leadership Is Not

While recognizing desirable characteristics for program leaders, we must also recognize that many school counseling and guidance programs have been handicapped by misconceptions of leadership requirements or roles. Examples of misuses of the leadership position include the following.

A Position of Reward. When school guidance programs were first authorized and funded on a large scale in the 1950s, many newly created directors of guidance positions were awarded to individuals for their long or loyal service, for outstanding accomplishments in other educational endeavors, or as a result of political patronage. Although stiffened certification requirements and professional guidelines have lessened such prospects today, we must recognize that they still do exist. Agency settings are not always exempt from such possibilities either. In such instances, programs and the pupils or clients they are designed to serve are bound to suffer when their leadership is rewarded to individuals for reasons other than professional competency.

A Consolation Prize. We have noted situations in which the director of guidance position has provided a convenient "consolation prize" or "escape hatch" for someone who is no longer effective in his or her present position but must be provided with an appropriate alternative. For example, the coach with too many losing seasons, the administrator who is inept in his or her duties, and even on occasion, the classroom teacher who cannot teach are all illustrative of individuals whom a school system may seek to "kick upstairs" to a counseling position. These "losers" provide little promise of improving themselves or programs in a counselor's role.

A Stepping-Stone. It is currently popular to misuse the counseling leadership position as a stepping-stone to better-salaried administrative positions. This is not to say that counselors should not seek or accept positions of greater leadership responsibility. They should, and programs of counseling and guidance in schools will surely be enhanced when chief school administrators have a counseling background and interest. What we are concerned with are those who use the position only as a stopgap or stepping-stone to the next position up the line, with little commitment to the professional goals of counseling and guidance programs. This person does not bring the dedication, professional motivation, and often the professional skill desired for program leadership.

A Junior-Grade Administrative Position. Somewhat related to the stepping-stone theory, though not necessarily synonymous, is the junior-grade administrator viewpoint. This is a viewpoint that suggests that any leadership or "titled" position, such as principal, department head, supervisor, and director of guidance, is primarily an administrative one. Whereas counselors themselves often complain that they have too many administrative tasks to perform at the expense of counseling, others may retreat behind administrative chores as a means of avoiding counseling. We must also be aware of those who view administration as a "status activity" and feel that their constant involvement in this activity is indicative of their importance and responsibility.

The "Peter Principle." Peter and Hull (1959) stated in their delightful best-seller, *The Peter Principle,* that "in time every post tends to be occupied by an employee who is incompetent to carry out its duties" (p. 8). They further state that "work is accomplished by those employees who have not yet reached their level of incompetence." In other words, given sufficient time, everyone will eventually reach his or her level of occupational incompetence. Although we cannot subscribe to Peter and Hull's rather pessimistic, though humorously presented "principle" as it applies to everyone, there are sufficient individual examples to alert us to this possibility when considering counseling program leadership. Thus, being a "good" counselor does not in itself suggest that one will be equally effective as a "good" counseling program leader. To exemplify the theory of Peter and Hull we note the following example.

"P.B." was recognized as one of the most effective and popular counselors in the Guidance Department of McGilton High School. Because of his reputation, his counseling case load was heavy, and many of his counselees were met after regular school hours and evenings. In summer, because of his demonstrated counseling skills, he was regularly employed as a practicum supervisor in the counselor education program of a nearby university. When a vacancy occurred in the department chairperson's position of the high school guidance program where he was employed, he was immediately recommended by his departmental colleagues. Others rallied to recommend him—parents, former students, teachers, and university counselor educators. The school board, as a result, offered "P.B." the position, and thus encouraged, he accepted. Here was a "good" counselor expected to be a "good" leader. But what happened in actuality?

While initially seeking to lighten his counseling case load, "P.B.," noting that counseling was his "first love," his forte, was in a few short months again deeply committed to an extensive case load. Routine administrative reports were usually late if completed at all. Communications between the guidance department and teaching faculty and parents decreased drastically. Even members of the guidance department staff found themselves increasingly unsure of their responsibilities. Program development came to a standstill. The McGilton High School Guidance Department still had a "good" counselor. They did not have a program leader. "P.B." had reached his level of incompetence!

The point of this example *is not* to suggest that *every* good counselor is a poor risk as a guidance program leader. Quite the contrary. What is suggested, rather, is that being a good counselor does not, in and of itself, promise good leadership. Although effectiveness as a counselor is certainly a prerequisite to effective guidance program leadership, other leadership qualities, plus the interests and attitudes of the prospective candidate, must be considered.

A Defensive Operation. Program leadership is not for those who, once attaining a position of leadership, view their position as one they must constantly defend against other would-be leaders. Fear and distrust are not the hallmarks of leadership; they are marks of lack of confidence in one's ability to lead. This lack of confidence can lead to the formation of cliques, the playing of favorites, and other politically oriented activities or games designed to protect the "leader." Such activities are defensive in nature and do not in any way contribute to program development.

Styles of Leadership

> Clifton and Dahms (1980) note that Robert Blake and Jean Mouton have developed a questionnaire that identifies leadership patterns. The questions deal with how one perceives decisions, convictions, conflicts, emotions, and goal achievement. Based on their responses to these questions, individuals are placed in one of five categories of managerial style. These categories are impoverished management, task management, middle-of-the-road management, country-club management, and team management. (p. 157)

They are described briefly as follows.

Impoverished Management

Neither achievement nor sound relationships are essential. This leader tries to remain uninvolved or neutral and see that established procedures are carried out.

Task Management

Good relationships are incidental and secondary to high achievement. This leader sees to it that goals are met by planning, directing, and controlling.

Middle-of-the-Road Management

A balance between high achievement and good human relations is the aim of the middle-of-the-road manager. This type of leader tries to find a middle ground in an attempt to achieve reasonable program accomplishments without destroying morale.

Country-Club Management

Program achievement is incidental, and it is secondary to good relations. This leader wants harmonious relationships and a work environment that is secure and pleasant.

Team Management

This leader attempts to encourage achievement by using participative involvement of staff members. Decisions are made collectively, and the administrator is, in effect, just another member of the team.

Robert Tannebaum and Warren H. Schmidt (1973) have identified seven styles of leadership. Each of these is identified by the specific actions a leader takes in arriving at a decision.

Low-trust level

1. Makes decisions and announces them.
2. "Sells" decisions to others.
3. Presents decisions and invites questions.
4. Presents tentative decisions.
5. Presents a problem, obtains suggestions, and then makes a final decision.

	6. Defines limits but allows staff members to make decisions.
High-trust level	7. All staff members participate in the decision-making process. (pp. 157–158)

Responsibilities of a Program Leader

Program leadership presumes the assumption of those responsibilities commensurate with this role. Although local differences will obviously result in some variations, some responsibilities appear to be common to program direction in most situations. These are discussed briefly in the paragraphs that follow.

Organization and Management

We have already commented on the desirability of the program leader being an organizer. We would add at this point that any smoothly functioning, efficient program requires organization in order that roles and responsibilities are clearly understood. It is also usually expected that program management will attend to, and be responsible for, the many administrative requirements that seem to "afflict" most organizations. The program leader also has the responsibility to specify and clarify roles and to delegate responsibility. His or her leadership position may be weakened if the leader allows any of these responsibilities to be assumed by or assigned to others. The leader must make provisions for the administrative management of the program in such a way that it will facilitate program achievement and not handicap his or her functioning as a leader. Additional discussion of this responsibility is presented on page 145 of this chapter.

Coordination and Communication

Program leaders are responsible for the coordination of the activities within the counseling programs. They also coordinate the program itself with other school and/or nonschool programs. The program leader in a school setting also sees that members of his or her "team" understand their roles, responsibilities, and relationships so that both personnel and programs complement, rather than complicate, other roles and programs in the school.

Communication goes hand in hand with coordination. In fact, communication is essential to practically all of the responsibilities of the program leader. It cannot be left to chance but must be planned for just like any other activity.

Decision Making

As mentioned earlier in this chapter, a program leader must accept the responsibility for decision making. In addition, the leader must be able to distinguish between those decisions for which she or he alone is responsible and those which should be shared. Leaders must also be prepared to accept and acknowledge the consequences of the decisions they make, recognizing that every program leader will have failures, as well as successes. An effective program leader is also aware that *how* decisions are made are just as important as *what* they are. When disagreements arise, as they inevitably will, the effective program leader works to keep differences out in the open and to use them for growth, rather than restriction of programs.

Identification and Utilization of Resources

The program leader is responsible for the identification and effective utilization of program resources. These include those that may be directly allocated through the organization; those which are available for the asking in the community; and those further removed, which may require some "extra" knowledge and skill to identify and secure. This latter category might include state and federal funding opportunities for counseling programs, foundation grants, and scholarship opportunities.

"Keeping Current"

The program leader has the responsibility of being up to date in his or her field. The leader must be alert to trends and their implications for his or her program, significant research and its application potential to his or her program, and promising innovations and current issues. A leader also has the responsibility of sharing knowledge with his or her staff and encouraging them to "keep current."

Evaluation and Program Development

Although "evaluation" often seems to carry a threatening connotation, it can and should be viewed as a positive process that leads to program improvement. The program leader must provide both the planning for evaluation and an atmosphere conducive to its being a positive experience. Program evaluation is discussed at greater length later in this text.

Supervision

The fact that individuals in organizations are subordinate to one another is a source of both serious resentment and personal satisfaction. Regardless of whether or not we personally like to supervise or be supervised, supervision is an essential activity of program management that seeks to ensure that individuals perform the roles and functions assigned to them and that they perform them to the best of their ability. The latter also implies a developmental role for the supervisor wherein one's supervisees are assisted in developing their fullest potential in relationship to the tasks to be performed. It is appropriate, then, that the counseling program manager have some understanding of both the objectives and techniques of supervision. The major objective of supervision, then, is to facilitate the achievement of program goals. This is achieved through supervision of performance and environment.

The supervision of performance focuses upon the relevance of the individual's activities to his or her designated role in the program and the ways in which she or he can be assisted or his or her performance improved. This process requires both professional understanding and personal tact on the part of the program manager. From the former viewpoint, the manager must clearly understand the role expectancies of those being supervised, what the outcomes to these expectancies should be, and the most effective techniques for goal accomplishment. Equally important, the supervisor must possess understanding necessary to assess the degree to which the supervisee is achieving the goals expected of him or her and the strengths or weaknesses she or he has exhibited in the process. Since supervision should be a growth process for the individual being supervised, the supervisee should also be able to suggest ways in which she or he can improve his or her performance. Effective supervision also requires tact on the part of the program manager, who must communicate clearly to his or her staff the objectives and processes of his or her supervision. The positive and growth aspects of the process should be emphasized. The manager should approach supervision encounters in a friendly and encouraging manner and at those times judged suitable for constructive results.

The supervision of the working environment seeks to ascertain its appropriateness to the activities of the program and its consistent conduciveness to individuals functioning well in its setting. The supervisor should note such features as lighting, heating, and ventilation, distracting noises, adequacy of space and furnishings, appropriate space utilization, cleanliness, convenience of location, and attractiveness of facilities.

Staff Morale and Staff Development

As suggested, the program manager is concerned with the professional development of his or her staff. The manager is also concerned with staff morale. The correlation between the two will be high. Although continuous program development is a planned-for expectancy in most organizations, it has become increasingly evident in recent years that the "morale" of those responsible for such development is a significant influence in the success or failure of a program's accomplishments. Although at one time morale seemed to be a descriptor reserved for those involved in a limited number of highly stressful situations, e.g., armies at war, populations in economic depression or famine, and explorers in difficult environments, in recent generations mental health professionals have (among others) become increasingly aware that large numbers of individuals are finding it increasingly difficult to cope with the everyday stress generated by their jobs, school, and home life. Popular publications such as Erma Bombeck's *Aunt Erma's Cope Book* (1979) have hit the best-seller lists and the expression "burnout" has become popular in covering a wide range of symptoms ranging from mild frustration to nervous exhaustion. The causes for "burnout" more frequently than not are attributed to one's job environment.

Nor can we assume that counselors are exempt from the

causes and symptoms of "burnout." In fact, articles in professional journals such as "Avoiding Counselor Burnout Through Role Renewal" (Boy and Pine, 1980); "Characteristics of Staff Burnout in Mental Health Settings (Pine and Masluch, 1978); and "The Ultimate Disappointment: The Burned Out Counselor" (Warnath and Shelton, 1976) suggest the presence of low morale, stress, and "burnout" in the ranks of counselors as well. Such possibilities pose a challenge to counseling program leaders to

1. Be aware of conditions that create stress and seek to prevent their existence;
2. Be able to recognize the symptoms that signal the potential of stress in staff members.
3. Be aware of preventive and remedial measures.

Although we hope that the causes of "burnout" would not thrive or be created by conditions in counseling programs, it is important that program managers, and counseling staff as well, be aware of the basic causes of stress-induced "burnout." Some of the common causes to be noted are

1. Seemingly unrelenting demands on an individual's time and energies coupled with a feeling of helplessness—no control—over the situations generating such demands.
2. The progressive loss of enthusiasm, idealism, energy, and purpose based on experiences and conditions associated with their work.
3. The consistent failure to achieve expectations imposed by self, and often others as well.
4. An emphasis on dealing with the needs of the job to the exclusion of one's own personal needs (e.g., rest, sleep, diet, relaxation, vacation).
5. The absence of any recognizable reward system, appreciation for a "job well done," or specific individual achievements. Often these "symptoms" are reinforced by unrealistic job goals, so-called high standards, bureaucratic constraints, and significant communications and supervisory gaps between management and staff personnel.
6. Individual traits such as "workaholism," perfectionist, au-

thoritarian, and other personal ego needs and an assortment of neurotic tendencies.

The resulting symptoms of individual burnout include

- accident proneness, physical difficulties, and susceptibility to illness
- indecisiveness
- personal doubts
- guilt
- personal and interpersonal withdrawal
- psychological rigidity
- longer working hours and lower productivity
- existential and philosophical doubts
- blame and resentment
- cynicism and griping
- apathy
- task avoidance
- unnecessary risk taking (Cleve, 1979 as seen in Argeropoulas 1981, p. 2)

Several authors suggest that the "burnout" candidate progresses through identifiable stages. For example, Edelwich and Brodsky (1980) suggest the stages as follows:

Enthusiasm—Stagnation—Frustration—Apathy—Intervention

Alschuler (1980) identifies three basic stages as alarm, resistance, and exhaustion.

A summarization of various preventive/remedial techniques suggests the following.

1. Encourage staff members to "shape up" physically. Evidence indicates that a sense of physical well-being is important in the deterring or remediation of stress. Proper physical exercise, a well-balanced nutritional diet, the avoidance of excesses in coffee, alcohol, drugs, sugar, and salt and personal cleanliness and neatness are important.
2. Help staff give proper attention to recreational activities and relaxation. Encourage their developing and/or giving

attention on a planned regular basis to hobbies, sports, travel and sight-seeing or whatever provides them with enjoyment. This includes time for relaxation as well—the art of doing nothing!

3. Work to eliminate or minimize job conditions that create stress. Encourage and compliment, rotate staff between counseling service and less stressful duties, and guard against individual counselor-client "overload." Insist on breaktimes (and set an example yourself). Create and use support groups.
4. Help staff members become more efficient and effective through time management, confrontation of problems and frustration, improvement of personal coping styles, and being accepting of and working with the "givens" of the job. Provide opportunities for professional (and maybe "personal" too) renewal through opportunities to attend workshops and conventions, "in-service" activities, and professional visitations or exchanges.

Program Management

Objectives

Program management may be viewed as that process which seeks to provide structure, order, and coordination of the activities of an organization. This management will exist at various levels. In an educational management structure, the superintendent of schools and his or her offices may be regarded as representing top management, the building principal and his or her assistants as middle management, and the directors of various programs, such as the school guidance program, as component management. (See Figure 5–1.)

The objective of management at all levels is the facilitation of the goal achievement of the organization. Thus, the objectives of such program components as the school counseling and guidance program must be consistent with and contribute to the accomplishment of the overall objectives of the institution. In other words, the school guidance program must contribute to the education of school-age youth in both the broad "education-as-growth-and-development sense" and the narrow "education-as-learning"

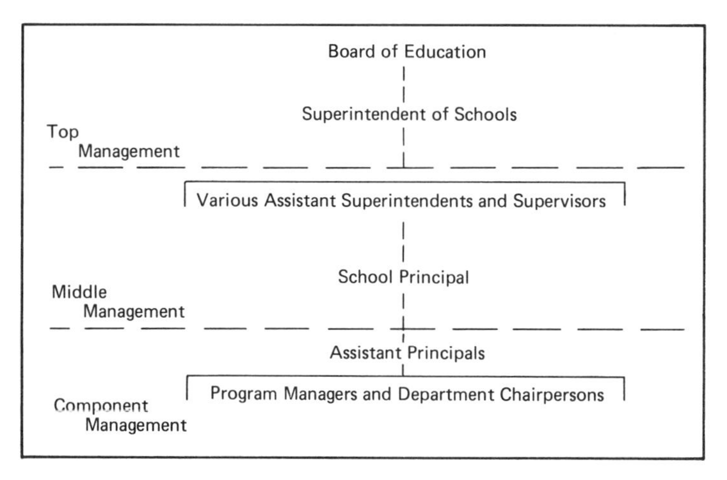

FIGURE 5–1. Management Levels.

sense. Helping "Harry High School" become a happy, well-adjusted (whatever this means) individual may be a commendable outcome of counseling; however, if in the process or as a result, "Harry" does not become better educated or more effective as a student, the counseling program may be viewed as of questionable value to the educational institution.

SOME GENERAL GUIDELINES FOR PROGRAM MANAGEMENT

The first general guideline for effective program management is that someone must be in charge. This must be more than the mere consigning of a label or the establishment of a "paper position" on an organizational chart. The program manager must be *recognized* as being in charge, and must have decision-making authority commensurate with his or her responsibilities. As previously emphasized, the manager of any counseling program at any level should be a professionally prepared counselor who should embody leadership as well as administrative abilities.

Effective program management demands efficiency. Where, for example, the school program manager also counsels; consults with teachers, administrators, and parents; and engages in other counseling and guidance-related activities—as a good manager should—efficient management will require planning. This may mean the scheduling of specific management-administrative activities at specific times with a "free-time" allowance for those activities that cannot be anticipated. If possible, these activities should be scheduled for a time when one works best at the tasks involved. In addition, the effective manager will discipline himself or herself to perform these duties on schedule. A "do-it-now" attitude is important to achieve program efficiency. The use of such aids as daily calendars, priority files, "tickler" files, and pocket notebooks are often helpful, unless the maintenance of such an "alarm system" becomes a major task in itself. This suggests that time should be managed so that it works for the program manager rather than against him or her. This further requires the establishment of priorities and the elimination of those activities that are not worth the time. In other words, efficient program management requires that one become a clock-watcher.

The importance of teamwork has been noted previously, but we again emphasize that the effective management of any organization, counseling programs included, requires the systematic input, involvement, and understanding of those who are members of that organization. Teamwork is essential to the establishment of a working organization pattern and to the development of related program policies and procedures. It is a prerequisite to staff morale and support for management. Teamwork does not simply happen. It results from the planning, actions, and attitudes of the program manager—from him or her doing those "things" that motivate individuals to work with him or her and with each other.

Management Activities

Effective program management requires a recognition of those activities that must be attended to if the organization is to function effectively. Most counseling programs require that management efforts be directed toward program operations, staffing, budgeting and facilities, and evaluation.

Program Operations. Program planning and development, the collection of resources, the resulting program activities, and the organization necessary to facilitate these undertakings are all a part of the operation of any counseling program. Policy development and program evaluation are additional and related aspects that must also receive the attention of the program manager. We again note that program planning, broadly viewed, develops from a recognition of the assessed needs to which the program can appropriately address itself within the environmental framework, the establishment of objectives and relevant priorities related to these needs, the identification of resources and procedures to achieve the established objectives, and the development of an operational plan that incorporates these factors. In chart form for a school program this overview can be depicted as in Figure 5–2.

At each point along the continuum A to G, the program manager assumes prime responsibility. The manager is the focal point from which direction of the school guidance program must emanate. The needs-assessment process (Point A) has been discussed in detail in Chapter 3. At Point B we note that the program manager will be involved initially with other educational leaders (and perhaps community leaders as well) in further clarifying and prioritizing those needs of the student body that the guidance program may best serve. The formulation of resultant appropriate program objectives and priorities within these objectives should involve other guidance workers as well.

Appropriate resources that may be utilized in the school counseling and guidance program should be inventoried preliminary to the detailed planning, whereas as at other points along the operational continuum, responsibilities may be delegated to other guidance workers. At all times, the program manager should

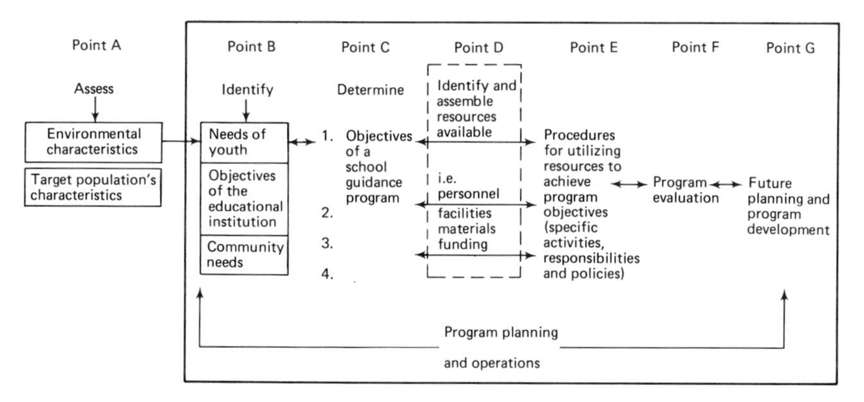

FIGURE 5–2. Check Points in Program Development.

be aware of the resources that are available for program operation.

The actual activities for achieving program goals and the planning that precedes these activities should involve the counseling and guidance staff and any others who can make meaningful contributions. However, here again, the program manager must exercise leadership and assume the ultimate responsibility for the operational plan that will encompass and coordinate the activities. This does not mean that the program manager should not delegate appropriate responsibilities for carrying out the program's activities; she or he must and should. Delegation is a technique for *effective* utilization of human resources, an art that characterizes the successful program manager.

Simultaneously with program planning, attention should be given to policy development. Again, the development of program policies should involve all of those who will have to "stand" with those policies, remembering that none will stand more alone with a disastrous policy than the program manager (and perhaps his or her superiors who sanctioned the policy, not exactly a comforting thought either). Policy development must therefore take cognizance of those influences that suggest or are affected by policy. In simple chart form these influences are depicted in Figure 5–3. The following are a few examples of areas in which school counseling and guidance program policies may be needed:

- faculty access to student records
- parents' access to their children's records
- students' access to their records
- who may have the results of psychological testing
- confidentiality of counseling interviews
- confidentiality of case studies
- role and involvement in student-faculty and student-administration disputes (either one-to-one or group versus group or individual)
- out-of-school counseling
- counseling of out-of-school youth (dropouts, graduates, move-ins), parents and other adults
- conducting or involvement in sensitivity groups
- drug counseling
- sex counseling

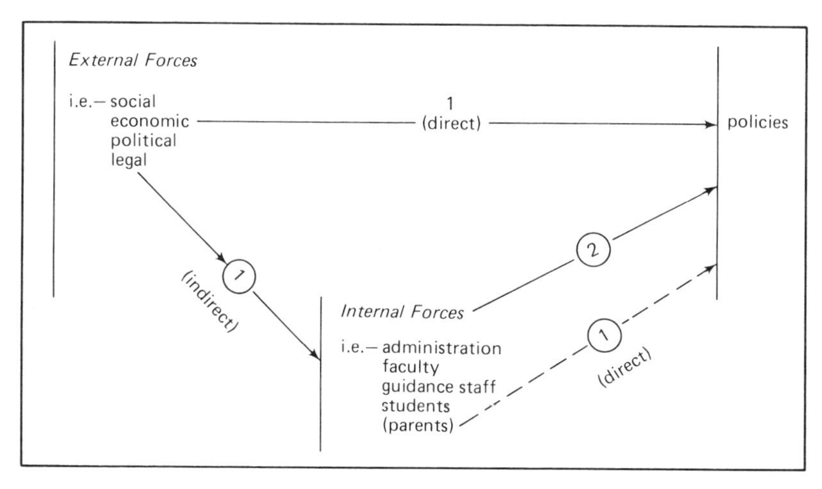

FIGURE 5–3. Forces Influencing Policies.

- teacher counseling
- job placement (especially if there is a local employment office)
- college advising (i.e., the recommending of specific institutions to the student or his or her parents)
- the staff's professional responsibilities (i.e. membership in professional organizations, attendance at professional meetings, adherence to a professional code of ethics).

In policy planning, it is better to anticipate a need and have a policy to meet it rather than attempt to develop a policy in the midst of some controversy. Although some policy flexibility is desirable, any notable exception should be noted. A policy stated in writing (and presumably communicated) is always more definite and defensible than policies that are only verbally understood.

Staffing. The potential for a program achieving its goals is dependent on many factors, but no single factor is more influential than staffing. The leader-manager of the counseling program is the key staff appointment. His or her qualities and many of his or her responsibilities have been discussed earlier in this chapter. This section therefore reviews, as an example, the personnel for the school counseling and guidance program from a total staffing viewpoint, although much of this section is equally applicable to nonschool settings.

The theme for staffing a school (or any) program might very well be the old personnel management slogan of industry—"getting the right person for the right job." This requires a skillful correlation of personal-professional characteristics of the potential staff member with the needs of the job and the characteristics of the school-community setting in which the staff member would live and work. There should also be a process that allows sufficient time and opportunity to secure the best candidates available. Characteristics of potential staff members may be examined in two categories: professional background reflected in training and experience, and personal characteristics.

Professional Characteristics. Both training and experience should be carefully examined in staff selection. Professional preparation is essential for appointment to any school guidance and student personnel position. The nature of this training, the institution in which the program was taken, how recently the training was completed or updated, the academic record achieved, and any specializations or outstanding accomplishments should be noted. Eligibility for any special licenses or certification needed should be considered. Once these characteristics become known, they must be examined as they relate to the unique needs of the job.

Experience is usually an important factor to consider in staff selection. The first consideration should not be "has the applicant had past counseling and guidance experiences?" but "how successful has the applicant been in previous experiences?" Many potentially capable counselors may come directly out of preparation programs with previous experiences only as students, classroom teachers, or perhaps even in noneducational occupations. The priority consideration is not "what" or "how much" but "how successful." (Poor teachers rarely make good counselors; poor administrators even more rarely make good counselors; poor counselor education or undergraduate students seldom develop into good counselors; and counselors whose past performances have been characterized by mediocrity will also seldom develop into outstanding professionals simply by changing jobs.) Once the criteria of "successful past experience" has been satisfied, the candidate's length and variety of experience should be reviewed in light of their relationship to job needs.

Personal Characteristics. Such personal characteristics as age, sex, marital status, race, religion, and background to mention but a few, may be relevant to staff selection. Personality and behavioral characteristics as they may affect both staff and community adjustment are important considerations. The attitudes and special interests—both professional and avocational—need to be examined in the light of school-community expectancies and opportunities. The candidate's own professional goals must also be discussed in light of the opportunity the position offers the individual to achieve or advance these goals. In summary, one is trying to match what one wants in a fellow staff member with what a candidate wants in a job and a work-community environment.

Staffing Procedures. The appropriate staffing of all counseling programs usually starts with a clear and detailed defining of the position for which candidates are being sought. This description should indicate the salary range and factors that affect the position. A general description of both the educational institution and the community should be prepared to accompany the job description. Once prepared, these announcements may be circulated through professional organizations, conventions, and placement services (such as the American Personnel and Guidance Association placement bulletin), university placement offices, counselor education departments in colleges and universities, and even direct contact with possible desirable candidates.

A review of the paper credentials of interested candidates should follow with the most promising being selected for interviews and the securing of additional information if needed. The importance of the interview, which should take place in the hiring school's setting, cannot be overemphasized. No amount of "paper" review can compensate for the insights provided both employer and potential employee through the visitation interview. Many school systems and universities fail to budget adequately, if at all, for this important procedural step in the staffing process, and suffer the results of their shortsightedness in the years that follow.

Once the total review process has been completed and the

candidates ranked in order of preference, the offer should be made immediately and definitely. In "selling" a staff position, do not hesitate to point out any important fringe benefits the school may have to offer as well as the obvious job features. The former, which is often left unmentioned, could include moving expenses, travel allowances to professional meetings, educational allowances for advanced training or workshops, scheduled time to just get acquainted and oriented the initial month on the job, group insurance plans, cooperative buying plans, community status, and community privileges.

Personnel "Pointers." The personnel selected for the counseling staff will determine whether a "winning team" can be developed. In concluding this section, a few tips for building such a team are listed.

a. Only pick winners. If you can't get winners, do without before accepting a loser or a doubtful producer. Two good counselors are better than six mediocre ones.
b. Look for initiative, imagination, and creativeness in selecting staff. Exciting people develop exciting programs. They will stimulate others and you as well. They are also more flexible and susceptible to change.
c. Strive for diversity in your staffing. Differences in age, sex, training, background, experience, personality, and so forth give you a broader range of capabilities as well as staff development potential. Do not, for example, only hire graduates from one school.
d. Pick "your" kind of counselor, that is, the kind who can relate, communicate, and work effectively with you, your staff, your faculty, your administration, your kind of student, and your kind of supporting community. It is ironical to observe counseling staffs who are not even relating to each other, much less demonstrating to others their art of improving human relationships. Remember, it is not sinful to like the people with whom you work.
e. *Do not select* pressured or "special" candidates. Nepotism discourages good people. In schools, do not encourage faculty members who want the job as a reward for years of service, or individuals who indicate they will be doing

> you a favor if they accept. The *only* valid basis for candidate selection is his or her professional-personal qualifications for the position.

In the last analysis you are looking for individuals who will add something to your program—not just maintain it; who will challenge you but not threaten you; who will like you but not worship you; and whose movement on to bigger and better challenges is a probability rather than a problem.

For an exercise in staff selection you may find it interesting to assume that you are responsible for hiring a counselor for your present setting (or one with which you are familiar). Brief vitaes are presented for five candidates. After your review of these vitaes, assume you must make a choice. Which candidate would you select and why?

Dr. Old Stuff	
Personal data	Age—58 H—5′9″ W—160 Marital Status—M
Educational data	PhD. Western Reserve U. 1971
	M.A. Bowling Green U. 1958
	B.S. Ohio Northern 1945
	Graduate academic average A−
Experience data	Two years as a college registrar
	Nine years as a high school principal
	Ten years as a high school industrial arts teacher
	Five years as a high school counselor
Professional data	Member APGA and affiliates, and the American Association of School Administrators
	Published—five articles in professional journals, period 1969–1974

Ms. Ima Sweetie	
Personal data	Age—30 H—5′2″ W—120 Marital Status—S
Educational data	Guidance workshop, West Virginia U. 1978
	M.A. Ohio State U. 1976
	B.Ed. Concord State College 1972
	Graduate academic average B+
Experience data	Four years as a high school counselor
	Four years as a junior high school teacher of history
Professional data	Member APGA and affiliates, NEA and affiliates.
	Published—one article based on master's thesis topic.

Mr. Hi Calory	
Personal data	Age—33 H—5′8″ W—260 Marital Status—S
Educational data	Professional diploma to be conferred, June 1983 Columbia U.
	M.Ed. Michigan State U. 1978
	B.Ed. U. of Toledo 1970
	Graduate academic average A−
Experience data	12 years as a high school physical education instructor and assistant football coach.
Professional data	Member, National Education Association
Mr. "Biggie" Flash	
Personal data	Age—24 H—5′7″ W—129 Marital Status—S
Educational data	Ph.D. Yale U. 1981
	B.S. Princeton U. 1977
	Graduate academic average—A
Experience data	None
Professional data	Member Phi Beta Kappa, American Psychological Association
	Published: Two articles in professional journals, period 1980–1981
Ms. G. O. Sloe	
Personal data	Age—39 H—5′5″ W—126 Marital Status—D
Educational data	Ed.S. Indiana State U. 1974
	M.A. Indiana U. 1969
	B.S. Ball State U. 1963
Experience data	Two years as a high school counselor
	Nine years as a high school teacher
	Three years in the Women's Army Corps
	Two years as a YWCA recreation worker
Professional data	None

Now, describe the qualifications of the "ideal" counselor you would liked to have hired for your setting.

Facilities. The physical setting in which we work is important to all of us. Many of us have daydreamed, perhaps even schemed unsuccessfully, for those luxurious settings usually seen in movies or on TV programs, with posh furnishings, color and closed-circuit TV, soft stereo music, library, built-in snack bar, desk-top dictating machine, computer system, and naturally a magnificent view from our big bay window. Although we usually fail to materialize these dreamings, perhaps it is because we have no evidence that our work effectiveness would be significantly increased by such lavishness. On the other hand, we do know that work effectiveness is handicapped when, for example, we see a counselor who is trying to counsel someone in the corner of the school cafeteria, function out of an office that is next to the band room, or work in an office next to a busy interstate highway.

We do not suggest either of these extremes. We would point out, however, that many counseling and guidance workers routinely spend at least half of their daylight hours in their work setting, and without question, their effectiveness during these hours will be influenced by the physical environment in which they must function. An important management activity is ensuring that physical facilities available to his or her staff are comfortable and functional, adequate for program role fulfillment, and managed in a manner that ensures their appropriate utilization.

Minimum Requirements. Every guidance worker should, as a minimum, anticipate having a private, unshared office with an adjacent reception area, either private or shared. The office itself should be adequate in size (at least 125 square feet), not something that restricts the size of the occupant on one hand or makes him or her look like the first fan in Yankee Stadium on the other. The office should provide necessary privacy and reasonable comfort. The reception area itself should be large enough to both protect and serve the adjacent office or offices (i.e., 250 square feet for a 125-square foot office or 300 feet for two 125-square-foot offices). Adequate filing and storage space should also be provided (roughly estimated at 20 square feet per 100 students). In large schools with sizable guidance staffs a conference room also becomes a necessity with the room size somewhat related to staff size. Other desirable physical facilities include testing facilities, a one-way vision room, an information library, "coffee corner," and toilet facilities.

Facility Management. Whereas securing minimum facilities for program function is a responsibility of management, it is also important that the program manager extract the maximum potential from those facilities she or he has at his or her disposal. Sometimes it is simply a matter of a more effective arrangement of furnishings and equipment. Envisioning such various possibilities can be aided by preparing scale models of both space and furnishings. The study of traffic patterns in and near one's offices may be also helpful.

Assignment of staff space in relationship to staff functions is an important though sometimes tricky task. For example, a counselor who is your group specialist may, barring the existence of a "group room," need a larger office than a staff worker who devotes his or her professional time to individual counseling. The program manager must not let his or her staff become preoccupied with facilities or furnishing as status symbols.

Facility management also presumes attention to the care of the physical environment. Cleanliness; orderliness; appropriate heating, ventilation, and lighting; and quick repair or replacement when needed are important in maintaining a facility where individuals want to work.

Budget Planning. The range of budget activities for counseling program managers appears to vary from simply picking up one's own pay check to planning and managing million-dollar budgets. The discussion in this section does not attempt to provide the details necessary to cover such a wide range of possibilities, lest this become a publication on fiscal management and budgeting. Rather, we briefly discuss a few basic considerations in budget planning, management, and know-how.

The significance of adequate financial resources to the success of any counseling program should be obvious. It determines, first of all, the caliber of staff that one can hire and hold. As previously indicated, good people are the key ingredient in successful program development, and they are not usually "bargain-basement buys." In addition, your budget allocation will also determine whether, once hired, you can furnish them with the tools to do the job and the fringe benefits to keep them happy. In racetrack terminology, there is a real relationship between the budget backing you have and the odds on your program coming home a "winner."

The probability of adequate budget support for the counseling enterprise is dependent on (1) potential support available and (2) the manner in which the budget request is developed and presented. Whereas the former may be beyond the direct influence of the counseling program manager, the latter will often provide him or her with the opportunity to directly influence financial support for the school counseling and guidance program. In order to enhance this possibility, the following planning and management guidelines are suggested.

- The formulation of an operational plan reflecting program goals based on assessed needs and related procedures is the first essential step.
- The budget should be prepared in a manner that reflects and can be clearly tied into this operational plan.
- Budget planning should involve the total counseling and guidance staff.
- Budget planning should be a continuous, ongoing process.

When the budget plan has been completed, it is the responsibility of the program manager to present and interpret the budget to the next higher authority. Both the preparation and presentation of the budget will be more effective if the program manager has some understanding of the total budget picture and the categories available to him or her for budget planning. For example, many school systems will categorize their budgets as follows.

I. Current Expenses
   1. Administration (salaries and supplies)
   2. Instruction (salaries and supplies)
   3. Plant operation (heat and other utilities, supplies, and salaries)
   4. Maintenance (repair and replacement)
   5. Services (attendance, health, transportation, food services)
   6. Fixed charges (employee retirement, insurance, rentals, interest on loans)

II. Capital improvement (purchase of sites, buildings, remodeling costs)

III. Debt services (debt retirement)

The school counseling and guidance budget is usually a part of the instructional or services categories and is frequently computed as a percentage of the instructional budget or on a cost-per-pupil basis. The major expenditure of the guidance program budget will be for salaries. Other common program categories may be for services, supplies, and travel. Included here is a sample departmental budget for a medium-sized (1,200 pupil) secondary school.

McGilton High School Guidance Department Budget Request for 1983–1984

Per Cent of Budget	Cost	
84.8	1. Staff personnel:	
	A. Director @ $18,950	
	B. 4 Counselors—2 @ $17,000	
	2 @ $16,550	
	C. Secretary-Receptionist @ $9,000	
	D. Clerk-typist half-time (50%) @ $4,160	
	Subtotal: Personnel	$99,210.00
7.7	2. Materials and supplies:	
	A. Office supplies ($352.38)	
	1. Stationery $2.78 ream × 3 = $8.34	
	2. Carbon paper $2.29 box × 5 = $11.45	
	3. Onion Skin $2.27 ream × 7 = $15.89	
	4. Mimeograph paper $2.75 ream × 20 = $55.00	
	5. Stencils $3.97 quire × 8 = $31.76	
	6. Correction fluid each $1.79 × 8 = $14.32	
	7. Pencils $.89 box × 14 = $12.46	
	8. Pens each $.43 × 28 = $12.04	
	9. Paper clips @ $.35 box × 28 = $9.80	
	10. Staples $.90 box × 28 = $25.20	
	11. Envelopes $.04 lot × 200 = $8.00	
	12. Note pads $.11 pad × 35 = $3.85	
	13. Appointment book $.28 each × 2 = $.56	
	14. Desk calendar refill @ $1.59 ea. × 6 = $9.54	
	15. Typewriter ribbons $1.00 each × 12 = $12.00	
	16. Rubber bands $.24 box × 14 = $3.36	
	17. Stencil wrapper $.04 each × 50 = $2.00	
	18. Duplicating master $4.48 box × 5 = $22.40	
	19. Duplicating paper $1.73 ream × 30 = $51.90	
	20. Duplicating fluid $1.33 gal. × 7 = $9.31	
	21. Scotch tape $.50 each × 28 = $14.00	
	22. Typing erasers $.12 each × 24 = $2.88	
	23. Mimeograph ink paste $2.72 lb. × 6 = $16.32	
	B. Tests $3.00 each student × 1600 = $4,800.00	
	C. Books ($375.00)	
	1. APGA $85.00	
	2. The School Counselor $30.00	

Per Cent of Budget	Cost	
	3. Vocational information reference books $200.00	
	4. Occupational information subscription series = $60.00	
	D. Film rental ($620.00) One film a month average at average fee of $62.00	
	E. Recording Tapes ($457.20) $2.54 each (1 tape per counselor per week = 5 × 36 wks. = 180 × $2.54)	
	Subtotal: Materials and Supplies	$6,604.58
2.4	3. Equipment and Maintenance	
	A. Tape recorders 2 @ $400 each = $800.00	
	B. Desk $850	
	C. Chair $150 for new director	
	D. Typewriter cleaning contract $125.00	
	Subtotal: Equipment and Maintenance	$1,925.00
1.7	4. Travel	
	A. Professional meetings for staff: 4 staff @ $200 Director @ $400 = $1200	
	B. Travel, home visits—average 40 miles a month × 9 months = 360 miles × $.20 a mile = $72.00	
	C. Travel referral agencies 300 miles × $.20 = $60.00 Students have to be taken to Indianapolis or Bloomington	
	Subtotal: Travel	$1,332.00
	5. Communications	
	A. Mailing costs $.24 each student 1600 = $384.00	
	B. Telephone charges—average $15. per month × 9 mos. = $135.00	
	Subtotal: Communications	$519.00
2.7	6. Research and Evaluation	
	A. Consultation services @ 2 external program evaluators @ $500 each = $1,000	
	B. Data processing costs @ $800.00	
	1. Questionnaire students, faculty, parents, represent perceptions 1st semester and second semester to evaluate effectiveness of new programs	
	2. Setting up data processing @ $300 for follow-up longitudinal study.	
	Subtotal: Research and Evaluation	$2,100.00
	TOTAL BUDGET:	$111,690.00

Upon receipt of the final budget, the program manager then assumes the responsibility for the accurate and appropriate management of the funds in accordance with authorized budgetary procedures. The manager should study and understand thoroughly these procedures. In the management of most budget expenditures, it is important to recognize the following.

- Expenditures can only be made for items that are identified in the budget.
- Expenditures can only be made after appropriate authorization (usually by signature).
- Receipts must be secured for any expenditure, regardless of how small or large they may be.
- When making major expenditures for supplies and equipment, you must be able to show you have made the best buy possible.
- "Slush funds" or "cash box" reserves (nonacountable funds) are usually not permitted.

In addition, budget managers should be aware of certain "common" opportunities for stretching the budget dollars. For example, many public discount houses, supermarkets, or national chain stores sell supplies and equipment cheaper than educational wholesalers. Many hotel chains, such as Hilton, Sheraton, and Albert-Pick, offer discounts to educators, and Hertz and Avis car rental agencies also offer educational discounts. Most test companies will provide free consulting services. A professional staff library may be developed by securing complimentary or wholesale copies of appropriate publications from textbook publishers. To quote a former university purchasing agent, "If you can't get it free, get it wholesale!"

Management Styles

Although budget management is important, people management is even more important. The personal style of the program manager—the way she or he communicates, relates to, and supervises his or her staff will have a tremendous influence on staff morale, efficiency, and effectiveness. Lefton et al. notes (1977) characteristics of four varying approaches or "styles" for the "management" of people. He identifies these as dominant-hostile management; submissive-hostile management; submissive-warm management; and dominant-warm management. The characteristics of these differing styles are now identified.

Dominant-Hostile Management. This is suggested as management that keeps "them in line" or "running scared." Some common notions that typically go along with this style of management are according to Lefton (1977):

- Give people half a chance and they'll mess things up.
- If you want something done right, do it yourself.
- When I want your opinion, I'll ask for it.
- Leave the thinking to me.
- Do it my way or else.
- Do this right and you'll get a reward; you'll get to keep your job.
- What matters is results, no matter how you get them.
- Nice guys don't win ball games. (p. 18)

Submissive-Hostile Management. This approach to management is based on a proposition of "let's not rock the boat" and is characterized by managerial viewpoints of

- Let's do it the way we've always done it.
- Managers who get good results are just lucky.
- Don't rock the boat.
- Why take a chance?
- Keep a low profile.
- I don't want to be a hero. I just want to hold on to what I've got.
- Play it safe.
- If you wait awhile, things usually take care of themselves.
- Let's wait and see what everybody else does. (Lefton, 1977, p. 20)

Submissive-Warm Management. "Take it easy on them" management, "let's be pals," or the "buddy system" is a way to characterize this approach. Other characterizations are

- This department is just one big, happy family.
- I don't think of myself as the boss. I'm just another one of the gang.
- Nice guys win ball games.

- I try to be a pal to my people.
- Always look at the bright side. Why dwell on problems?
- What really matters is positive thinking.
- My door is always open.
- High morale is 90% of the ball game.
- A pat on the back goes a long way (Lefton, 1977, pp. 20–21)

Dominant-Warm Management. An approach that seems to have the most promise and be the most consistent with the counseling profession is that of the dominant-warm manager. This "get the best out of them" management usually is associated with the following ideas.

- I don't manage people. I manage individuals.
- Any manager who thinks he can do it all on his own is kidding himself.
- Don't turn your back on disagreements, welcome them. Differences generate ideas.
- I want to hear what *you* think.
- Don't be afraid to make a mistake. But learn from it so you don't repeat it.
- You can't expect a guy to do his best if he doesn't understand what's in it for him.
- I have some ideas about what should be done, but I want to hear yours.
- I don't have all the answers. (Lefton, 1977, p. 21)

Consultation

In the past decade consultation as an appropriate counselor activity has developed rapidly. The demand for, and utilization of, consultation services has reached the point that the effective program manager must understand the processes of consultation, be capable of offering such services both within and without the organization with which the program manager is affiliated, and recognize those occasions when consultants are needed by his or her own organization. It is particularly significant that many authors have suggested that the appropriate role for the elementary school counselor to play is that of a counselor-consultant. For example, early in the development of suggested formats for elementary school guidance programs, articles and textbooks such as Abbe, *Consultation to a School Guidance Program,* (1961); Crocker, *Depth Consultation with Parents,* (1964); Eckerson and Smith, *Elementary School Guidance: The Consultant,* (1962); and Faust, *The Counselor as a Consultant to Teachers,* (1967) dealt with consultation in elementary school guidance programs.

In discussing consultation in *The Counselor-Consultant in the Elementary School,* Faust (1968) noted, "Although counseling has been described and researched for many years, this is not true of consultation. The latter has been practiced for as many years as counseling, if not longer, but the literature is strangely sparse in its treatment of this role." Faust (1968) goes on to note that

> Counseling and consultation differ in several ways. These primary differences can be found in (a) focus and (b) the kinds of relationships that are developed within the employing school. The consultant focuses on some unit external to the consultee. In the case of a consultant to a teacher, the external unit may be a child, instructional method, course content, etc.
>
> A second major difference between consultation and counseling is found in the kinds of relationships established outside the consultation and counseling settings. Since in consultation the chief focus is on a unit external to the self of the consultee, the personal risk is not as great as it is in counseling, where internal units (the person of the counselee) receive a majority of attention. Personal investment, exposing one's personal self, is not as extensive in consultation. Therefore, risk is not as great, and the consultee need not invest as much trust in the counselor. The consultant is freer to move in many of the normal, day-to-day competitive environments of school personnel. (p. 33)

Goodstein (1978) noted that Caplan (1970), in a book on mental health consultation oriented to community-industrial models, restricted his use of the term *consultation* to

> the process of collaboration between two professional persons: the consultant, typically the specialist, and the consultee, who requests the consultant's help with some professional problem which he or she is having difficulty solving and which is seen as within the consultant's area of specialized competence.
>
> The professional problem may involve the management or treatment of one or more of the clients of the consultee, or the

planning or implementation of a program to cater to such clients. Caplan uses the concept of *client* to denote the lay person who is the primary focus of the consultee's professional practice, such as the teacher's student, the psychologist's, psychiatrist's, or social worker's patient, the minister's parishioner, or the lawyer's client.

Caplan's definition of consultation is further restricted to those professional interactions in which the consultant has no direct responsibility for the client and the responsibility for implementing any remedial plan developed through the course of the consultation remains with the consultee. This type of consultation is aimed not only at helping the consultee with the particular problem under scrutiny, but also at increasing the general level of the consultee's competence in this area. While this definition of consultation is obviously applicable to any kind of professional work, Caplan restricts his discussion to work in the mental health field, that is, the promotion of mental health, and the prevention, treatment and rehabilitation of mental disorders. (pp. 23–24)

As we have previously noted,

In school settings, counselors who function in a consulting role are, in effect, giving their special expertise to teachers, school administrators, and other appropriate personnel. In this role, they become a resource professional for the developmental or adjustment needs involving third parties, usually students. For the counselor to function effectively as a consultant in the educational setting, one must possess special knowledge or skills appropriate to the consulting need. Among the relevant skills the counselor can bring to consulting with teachers and other educational providers and planners are the following. (Gibson and Mitchell, 1981, p. 332)

- An understanding of human growth and development and the influences on this growth and development, including the impact of the school.
- A recognition of the needs of individuals related to the various processes and stage of human growth and development and how institutions (i.e., schools) and agencies can contribute to the satisfaction of these needs.
- Knowledge of the impact of the school environment in general and the classroom in particular on the individual and how this environment can be structured to bring about the most positive results.
- Special ability and understandings promoting desirable human relations and communications skills.

- Training in assessment to identify individual traits and characteristics related to the development of the individual's potential.
- Special understanding regarding career development, planning, decision making, and opportunities and relating this understanding to the individual and the school and its curriculum development and subject-matter areas.
- An understanding of the dynamics and processes of groups and how these may be used to create motivation and change in groups.
- An ability to communicate, counsel, and consult with fellow educators, parents, and the community.

Blackham (1977) noted consulting activities that counselors might perform with administrators, teachers, and parents, as suggested in Figure 5–4.

With Administrators	With Teachers	With Parents
1. Plan a schoolwide educational assessment program. 2. Identify children with special needs. 3. Facilitate community and parent-school relations.	1. Identify and analyze deficiencies in the academic and psychological development of children. 2. Develop skill in understanding child behavior, in classroom management, and in conducting parent-teacher conferences. 3. Develop remedial or prescriptive programs for individuals and groups. 4. Help develop more effective teaching strategies. 5. Help teachers develop effective career education programs.	1. Facilitate positive school-parent relationships. 2. Enhance parent understanding of children's development, abilities, and difficulties. 3. Help parent to modify child learning and behavior problems. 4. Conduct parent education groups.

Source: Garth J. Blackham, *Counseling: Theory, Process and Practice* (Belmont, Calif.: Wadsworth Press, 1977), p. 361.

FIGURE 5–4. Consulting Activities Counselors Perform.

Kurpius (1978) identified nine stages of the consulting process that provide an understanding of how counselors and counseling program managers can function effectively as consultants: (1) Preentry; (2) Entry; (3) Gathering Information; (4) Defining the Problem; (5) Determining the Problem Solution; (6) Stating Objectives; (7) Implementing the Plan; (8) Evaluation; (9) Termination. These nine stages indicate that consultation is an organized, systematic process in which each step logically leads to the next. In utilizing the consultation process, counselors may find it helpful to their consultees to identify these stages as guidelines for the process they will be sharing. This will further assist both the consultant and consultee in keeping the consulting activity "on track."

Community Relations

Counselors in both school and nonschool settings have increasingly realized in recent years the vital importance of "taking their case to the public." By this we mean making the public aware of the nature and role of counseling services and their contributions to human welfare through a variety of institutional and agency settings. In times of budgetary limitations those programs supported by the public, either through taxation or patronization, that are most likely to be trimmed are those which have little understanding or recognition for their importance.

As Miringoff (1980) notes

> Every human service organization is surrounded by a community to which it must respond. The community may include a variety of publics, including potential clients, the general public, political bodies, other human service organizations, and other organizations and groups. The relationship of this community to the human service organization is an important one, and one that influences the functioning of the organization and the quality of its service (p. 159)

Community relations ought not be viewed in the same terms as an advertising campaign; i.e., selling a product through such techniques as newspaper publicity for image building; social activities involving key political and/or community figures. Rather, community relations from a program management perspective should be viewed in terms of increasing the program's service effectiveness which means reaching the optimum number of clients the program is designed to serve. In this vein, community relations may be viewed in terms of three major tasks: education, outreach, and advocacy.

"A program of education about social problems represents a direct way in which human service organizations can achieve some degree of official goal achievement. If effective, such education programs can lead to the prevention of some social problems before they reach the point at which treatment is necessary" (Miringoff, 1980, p. 161). In this regard, it is usually better to stress the human aspects of a social problem and its treatment, rather than program details and/or descriptive statistics.

Outreach programs are designed to increase the likelihood that those individuals in need of and entitled to the counseling service are, first, aware of the availability of the service and, second, inclined to utilize the service. Schools and agencies often "duck" their outreach responsibility by the rationalization that they already have more clients than they can handle. According to Miringoff (1980):

> outreach is a specific kind of educative task, which is education directed not to the general public but at potential clients. Many clients who could be successfully served by an agency are often not sufficiently informed about the organization's service capabilities to realize that their problem could be treated or alleviated. Many may feel that their problem is unique, or that they need to face their problem alone. (p. 162)
>
> In advocacy, the task is to persuade the community that something needs to be done. In the case of advocacy, the audience may be the general public, but it may be aimed at a more specific audience as well. Advocacy may be designed to convince those who have access to, or control of, resources that the organization requires in order to function. Hence, a local legislature may need convincing that a particular program or organization is a worthwhile recipient of funding. This might require direct lobbying or the organization of community support.
>
> The role of advocate has a long history of conceptual development in the literature of community organization practice in social

> work. In recent years, community mental health has adopted it as a basic concept. (p. 163)

Another increasingly important aspect of community relations is that which might be labeled "political activity." This activity has become important during times of economic cutbacks when adequate funding for counseling services is threatened, particularly for school counselors, whose programs may be viewed as ancillary or "nonessential" and, therefore, subject to the economic fortunes of the school system.

DiSilvestro (1980) notes that in the case of school counselors,

> The most immediate access many have to policy makers who affect their work is their local school board. The local school board determines those educational policy decisions that most directly affect the counselor's work. More specifically, decisions concerning counselor staffing, as well as counselor funding, are determined predominantly by the local school board. Not only are staffing ratios and funding priorities determined by the school board, but policy decisions that affect the role and function of the school counselor are significantly determined by the school board. (p. 351)

DiSilvestro concludes that "Three effective approaches for counselors to employ in dealing with school boards are (a) making personal contact with board members; (b) having needs assessment information available to support proposals; and (c) presenting options when making requests for board consideration." (p. 356)

In both school and agency settings, effective program managers generally can "read" their community well. They can identify the community's major concerns and how the community views their program and the community leaders who shape public opinion and policies. They can identify the most effective means to communicate a program's services, achievements and needs, and their importance to the community.

Ethical and Legal Considerations

In any activity where one human being is professionally concerned with the well-being of another, consideration must be given to providing ethical guidelines for the guidance and protection of both the profession's membership and the clients they serve. The school counselor and student personnel worker may sometimes be confused by the fact that she or he seems to be professionally responsible to several groups (e.g., educators, psychologists, counselors); however, an examination of the codes of ethics of the National Education Association, the "Bill of Rights" of the American Federation of Teachers; The American Psychological Association; and the American Personnel and Guidance Association would reveal little that is in conflict and much that is related. Professional membership in all relevant professional organizations is encouraged. The American Personnel and Guidance Association is the professional organization to which most school counselors and student personnel workers should be committed first. The Ethical Standards of the American Personnel and Guidance Association are presented in Appendix D. Most nonschool counselors belong to the American Psychological Association, Division 17. The Ethical Principles of Psychologists are presented in Appendix E.

Whereas counseling program managers should insist that their staff members be fully aware of the ethical standards of their profession, they should also understand that these standards are not in themselves legal guidelines. There is, however, a growing concern for legal responsibilities and limitations affecting the role and function of counselors in schools and other settings. Counselors' responsibilities to themselves, their clients, and society will require continuous analysis and synthesis of the law by legal experts for understanding by counselors.

These legal-ethical concerns and conflicts affecting counseling personnel and their programs are many and varied. However, some of these are more universally recognized and of greater concern to the profession than others. Included are such concerns as the right of privileged communication, confidentiality of counseling records, ethical standards for group leaders, third-party payments, and licensure for private practice.

Of all the ethical concerns of counselors, none has been greater or more consistently examined in a legal context than the confidentiality of the counseling relationship. This relationship—"the right of privileged communication"—is considered by many as the criteria for establishing counseling as a profession. Attorneys have long possessed this right of privileged communication by common law. In addition, most states (and countries) have, through statutory law, extended this privilege to physicians and clergy, and in some instances to psychologists. However, though counselors usually suggest that confidentiality is a condition of the counseling relationship, they have attained only limited legal guarantee in terms of statutory provisions or favorable court decisions on which to base such a privilege. Even when this privilege is possessed, counselors should be aware of these exceptions that unequivocally require the disclosure of information in a court of law such as knowledge of a planned crime or fraud.

The Program Manager as an Agent of the Profession

The recognition of counseling as a profession has been discussed from the standpoint of legal implications. As inferred, the achievement of certain legal privileges, e.g., privileged communication, is contingent upon counseling reaching a level of professionalism that will result in society bestowing upon counselors "all the rights and privileges pertaining thereto." In this pursuit of professionalism, it is essential that those counselors who hold leadership roles become actively involved in the upgrading of themselves, their programs, and their profession. It is in this sense that the guidance program manager must function as "an agent of the profession" within his or her own professional setting. Responsibilities in this role focus on professional membership and activities.

To function as an agent and licensed practitioner of the profession, it is important that the counseling program manager hold membership in his or her primary professional organization. For example, the vast majority of school counseling and guidance workers view the American Personnel and Guidance Association as their "home organization." Within the parent organization, A.P.G.A., there are branch organizations that cater to various levels or special areas of interest such as The American College Personnel Association, the Association for Counselor Education and Supervision, the National Vocational Guidance Association, the Association of Non-White Counselors; the American School Counselor Association, the American Rehabilitation Counseling

Association, the Association for Measurement and Evaluation in Guidance; the Association of Specialists in Group Work; the Public Offenders Counselors Association and the American Mental Health Counselors Association. There are also state and local chapters of many of these branches, in addition to state and local chapters of A.P.G.A.

Although membership is important (and a prerequisite to many professional activities), it is not in and of itself the hallmark of the professional. The true professional identifies himself or herself through active participation in his or her professional societies and the utilization of the professional route to program and self-improvement. The professional attends and participates in professional meetings; reads professional publications; and contributes his or her own ideas, successful practices, or research findings through program presentations, contributions to professional publications, or through more informal means.

As an agent of the profession, the counseling program manager must accept several responsibilities. The program manager must demonstrate that she or he believes in what she or he stands for by being an active member of his or her professional organization and by representing in practice the ethical standards espoused by the American Personnel and Guidance Association and/or the American Psychological Association. Beyond this, one should also actively encourage—not pressure—one's fellow guidance workers to become members and to actively participate and adhere to the stated ethical guidelines of the profession. The most effective program managers are, in reality, program leaders. As suggested previously, this requires one to believe in, and to be committed to, the profession in the fullest and truest sense. Effective counseling program managers will also be effective agents of their profession.

Program Management and Technology

A program manager is constantly seeking means of improving the efficiency and effectiveness of his or her program. Whereas counseling and guidance programs are people-oriented, this orientation should not be permitted to obscure the potential contributions of technology to program operation. As Walz (1970) suggests:

> Guidance technology has the potential to enable counselors to reach new goals and to accomplish old goals in new ways. The appropriate guidance use of technology, however, is not just one of designing machines but rather of discovering how to use technology to realize counselors' personal and societal goals in particular settings. The future of guidance could well depend on the capacity of the counseling profession to utilize technology effectively. (p 175)

Educationally, the physical manifestations of this technology are most commonly recognized in computers and automated data processing machines, television, videotaping, and other audio-visual equipment and teaching machines. Of these perhaps the most awe-inspiring, controversial, and confusing are the computers and their utilization in data processing. An article on computers in the *Personnel and Guidance Journal* (1970) described their components and functioning, as follows:

> Data processing is the use of computers to rapidly store, retrieve, and display information. The two essential components of data processing are: (a) the computer equipment, or hardware; and (b) the systems of programs, or software which enable the computer to perform its job.
>
> A computer operates through five main functions: input, storage, control, processing, and output. A person solving a problem with a calculating machine uses these same five functions: (1) When s/he punches the keyboard he enters numbers into the machine as input. (2) He manipulates the keys in a sequence of steps to achieve his answer (control). In a sense, the sequence of steps is his program. (3) He writes any intermediate calculations on paper, which represents one of his means of storage. (4) Movements of gears and counters in the machine amount to processing. (5) The final result—numbers showing on the dial—is the output.
>
> Though this explanation is highly simplified, a computer does the same thing, except at higher speeds, automatically, with stored programs, and without an operator.
>
> Briefly, this is how a computer works:
>
> *Input.* The computer takes in data by sensing or reading information from one of many sources: punched cards or paper tape in which information is represented by the presence or absence of magnetized spots; and magnetic or conventional characters printed on paper, read by a variety of scanning or other devices.
>
> Another form of input is data entered into the computer by a

keyboard that looks much like a typewriter. All input data—numbers and letters—are converted into electronic pulses that can be understood by the machine.

In addition to information to be processed and stored, input can take the form of step-by-step instructions of the computer program itself. It is the human programmer's task to prepare such a program of instructions.

Storage. Several types of storage devices in computers make it possible to store (a) program instructions; (b) the data to be processed (this could be fresh data or data already processed and stored in the computer's memory); (c) reference data used repeatedly, such as mortality tables used in insurance problems.

Control. The computer starts by obeying the first instruction, then proceeds through all the instructions of the program in a sequence directed by the instructions themselves.

Processing. Processing involves the manipulation of data within the machine. Typical operations include assembling, classifying, calculating, and summarizing.

Output. The result of processing is output, which takes many of the same forms as input: punched cards, punched paper tape, and magnetic tape. It also has some forms of its own: printed reports, electronic display on cathode ray tubes, and even audio devices that use prerecorded human voices to answer anticipated questions.

When reduced to bare fundamentals, computers are capable of only two arithmetic operations—adding one number to another and comparing two numbers to see if they are equal. But they can perform these simple operations so rapidly and in so complex an interacting network that they can solve enormous problems when those problems are properly stated by men.

Before a single instruction is written, then, analysis and planning are in order. It frequently takes months of effort to define the problems a computer must solve in order to achieve a worthwhile data system. The activity itself is called systems analysis or systems development. The fact that such human insight and knowledge are required will ensure man's place among machines for some time to come. ("A Brief Look at Computers," *Personnel and Guidance Journal,* vol. 49, no 3, from material published by the American Federation of Information Processing Societies, p. 173)

This processing of information through a computer could be charted as in Figure 5–5 from Gibson and Higgins, 1966).

In an earlier publication, we pointed out that the potential

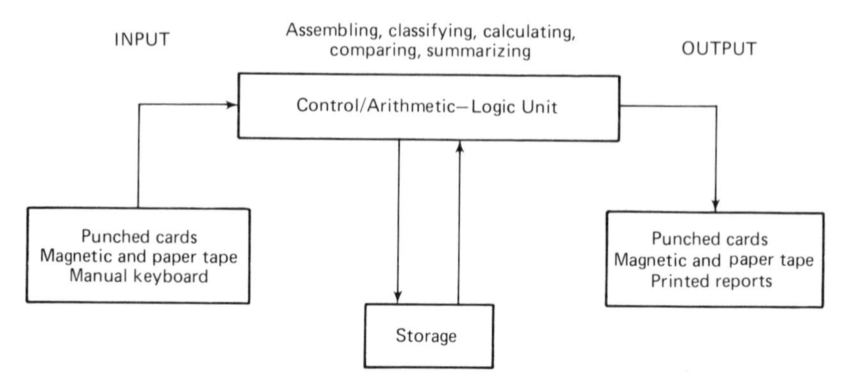

FIGURE 5–5. Processing.

advantages of automated data processing for the school counseling and guidance program included the following:

- Permits data to be assembled and made available more readily and in greater amounts than ever before.
- Facilitates the rapid synthesis of data from different sources.
- Frees counselor time for nonclerical duties.
- Promotes standardization and accuracy.
- Aids the development of more valid criteria for predictive, analytical, and other decision-making purposes.
- Encourages research.

Although computer-assisted data processing is becoming a common tool for counselors, developments have progressed beyond these systems. Loughary (1970) describes these as follows:

> designed to go beyond information-processing, and replace counselors in performing different tasks. Just like those at the first level, these systems are totally controlled by the counselor or his designate. The machine can be turned on and off by him, and more important, the memories of such systems are completely available to the controlling counselors. That is, they can interrogate the machine to find out what it has said to the counselee, and vice versa. (For descriptions, see *Computer-Based Vocational Guidance Systems, 1969; Educational Technology,* 1969.)
>
> Some of these systems are similar in design to traditional manual systems. For example, the user indicates a subject of interest to the system, and the computer provides him with a list of resources or references. These are essentially automated reference

systems. There are a few occupational and educational information systems which permit the user and the computer to conduct a dialogue for purposes of identifying materials that seem appropriate for the user. Some of these systems also intend to provide the user with decision-making practice. The dialogue is usually an interrogation of the user by the computer, essentially a function of the computer having a less sophisticated vocabulary and fewer statements than the user.

There are other systems of this second level which claim to assist the user in identifying educational opportunities suited for his needs and interests. These systems match a collection of user interests, needs, preferences, financial resources, and other characteristics with institutional descriptor characteristics. What shakes out is the institution(s) which seems to make the best match with the user's statement of needs. Several commercial services of this nature are now on the market.

There are also systems using the model just described to match workers with job opportunities. Another attempts to assign a rehabilitation client to a counselor and counseling office for which counselee success is most likely. In addition to the above references, the *Journal of Educational Data Processing* frequently includes papers on computer-assisted counseling systems (e.g., *Journal*, 1969; see also Tondow and Betts, 1967). (pp. 185–186)

Loughary's third level of systems is labeled "substitute counselors." He indicates: "The uniqueness of these systems is that their designers and operators would ascribe to them a particular characteristic found in human counselors specifically, privileged communication or privacy. The memories of these systems would be controlled totally by the user, i.e., the counselee" (Loughary, 1970, p. 186). Although Loughary states that he knows of no system which fits his third level because they do not provide privileged communication, several do appear to be substitute counselors in every other respect.

Although the major emphasis in this section has been on the computer and automated data processing, there are also demonstrated values for school guidance programs in the use of educational and closed-circuit television and for both audio- and videotaping and teaching machines. Publications such as Super's *Computer Assisted Counseling* (Teacher's College Press, 1969); the U.S. Office of Education's *Computer-Based Vocational Guidance Systems*, and the November, 1970, issue of the *Personnel and Guidance Journal* (theme: Technology in Guidance) are among those publications that guidance program managers can use to further acquaint themselves with the potential of technology for their school's counseling and guidance program.

Summary and Implications

In any setting counseling program development and management is dependent upon the caliber of professional leadership and management. Even though styles and characteristics of program leaders vary, some general characteristics appear to apply to most leaders. These include being competent and knowledgeable in one's professional field; being adept at identifying and utilizing the good ideas of colleagues as well as contributing worthwhile ideas of one's own; being professional and ethical at all times; being willing to assume responsibilities and make decisions; creating an atmosphere conducive to professional accomplishment; being insightful, reasonably likable, and well organized. The responsibilities of program leaders are also broad and varied, but, in general, they encompass overall program management, including coordination and communication; resource utilization; program evaluation; supervision; decision making; and responsibility for staff selection, morale, and development.

Program managers also have consultation opportunities and responsibilities. They must recognize the vital importance of public relations, be aware of the ethical and legal guidelines for their profession, and, in general, be an active agent for the profession. Too, the effective program manager is constantly seeking means to improve the efficiency and effectiveness of his or her program and therefore is alert to the potential of technology which may enable programs to reach new goals and accomplish old goals in new ways.

These expectancies and responsibilities imply that in today's accountable and publicly scrutinized programs, the counseling program leader must not only be a specialist in the field of counseling but also a specialist in program leadership and management. Such specialization results from both experience and preparation.

CHAPTER 6

The Elementary School Guidance Program

Introduction

The necessity of providing guidance services for secondary school students is rarely questioned today. Most state departments of education and regional school accrediting associations *require* the provision of guidance services for secondary school students. Although questions may be raised about the secondary school counselor's most appropriate functions, and disagreement may arise over which guidance objectives should be given precedence, at least the adolescent's need for the kinds of assistance provided through school counseling and guidance programs has been widely recognized.

Unfortunately, judging by the relatively small number of school systems that require the employment of elementary school counselors, the needs of elementary school students for the kinds of developmental assistance that school counselors could provide apparently have not been as widely recognized. Or, if recognized, attempts to convince school patrons and school personnel of the vital importance of providing developmental guidance services for elementary school students have been relatively unsuccessful. Yet, it is becoming increasingly more obvious that if our society is to have healthy, stable, productive, and fully functioning adults, special assistance in fulfilling affective and cognitive needs must be provided through our schools for our children and preadolescents.

THE ELEMENTARY SCHOOL: STARTING POINT FOR GUIDANCE

The provision of formalized, structured programs to assist the child to meet basic developmental needs cannot be deferred until the individual reaches high school. As Dinkmeyer and Caldwell (1970) pointed out:

> It is increasingly recognized that the elementary school child is at a crucial stage in his development. He is engaged in the formulation of a style of life. He is in the process of establishing an identity and a self-concept. He must deal with the problem of adequate social relationships and also meet the challenges which occur in the world of educational achievement. There is an increasing amount of evidence that the early elementary grades are crucial for both the educational and personal development of the child. (p. 5)

And as Myrick (1977) stated:

> The most favorable time for attacking school and social problems is during the early formative years. Research shows that about 50 percent of a child's intellectual development occurs between conception and age 4, 30 percent between ages 4 and 8, and 20 percent from ages 3 to 17. Other studies of child development have shown that children establish lifelong behavioral patterns during ages 6 through 10 . . . the first four years of school!
> . . . Parents and teachers and principals need help in resolving problems. Out of frustration many parents are turning to the school for support and assistance in child rearing practices. They want to be better parents and many are frustrated with the problems that confront today's youth. In addition, teachers and principals often lack the necessary preparation and time to cope with problems of the contemporary child. In many instances they are overwhelmed by pressures to update materials, expand the curriculum, develop new learning approaches, relate with large numbers of students, and, at the same time, meet individual needs. Because of these responsibilities they need help in developing an organized guidance program which can be incorporated into the curriculum and give more intensive help to children. (p. 47)

The crucial need for initiating elementary school guidance programs has long been recognized. As Meeks (1962) noted several years ago:

> The urgency of the demand for guidance in the elementary school has become greater as the greater complexity of modern living has increased the pressures which can be factors in a child's maladjustment and which hinder learning. Teachers have seen, for example, that emotional pressures upon the child by the school, his parents, or his peers may create an emotional block which will prevent his learning to read until, through counseling or other help, the block is removed.
>
> More significant than the recognition of the usefulness of guidance in the correction of maladjustment has been the acceptance of guidance as an integral part of the whole educational program. Guidance is now regarded as much more than a privilege accorded the maladjusted; it is also needed by other children and requires programs that have as their major objective helping all children to be at ease with themselves and with others. (p. 30)

Additionally, the importance of elementary school guidance both to the child and to the basic purpose of the school in our society is increasingly reflected by the findings of research pertaining to self-concept and academic achievement. Purkey (1970), for example, summarized his review of such research with these conclusions:

> We have seen that there is a persistent and significant relationship between the self-concept and academic achievement at each grade level and that change in one seems to be associated with change in the other. Studies have been presented to indicate how the successful student sees himself, and how his self-concept contrasts with the self-image of the failing student. Although the data do not provide clearcut evidence about which comes first—a positive self-concept or scholastic success, a negative self-concept or scholastic failure—it does stress a strong reciprocal relationship and gives us reason to assume that enhancing the self-concept is a vital influence in improving academic performance. (p. 27)

The importance of the counseling and guidance function to the total educational effort is frequently misunderstood. In the elementary school this misunderstanding has resulted in the lack of support for the development of school counseling and guidance programs at this level. When the National Defense Education Act was amended in the mid-1960s to include provisions for the support of junior high and elementary school counseling and guidance program development, it appeared that the need for continuous guidance services at all educational levels had been established. However, in spite of the strong support provided by that and subsequent federal legislation, the provision of guidance services for all elementary school children has not been accomplished; in fact, such services have not been provided for even a majority of these children. Basically, these services have not been provided because school patrons and administrators—and many teachers—have not been convinced that services provided by elementary school counselors warrant the additional expenditures that such services require. Thus, a guidance program cannot be superimposed upon a school; instead, it must evolve from a planned program of environmental and pupil needs assessment. Most importantly, the identified needs must be communicated to the total school community as a first step in the initiation of a guidance program.

Characteristics of the Elementary School

Elementary schools are becoming larger, more complex, and more urban, and they are placing greater stress on individualized instruction than has been true in the past. The size, complexity, and urbanization of the school make it more difficult for teachers to develop the knowledge and understanding of each child required for optimal learning and adjustment; this is especially necessitated by the stress on individualized instruction. All of these factors dictate a need for professional counseling personnel in the schools.

The increasing size and complexity of our schools—resulting from population shifts, school consolidation, and school integration—coupled with inadequate budgets and proportionally smaller teaching staffs have resulted in larger classes than has been considered desirable. Even with teacher aides, team teaching, and other innovative practices, the classroom teacher has little time for determining the individual characteristics and needs of each of the students. The increasing urbanization of our society has made this task even more difficult. In rural and small neighborhood schools, the teacher usually knew the families from which the children came, and hence had or could quickly get a much better understanding of the children than is possible in the schools of today. In the typical urban school, little is known about the child's family or nonschool life. Also, there is the increasingly complex task of assisting the student in understanding and accepting classmates who come from widely divergent social, cultural, and ethnic groups. Although this problem is not new—actually it has been too long ignored—it was not too visible in the small neighborhood school, which largely served children from relatively homogeneous cultural groups.

In addition to the increased movement toward individualizing instruction, there is also a great thrust toward performance-based evaluaton. Both of these trends require in-depth knowledge of each student and the carefully coordinated efforts of the teachers and other educational specialists.

As a result of these changes in the educational system, the hard-pressed teacher finds it increasingly difficult to cope with students' academic or cognitive needs, let alone find time to assist with their affective needs. However, if a student's classroom climate is the key to his or her maximal affective and intellectual development, as many educators theorize, the teacher *must* consider the student's affective needs. An important role of the counselor is to assist the teacher in the fulfillment of obligations related to both categories of student needs, cognitive *and* affective.

Characteristics of the Elementary School Student

Most adults, once their own children leave the elementary school, cease to have an interest in the elementary school or the elementary pupil. Unlike high schools, whose athletic teams, marching bands, drama presentations, and so forth constantly remind the public of their existence, the elementary school and pupil would appear to be dealt with only in memories of the distant past by the tax-paying public. Although much concern and some action is targeted on the problems of adolescents, especially as they may interfere with the tranquility and enjoyment of adulthood, the elementary school pupil does not threaten us on the highway, crowd into our places of entertainment, deface our property, steal our hubcaps, or challenge our assumptions, as the adolescent frequently does. The elementary age pupil is easy to overlook and to ignore (unless she or he is your child). Their problems, if they do exist, it is usually assumed, can be dealt with adequately by the parent and by the traditional elementary school. Although educators, psychologists, and other human development specialists are in agreement regarding the importance of the developmental years of the elementary school pupil in his or her later behavior as an adolescent and adult, little attention is given to the nurturing and growth of positive attitudes and behaviors. The preventive and developmental potential of elementary school guidance programs is all too frequently viewed as a "frill" that can be done without. It is better to save these dollars now and pay them later threefold in the cost to the public of juvenile delinquency, vandalism, teenage substance abuse, school dropouts, and so forth. During the elementary school years, the child is still modifying and developing a self-image, an image that has been developed since birth. It is a search for identity. If one is treated as a member of a homogeneous, competitive classroom group, one's search for identity is further compounded, and any negative self-images held will be greatly strengthened. If one is seen as a highly unique individual, responded to in terms of specific needs and assisted to form a positive and realistic self-concept, not only will his or her self and social adjustment have been enhanced but also the development of his or her academic potential will have been greatly facilitated. As Purkey (1970) pointed out:

> Gradually, it is becoming clear that many of the difficulties which people experience in most areas of life are closely connected with the ways they see themselves and the world in which they live. The evidence presented in this book indicates that students' failures in basic subjects, as well as the misdirected motivation and lack of commitment characteristic of the underachiever, the dropout, and the socially disabled, are in large measure the consequence of faulty perceptions of themselves and the world. (p. 2)

Every teacher is aware of the great differences that exist among the children in any classroom, including the elementary school. They differ in academic and other aptitudes; in levels of achievement in all areas; in motivation; in temperament; in attitudes with regard to self, family, peers, school, and society; in size, weight, height, maturational rate, color, race, ethnic group background, *ad infinitum*. Obviously, every child is truly unique. The divergency of these characteristics, or stated differently, the uniqueness of each child, would appear also to necessitate the placement of counselors in our group-oriented elementary schools.

What Is Elementary School Guidance?

There is no universally accepted definition of elementary school guidance. However, there is considerable agreement that elementary school guidance programs should be developmentally oriented. Many approaches to elementary school guidance are labeled "developmental," but no single approach has emerged that could be called *the* developmental approach.

As applied to elementary school guidance, the developmental concept is envisioned as assisting all children to develop normally, to go through the developmental process without undue anxiety, self doubts, or threat. The concept of developmental guidance is perhaps more readily understood if a continuum is envisioned ranging from crisis or remedial counseling to counselor intercessions to improve the learning and home environments of children. Whereas the solely remedially oriented counselor is occupied full time on a one-to-one basis with children who have problems (thus the term *crisis centered*), the counselor at the other end of the continuum—the developmentally oriented counselor—works virtually full time with teachers and parents to assist them in providing environments that are conducive to normal child development. Given the realities of most schools and most communities, today's developmentally oriented counselor functions somewhere around the middle of that continuum. As much time as possible is spent in assisting teachers and parents to understand and provide for children's needs, but some time must also be spent assisting children to resolve problems.

Basically, developmental guidance is an attempt to provide an *organized* structure of services designed to assist the school to meet more effectively the students' developmental needs. The types of needs with which developmentally oriented guidance programs are concerned were identified by Dinkmeyer and Caldwell (1970) as follows:

> The child needs to mature in self-acceptance and in an understanding of self, in a comprehension of his assets and liabilities. He must develop a more realistic self-evaluation. At this stage of life he needs to mature in social relationships, to be able to identify and belong with his peers. He must develop independence and take responsibility for his actions, make choices, and be responsible for the consequences of these choices. The child must also come to understand the role of work in life, as it first appears in educational achievement and then in terms of long-range career development. It is vital that he come to understand opportunity in the environment and the way in which it relates to his own development. (p. 5)

Elementary School Guidance Program Objectives

Children's developmental needs—such as those identified by Dinkmeyer and Caldwell (1970)—lead to the derivation of elementary school guidance program objectives. The broad goals of their counseling and guidance programs are highly similar. However, the specific nature of a program will be governed by the needs that exist in a specific school population. These needs will vary from school to school. Among the many factors responsible for the variation in needs is the variation in cultural demands on children. Cultural demands and expectations become children's developmental needs. As cultural demands vary from one community to another, variation in some of the specific developmental needs of children will occur from one school to another. The identified high priority developmental needs of the students in a specific elementary school will, therefore, become that school's guidance program objectives. Abundant examples of derived objectives are found in the elementary school guidance literature. Little variation is found among the listed objectives, which suggests that there is widespread agreement about the broad objectives (or goals) of elementary school guidance programs. The kinds of objectives typically found in such listings may be seen in the following list published by the Ohio State Department of Education's Division of Guidance and Testing (1976).

Objectives of Elementary Guidance Services

Specific objectives of elementary guidance services are the

- provision for the early identification of individual differences so that necessary educational programs may be designed to meet the needs of every student.
- assistance to students to develop a positive self-image through efforts to improve their self-understanding, self-direction and skills in problem solving and decision making.
- involvement of teachers and other school staff members in developing a clearer understanding of the growth and development of students and a learning climate which facilitates that development.
- involvement of parents in ways which will help them understand the educational, career, personal and social development of their children.
- cooperation and work with administrators, teachers, counselors, pupil personnel specialists and parents in order to bring into focus a school's total effort for every student.
- coordination and utilization of the resources of the school, home and community to increase the students' opportunities for successful achievement in school.
- contribution to ongoing educational planning by examining the learning conditions and seeking improvements in the learning climate.

Guidance Should Be Programmatic

The nature of educational systems and the needs of elementary age children dictate that guidance programs be developed for elementary schools rather than just making available a variety of guidance services. In differentiating *programs* from *services,* Shaw (1977) stated:

> The idea that a counseling *program* is different from counseling *services* may be new to some. As applied to counseling staffs, the basic concepts of a programmatic approach are that there is agreement on the outcomes that the staff should help to bring about; that all members of the unit carry out functions leading toward the attainment of the commonly agreed upon goals; and that they co-

> operatively assess the extent to which the specified goals have been achieved with a view to using such information to modify either the goals or the functions utilized to achieve them. Inherent in the process is an agreement that the staff will function in an active (goal-seeking) mode rather than a reactive (service-providing) mode.
>
> Services versus programs. What are the operational differences between services and programs? Service-centered staffs tend to hold themselves ready to provide whatever services may be demanded by a student, parent, teacher, or administrator. This meets our notions of service to others, but the services approach tends to vitiate our efforts, to involve us in a variety of subprofessional or administrative responsibilities, and to put us on too many sides of too many fences. One junior high school administrator described this behavior as an attempt to be perceived as the "building good guys." The general notion is that there is an essentially unlimited smorgasbord of services from which any potential consumer may pick.
>
> The program idea, on the other hand, implies that the counseling staff, in conjunction with others, will define specific program objectives and then will actively seek to attain these chosen objectives. A program defines a full work load for every counselor. Therefore, by implication, counselors cannot and will not become involved in activities unrelated to the attainment of program goals. The program idea thus introduces the concept of *focus* to guidance activities. The attempt to be all things to all people is dropped in favor of attempting to achieve certain generally agreed upon goals and objectives. Further, the notion of *effectiveness* is clearly implied. (p. 339)

Given the vital importance of the programmatic factor, it is then relevant to ask, "What constitutes a program?" According to Shaw (1977): "The minimal components include a rationale, a statement of goals and objectives, a description of the functions to be utilized in achieving objectives, and a description of the evaluation strategies needed to determine whether objectives have been achieved." Shaw (1977) emphasized that no program element stands alone. Each is "dynamically interrelated" to other program elements. The most defensible rationale for a counseling and guidance program in any setting, including the elementary school, is an objective environmental-organizational-clientele assessment.

Thus, the guidance services provided must be carefully determined, planned, structured, and systematized. Without this, the guidance offerings are made available on a haphazard, crisis-oriented, catch-as-catch-can basis.

Initiating an Elementary School Guidance Program

Once a needs and environmental assessment has been completed, the key to the development and successful implementation of an elementary school guidance program is involving the school staff in determining the specific priorities and related objectives of the program and, as noted earlier, the specific program responsibilities required of each member of the staff to achieve the desired objectives. The teaching staff of the school for which a program is being planned must obviously be utilized in both the design of the program and its implementation. Without such close cooperation and coordination, the guidance services will lose much of their effectiveness.

In stressing the importance of involving the school staff in the development of a program of guidance services for a school, Worzybt (1978), in a Pennsylvania State Department of Education publication, stated:

> If an elementary school guidance program is to be effective, then those who are expected to make use of the services will need to (a) understand them, (b) see a need for them, (c) desire to use them, (d) understand their role responsibilities in relationship to the services, and (e) be prepared to alter their existing roles and functions where necessary so that services can be maximized. (p. 43)

Primary responsibility for guidance program development, coordination, and implementation, however, must be assigned to a specialist—a specifically prepared elementary school counselor. We have previously noted the importance of the professional counselor as the program leader-manager. In the elementary school we further emphasize his or her special qualifications to function in the elementary school.

This counseling specialist should be involved from the beginning in the planning and initiation of the schools' counseling and guidance program. Obviously, the specialist will involve administrators, teachers, and other pupil personnel specialists—and may consult with parents and community leaders as well—but the specialist must be responsible and accept the responsibility, to take the initiative and lead in program planning and development.

We also emphasize the importance of school-oriented planning—planning a program to meet the unique needs of a unique elementary school and its population. In other words, it is important that the guidance program be developed for a *specific* school.

In some school districts with several small elementary schools, budget limitations may require shared counselor time by two schools. If so, the plans for counselor utilization should be determined for *each* of the involved schools in consultation with the assigned counselor. Shared counselor time will severely limit the objectives that can be achieved through the counseling program, and the derived program goals should reflect this.

To initiate a guidance program, the following steps seem minimally essential.

Step 1. The Formation of a Guidance Committee*

The committee, selected by the principal and/or the counselor should include three or four teachers whose judgments are respected by the faculty, the principal or an assistant principal, and the counselor. The responsibilities of the guidance committee cannot be underestimated. The success or failure of the guidance program depends in large part on this committee. The committee will make the ultimate decisions about the specific populations to be served by the counselor, the primary objectives of the guidance program, the methods and criteria by which the program will be evaluated, and the most promising approaches for informing the total staff, the students, and the community (especially the parents) about the guidance program once it has been derived. The informational aspect will be much simpler if *all* of the following steps have been taken.

Step 2. A Determination of Needs

As previously indicated, step two requires that a needs and environmental assessment be made. Chapter 3 has detailed pro-

*The "world" seems to be aware of the ineptness that committees seem to bring out in individuals—e.g., "The pooling of ignorance; a camel is a horse designed by a committee; I can do it in one day by myself and it will only take five days if we appoint a committee." We make the basic assumption here that guidance committees are among the rare exceptions to the committee theory.

cedures for such an assessment. Many state departments of education, through their guidance divisions, provide examples of recommended assessment forms for elementary schools and will furnish consultative assistance. An example of an assessment approach utilized by one school system is provided following the listing and discussion of the program initiation steps.

Step 3. A Determination—by the Guidance Committee—of the *Most Pressing* Needs Identified Through the Needs Assessment Study

If step two has been carefully implemented, step three is primarily a matter of examining the relative priority assigned—by each of the school's populations surveyed—to the identified needs, and then subjectively determining which needs should become the initial focal points of the guidance program. Examples of needs' listings are given at the end of this sequence.

Step 4. A Formulation by the Guidance Committee of a Hierarchy of the Specific Objectives of the School's Guidance Program

This step, although based on the needs identified in step three, will require considerable input from the counselor and the assistance of the principal if that individual has not been a member of the guidance committee. However, the determination of the program's specific goals is made *by* the committee. Care should be taken to assure that the objectives are attainable with the resources available or readily obtained, and that they are defined in a manner that will permit objective evaluation to determine the degree to which they are achieved.

Step 5. A Determination by the Guidance Committee of the *Most Immediate* Guidance Needs Evolving from the Derived Objectives

Although step five overlaps step four, it is a different task. Step four requires the identification of the objectives of the total guidance program. Step five resolves the problem of "where shall we begin?" To initiate a program on the assumption that efforts to achieve all of the specific objectives will be undertaken simultaneously is to invite probable failure. Instead, it must be decided which is the *first* guidance task to be undertaken, the second, and only as many others as the counselor's time permits. A tentative schedule for phasing in additional objectives can be constructed, but *always*, the primary goal is to obligate the counselor *only* for those objectives that *can* be attained. If goal attainment is reached in less than the time anticipated, new objectives can be introduced. If a more global effort is undertaken and success is *not* obtained, the guidance program may be placed in jeopardy.

Step 6. The Presentation of the Committee-Determined Objectives and Most Immediate Guidance Needs to the Total Faculty for Their Revision and Acceptance

Although every step in the sequence is important, step six may be one of the most crucial. To be successful a guidance program must be understood and supported by the faculty. Step six provides a forum for a discussion of faculty feelings about the developing guidance program, for providing answers to their questions, for letting them see that the program *is* necessary, and for enabling them to become active participants in the *development* of the program rather than to be simply recipients of guidance services. It should also be noted that the faculty are not merely *informed* about a "developed" program. The rationale, objectives, and initial goals are *discussed* with them and appropriate modifications of the plan are made based upon the input from the faculty. It would be highly unusual to accomplish the purposes of step six in one faculty meeting. A series of meetings should be anticipated and planned for.

Step 7. A Determination of the *Specific* Functions and Activities Required of the Counselor and of the Other Members of the Faculty and Staff for Program Implementation

Unless the counselor's specific activities are carefully delineated, the counselor may quickly be drawn into a series of seemingly crisis-oriented activities that would preclude activities pertaining to the specified objectives. If the guidance program is to be truly developmental, provisions for handling crises should be determined and publicized *before* the guidance program is initiated. To the degree possible, staff members other than the counselor should be assigned to cover the crises. If the counselor is to be utilized at all for crises, time for handling crisis-related activities should be built into the guidance program structure.

Step 8. The Development by the Guidance Committee of a Formal Statement for the Faculty in Which *Their* Guidance Program Responsibilities or Functions and Those of the Counselor Are Described

Faculty and administrators also have important guidance program responsibilities, and these *must* be drawn from the decisions reached by the guidance committee at step six. The faculty and administrators must see that the program responsibilities are not just being superimposed upon them, but that the added functions are necessary to implement the guidance program which *they* helped to devise. Also, the total school staff must understand what the counselor is attempting to do. The statement called for in step eight will enhance total staff support of the guidance program.

Step 9. The Counselor Should Orient the Students to the Program Through Classroom Discussions, and Assist Them to See How Specific Counselor Services May Be Utilized. Also, the Counselor Should Orient Parents to the Program Through Prepared Printed Statements, Parent-Teacher Meetings, and Individual Parent Conferences as Requested

The content of the orientation meetings will obviously be determined largely by the guidance program rationale and objectives as developed by the committee and revised by the school staff. However, the students—the primary beneficiaries of the program—should be apprised of the guidance services being made available and how one can take advantage of them, especially in those instances when self-referrals would be expeditious.

Step 10. The Establishment by the Guidance Committee of Procedures for Gradual, Steady Expansion of the Program to Fulfill All Objectives in Order of Their Established Priorities

The key element of step ten is the *gradual* expansion of the program to include the additional objectives deemed desirable by the guidance committee based upon the input from faculty, students, and parents. *No* expansion should occur until the initial aspects of the program are being successfully achieved, and then only those elements should be added for which there is reasonable assurance of success. Grandiose, highly generalized programmatic goals may look appealing on paper, but failure to achieve the stated goals will likely result in a lack of confidence in the program that may even place in jeopardy those aspects of the initial program which had been achieving success.

Step 11. The Formulation by the Guidance Committee of the Specific Approaches to Be Utilized for the Evaluation of the Guidance Program

A vital component of any educational program is evaluation. Developmental guidance programs cannot be an exception to this basic principle. The guidance program has been carefully structured to achieve specified objectives. Without valid evidence obtained through predetermined evaluational approaches, it will be difficult to determine whether or not the objectives are being achieved.

Therefore, the guidance committee must establish procedures and a schedule for testing the derived guidance program objectives. An important aspect of the selection of procedures will be the identification of the specific criteria to be used for determining the success or failure of each of the guidance approaches that comprise the guidance program. The implementation of the adopted evaluational procedures will typically be the counselor's responsibility, but the obtained evaluational data will be given to the guidance committee to enable that group to determine program successes and failures as well as needed program modifications.

Step 12. Periodic Meetings of the Guidance Committee and the Total Faculty Must Be Held to Disseminate the Evaluational Findings and to Explain Needed Program Modifications

The findings of the evaluations must be shared with the faculty, and the implications derived from the evaluations must be discussed with the faculty not only to maintain the support of the faculty but also to obtain possibly new insights from faculty members about programmatic strengths and weaknesses. By involving a school's faculty, staff, students, and parents to the degree required by these twelve steps, the school's developmental guidance program should indeed be a program developed by and for the unique but specific needs of that school.

Examples of Guidance Program Initiation

THE BOULDER VALLEY APPROACH

A description of the steps taken in initiating pilot counseling programs in two Boulder Valley, Colorado, elementary schools was reported by Stiltner (1978). The Boulder Valley guidance program implementation plan provides an excellent example of the efficient utilization of needs assessment as a foundational step in guidance program development. The plan also demonstrates the importance of procuring—through involvement and communication—the support of the school's faculty, students and parents.

Stiltner (1978) described the initiating process as follows.

> With the encouragement of the Colorado State Department of Education, the Boulder Valley Public Schools decided to use a portion of their Title IV B funds to establish a pilot counseling program in two elementary schools. The schools were selected on the basis of the following criteria: a student population of approximately 600, a demonstration of a need for elementary counseling, and willingness of the faculty to support a counseling program in other schools as well as in their own.
>
> The first steps were explaining the possibilities of an organized elementary guidance program to the students, staff, and parents of the schools and developing a comprehensive plan to meet their needs. One method used in this program development was a needs assessment of the guidance and counseling needs in the pilot schools. The assessment provided a data base for developing activities and involved all of the people with whom the counselors worked. The needs assessment was also used to inform parents, students, and teachers of the possible functions of an elementary school counselor. (pp. 239–240)

In the Boulder Valley approach, a committee was formed to implement the needs assessment, to identify the basic assumptions foundational to the development of the assessment instruments, and to develop a plan for the evaluation of the resultant counseling program. Three needs assessment instruments were developed: one each for students, teachers, and parents. The administration of the instruments was meticulously planned and implemented. Although the details are not given here, the Stiltner (1978) report provides a very helpful summary of the specific administration procedures. An illustration of the primary needs identified by each of the three groups surveyed is provided in Table 6–1, which was published by Stiltner (1978).

The value of the approach utilized by the Boulder Valley schools—and which is very similar to that recommended herein—is seen in the conclusions derived by Stiltner (1978).

> There are several factors that other schools should consider in implementing such a needs assessment. The involvement of teachers, parents, and students should be encouraged. This involvement serves to increase not only the validity of the needs-assessment results but also the participants' commitment to developing and implementing plans to meet the identified needs.
>
> Needs-assessment instruments are available from commercial sources and from other schools. These instruments are helpful in generating ideas for items and formats that a school can use. Any instrument will, however, be more effective if it is specifically adapted for the particular school and community using the instrument. The counselors, principals, teachers, students, and parents all can provide helpful suggestions about items and formats that they feel will yield the most meaningful results. (p. 246)

The Euclid Approach

The importance of involving the total school staff in both planning and implementing a guidance program may also be seen from the report by the Euclid, Ohio, City Schools (1967–1968) of their 1967–1968 Title V-A guidance project. Euclid, with a population of 75,000 persons, has eleven elementary schools. A series of in-service meetings featuring four nationally prominent authorities were held throughout the 1966–1967 school year to orient the elementary school's staff to guidance concepts. The second year of the funded project involved the placement of a full-time counselor in two of the city's elementary schools. One school contained 672 children and 28 teachers, and the other 574 children and 23 teachers. Both counselors had elementary teaching backgrounds and were certificated in guidance. The stated objectives of the program were:

TABLE 6–1. ***Items Ranked Most Highly by Intermediate Students, Teachers, and Parents ‡***

Questionnaire Number	Item	Student's % *	Student's Rank	Teacher's % †	Teacher's Rank	Parent's % †	Parent's Rank
19	learning about jobs I'd be happy in	50	(1)	54	(32)	78	(22)
11	finding out what things I can do best	50	(2)	84	(16)	88	(6)
29	finding out how people feel about me	49	(3)	77	(24)	75	(28)
37	learning to solve my problems	46	(4)	95	(5)	89	(4)
12	finding out what different jobs I like	45	(5)	60	(30)	80	(18)
36	learning to make good choices	44	(6)	89	(10)	83	(14)
25	learning how to get along with people who "bug" me	44	(7)	87	(13)	81	(17)
20	finding out things I do that "bug" others	44	(8)	91	(7)	75	(27)
33	knowing what to do when I am with kids who are doing things I know they shouldn't do	42	(9)	88	(12)	92	(1)
17	getting along better with my brother or sister	42	(10)	53	(33)	69	(30)
	learning to resolve conflicts	—		97	(1)	—	
5	learning to keep my mind on my work until I finish it	40	(11)	97	(2)	88	(7)
7	learning to organize my time better	38	(12)	97	(3)	—	
4	learning to listen better in school	23	(30)	96	(4)	87	(8)
22	being more aware of the feelings of others	—		91	(6)	83	(13)
28	being more sure of myself	31	(23)	90	(8)	88	(5)
34	feeling satisfied with what I do	32	(30)	90	(8)	90	(2)
31	learning how my feelings change (affect) what I do	34	(22)	90	(9)	90	(3)
24	being able to accept criticism better	25	(30)	78	(23)	87	(9)
6	feeling more comfortable in class discussions	27	(28)	68	(25)	86	(10)

* Students selected from the responses "yes," "maybe," and "no." The percentage reported here is the percentage of students selecting the "yes" response.

† Teachers and parents responded on a four-point scale from "of great importance" to "of no importance." The percentage reported here is the percentage selecting the two responses "of great importance" and "important."

‡ As seen in Barbara Stiltner. "Needs Assessment: A First Step" *Elementary School Guidance and Counseling* (April 1978), p. 244.

a. To further develop in the Euclid Public Schools an organized program of elementary guidance services.
b. To develop an elementary guidance program that will increase student opportunity for self-development and educational success.
c. To help teachers better understand and work with students.
d. To help parents understand and work with their children in school-related problems.

To evaluate the program a twelve-item questionnaire was given to the classroom teachers in early April 1968. Forty of the forty-eight teachers returned the questionnaires. The reported results of the teacher survey provide information of much value for guidance program initiation and development. Although the length of the total report does not permit its inclusion herein, excerpts from its "Summary and Conclusions" section are given to emphasize the importance to a successful guidance program of teacher involvement and effective teacher-counselor communication.

> From the results of the questionnaire, it seems that the elementary school guidance program had a successful first year. One of the most important aspects of the program was the acceptance of the counselor in the total school program. 93 percent of the teachers felt it was an advantage to have him on the staff. Most teachers seemed to feel that having someone available to more adequately meet the needs of individual students was highly desirable. . . .
>
> A major part of the guidance program is the developmental groups guidance program from kindergarten through grade six. Here the counselor teaches specific guidance lessons at the various grade levels. Fifty-five percent of the teachers said that the lessons taught were appropriate for their grade level and that they were beneficial to their students, while thirty-five percent said that it was either too early to judge or that they were not presently involved in the program as of April 5, 1968. Ten percent felt that they could carry on the guidance lessons for their class as well as the counselor could. It should be noted, however, that one major objective of the developmental guidance program was to get the counselor to meet and to know the children throughout the school. Unfortunately, in some cases, the teachers focused on the quality of the lesson being taught and not on the getting acquainted with the counselor objective when they judged the total developmental program. It is hoped that through better communication with the teachers and more

grade-level teacher involvement, the total developmental program can be improved and expanded. . . .

No matter whether the counselor is working with the developmental guidance program or counseling students, there always seems to be the difficulty of feedback of information to teachers. The amount of feedback to teachers of pertinent information gathered in counseling certain students is questionable in the sense of what is desirable to tell to the teacher without betraying the counselee's confidence and trust in the counselor. During the 1967–1968 school year, the counselors tried to use general terms in relating counseling events to the teachers. Fifty percent felt that this was satisfactory and that they had received enough information. Twenty-five percent of the teachers felt that the amount of feedback was not adequate. The questionnaire did not discriminate whether these teachers wanted more specific information or if they felt they were not getting enough information in general terms.

Because of its very nature, the elementary guidance program is bound in some cases to overlap into jobs being done by the principal, psychologist, visiting teacher, and nurse. About half of the teachers in each building involved in the survey felt that this overlapping of job responsibility was confusing and should be made clearer to them. A small percent, however, were opposed to any rigidly defined role of the counselor for fear that such regimentation would eliminate the informality, approachability, and flexibility of the elementary guidance program. One example of this informality and flexibility would be the present practice of making oral referrals, where the vast majority of teachers preferred this practice to some other procedure. . . .

Thirty-one of the forty teachers returning questionnaires listed ways that the present program could be improved for next year. This was a very encouraging sign because the general overall tone of the teachers' responses on their questionnaire was very favorable toward the elementary guidance program. It would then seem that these suggestions for improvement can be interpreted as an involvement on the part of the teachers in the program and a desire on their part to see it improved and continued. (Final Report: Elementary Guidance Program: Euclid City Schools, Euclid, Ohio. 1967–1968)

Implementing a Developmental Guidance Program

We have seen that the implementation of a developmental guidance program is not an easy task, nor is it the sole responsibility of the school's guidance specialist, the school counselor. We have also seen that a successful program requires the involvement of the school's administrators, teachers, and specialized personnel, as well as its students and their parents, and the utilization of community resources. Although the counselor must assume the primary responsibility for program development and operation, she or he must be permitted to assume functions in keeping with developmental guidance program objectives. It is not uncommon to find elementary schools that are simply overwhelmed with attendance and minor behavioral problems; with children who need psychological testing; with problems which require school liaison with parents, juvenile courts, and social agencies; and with a myriad of semiadministrative needs. Overburdened teachers and administrators who are unfamiliar with appropriate guidance functions look to the counselor for assistance with these crisis-oriented, administrative, or classroom-management problems. Although the counselor can undoubtedly provide assistance with problems such as these, to use this specialist primarily for those functions is a most inefficient practice. The counselor, too, will quickly be overwhelmed with administrative tasks and "brush fires," and will have little if any time to devote to developmental guidance concerns. It is important, therefore, that the counselor's guidance program and other school responsibilities be clearly delineated. An obvious first step in counselor role delineation is to specify the counselor's guidance program responsibilities.

The Responsibilities of the Elementary School Counselor

The guidance program structure has been created to fulfill the objectives that have been derived from the assessed needs of students, faculty and staff, and parents. It follows, then, that the counselor's areas of responsibility will be dictated by the derived objectives of the program. It is the counselor, though, who must translate the areas of responsibility into specific counselor functions. The task of specifying functions is made much simpler when the functions are categorized in a meaningful fashion. The categorization of counselor functions should also produce a more effective use of counselor time. The ASCA (American School Counselors' Association) Role Statement which appears in Appendix F has suggested a very meaningful system for the categorization of counselor functions.

Counseling Functions

It is the responsibility of the elementary school counselor, according to the ASCA statement, to counsel not only students but teachers and parents as well. Counseling may be provided to individuals or may occur through the utilization of groups. The counselor may understandably ask at this point, "Where does one find the time for such time-demanding responsibilities?" Time is indeed a critical factor. Individual counseling *will* require considerable time, and the proportions of counselor time to be devoted to the counseling of individuals—whether they be students, teachers, or parents—must be determined by the results of the needs analyses which were made. If attainment of the accepted guidance program objectives for a specific school requires extensive individual counseling, the counselor will have little time left for undertaking other guidance program responsibilities. It is, therefore, imperative that the counselor maintain a log of his or her daily activities. If too much time is being required to meet the demands for individual counseling, the program objectives must be reexamined and modified if possible. Although some individual counseling will be necessary in almost any school setting, in developmentally oriented guidance programs utilization of the counselor in such one-on-one sessions is held to a basic minimum because, typically, individual counseling is more crisis than developmentally oriented. Crisis counseling may be viewed as a utilization of a "Band-Aid" approach to guidance. Developmental counselors recognize the need for some proportion of counselor time being spent to assist with problems requiring immediate attention, but optimally less than one-half of the counselor's time will be expended for crises resolution. Developmentally oriented counselors are neither unmindful of individual's needs for counseling assistance nor unsympathetic to those individuals. It is believed that the numbers of students needing such assistance would overwhelm the counselor (assuming that each elementary school has at best only one counselor), and that rather than attempting to ameliorate problems, the counselor's time should be used as much as possible to assist the faculty to create a school and individual classroom learning climate that would assist in the prevention of student traumas.

Group counseling approaches may be used very advantageously with students to reduce the need for individual counseling. More effective expenditure of counseling time will be one of the benefits to be derived from the use of counseling groups. Moreover, much of the vital information pertaining to children's developmental needs (such as the understanding of self and others) is more effectively acquired through group sessions than through individual sessions with a counselor.

Although group counseling can be provided by the counselor for parents and for faculty, it probably should not be. If the program objectives seemingly mandate this type of activity, then the school administrator should bring in specialists to conduct counseling groups for parents and faculty. Informational (or guidance) groups can be held by the counselor for faculty and parent groups, but it should be recognized that conducting informationally oriented groups is a consultative function of the counselor, not a counseling function.

Consultative Functions

In a developmental guidance program consultative functions will require a greater expenditure of counselor time than either counseling or coordination responsibilities. In fact, the rationale underlying developmental guidance programs requires that the counselor—the school's child development specialist—help faculty and parents to understand and help fulfill the diverse developmental needs of elementary schoolchildren. Although consultation occurs with parents both in individual and group sessions, the primary recipients of consultative functions are members of the school staff. Through consultation—which must be handled with the utmost tact and diplomacy—teachers are assisted in modifying the curriculum as indicated by student needs and developmental levels, in conducting appropriate developmental guidance activities in the classrooms (e.g., career awareness activities, activities to facilitate self-concept development, and activities to facilitate the development of interpersonal relations skills), and in understanding and meeting the unique needs of individuals in their classes.

A major consultative function of the elementary school counselor in many schools has resulted from federal legislation (PL 94-142) mandating the provision of free, appropriate education for all handicapped children. A basic requirement of PL 94-142 is that an Individualized Educational Program (IEP) be developed for each handicapped child. The IEPs are developed by a team minimally composed of (a) a representative of the school, other than the child's teacher, who is qualified to provide or supervise special education, (b) the child's teacher, (c) the child's parent or guardian, (d) the child when appropriate, and (e) other individuals as invited by the parents or school. Because the counselor is a child development specialist, school administrators call upon the counselor for either preparation or consultative assistance in the development of IEPs. Some special education and pupil personnel specialists believe that counselors *should* be involved in the implementation of PL 94-142, especially in those aspects of the IEP pertaining to a child's affective and social needs. There may be counselors who prefer to avoid activities pertaining to IEP development for any number of reasons (i.e., a lack of formal training in working with handicapped children, a fear that the time demands of IEP child study team involvement may preclude a continuation of the developmental activities evolving from their adopted guidance program objectives, etc.). However, given the realities of school personnel budgets, it is probable that a number of school systems will either have to utilize counselors for IEP consultation or replace them with special education personnel specifically employed to assist with the IEPs and other facets of PL 94-142 implementation.

Elementary school counselors *are* (or at least *should be*) qualified to provide invaluable contributions to IEP development, especially in the affective and social needs' areas. Therefore, assisting a school's child study teams is a legitimate professional function of the counselor. The counselor should *not* be given priority responsibilities for IEP development; instead, the counselor's role should be consultative. To assure minimal inference with the structured guidance program developed for the school, the IEP's consultation should have been provided for in the program objectives and counselor time allocated for such consultation.

Career Guidance Function

The career education movement launched in the 1970s emphasized the establishment of comprehensive career education models at all educational levels, including the elementary school. These comprehensive models viewed the individual's career development, his or her career education and career guidance as integral and complementary and interwoven components of the whole. Because of this important role of the elementary school in the individual's career development, special mention is merited here on the premise that counseling and guidance program developers in the elementary school must give appropriate attention to this area in their planning. The justification for both career education and career guidance in the elementary school can be derived from the following basic assumptions:

Career Development Is a Part of the Individual's "Total" Development

All aspects of the individual's total development, whether they be social, physical, emotional, or educational are interwoven and often difficult to separate and distinguish from each other. Career development is no exception. This implies, as with all other aspects of the individual's development, that his or her career development must be planned for, nurtured, and enhanced by effective programs at all educational levels, programs which are cognizant of his or her physical, emotional, and intellectual development.

Career Education and Related Career Guidance Programs Should Have a Developmental Emphasis in the Elementary School

The individual's stage of development would suggest that the elementary school years should provide opportunities for pupils to develop an awareness of the meaning and significance of work and of the inevitability of career decision making. Too, these are the years when natural curiosity and inquiry are high, when youth are prone to explore and "try out," and when they can examine careers relatively free from prejudice. Elementary school programs should educate pupils to the relationships between educational opportunities and ultimate career planning. The elementary school pupil should also be assisted in developing basic habits and attitudes of value to both his or her education and eventual world of work. The elementary school years are the years for developing the foundations for one's eventual career planning and decision making.

Career Development Programs Are Most Effective as Planned and Coordinated Total School Efforts

The career development "team" for the elementary school would list the teacher, counselor, and administrator as starters with the parent as an important "back-up" player. All have important roles to play in the elementary school pupils' early career development. Each is less effective without the cooperation and involvement of the others.

As Gibson (1972) noted, the teacher has

> daily contact and in the school works closest with the pupil. She or he has the opportunity to observe the child on a daily basis and answer his or her many spontaneous questions.
>
> In a more structured sense, the classroom teacher also can and should incorporate career development and guidance activities into the planned program of pupil learning experiences. (p. 21)
>
> For classroom guidance the counselor can provide suggestions and perhaps even materials to assist the classroom teacher and in general work closely with him in the preparation of an effective educational-career guidance and development program. The elementary school counselor can also take responsibility for planning special activities which are appropriate to the on-going classroom experience of the pupil. The elementary school counselor is responsible for the development and coordination of the school's program of career guidance, but the elementary classroom teacher is, as always, the indispensable person in any program of pupil development. (p. 21)

Summary and Implications

The elementary school should be the starting point in any school system's planned program of continuous and comprehensive counseling and guidance services. The importance of the developmental years of the elementary school pupil coupled with the unique characteristics of this age group have implications for the nature of programs of counseling and guidance in the elementary school. Additionally, the uniqueness of the elementary school as an educational organization also suggests differences in counseling and guidance program development at this level.

Regardless of the differences in pupil population and organization that distinguish the elementary school, the basic fundamental procedures—assessment; formulation of objectives; determining procedures; and evaluation—apply. A major difference in counselor functioning, however, would see the elementary school counselor more frequently in a consulting role with parents, teachers, and administrators and perhaps less in an individual counseling role than in the secondary school.

As the elementary pupil himself or herself will do in time, let us proceed to the middle school and to counseling and guidance programs at that level. Chapter 7 examines guidelines and activities for such programs.

CHAPTER 7

Guidance in the Middle School

Introduction

Since the inception of a twelve-year format for U.S. public education, various organizational plans have been developed in attempts to provide students with functional and age-appropriate educational experiences. Among school patterns utilized have been an eight-year elementary school and a four-year high school; a six-year elementary school and a six-year high school; and a six-year elementary school, a two- or three-year intermediate or junior high school, and a three- or four-year high school. A movement to replace the junior high school with a different intermediate or "middle" school developed in the 1960s and 1970s and appears to be the current "in" arrangement. As middle schools were incorporated into the school structure, the typical six-three-three organization plan for grades one through twelve was replaced by a four-four-four or five-three-four plan; the middle school thus encompasses either grades five, six, seven, eight or six, seven, eight. In essence then, the middle school is typically an educational structure for students between the ages of ten through thirteen. As the middle school concept heavily emphasizes guidance services, it is most important that school counseling and guidance specialists become familiar with the middle-school rationale and that they be utilized in the development of middle-school programs. Those counselors who practice in community agency settings where school-age youth are potential clients should also be aware of the nature of school counseling and guidance programs that are available to middle-school youth.

The Middle School

BASIC CONCEPTS

The development of the middle school has involved much more than adding the sixth grade to the junior high school and dropping the ninth grade; it requires an entirely different curricular and organizational approach. The rationale for the middle school concept is primarily based on the beliefs that today's developing youth reaches physical, social, and intellectual maturity at a younger age than did previous generations, and that the junior high school as typically organized does not meet the developmental needs of these students (Eichborn, 1967). In fact, the middle school movement throughout the United States has been viewed in part as a movement based on the rediscovery and reintroduction of the basic principles of adolescent learning upon which the junior high school was established almost seventy years ago. Proponents of the middle school support the rationale that children ten to fourteen years old constitute a distinct stage of development involving unique physical, emotional, social, and mental characteristics.

It is additionally believed by some proponents that the middle school will (1) provide for more appropriate curricula for the age groups now in middle school programs; for example, fifth and sixth grade pupils will have a more adequate curriculum than that provided in the traditional elementary school, whereas seventh and eighth grade pupils may have more age-appropriate experiences than provided in the traditional junior high school; (2) promote programs designed to accommodate individual differences among students; and (3) increase the effectiveness of programs designed to meet the counseling and guidance needs of this particular age group of students.

The programmatic features characteristic of the middle school were found by Alexander (1971) to be:

1. A home base and teacher for every student to provide for continuing guidance and assistance to help students make the decisions they face almost daily regarding special needs and learning opportunities.
2. A program of learning opportunities offering balanced attention to three major goals of the middle school: (a) personal development of the between-age; (b) skills of continued learning and (c) effective use of appropriate organized knowledge.
3. An instructional system focused on individual progress, with many curriculum options and with individualized instruction in appropriate areas.
4. The use of interdisciplinary team arrangements for cooperative planning, instructing, and evaluating.
5. A wide range of exploratory activities for the socializing, interest-developing, and leisure-enriching purposes of the bridge school. (p. 10–11)

A specific, universally accepted model for the middle school has not yet been achieved. Instead, middle-school designs vary with community needs and philosophies. Moreover, some middle schools are "middle schools" in name only. Although they contain new groupings of grade levels, they have not provided new programs attuned to the developmental needs of the students they are to serve.

Goals and Objectives

A basis for middle school goals has been proposed by Stamm and Nissman (1979) who suggest that in order to respond to any educational program, a person must have a quality of self-direction—a good feeling about himself or herself. Each child and teacher involved in the program has to discover and accept his or her strengths and weaknesses to work up to his or her fullest potential. Further, a person needs experience in making rational and responsible decisions, to understand and develop a tentative system of values, and to begin to appreciate himself or herself as a thinking being worthy of active participation in society. The person must have enough confidence in himself or herself to try and, if she or he fails, to try again. The middle school's primary goal should, therefore, be to reflect this attitude as a supportive measure through fair rules and regulations and realistic evaluative procedures.

Stamm and Nissman suggest other goals of the middle school as

- a commitment to learning skills
- concern for social development and interpersonal relationships
- emphasis on physical well-being
- emphasis on creativity—consideration of a variety of options, experiences and awareness of the multitude of horizons to be explored;
- a help for each child to grow confidently and look to the future as an exciting experience yet to be met.

The Middle School Counseling and Guidance Program

Considerations in Program Development

Whether or not the middle-school pattern provides more effectively than other organizational patterns for meeting students' guidance needs at this age level, as its proponents theorize, if it is to succeed in attaining its intended objectives, it *must* provide effective guidance services. The emphases on student responsibility and self-direction, on programs individually designed to accommodate differing maturational rates and developmental levels, and on personal-social development make student self-understanding and staff understanding of students mandatory. Most middle-school advocates agree that guidance services are basic to the operation of a middle school, but there are differences of opinion about how such services should be implemented. Alexander (1971) envisioned problems in obtaining sufficient numbers of trained counselors with which to staff adequately the middle school; hence, he would assign major responsibility for personal development aspects of the program—including counseling—to teacher-counselors. To facilitate this he recommends that the home-base group be led by a teacher-counselor and that this group be assigned a regularly scheduled block of time to be used by the teacher for both individual and group activities relating to personal development. It would seem that attempts to find a sufficient number of teachers with adequate preparation for their required guidance responsibilities would be even more difficult than finding counselors, but that is a personnel problem which should be resolved before the final draft of a middle-school program is completed.

Others have similarly advocated the use of core teachers for the provision of individual guidance in classes scheduled in multiple time-modules, coupled with full-time counselors and other specialized personnel. Some have recommended limiting middle school enrollment, eight hundred to one thousand pupils, divided into three "houses" of equal size with a counselor each, plus a school coordinator. In any event, programs of counseling and guidance would appear central to the concept and success of the middle school, and although the goals and objectives for middle school counseling and guidance programs will obviously vary, dependent on differing needs and environmental settings, many programs will share broad general goals in common. By way of example, we note the following comprehensive goals prepared by the Florida Department of Education (1974):

GOALS AND OBJECTIVES FOR MIDDLE SCHOOL GUIDANCE SERVICES

1.0 To help middle school students develop their maximum personal potential and to acquire appreciation of all persons as members of society.

1.1.1 Students will be knowledgeable of various value concepts and understand the processes for forming and changing values.

1.1.2 Students will understand the relationship between personal values and specific behaviors exhibited by individuals.

1.1.3 Students will identify their personal values and relate them to their response in various life situations.

1.1.4 Students will recognize values that differ from their own and tolerate behaviors based upon those values.

1.2 Students will be able to cope with problems that interfere with their personal growth and development.

1.2.1 Students will be knowledgeable of the typical physical, emotional, and social characteristics, concerns, and problems of persons their age.

1.2.2 Students will understand the factors that contribute to typical problems of persons their age and be aware of potential methods of resolving such problems.
1.2.3 Students will alleviate their personal, social, and academic problems and reduce the likelihood of their recurrence.

1.3 Students will exhibit attitudes and behaviors that indicate respect and caring for themselves and others.
1.3.1 Students will be concerned with their personal welfare.
1.3.2 Students will be concerned with the welfare of other individuals.
1.3.3 Students will respect school property and the possessions of others.

2.0 To help middle school students maximize their academic potential and incorporate exploratory career-development concepts into their educational experiences.

2.1 Students will adjust positively to the environment, structure, and program of the middle school.
2.1.1 Students will be familiar with the facilities, program, and management of the school.
2.1.2 Students will have pride in, and a sense of belonging to, their school.
2.1.3 Students will have meaningful interpersonal relationships with teachers and students including those with different backgrounds.
2.1.4 Students will be independent in their personal, social, and academic endeavors.

2.2 Students will develop interests and capabilities that contribute to their future success and happiness.
2.2.1 Students will understand the goal-formation process and how interests and abilities contribute to the development of personal goals.
2.2.2 Students will be aware of their relative strengths and weaknesses in both academic and nonacademic areas.
2.2.3 Students will plan and achieve in academic and nonacademic programs in accordance with their personal interests and abilities.
2.2.4 Based upon the exploration of their interests and abilities, students will begin developing realistic personal goals.

2.3 Students will acquire information and experience that will enhance their career-development process.

2.3.1 Students will be knowledgeable of general career alternatives available to them.
2.3.2 Students will be knowledgeable of the personal characteristics that generally contribute to job success.
2.3.3 Students will identify their personal interests in various career alternatives available to them.
2.3.4 Students will be knowledgeable of the personal and educational requirements for the occupations of interest to them.

3.0 To assist parents in understanding the behaviors, abilities, and interests of middle school students and in coping with the concerns and needs of their children.
3.1 Parents will understand the unique needs and concerns of middle school students and explore alternative methods of relating to them.
3.1.1 Parents will be knowledgeable of the middle-school concept and of the unique goals of the middle school.
3.1.2 Parents will have a genuine concern for the development and welfare of their children.
3.1.3 Parents will acquire and utilize information and skills that enable them to meet the needs of their children.
3.2 Parents of students who are referred for guidance services will learn effective means of coping with the problems and needs of their children.
3.2.1 Parents will be aware of the behavioral characteristics of their children that resulted in the focusing of special attention upon them.
3.2.2 Parents will cooperate with efforts to identify the factors that may have led to their child's referral.
3.2.3 Parents will cooperate with efforts to solve their child's behavioral problems.

4.0 To assist the school staff in the identification of, and provision for, the physical, emotional, social, and academic needs of middle school students.
4.1 Instructional personnel will be sensitive to the needs of students and will assist them with potential or actual educational and personal problems.
4.1.1 Teachers will be knowledgeable of the general characteristics and needs of middle-school-aged children.
4.1.2 Teachers will be knowledgeable of the problems that are frequently experienced by middle school students and of the specialized services available in the

school and community to assist students with problems.

4.1.3 Teachers will identify students with potential educational or personal problems and make appropriate referrals.

4.1.4 Teachers will assist students in solving their educational and personal problems.

4.2 Instructional personnel will provide opportunities for students to explore career development concepts in the middle school.

4.2.1 Teachers will be knowledgeable of the career development process and of appropriate activities for facilitating the exploratory stage.

4.2.2 Teachers will assist students in acquiring occupational information and in developing positive attitudes toward the world of work.

Program Activities

As we examine suggested goals and objectives, we may suggest that the functions of middle school guidance personnel will include, in addition to regular guidance program development obligations, the following basic responsibilities:

a. Orienting incoming students and their parents to the policies, procedures, and facilities of their new school.
b. Preparing profiles of the new students. This function is an implementation of the appraisal aspect of guidance services and will require data from elementary school records, tests, and student interviews.
c. Orienting staff to the new students. The counselor reviews the student profiles with the core or home-base teacher and other members of the teaching team and assists them in determining appropriate academic and personal development activities for each student.
d. Consulting with core leader and other faculty about difficulties encountered by individual students.
e. Counseling students, individually and in groups, whether self- or teacher-referred.
f. Coordinating of career-orientation programs. This involves working with the library personnel and other staff

members in both the procurement of informational materials and their appropriate utilization.

g. Conducting group guidance sessions for students as needed and as in-service training demonstrations for teachers.
h. Facilitating the transition from the middle school to the high school by arranging meetings between students, their parents, and high school counselors for high school orientation, and for program and course selection.
i. Assisting in middle school program research, evaluation, and modification.

These guidance responsibilities are not unique to the middle school; they are based on student and program needs that exist in *any* intermediate school. However, the nature of the middle school program gives them even greater magnitude.

Another view of the activities actually reported by middle school counselors are contained in a study by Miller and Pappas (1978) in which 110 middle school counselors reported their priority "on the job" functions. The rankings of these functions are presented in Table 7–1.

The Middle School Counselor

Perhaps one of the reasons that the junior high school never achieved the success anticipated by its early advocates was that it never became a truly unique educational institution. The junior high school simply became what the name implied—high school, junior. It mimicked in nearly every detail—from varsity sports and cheerleaders to academic honoraries—their senior high schools, and their teachers and principals looked to the day, like their students, when they would be "advanced" to the high school level. Junior high school counselors were, like their teaching colleagues, trained and certified for services in secondary schools. Special courses focusing on the junior high school were a rarity and junior high school "specialists" were rarer still.

If we can learn from the lessons of history, it would seem apparent that the middle school and the middle school professional staff, must indeed reflect the uniqueness of the student population that forms the theoretical basis for the middle school

TABLE 7–1. ***Combined Rankings of Ten Highest Middle School Counselor Functions (N-110)***

Ranking	Per Cent	Function
1	98	Providing individual counseling for students with personal-social concerns.
2	94	Communicating the guidance program and its services to students.
3	89	Organizing and administering the guidance program.
4	87	Communicating the guidance program to school personnel.
5	85	Consulting with teachers on student developmental needs and concerns.
6	84	Identifying students in need of special assistance
7	80	Conducting small group counseling for selected student populations
8	78	Communicating the guidance program to parents.
9	76	Identifying and making referrals to other school personnel.
10	74	Interpreting standardized test results to students and parents.

Source: Judy Tindall, Ed., Middle/Junior High School Counselors' Corner. "Middle School Counselors View Their Priorities" by Gary M. Miller and John G. Pappas. *Elementary School Guidance and Counseling* (April 1978), 291.

concept. The middle school will not achieve its anticipated uniqueness as either a "grown up" elementary school or an embryonic high school. Furthermore, if counselor education programs do not make special training provisions for middle school counselors, and state school certification boards do not specify special requirements for middle school counselor certification, the middle school counselor in practice may then become either a trained elementary or secondary school counselor, practicing in a middle school—a "duck out of water"—a facsimile of his or her junior high forerunner!

The question must then be asked, What is the role of the middle school counselor and how does it differ from that of the elementary or secondary school counselor? The American School Counselors Association position statement, Appendix F, describes the unique role of the middle/junior high school counselor. Additionally, the basis for responding to the question must surely be grounded in the unique needs and nature of the middle school student-client population. In this regard, one might begin by noting that Havighurst (1968) suggested three specific developmental tasks of children in the middle school years: (1) organizing one's knowledge of social and physical reality; (2) learning to work well in the peer group; and (3) becoming an independent person. We also note as further examples that eleven-year-olds frequently exhibit physical exuberance, intense emotions, competition, curiosity, peer interest, and behavior that appears silly to adults. Twelve-year-olds have been described as an age of in-between childhood and adult behavior characterized by "spirit," increase in patience, marked physical-sexual development for many, especially girls, increase in self-confidence, and continued importance of peers.

How, then, can we further examine the role of the middle-school counselor? In light of the nature of the middle school, its basic concepts and goals, and the general characteristics of the middle school eleven and twelve-year-old students, it would appear that the middle school counselor must certainly also become a "transitional consultant"—a professional specialist in helping his or her youthful client population negotiate their "passages" through these crucial years. We further suggest that the middle school offers the middle school counseling program a unique opportunity and setting to provide realistic developmental, growth, and preventive activities. The counselor may also function as a human resource developer through the assessment of individual potential, with related feedback and counseling, although serious future planning is probably premature. Individual counseling may be desirable on occasion, but client interaction, time commitment, and insight will be limited. Certainly, group counseling and guidance activities will be important in the development of human relationship skills with one's peers. Whatever unique role for the middle school counselor will eventually emerge, it is important that such a role does emerge. As Miller and Pappas (1978) noted:

> Developing a role identity, gathering support for one's efforts, and expanding the scope of one's services can be an overwhelming task for any professional. Obviously, more precise clarification of one's role and function is needed to assist the middle school counselor in

> becoming a viable component of any school's guidance team. Without such clarification counselors in middle schools can easily flounder and lose their creditability. (p. 291)

Teacher Guidance in the Middle School

Many advocates of the middle school, and many middle schools in practice, have emphasized the significant role of the middle-school teacher in their pupils' social-emotional-educational development. Although, as we have noted, the teacher is critical in any program of pupil guidance at any level, the basic concept and philosophy of the middle school suggests a particularly important and unique teacher-student relationship.

The importance of this relationship merits additional discussion in this chapter. Alexander and George (1981) have suggested that the teacher-student relationship is the starting point of the middle school's program for counseling. They further emphasize the importance of every middle school student having a close advisee relationship with at least one teacher in his or her school. In this advisor-advisee program of pupil guidance, Alexander and George (1981) suggest the following teacher/adviser roles.

> The Advisor is the Academic Expert on Each of His Advisees. As such the advisor:
>
> - Assists the student in the planning of exploratory, extracurricular, independent study and other academic choice activities. The advisor keeps a record of electives chosen by each advisee.
> - Communicates information about facilities, materials, and personnel to students and parents.
> - Maintains and utilizes cumulative records, personal profile sheets, and other information-gathering options.
> - Prepares report cards.
> - Assists students in studying and learning how to study.
> - Assists students in the process of developing and clarifying special interests and aptitudes.
> - Will be able to identify and take into account any physical handicaps the student may have.
> - Will be able to identify and take into account reading level of the student, and the mental and chronological ages of the student.

- Contributes to the understanding of other staff members of the academic strengths, weaknesses, problems, and interests of each student.
- Controls the student's overall academic schedule, assisting in decisions as to whom the student will study with, at what times, and in what groupings. The advisor will assist in determining the degree of responsible independence each student can assume, and what learning styles seem appropriate.
- Prepares for and participates in parent conferences with reference to the student's academic progress.

The Advisor is the School Advocate and Guide for Each Student. As such the advisor:

- Attempts to build a relationship with each student that is characterized by caring, trust, and honesty.
- Is, in general, an available buffer between student, general faculty, administration, parent, and community.
- Attempts to see that each student acquires an increasingly positive self-image during his enrollment at the school.
- Knows each student and his background as thoroughly as possible.
- Contributes to and supports the school guidance program.
- Contributes to the other staff members' understanding of the personal strengths, weaknesses, problems, and interests of each advisee.
- Maintains an attendance record of each of the advisees.
- Is responsible for parent-school communication, and for participating in and planning for parent conferences concerning the personality and behavior of the advisee.

The Advisor is the Person Most Directly Responsible for the Social and Emotional Education of His Advisees, and for Assisting in the Social and Emotional Maturation of Each Advisee. As such the advisor:

- Attempts to create a sense of belonging and responsibility through participation in home-base activities.
- Conducts activities during the advisor-advisee program which focus on increasing social skills of advisees and on growth in personal and interpersonal understanding.
- Assists students in clarifying their values and in developing more mature reasoning abilities.

- Places increased emphasis on the prevention of problems in the lives of the students.
- Participates in outings, field trips, and after-school activities which promote opportunities for emotional and social education.
- Helps students learn to work in a group and to realize the need for getting along with others in order to meet individual and group needs.
- Assists students in the appreciation of individual differences.
- Helps students develop appropriate attitudes toward competition and cooperation as the advisor-advisee group participates as a group in intra-school programs. (pp. 95–97)

Obviously, such advisor-advisee programs will be enhanced if they are viewed as a part of the school's total counseling and guidance effort. Clearly teachers and counselors working together as "team" members, serving each other as consultants, and coordinating their respective efforts will result in increased "payoff" for their mutual concerns—the student.

Summary and Implications

The American middle school is a relatively new but very popular concept in our educational format. This school usually involves two or three of the traditional sixth,- seventh-, and eighth-grade levels. Since the middle school is viewed as an arrangement for helping students making the transition between their elementary and secondary school years, this is an important consideration in determining the appropriate role and function of the middle school's program of counseling and guidance and the professionals who staff their programs. The Florida Department of Education suggested comprehensive program goals as

1.0 To help middle school students develop their maximum personal potential and acquire appreciation of all persons as members of society.
2.0 To help middle school students maximize their academic potential and incorporate exploratory career-development concepts into their educational experiences.
3.0 To assist parents in understanding the behaviors, abili-

ties, and interests of middle school students and in coping with the concerns and needs of their children.

4.0 To assist the school staff in the identification of, and provision for, the physical, emotional, social, and academic needs of middle school students.

In achieving these goals we have suggested that a major function of the middle school counselor may be that of a "transitional consultant." In this role the counselor may work closely with the classroom teacher and vice-versa because of the significant adviser-advisee teacher-student relationship suggested as the core of the middle schools' comprehensive program of counseling and guidance. This uniqueness of the middle school counseling and guidance program may be noted even more as we contrast it to the more traditional programs found in many secondary schools as discussed in the next chapter.

CHAPTER 8

The Secondary School Guidance Program

Introduction

The Secondary School and the Traditional Counseling and Guidance Program

Since their initial development in the period just before and following World War I and until recent years, school counseling and guidance programs have been almost the sole prerogative of the American high school. During the past fifty years, educators have noted trends in secondary school guidance programs that have emphasized at different times in our history vocational guidance, educational guidance, testing, pupil mental health, group guidance activities, individual counseling, placement and manpower needs, guidance for the gifted, guidance for the disadvantaged and cultural minorities, and career guidance. Out of these varying emphases, a traditional set of basic services developed. These services have been reinforced in counselor training programs, counselor certification requirements, accreditation criteria, and governmental support programs. The following sections describe these services and activities.

Individual Analysis. This service has emphasized the gathering of pupil data for both individual and group analysis. The results of these analyses presumably would be used for identifying the characteristics and potential of every student, for pupil advising and counseling, and school program development. Typically, the bulk of the data is collected from school records and the results of standardized testing programs. Nonstandardized instruments, such as autobiographies, rating scales, observation techniques, and questionnaires have also been used on occasion to implement the more standardized data. This basic service is intended to promote student self-understanding as well as better understanding by his or her teachers, counselors and parents. In this area of pupil analysis the counselor will often consult with school psychologists and psychometrists as specialists in psychological assessment and with social workers as specialists in environmental and case study analyses. This area is often referred to as the individual inventory or pupil appraisal, although individual analysis appears to be more currently popular. Belkin (1981) suggests that assessment and appraisal are integral yet separate tasks of the counseling function in schools, with assessment referring to the collection of information about the individual and appraisal referring to the use of the information to form certain judgments or conclusions about the individual. In recent years and for the future, the process of such data collection and analysis has been drastically altered and significantly enhanced by the increased utilization and sophistication of computers and other means of data processing.

Individual Counseling. Individual counseling according to Warner (1980) is a

> therapeutic and growth process through which individuals are helped to define goals, make decisions, and solve problems related to personal-social, educational, and career concerns. Specialized counseling provides assistance with concerns related to physical and social rehabilitation, employment, mental health, substance abuse, marital and family problems, human sexuality, religious and value choices, career development, and other concerns. (p. 2)

The individual counseling service has been frequently referred to over the years as "the heart" of the school counseling and guidance program. Without engaging in this particular activity, counselors cannot really be called counselors. Further, as Hansen et al. (1982) note "Counselors must understand both the why and the how of counseling. A counselor who has knowledge of one but not the other is lacking as a professional." Although the emphasis in practice has tended to be that of counseling the individual with adjustment or behavioral problems, we suggest that school counseling should also give equal attention to the developmental needs of the adolescent. "Counseling does not attempt to restructure personality, but to develop what already exists. It is chiefly concerned with individuals' adjustments to themselves, to significant others in their lives, and to the cultural environment in which they find themselves." (Hansen, Stevic, and Warner, 1982, p. 14). Effective counseling not only requires counselors with the highest levels of training and professional skills but a certain type of person as well. Counseling programs will suffer in effectiveness and credibility unless counselors exhibit the traits of understanding, warmth, humaneness, and positive attitudes toward humankind. Counseling programs will also suffer in credibility if their major emphasis and priority activity is not counseling.

Group Guidance and Counseling

> The term group guidance is most often used to refer to any part of a guidance program that is conducted with groups of students rather than with an individual pupil. A basic purpose of group guidance is to provide information and data to facilitate decision making and behavior. The approach of group guidance is preventive in nature; the group's members are most directly concerned with acquiring information, becoming oriented to new problems, planning and implementing student activities and collecting data for occupational and educational decisions." (Shertzer and Stone, 1981, p. 200)
>
> Group counseling is a process in which one counselor is involved in a relationship with a number of clients at the same time. (Shertzer and Stone, 1981, p. 200).

Traditionally, group guidance activities have sought to provide information, advice, orientation, and meaningful experiences to groups of students. In recent years, group counseling has been increasingly utilized in schools to assist the problem solving, decision making, routine adjustment, and growth of students. The latter emphasis (growth groups) again reflects an increasing emphasis on the developmental potential of the counseling enterprise. Moreover, school programs of counseling and guidance, with high pupil-counselor ratios, have increasingly used group techniques as a means of serving more students with limited staff. Many counselors consider group techniques more effective with many students than individual counseling, while recognizing that it is not an effective or appropriate intervention strategy for all clients.

Career Development. Because of its emphasis on vocational guidance the career area is probably the oldest of the various basic activities in schools. The original purpose of this particular activity has been to provide pupils with the necessary vocational and educational information to make appropriate occupational choices and related educational decisions. In recent years this service has been expanded to also include information that would be characterized as social or personal in nature and to emphasize "career planning and decision making as a developmental process." This process suggests certain experiences and understandings should occur across the various life stages as a means of building an appropriate foundation for career planning and decision making. The career-education movement of the 1970s provided a new impetus for this specialized area of the school's counseling and guidance program through its recognition of the inseparability of career education and career guidance. Srebalus, Marinelli and Messing (1982) stated that

> career guidance, like career education, is an organized, systematic program to help the individual develop self-understanding, understanding of societal roles, and knowledge about the world of work. Whereas career education is the lifelong totality of experiences through which one prepares to engage in work, career guidance is one aspect of the preparation; it entails active assistance with the development of decision-making skills and the framing of occupational and educational plans. While there is some overlap between career education and career guidance, career education stresses direct experience and activities related to occupational skills and attitudes (Hoyt, 1977). Career guidance emphasizes the process of planning, decision-making, and implementation of decisions. (p. 255)

Placement and Follow-up. Although the term *placement* connotes placement in an occupation, the traditional concept of placement in secondary school programs has been considerably broadened, emphasizing placement in a variety of settings. Perhaps the greatest emphasis in most schools has been on the placement of students in collegiate institutions or into jobs upon their graduation. In a broader sense, placement has often meant curricular placement or scheduling, placement in appropriate activities, environmental placement, placement for personal development, and part-time job placement. Studies such as that by Prediger, Roth, and Noeth (1974) and Gibson and Mitchell (1976) have indicated the need for more effective placement activities in school counseling and guidance programs. Most studies seem to indicate that there is far greater emphasis on the placement of students than on follow-up. Nonetheless, follow-up is viewed as a means of evaluating the effectiveness of the placement activities and also as an opportunity, in some settings, to make adjustments or necessary reassignments.

Research and Evaluation. In recent years research and evaluation have frequently been identified as a needed basic activity for school programs. The dearth of research emanating from school counseling and guidance programs, however, would seem to indicate that for the most part this is an activity in writing only. However, as we have stated elsewhere, for general practitioners in counseling and other helping professions, the most positive general outcome of "practitioner research" is the improvement of one's professional skills and understanding. Research can provide answers to professional questions, dilemmas, and failures. Research enables practitioners to become better at their "art." It can enable us to verify what works and what doesn't and, if pursued, why. It can eliminate much of the guesswork, "hunch," and uncertainty from practices. Engaging in practical research can increase our insights and deeper understandings of ourselves, our profession, and relationships between the two. Our own research can help us as individual professionals become better at what we do. Moreover, practitioner's research tends to focus on "local" problems or concerns and may, therefore, have opportunities to provide results that are immediately applicable (Gibson and Mitchell, 1981).

Although as a basic activity evaluation fares a little better, because of the periodic accreditation reviews to which most secondary schools are subjected, there is little indication that in practice it is a major concern of most secondary school counseling and guidance programs. The increasing relationships between evaluation, accountability, and program support suggest a significant heightening of interest and activity in this aspect of the schools' counseling and guidance programs as a "survival technique" if nothing more.

Consultation. Although consultation as a basic activity in school counseling and guidance programs appears to have been initially consigned to the elementary school, it is becoming increasingly popular as a secondary school activity as well. The consultation service enables the school counselor to share his or her special knowledge and expertise with others such as teachers, administrators, and parents in the process of helping their mutual "client"—the student. A variety of consultation models are available to the counselor who must understand and develop the processes and skills needed for effective consulting.

The counselor's role as a consultant in the schools was formally acknowledged for the first time in 1966 when the American School Counselor Association (ASCA) and the Association for Counselor Education and Supervision (ACES) specified that counseling, coordination, and consultation should be the three primary role responsibilities of the elementary school counselor (Aubrey, 1972). The consulting role is perhaps more integral to the functioning of the counselor on the elementary level, but it is appropriate and becoming increasingly popular for secondary school counselors as well.

The consulting relationship is perhaps best described as a collaborative relationship in which significant others in the student's life communicate about him or her. *Collaborative* is a key term; it implies that the counselor and significant others relate to each other as equals. Thus, the counselor does not present himself or herself as an expert who has all of the answers (George and Cristiani, 1981).

Characteristics of Secondary Schools

In discussing the development of guidance programs in secondary schools, an obvious, but nonetheless important, consideration are those characteristics common to most secondary schools. These are as follows.

Secondary Schools Are Generally Large, Complex Institutions Populated by a Heterogeneous Student Body

The size and complexity of the secondary school have implications for both program development and program activities. Since the larger student bodies tend to be more heterogeneous in composition, often representing many cultural minority groups, the identification of these groups and responding to their needs can represent a major challenge to the counseling and guidance program.

Secondary School Faculties Represent a Variety of Academic Specialities

The secondary school faculty member tends to concentrate on a particular subject area. As a result, the secondary school faculty represents a variety of specializations. These "specialized" faculty members provide a reservoir of resources that the counseling and guidance program may use in the career, educational, and personal-social development of the student.

Secondary School Years Are Important Decision-making Years for the Individual Student

During a student's secondary schooling, she or he is usually confronted with at least two lifetime influencing decisions. The first of these decisions occurs when one must select a curriculum to follow upon entering secondary school. This curriculum may determine both one's vocational and educational future. A second important decision that many youths make during this period of time is whether to complete their secondary schooling. Various dropout studies indicate that approximately one fourth of American high school youth make the decision to leave school prior to finishing their secondary school program. In addition, many students make important decisions regarding job or college choice during their senior year. The wide variety of course offerings and activities available in most secondary schools prompts a nearly continuous series of minor decisions for the student. They may also be confronted with significant personal decisions regarding sex and marriage; use of tobacco, alcohol, and drugs; and friends and friendship.

Secondary Schools Are Subject-matter Oriented

Schedules and classes still tend to be formal and rigidly organized in most secondary schools, with considerable emphasis on academic standards, homework, and grades (and little planning for personal-social growth). The homeroom that many students have experienced in the elementary school years ceases to exist in most high schools, except as an administrative checkpoint. As a result, at a time when the student is accelerating his or her development as a social being, the secondary school structure often tends to inhibit this growth and development by placing students in a series of formal, academically oriented subject-matter class experiences. At the same time, many schools fail to provide students with an organized scheduled group (such as homeroom) where the individual student might develop social skills and attitudes. This suggests a challenge to the subject-matter teacher and the counselor to work cooperatively to incorporate both social development and career development experiences into the academic program.

School Spirit, or Esprit de Corps, Is Usually More Evident in Secondary Schools Than in Any Other Educational Institution

This school spirit is usually reflected in the quest for winning athletic teams, championship bands, and other public indications of excellence. The competition among students for participation in significant school events is often keen. Social divisions may often arise between those who have "made it" and those who have not in terms of these activities. On the positive side, however, school spirit in competitive activities can often be a potential factor in motivating students to remain in school, in making them seek higher academic achievements, and in promoting pride in the school. Moreover, for many communities, pride in their high school becomes a major source of community pride. School spirit and its impact on school environment and community support cannot be overlooked in counseling and guidance program planning.

Characteristics of Today's Secondary School Student

In addition to the characteristics of the secondary school just discussed, characteristics of the secondary school student must also be considered in the development of secondary school guidance programs. It must be recognized, however, that any attempt to describe the "typical" adolescent or predict his or her behavior is fraught with peril. Probably the best single prediction would be that he or she is unpredictable. Some generalizations may help us recall that fascinating period of life; we cautiously mention the following.

It Is a Transitional and Rapid Physical Growth Period

> Physical changes are, of course, the most readily observed and easily measured. Only once before (early childhood) and never again will the individual experience such rapid and significant physical growth. In a short space of years childhood is left behind and the physical adult arrives complete with voice changes, sexual characteristics, and impulses. This new physical self is a source of anxiety, frustration, and uncertainty as it develops. Its impact on the adolescent's ego and self-concept cannot be underestimated. Girls are concerned about their figures, complexions, and general feminine beauty, while boys worry about their physical growth and coordination and their general appearances of manhood. To be a late physical maturer—to not develop at the time when one's peers are "growing up,"—can be disastrous to the adolescent's image of himself or herself. (Gibson, 1979, p. 18)

It Is a Period of Rapid Intellectual Growth

> Perhaps, equally startling but not as readily observable are the intellectual developments of adolescents. New ways of using one's intellect are brought into play as the adolescent sees and solves problems from a broader frame of reference, becomes more aware of alternatives and options, learns to hypothesize and to make his or her own interpretations rather than rely on others. Dusek (1977) notes that "Currently available research demonstrates that advancements in cognitive competencies permit children and adolescents to view moral dilemmas and moral situations in more diverse and abstract ways. Higher levels of moral thinking become possible with the onset of formal-operating thinking." (Gibson, 1979, p. 18)

There Is a Growing Awareness on the Part of the High School Student of Societal Problems and Issues, Especially as They May Affect One Individually

Recent generations of high school students have been characterized by their awareness of, and often active involvement in, politics, civil liberties, and other national issues. Related to the latter have been the adolescent's reactions and uncertainties regarding the draft and what many viewed as inequities between military responsibilities and political privileges. Minority youth of high school age became increasingly active in the late 1960s and early 1970s in calling attention to their grievances. It is not uncommon for student publications to editorialize on political and social issues, for adolescents to be active in political campaigns, and to speak out or act forcefully on such concerns as nuclear energy, rearmament, and conservation. The "discovery" by adolescents of their new intellectual powers increases their motivation to become involved in and solve the problems of the universe.

New Behavioral and Personality Traits Also Emerge

They are observable in the form of new interests, values, and attitudes, and a "mode of operation" that seeks to model adulthood. Much of the adolescent's new behavior patterns are designed to establish one's own identity, individuality, integrity, and above all, independence. These are not without influences from the developing physical and intellectual characteristics of the individual. For example, these may include (Dusek, 1977) "Changes in attitudes about trial marriages, communal living, and the like, reflecting reinterpretations of existing social mores. Although these reinterpretations depend upon the broad changes occurring within the culture, they also reflect the development of cognitive competencies necessary to understand the flexibilities of social mores." (Gibson, 1979, p. 18)

Much of the adolescent's behavior which adults view as unacceptable is, in fact, seeking to emulate adult behavior. In seeking to enhance his or her image as an adult, the adolescent seeks "the adult experience." He or she is anxious to drive—even own—a car and to drive it in such a way as to draw attention to the fact he is driving—usually by driving fast, with attention-getters like tire squeals, rapid acceleration, horn honking, and so forth. For many there will be a significant increase in the use of profanity. Cigarette smoking becomes another symbol of adulthood. Alcohol and drugs may be experimented with and increasingly used. Sex becomes a popular topic of conversation and sexual activity increases. (Gibson, 1979, p. 19)

There Is a Significant Increase in Conflicting and Aggressive Behaviors

Parents, teachers, and other adult authority figures will be the recipients of much adolescent aggressiveness, although brothers and sisters will usually come in for their share. This aggressiveness will include bickering, talking back, sarcasm, and other signs of irritability. Much of this hostile behavior will stem from his or her quest for recognized independence and his or her challenges to those who, in his or her mind, would deny or limit that independence. (Gibson, 1979, p. 19)

She or He Shares Many Problems with His or Her Peers Unique to Adolescence

A multitude of studies have investigated the priority concerns of youth. Most of these tend to be outdated immediately following their publication. Recognizing this limitation, we use four categories to classify a consensus of common adolescent problems, including one in which we previously participated. (Gibson and Mitchell, 1970)

Developing as a Social Being. This includes problems of one-to-one personal relationships, particularly dating, love, sex, and marriage. It also involves group living and acceptance and, in general, the development of human relationship skills.

Developing as a Unique Being. The adolescent is concerned with the development and recognition of his or her own uniqueness as an individual. It is a time when the adolescent is seeking to develop his or her own value system, and the adolescent often finds that she or he is faced with value conflicts. Anxieties are often created as a result of constant demands on him or her to "measure up" made by evaluative testing and other appraisal techniques that appear to standardize him or her. The adolescent is concerned when she or he fails to gain parental or other support for his or her "new self."

Developing as a Productive Being. In this regard, youths are concerned with their educational adjustments and achievements, their career decisions, future educational directions, impending financial needs, and employment prospects. Many become concerned because school is not providing them with a marketable skill. Others feel that staying in school is delaying earning a living.

> *Developing as a "Societal" Being*
> While the adolescent is busily coping with various physical, intellectual, and personality changes, he or she must also deal with the expectancies which our culture imposes. While these expectancies or tasks will vary to some extent due to the social-cultural context in which the adolescent develops, we can assume most of the following are anticipated for most adolescents. (Gibson, 1979, p. 18)

1. "Growing up and maturing—physically, emotionally, intellectually, socially, morally, economically, and spiritually.
2. The achievement of independence, including independence of thought, decision, and action.
3. The development of a deep sense of personal responsibility, particularly responsibility for self.
4. The achievement of self-discipline.
5. The development of worthwhile goals, including an education suited to his/her personality, and the acquisition of a dependable set of values.
6. The achieving of selfhood and self-identity." (Schneider, 1967, pp. 10–12)

The Secondary School—Hub of a Continuous Counseling and Guidance Service

It has frequently been stated that guidance is and should be a continuous process and that the school counseling and guidance program should contribute to the individual's development from the time one enters kindergarten until one completes his or her formal education. This presumes that school guidance and counseling programs function in the elementary school, middle or junior high school, secondary school, and postsecondary school institutions, including colleges and universities. Because of its central location in the developmental process of the individual, the secondary school counseling and guidance program might be said to be the center point, or hub, of the continuous guidance process.

In a sense, the secondary school is a link in the continuous educational process in that it is an institution that is both a receiver from and a sender to other educational levels (the middle and junior high schools also qualify in this regard). Therefore, the secondary school counseling and guidance program must emphasize a facilitative and developmental process that readily integrates the entering students and their needs on one hand and at the same time gives attention to the existing needs of students preparing to move on to other educational or vocational opportunities. In this pivotal position, the secondary school program can neither function in the foundation and development sense that the elementary school program can, nor in the terminal and professional preparation sense of higher education programs. Although secondary school programs have been characteristically different, it would appear that the time is at hand to reexamine their need to function more effectively as the hub of the continuous guidance process and what this may imply for program objectives and practices. Appendix F presents the ASCA (American School Counselors' Assocation) Role Statement," The Practice of Guidance and Counseling by School Counselors, which has a section for secondary school counselors.

Patterns of Organization for Secondary School Counseling and Guidance Programs

Over the years a variety of organizational patterns for secondary school guidance programs have become recognizable. Although many variations of these patterns have existed, most readers will easily identify one or more of them—deans of men and women, student personnel services, director of guidance, and class counselor. These are briefly discussed, and organizational charts depicting these programs are presented in Figures 8–1 through 8–6. In recent years a wide variety of new experimental and innovative programs has been noted. Although no attempt is made here to present even a representative sample of these, several examples are briefly described. These are the counselor-consultant model and the counselor-as-a-youth-community-developer model.

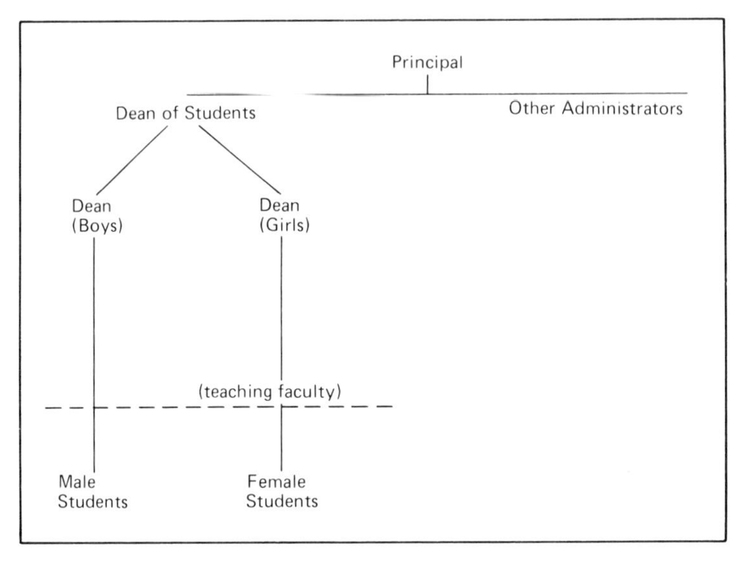

FIGURE 8–1. Deans.

COORDINATE DEANS MODEL

The coordinate deans program has been characterized since its inception in the early 1920s as a program in which two counselors are designated: a male counselor, the dean of boys (men), who works primarily with the male students; and a female counselor, the dean of girls (women), who works with the female students. As previously noted in Chapter 2, the roles of these deans frequently appear to overemphasize disciplinary and administrative tasks rather than counseling and other guidance functions. Because of the titles assigned, noncertified individuals are more likely to be appointed to such positions than if the person were labeled a school counselor or guidance worker. In recent years we have noted a trend away from such sexist titles as Dean of Men/Boys and Dean of Women/Girls.

COUNSELING AND GUIDANCE SERVICES (SPECIALIST MODEL)

The student-personnel-services pattern of program organization originally reflected the trend toward specialization in the 1930s and 1940s; a trend that we are once again experiencing in education. As noted in the organizational chart, Figure 8–2, titles such

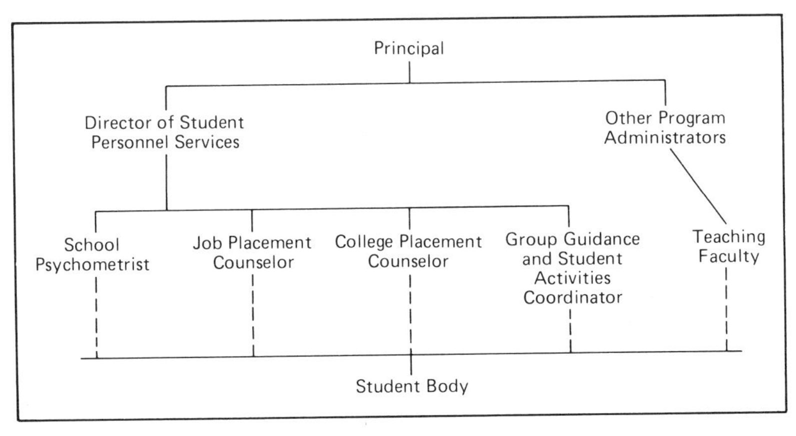

FIGURE 8–2. **Counseling and Guidance Services (Specialist Model).**

as school psychometrist and student activities coordinator are common to such programs. Although this pattern of organization enables individuals to become especially competent in their area of specialization, the directors of such programs must be careful so that students do not become compartmentalized and treated only as parts rather than as complete individuals.

SCHOOL COUNSELOR (GENERALIST) MODEL

The director-of-guidance or school-counselor pattern of organization is generally found in the small school where a single individual is designated to handle the counseling and guidance responsibilities. In contrast to the student personnel specialist,

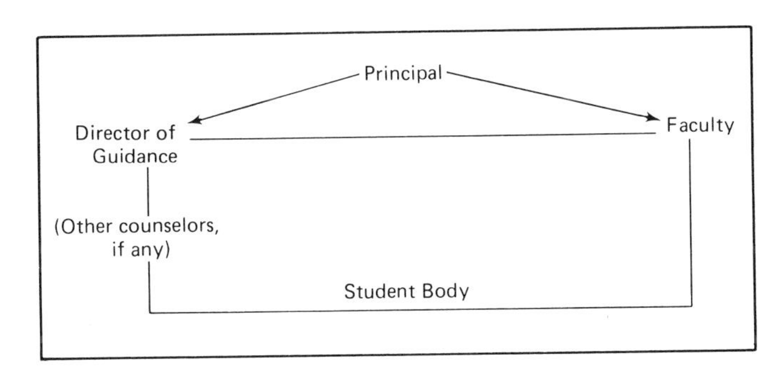

FIGURE 8–3. **Director of Guidance.**

individuals functioning in these solo operations must be viewed as generalists. Although this type of program may be quite satisfactory for small schools, it is not uncommon to find only one guidance specialist in medium-sized or even large schools—a situation that usually is less than satisfactory.

Class Counselor Model

Programs organized along lines that assign class counselors may in one sense be considered specialized and in another sense, generalized. In those programs that assign a given counselor to a grade level, she or he may tend to become a ninth-grade or tenth-grade specialist. On the other hand, many programs will assign the counselor to an incoming class, and she or he will function in this role until "his" or "her" class graduates, at which time the counselor will revert to another incoming class and repeat the process again. The latter arrangement is probably the more desirable of the two, since it seems to be more closely related to the principle of guidance as a continuous process. Further, it provides the opportunity for the counselor to work with the same students during the three- or four-year period in the secondary school.

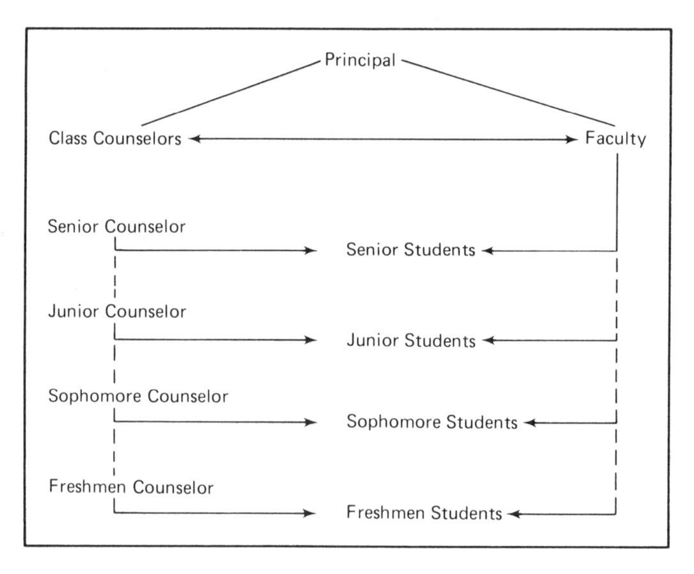

FIGURE 8–4. Class Counselors.

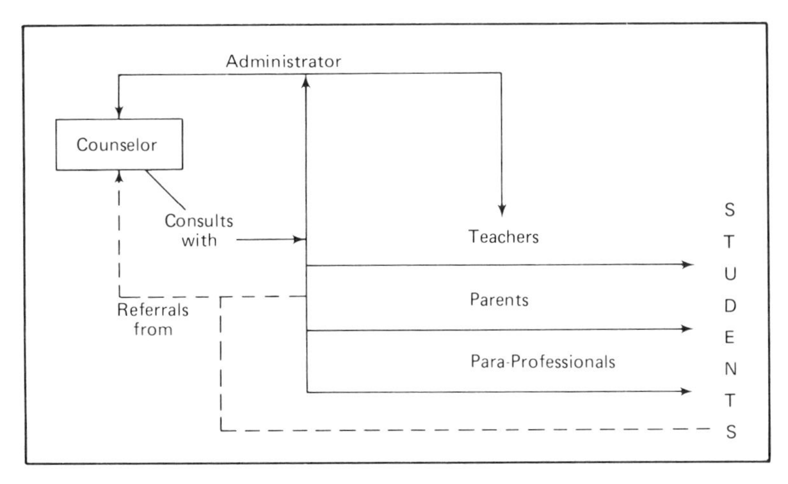

FIGURE 8–5. Counselor as a Consultant: Trainer, Supervisor, Referral Source.

THE COUNSELOR-CONSULTANT MODEL

One of the most popular of the recent models for school counseling programs is the one in which the counselor functions primarily as a consultant. In this role the counselor serves as a guidance consultant to the school administrator, teachers, parents, and paraprofessionals in his or her school or school system. The counselor is also envisioned as a referral agent for these personnel and will handle direct student self-referrals. In this capacity the counselor also tends to function as a guidance supervisor of those working directly with students and as a trainer of teachers, paraprofessionals, and, on occasion, even parents, preparing them to work more effectively as agents of the school guidance program in meeting the needs of youth. Although this model has achieved some popularity at every level, it is even more common at the elementary and middle school levels. Figure 8–5 depicts this pattern of program organization.

THE COUNSELOR AS A COMMUNITY-YOUTH DEVELOPER

Within the counseling and psychological professions, some individuals have suggested that the counselor could function more effectively in a school and community agency setting where he or

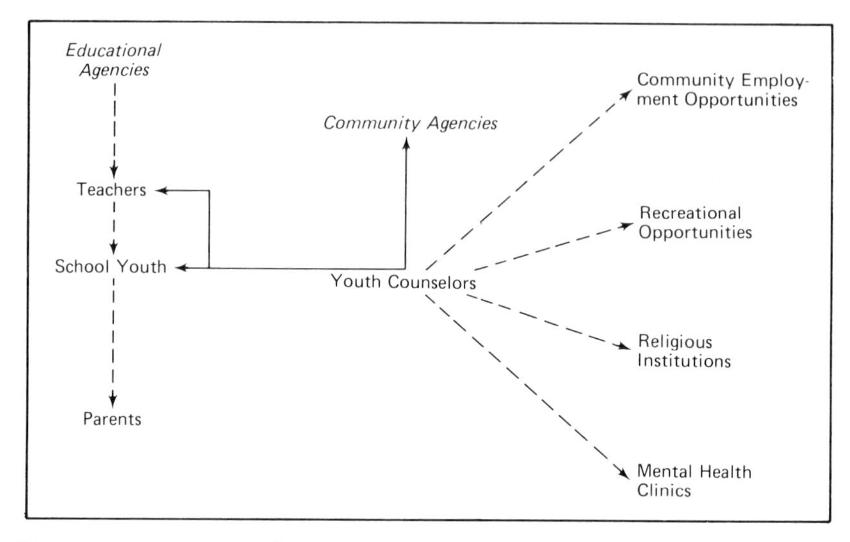

FIGURE 8–6. Counselor as a Community-Youth Developer.

she could more appropriately coordinate the resources of the entire community to meet the needs of youth. Whereas one's contacts with youth would come primarily through the educational setting, one would tend to be less restricted by educational policies, and would probably not be viewed by youth as a member of the Establishment. This pattern is popular in the British Isles, where "careers officers" divide their time between school settings and local employment offices. Figure 8–6 depicts this pattern of organization.

Secondary School Programs and the Challenges of Contemporary Society

From an adult perspective, the adolescent often appears to be a carefree, happy individual with few concerns or worries other than a Saturday night date, the availability of one's parents' automobile, or victory for the home team in the state tournament. Yet, we are aware, often painfully, that our schools, especially our secondary schools, are themselves a reflection of our society, with not only the "plus's" but the problems of society to contend with as well. Thus such society-wide concerns as human substance abuse, sexuality, marriage and family, stress management, and women and minority rights, to mention but a few of the obvious, are also of concern to school counselors and their programs. If the secondary school program is to maintain relevance, it must include planning that takes into account these and other timely societal, and adolescent, concerns.

Sexuality

Adolescents and young adults have always been confronted with problems arising from their developing sexuality. These have typically included concerns regarding their individual sexual development, curiosities, attitudes, and experiences. Although in theory many schools have provided for sex education, these programs have been often grossly inadequate to the needs of their student enrollees. Many school counseling programs have functioned in the past in a way that suggested that problems in this realm either didn't exist or were "off limits." Related to this is the fact that counselor education programs rarely provided any special training to prepare counselors to cope with this most common of all problems. In recent years these problems have tended to be more openly recognized, and despite some areas of public resistance, schools are moving forward to provide more relevant educational and counseling programs to meet the needs of the students. From the standpoint of the school counseling program, we must recognize that many adolescents have problems in the area of sexuality that are just as intense and crucial to their adjustment and development as those in the more openly recognized areas of career and educational decision making. Although statistical data regarding sexual activity may frequently be conservative, in 1976 over 40 per cent of unmarried seventeen-year-olds reported that they had had sexual intercourse at least once and 18 per cent of the fifteen-year-olds reported having engaged in sexual intercourse. In the same year (1976) nearly twelve thousand babies were born to girls who were not yet fifteen. These and other data consistently indicate the need high school students have for sexual information and sexual counseling. However, reinforced by adult attitudes, the stigma often attached to problems of a sexual nature will usually drive youth to discuss them only with their closest and usually equally uninformed peers according to Tegtmeyer (1980).

> School counselors can play a major leadership role and act as catalysts in the acceptance and expansion of the concept of sexuality in human liberation. This process involves viewing sexual development and expression as a normal and integral part of being human and as important to the formation of a valuable relationship. Implicit in this approach is the need for greater individual integrity, responsibility, and respect for the rights of others. As school counselors become more aware of and receptive to the sociosexual needs of their students and more accepting of their own sexuality, they will help promote a more realistic sexual climate—by acting as models and by offering counseling services and programs. (p. 433)

School counseling programs must openly indicate their recognition of young people's sexual concerns and must demonstrate a willingness to assist students, both individually and in groups, in coping with these concerns. Community groups however, frequently religious or parental, will often strenuously resist any school efforts to recognize, much less deal with, sexual concerns, issues, and education.

Substance Abuse

Although alcohol abuse has long been a national problem, only within recent generations has drug abuse aroused similar public concern. Limited largely in the past to urban and inner-city ghetto areas, and usually to adult members of minority groups in these areas, it has suddenly spread to all socioeconomic and age levels, including wealthy suburban communities. As drug abuse spread to all levels of society, it imposed its problems on both our privileged and our deprived youth. Thus, in a short period of time, the drug phenomenon has become a priority concern to all segments of the American public. The sudden increase in drug addiction on the part of American youth and the creation of the drug culture of the 1960s and 1970s caught educational institutions completely unprepared. In many high schools, the school counselors were called upon to take the lead in "doing something about the drug problem." Yet, with rare exception, school counselors were completely unprepared, and frequently still are, to effectively assist youth in preventing drug abuse or coping with this problem. The continued existence of the problem among marijuana users alone is clearly indicated from the data in the following paragraphs.

> In 1969 only 4% of the American population had ever used marijuana (Gallup, 1977). In 1973 the figure rose to 12%, and in 1977 the figure was up to 24% (a 100% increase in four years) (Gallup, 1977). As the following statistics on age of users in 1977 indicate, frequency of use is related to age; 18 to 24 years old, 59%; 25 to 29 years old, 51%; 30 to 49 year old, 16%; 50 years and older, 5% (Gallup, 1977). In particular, it is the 12 to 25 years old group that has been showing the greatest increase in marijuana use (Cohen, 1979a).
>
> Since 1975 the National Institute of Drug Abuse (NIDA) has conducted an annual survey of the use of marijuana by high school seniors in the U.S. The 1975 survey reported six percent of high school seniors admitted to smoking marijuana daily (defined as 20 or more times in the past thirty days) during their senior year (Johnston, Bachman, and O'Malley, 1978). The number of seniors who are daily users rose to 8.2% in 1976, 9.1% in 1977, and 10.7% in 1978 (Johnston et al., 1978), which means that in 1978 approximately one of every nine high school seniors in the U.S. smoked marijuana daily (as defined above). In addition, daily marijuana use among high school seniors now exceeds daily alcohol use by the same group (6%) (Johnston et al., 1979). Because the NIDA survey does not include high school dropouts, the percentage of teenagers who are daily users may well exceed 10.7%.
>
> Over the course of three years, 1975 to 1978, the daily use of marijuana has doubled among high school students. Another concern is the substantial and continuing increase in the prevalence of early use—in the class of 1975, anywhere from 30% to 90%. For many users, one drop of high potency hash oil is enough to produce an hallucinogenic effect ("Street drug analysis . . .", 1977). The escalation of the THC potency in marijuana products over the past decade indicates a shift toward the abuse of a stronger drug—highly potent marijuana. (Margolis and Popkin, 1980, p. 7)

Concern over teenage alcoholism has also received renewed and increased attention, and well it should. The reports of usage of both alcohol and drugs among teenagers is alarming and on the increase. For example, according to Spoth and Rosenthal (1980):

> a review of survey data clearly shows a considerable increase in alcohol use/abuse among adolescents during the past three decades. Researchers examining alcohol use during the 1950s and 1960s consistently reported that between two percent and six percent of high school students consumed one drink or more a month on the average, and ten percent experienced drunkenness over the course of their high school years (Globetti, 1964; Maddox and McCall, 1964; Slater, 1952). In contrast, a nationwide survey conducted in 1974 (Rachal, Williams, Brehm, Cavanaugh, Moore, and Eckerman, 1975) presents a clearly different picture. The proportion of adolescents reported being intoxicated at least once a month increased from ten percent before 1966 to 19% between 1966 and 1975. Nearly one-quarter of the teenagers interviewed were classified as "moderately heavy drinkers" (13.7%) or "heavy drinkers" (10.6%). Even more recently, Abelson, Fishburne and Cisin (1977) found that more than 31 percent of adolescents between the ages of twelve and seventeen were "current drinkers." None of these survey data indicate that the current drinking trends will reverse. (Spoth and Rosenthal, 1980, p. 212)

In order to more effectively meet these responsibilities, school counselors must first learn all they can about the nature of alcohol and drugs and those who use them. It is also extremely important that the counselor keep the lines of communication open to youthful substance users, who often have a tendency to withdraw into their own subculture. In addition, school counselors should also seek closer liaison with other community agencies and medical personnel who are actively engaged in working with these problems. The counselor can also play an important role in helping to reeducate parents and other adults concerning the significant factors involved in substance use and abuse.

Stress

Stress occurs when individuals believe that the demands from the environment are more than they can handle. (Alschuler, 1980). It is the "burning out" of one's psychological ability to cope adequately with the expectancies and demands of everyday living. It is reflected across the country in statistics of crime and delinquency, mental health treatment and confinement, career and school leaving, suicide, and the previously discussed extent of substance and sexual abuse. In other words, individuals react to stress in a variety of ways, most of which are unhealthy and counterproductive to both the individual and society. Let us examine some of the more common of these outcomes.

If we examine stressful outcomes in the context of the secondary school student, we would begin by noting that although the problem of juvenile delinquency has existed in the United States for many years, a report from the Federal Bureau of Investigation (1973) suggested both the prevalence and seriousness of the problem. This report noted that persons ten to eighteen years of age were represented in 44.5 percent of all arrests for crime. The arrest rates of persons under eighteen has gone up 123.9 percent from 1960 to 1972. Since the age group from ten to eighteen years constitutes only about 15 percent of the population, the arrest record of this group is disproportionately high. It can be predicted that over one million people under the age of eighteen will be arrested in the United States annually. The resulting cost to individuals and to society is staggering.

Vandalism alone now costs schools over a half billion dollars yearly. Each year, students commit seventy thousand physical assaults on teachers and hundreds of thousands on other students. (Moorefield, 1977). In a limited California study, twenty-three California school districts responded to a burglary and vandalism survey conducted by the Fresno Unified School District, Burglary and Vandalism Prevention Project (1978). This summary compiles survey data on eighteen thousand occurrences of damage or loss to buildings, glass, equipment, buses, and nonspecified areas amounting to $4,500,000.

Big city vice data indicate a continued increase in drug peddling to secondary school age youth. Although the true extent of drug usage among teenagers and preteenagers is difficult to estimate, it is believed to be extensive. As evidence, a report by Kovar (1979) indicated that nearly two thirds of the graduating high school class of 1977 had tried one or more illicit drugs.

Excessive alcoholic consumption is also a problem that frequently stems from adolescent and preadolescent problems. According to a U.S. Department of Health, Education and Welfare report, "twenty-five per cent of all seventh graders report getting drunk one or more times a year" (Alcohol and Health Report, 1974). This youthful intoxication is a symptom or "signpost" of later problem drinking. In addition to data previously cited, figures released by the National Institute on Alcohol Abuse and Alcoholism (1973) indicate that one out of ten teenagers is presently or will become an alcoholic. Additional figures indicate that some four hundred fifty thousand people under the age of twenty-nine years are already alcoholic (*Editorial Research Reports*, vol. 11, 1973).

Another result of the failure of youth to enter adolescence well adjusted has been the increase in adolescent and young adult suicides over the last twenty years in the United States. Suicide is the third most common cause of death among teenagers. For example, in the age group of fifteen to twenty-four years, from 1950 to 1970, the suicide rate doubled from 6.6 to 13.9 per 100,000 (U.S. Bureau of the Census, 1976). Suicides and attempts at suicide have continued on the rise in recent years, especially among young people, women, and members of ethnic minority groups (Lee, 1979). As an indication of the full impact of this tragedy on our country, at least 20,000 people commit suicide in the United States each year, making it the tenth leading cause of death (Klagsbrun, 1976). Many other suicides go unreported and do not show up in the statistics. Authorities (Klagsbrun, 1976) put the total number of suicide deaths closer to 100,000 per year, and the number of suicide attempts at ten times that figure. This means that approximately one million Americans a year make the decision to take their lives and then take steps to implement that decision (Morgan, 1981).

In a broader sense, the stress or mental health of our adolescent school population relates to the need to develop to the fullest our human resource potential. The development of a positive societal outlook further underscores the need for an emotionally healthy society. As noted in the classic UNESCO publication of over twenty-five years ago (Wall, 1955),

> To survive without hostility to others, the whole mass of a society must be fundamentally healthy, composed of stable men and women free of neurotic fears, anxieties and tensions, aware of their own prejudices and with positive attitudes of friendliness to others. Such a healthy society is likely to reject, as eccentric and unbalanced, individuals, however gifted, who are themselves maladjusted and who claim leadership. The danger to peace is at its most acute, as

> we have seen, when a nation of predominantly unbalanced people seeks and finds maladjusted leaders who, by playing on deep fears and anxieties, rouse and maintain hostility to other groups. Anything therefore which contributes to the healthy emotional development of human personality is a direct contribution to the maintenance of peace. (p. 19)

It is clear that school counselors need to increase their understanding of the causes and effects of stress on the normal developmental processes of young people.

Whereas the mental health of school-age youth and adults has been a concern for most of this century, a proliferation of articles calling public and professional attention to mental health problems under the labels of "stress" and "burnout" have made us increasingly sensitive to such problems in the 1970s and 1980s. It would appear that secondary school counseling and guidance programs, therefore, have the responsibility to develop stress prevention and reduction programs for their student client population.

Additionally, and perhaps for the first time, school counselors may also consider providing a service for their "burned out" faculty colleagues as well. Whereas the dramatic evidence cited earlier in this section testifies to the extent and loss to society resulting from youth under "stress," less dramatic but nonetheless impressive evidence points to the extent of stress in the teaching profession. In fact, many of the in-school factors that create stress for teachers result from student behavior under stress. The statistical evidence notes that each year over fifty-two thousand (5 %) of the nation's one million secondary school teachers are attacked by students, ten thousand of whom require medical treatment; sixty thousand teachers (6 %) are robbed; and every month one hundred and 20 thousand (12 %) have something stolen (National Institute of Education, 1977).

If these internal pressures from the work load and students were not enough to cause stress in teachers, numerous external pressures are exerted on schools: to mainstream students with special needs; to provide multicultural and bilingual education; to reduce expenses in a period of rapid inflation; to respond to the questions of parents, the concerns of supervisors, and the achievement objectives of school boards and administrators (Alschuler, 1980). Simultaneously, declining school enrollments foreshadow the strong possibility of reductions in the teaching force, including layoffs. Beyond these pressures, which affect all teachers, there are usually one or more intense stresses in teachers' personal lives, such as death, an accident, or an illness of a family member; divorce; debts; trouble with in-laws; and changes in their living conditions and personal habits. Not surprisingly, the combination of these job-related and personal pressures makes stress the number one health problem of teachers. (Sylwester, 1977)

Other studies indicate that the problem of stress in teachers could be reaching epidemic proportions. A recent Chicago teachers' union survey (Walsh, 1979) indicated that of five thousand five hundred respondents to a stress questionnaire, 56.5 per cent reported physical and/or mental illness as a direct result of their jobs. Physical symptoms singled out by the teacher respondents included high blood pressure, ulcers, digestion problems, depression, headaches, heart disease, and kidney problems. A further measure of job dissatisfaction among teachers is a National Education Association Teacher Opinion poll (McGuire, 1979) that found that one third of those now teaching would not reenter the field if they could start over. Only 60 per cent reported that they planned to remain in the profession until retirement.

Recognizing that pupils under stress can create teacher stress, and vice versa, school counseling programs should have the broader responsibility in this instance to assist both students and teaching colleagues in the prevention and alleviation of stress.

Inasmuch as this book does not deal with counseling in the theoretical or process sense, we avoid a detailed analytical-theoretical discussion of the topic, but do, however, briefly indicate a few of the basic causes, symptoms, and treatment approaches related to stress.

COMMON CAUSES OF STRESS

- a variety of pressures and demands, coupled with a feeling of powerlessness, of being trapped without options.
- constant feelings of fatigue and/or frustration
- the feeling that one is not respected, including no "strokes," no positive feedback, rejection even hostility from others
- the failure to achieve or lack of recognition for efforts and achievements

- failure to see meaning in time-consuming activities (such as homework for students, paperwork, and meetings for teachers).

RESULTS

- lethargy
- depression, withdrawal
- chronic anger, cynicism, hostility, sarcasm, and so forth
- constant worry, anxiety, paranoia
- developing interests that result in "going to school" or "teaching of school" becoming of secondary or little interest to the student or teacher.

REDUCTION/PREVENTION/TREATMENT

- develop stress management programs
- help those under stress form support groups with peers with whom they can share their concerns, develop "mutual assistance pacts," and plan coping strategies
- generate positive feedback and reinforcement to individuals under stress
- Assist individuals in identifying positive outlets such as hobbies, recreational activities, and rewarding new experiences
- Assist students and/or faculty under stress to identify the stressors in their situation and develop plans to deal with each.

Summary and Implications

More counselors are employed in secondary school programs than any other single setting in this country. These programs have, over the years, focused on a series of basic services emphasizing individual counseling, individual analysis, group counseling and guidance, career development, consultation, placement and follow-up, and research and evaluation.

Important to the development of counseling and guidance programs in secondary schools are their unique characteristics. For example, secondary schools are generally larger and more complex than elementary or middle schools. The secondary school faculty tend to be subject-matter specialists and thus, the secondary school is subject-matter oriented. From the students' (and often public's) viewpoint school spirit is usually more in evidence at the secondary school level.

Secondary students also exhibit new and unique characteristics, as it is a period of rapid physical and intellectual growth, an increasing awareness of societal problems and issues, and emergence of new behavioral and personality traits. This is also a period of time when youth exhibits increased aggressive and conflicting behaviors, with adults often the recipients of this behavior.

Recognizing both the uniqueness of the secondary school and their student populations, and further noting the differences from school to school, a variety of models for program organization must be expected. Whatever model is selected for a given school, it should be the one deemed most appropriate for that setting and clientele. It should also be anticipated that common concerns in the broad areas of human sexuality, substance abuse, and stress are likely and must be planned for in most settings.

The overall implication is that secondary school counselors must be prepared for both relevancy and flexibility if programs themselves are to change as needs and environmental factors change.

CHAPTER 9

The Student Personnel Function in Higher Education

Introduction

Some twenty years ago Mueller (1961) described a typical college campus and identified some of the areas of college life with which students will need assistance.

> The swarm of anxious, ambitious human dynamos which converge each September on every college campus must be organized into a "community of students" and nurtured in the "collegiate way of life." Although the student's education is the heart and center of this life, his initiation begins long before his actual classroom experience. He must first be admitted, classified, housed, fed, advised, and perhaps financed. And if his campus years are to fulfill their promise, no aspect of his college experience must be overlooked. His health, his manners, his leisure time, his social or marital adjustment, even his final placement must be considered. Only mature, efficient and persistent attention to all parts of his personality and to his place in the total campus milieu will promote his own and society's welfare. (p. viii)

To that list today could be added many additional needs of students that, on most campuses, are addressed by student personnel workers. It may correctly be deduced from Mueller's campus description that the student personnel function in higher education consists of two—not necessarily exclusive—aspects:

1. Providing for student needs pertaining to such aspects of college life as admissions, advisement, housing, health, leisure-time activities, financial concerns, interpersonal relations, social skills, et cetera.
2. Assisting the institution to fulfill its obligation toward the development of the *total* individual, i.e., to provide ". . . mature, efficient and persistent attention to all parts of his personality. . . ."

There seems to be little disagreement among current student personnel workers about the validity of those two functions. There has been considerable debate, however, about the campus "structure" through which the requisite services are provided, as well as questions as to the success being achieved in fulfilling the second function. The issues, which are by no means resolved, are explored in depth in this chapter.

To understand the issues so that one is more able to contribute to the development of meaningful student personnel programs, an understanding of student personnel history and philosophy is required. Therefore, the following overview of historical and philosophical foundations is provided.

An Overview of Student Personnel Development

Student personnel services have become essential to the successful operation of virtually every American college and university. Although the kinds and numbers of these services provided vary from campus to campus, the rationale for the inception of the services is the same everywhere. That rationale, the reason for the provision of *any* higher program or service, is to assist the institution to achieve its stated objectives. The American college or university today that does not list among its objectives one alluding to "the development of the *total* student" is very rare, if it exists at all. The achievement of that objective on the contemporary college campus requires that the institution provide services which address student needs arising from both curricular and noncurricular aspects of college life. Moreover, the provision of the needed services requires specialized personnel—student personnel workers.

There was no need for specialized student personnel staff during the pre–Civil War period of American higher education and little need for personnel specialists until this century. Assistance with all aspects of the students' development was provided by the college president and faculty during Colonial days even though the college's obligations did not pertain just to the students' intellectual development. As Ayers, et al. (1966) noted ". . . the colleges took responsibility not only for their students' intellectual growth, but also for their moral, spiritual, and social development" (p. 4). In essence, the college president and faculty were acting *in loco parentis*. They were enabled to fullfill the various student "oversight" functions arising from their paternalistic concerns by the small numbers of students on their campuses and by virtue of the prevailing campus life style—the "collegiate way."

According to Rudolph (1962)

> The collegiate way is the notion that a curriculum, a library, a faculty, and students are not enough to make a college. It is an adherence to the residential scheme of things. It is respectful of quiet rural settings, dependent on dormitories, committed to dining halls, permeated by paternalism. It is what every American college has had or consciously rejected or lost or sought to recapture. . . . (p. 87)
>
> For the adherents of that tradition [the "collegiate way"], the college was "a large family, sleeping, eating, studying, and worshiping together under one roof." (p. 88)

From Rudolph's depictions of the prevailing life style on the self-contained Colonial college campuses, it is apparent that the college president and faculty could address most aspects of students' developmental needs themselves; there was no need to employ the type of staff person who would in later years be known as a student personnel worker.

Higher education historians view the beginning of the post-Civil War era of American history as a major turning point in American higher education. Rudolph (1962), for example, referred to the years immediately following the Civil War as "The Dawning of a New Era" (p. 241). The "new era" was highlighted by:

1. A renewed emphasis upon technological and scientific education, thus "spawning" new colleges and institutes. (Rudolph, 1962, p. 244)
2. The passage of the Morrell Act of 1862, which enabled the development of the land-grant colleges. (Rudolph, 1962, p. 244)
3. The development of the elective curriculum. (Rudolph, 1962, p. 290)
4. The expansion of the extracurriculum disproportionately to the curriculum. (Brubacher and Rudy, 1968, pp. 199–120)
5. The introduction of an impersonal, intellectualistic faculty approach to students. (Brubacher and Rudy, 1968, p. 330)

The impact of the post-Civil War changes on American higher education was aptly described by Brubacher and Rudy (1968)

> After the Civil War, American Ph.D.'s, who had been trained in Germany, tried to introduce a more impersonal, intellectualistic approach modeled on the Continental European university. However, the paternalistic tradition had by this time attained such a strong influence upon the American college that it could not be completely eliminated. To be sure, the unity of the old-time college was shattered as the curriculum grew broader and more diversified, as the elective system spread, as the undergraduate population became larger and less homogeneous, and as secular influences became stronger. Many of the new faculty members were more interested in scholarly research than in personal dealings with students, and it was becoming increasingly apparent that promotion depended upon published research, not on student counseling. In the main, however, American college students were not converted to this intellectualist view of the higher learning. They were not interested in taking advantage of the opportunity to become mature scholars, European style. In the activist atmosphere of the American campus, they considered this to be an approach suitable only for professors and "grinds." Instead they developed enthusiastic support for strenuous extracurricular activities and contented themselves with a "gentleman's C. . . ."
>
> The American college, at this point, showed signs of developing a split personality. The old "college life" continued to flourish. But now it was developing distinctly apart from, and frequently in

> opposition to, the intellectual side of higher learning. "Campus opinion" came to exercise a sway more imperious, more tyrannical, than anything the old paternalistic college rules had been able to impose.
>
> When the personnel movement arose in the twentieth century, it thus represented not only a major effort to restore a unified life to the American college but also a revival of the old-time college's concern for the nonintellectual side of the student's career. This reaction to the temporary vogue of German impersonalism expressed itself, however, in different ways from the clerically dominated pattern of earlier times. As a result of the greater size and complexity of American institutions of higher learning, it was no longer possible for the president and teaching faculty to function as active personnel officers. This task now had to be assumed by special staff members who devoted all of their time to it. (pp. 330–331)

The pressures that were to necessitate the employment of student personnel workers were being felt by college and university presidents by the late nineteenth century. For example, President Gilman of Johns Hopkins University appointed higher education's first "Chief of the Advisors" in 1889 (Peterson et al., 1980, p. 8), and at Harvard University in 1890 a professor was appointed ". . . to serve as what Cowley called a 'dean of student relations' " (Williamson, 1961, p. 5). Although individuals had been employed by colleges prior to these appointments to assist with discipline, with women's housing and social supervision, and with activities pertaining to the extracurriculum, the Johns Hopkins and Harvard appointments seemingly signified the formal recognition of the obligation of higher education institutions to provide a specifically designated *counseling* service for students.

Thus, the practice of assigning special staff to address student needs and problems, especially those not directly related to the institution's academic programs, was being established. The "special staff" employed were the forerunners of the contemporary student personnel specialist.

Two factors appear to have been largely responsible for the employment of the "special staff": the need to facilitate the development of the *total* student, and administrative necessity. These factors should be carefully noted; they play important roles in the determination of appropriate or requisite student personnel functions for the 1970s and 1980s. From a contemporary *student development* perspective it is perhaps unfortunate that, of the two factors, "administrative necessity" was apparently viewed as the more important factor. The services provided by the special staff were apparently developed primarily in support of, and peripheral to, an institution's academic program rather than being made integral, developmental aspects of the curriculum. As Williamson (1961) noted

> it is clear that personnel work is related to, or extends from, that philosophy of education which concerns itself with the total development of the individual student. But we note that many of our services were empirically developed before such an explicit philosophy was formulated. This sequence of evolvement is of great significance because it means that our work has had a grass-roots development in the daily experiences and difficulties of students and teachers. (p. 11)

By the end of the nineteenth century the foundations for higher education student personnel programs had been laid and the roots of a new profession had been established. Mueller (1961) wrote

> It has been customary to consider the history of the profession of personnel work as one which lies wholly within the twentieth century. The identification of a new profession begins when official titles are applied to specialists in the field, when formal statements of purpose are written and issued to the public, when workers come together in national associations, and when the first pamphlets, journals, and textbooks are published. For personnel work all these events occurred shortly after 1900. Although it is clear that what we now know as personnel work with students had been in operation for at least seven hundred years, such work took a tremendous leap forward to self-consciousness in the present century and made itself known as *the personnel movement.* (p. 50)

The "personnel movement" accelerated rapidly once it was initiated. Two of the many factors that influenced the development of personnel services during the formative period of the personnel profession significantly stand out: the vocational guidance movement and the mental hygiene movement. Both movements were begun around 1908. The vocational guidance thrust was propelled by the work of Frank Parsons, and the mental hygiene movement by the National Committee for Mental Hygiene (which was founded largely because of the publication of *A Mind That Found Itself*, written by Clifford Beers, a former mental hospital patient).

Also providing impetus to the "personnel movement" were the increasing industrialization of American society, the higher standards of living that workers were attaining, complexities of the "world of work" that necessitated assistance with career selection, and the contributions of the "rapidly developing sciences of psychology and sociology" (Mueller, 1961, p. 51). According to Brubacher and Rudy (1968)

> After the First World War the personnel movement received a tremendous impetus all over America. Mental testing and counseling had been developed on a large scale by the Army, and as soon as peace came "army psychologists transposed to the colleges the many techniques of counseling and diagnosis perfected in army personnel." The field assumed more and more of the aspects of a distinct profession, growing out of the stage of "sentimentalized intuition" and entering that of systematic differentiation and specialization of personnel functions. A solid body of scientific knowledge was being built up that could be applied in counseling situations. Personnel workers of every variety—psychiatric, religious, social, vocational, educational—began to appear in large numbers. At institutions such as the University of Minnesota under President Lotus D. Coffman an independent and comprehensive personnel program was put into effect (at the same time as the "General College" experiment) and professional counselors were given extensive powers of waiver and assignment over students. Great national foundations were becoming interested in coordinating and stimulating the personnel work that was going forward at dozens of campuses across the nation. With the backing of the Rockefeller Foundation and the General Education Board, the American Council on Education initiated an extensive study of personnel practices, achievement tests, rating scales, and vocational monographs. As a result, not only were personnel procedures standardized all over the country, but in 1948 the council joined with the Carnegie Foundation and the College Entrance Examination Board in creating the Educational Testing Service, a nationwide cooperative experiment in the use of achievement tests. To sum up, then, in the

> years following 1918 the student personnel movement in colleges had gained national recognition and professional stature; it was becoming self-conscious, confident, and widely influential. (p. 335)

In the 1930s the "personnel movement" lost momentum that it did not regain until after World War II. The setback in the 1930s was primarily a product of two influences: monetary problems stemming from the country's economic depression and the revitalization of the philosophical position that the primary function of higher education was to develop students' intellect (Fenske, 1980, p. 21).

Following World War II, the "personnel movement" began its peak growth period. "The advent of the G.I. Bill, with its surging need for academic, personal, and financial advising on nearly every campus in the country, exemplified the postwar trends that breathed new life into student-oriented services of all kinds" (Fenske, 1980, pp. 21–22).

The growth of student personnel services continued at a rapid rate through the 1950s, 1960s, and 1970s. Today, as a glance at almost any college or university directory will reveal, student personnel services are being provided for almost every facet of college life.

Philosophical Foundations

The term commonly employed to denote the philosophical foundations underlying student personnel is *the personnel point of view.* The utilization of that term to convey the underlying "spirit" of student personnel work was popularized through the publication by the American Council on Education (1937) of a pamphlet describing personnel work at the college level (Mueller, 1961, p. 56). The A.C.E. publication, *The Student Personnel Point of View,* did not introduce the term to the profession. Strang (1935) had earlier stated: "The personnel or guidance emphasis in education . . . is manifested in a philosophy and in concrete programs. The philosophy is sometimes called the *personnel point of view*" (p. 16).

The "personnel point of view" is based upon three major assumptions:

1. Each student is to be considered as a functioning whole. Thus the development of the student as a *person*—not just his or her intellect—should be emphasized.
2. Individual differences are anticipated; each student is unique. Thus "mass education," the practice of treating all students as though they were alike, must be avoided.
3. The most significant factors in the development of a student services program are the drives, interests and needs of each student for whom the services are to be provided. Thus, to the extent needed, remedial and other services designed to assist the student to overcome developmental obstacles should be provided. (Mueller, 1961, p. 56; Williamson, 1961, pp. 13–15; Strang, 1935, pp. 16–19)

The "personnel point of view" in essence evolved out of reactions to the philosophy of rationalism, which has as its sole aim ". . . the development of intellect and reason" (Crookston, 1980, p. 27). The philosophical foundations underlying the "point of view" come from the philosophies of instrumentalism, humanism, and pragmatism. Instrumentalism—the philosophical opposite of rationalism—"emphasizes the full and creative development of the whole person" (Crookston, 1976, p. 27). Humanism stresses the dignity and worth of a person and suggests the principle that the learner is at least equally as important as the materials to be learned. Dewey (1916) stated that the essential feature of pragmatism ". . . is to maintain the continuity of knowing with an activity which purposely modifies the environment" (p. 400). Thus, pragmatism—based on the premise that the function of thought is to guide action—suggests that knowledge is acquired by the learner's being involved in meaningful activities.

Building the basic premises of instrumentalism, humanism, and pragmatism into the "point of view" provided student personnel with an excellent philosophical foundation. That foundation, the "personnel point of view," has served as a basis for the development of student services since the mid-1930s, and almost a half-century later, the philosophical principles manifested by the "point of view" still seem firmly entrenched.

Despite the general acceptance of the philosophy, however, there has been increasing concern about its implementation. As we have seen, student services evolved through a "grass-roots" developmental pattern and consequently were perceived as being peripheral to academic programs. As the student services' programs grew, they were administratively organized into a structure parallel to, but separate from, the academic structure. Questions about the effectiveness of the resultant "dualistic" academic and student services' programs in complying with the intent of the "point of view" philosophy were appearing by the late 1940s and led in the 1960s to the emergence of the concept of student development (Crookston, 1976).

> Student development has been defined as the application of the philosophy and principles of human development in the educational setting. Human development refers to the knowledge, conditions, and processes that contribute both to the growth, development, and fulfillment of the individual throughout life as a realized person and effective, productive citizen, and to the growth and development of society. (pp. 27–28)

As may be seen from these definitions, a revitalization of the goal of "education of the whole student" was being sought by the student development advocates, and as was indicated by the questioning of the established parallel structure, the supporters of a student development approach believed that to attain the "whole student" objective, the academic and student services' programs needed to be integrated into one unified program. In other words, the student services had to become integral aspects of the institution's educational process.

Dissatisfaction with the campus roles assigned to student services did not stem from differences about basic student personnel philosophy. Proponents of the "complementary functions" approach (Cowley, 1964, p. 68), as well as proponents of the "student development" approach, have reaffirmed the principle of "total student development." Brown (1972), an advocate of the student development approach, stated "One major assumption underlying the entire discussion here is that total student development has been and must remain one of the primary goals of higher education" (p. 7). Cowley, who in the previously cited 1964 statement defended the noncurricular approach, was credited by Williamson (1961) for the introduction of the term "holism" ". . . to devote our central concern with all aspects of the development of human individuality" (p. 13).

The questions raised by student development advocates arose from the seeming failure of higher education institutions to meet their stated objectives pertaining to the development of the total student. For example, Brown (1972) asked: "Has student development ever been a real goal of higher education or is it a myth? Is it a viable goal for the future? If the starting place is the student, what does higher education want to achieve?" (p. 28).

About ten years have passed since Brown raised those questions. If activity in a professional field is a criterion, the numbers of developmental-oriented position papers and research reports appearing in student personnel literature in the last ten years along with the numerous studies being undertaken by student personnel professional organizations indicate that "student development" has indeed remained "a real goal" of higher education personnel workers. In essence, the controversy is being resolved by providing requisite services for students, by structuring those services around developmental approaches, by involving faculty as much as possible in the provision of developmental activities, and by preparing prospective student personnel workers to understand and utilize student development concepts in their professional practice. As Packwood (1977) noted

> Many college student personnel workers are hired because they are experts in a given service or can do the job in the service that the college wants done. The basis for employment then is professional and technical skill, just as a surgeon is hired for surgery. Of course there is much more than the skill of surgery that is included in the professional surgeon's activities. That "much more" for the college student personnel worker becomes the implementation of student development principles. (p. xxv)

The Necessity of Student Personnel Programs in Higher Education

In this era of very essential cost consciousness a basic question must be asked. Are student personnel services necessary? There is really only one satisfactory approach to obtaining an answer to that question, and that approach is to ask another question: Can the institution's goals be achieved without the provision—by specially prepared professionals—of those services?

Higher education history suggests that, depending upon the stated goals, the answer to the second question is "No."

Student personnel services were created because college academic personnel could not or did not cope adequately with students' nonacademic developmental needs. There is little if any reason to believe that students on contemporary campuses would fare any better than did students of the post-Civil War era without aid from personnel workers. In contrast with higher education at the beginning of this century, campuses today and the society they represent are much more complex, the student bodies today are much more diverse, and academic and technical programs today are more numerous and more complex.

The elimination or drastic curtailment of student services on most campuses would seemingly signify a return to a philosophy of rationalism. Yet, as Brubacher and Rudy (1968) pointed out

> The higher learning in the United States has always been organized for informal "education" as well as formal "instruction." It has come to be interested in "the whole student"—in forming character as well as intelligence, in preparing men and women to be desirable citizens and persons as well as specialists and savants. Here again, we may well see in this unique "college life" the powerful influence of the democratic American community upon patterns of higher education. Certainly these characteristics mark off American student life from that of Continental Europe and even from that of the parent universities in England. (p. 400)

Does the democratic American community today want its higher education institutions to be governed by a philosophy that ignores all aspects of students' developmental needs except those which pertain to the intellect? Williamson (1961) provided examples of students whose needs likely would *not* be addressed if student services' personnel were not part of the institution's staff.

> The rehabilitation of failing students of high potential ability and the prevention of misuse of abilities are important areas of service. We seek to avoid, if possible, wastage of human resources by organizing both preventive and remedial services in education.
>
> Our advocacy of such a plan has drawn the charge that we desire or seek to coddle students, particularly those possessing modest or limited scholastic aptitude. In many instances, such a

> charge may be appropriate. However, when we operate at our best, we seek to help each individual achieve that level of effectiveness of which he is capable. We must admit that, to some of our critics, it may seem that we frequently help low-ability students find easy courses in which to enroll. Then, too, it may very well be that our efforts to help superior students achieve the optimum of their potential are not sufficiently visible to our faculty colleagues. Indeed, we readily observe that a tremendous amount of our effort is devoted to the failing and the near-failing student, who desperately comes for counseling or some other kind of service to avoid severance from alma mater. In spite of such partial observations, the record indicates that our complementary services have helped salvage and conserve human resources at all levels of capability. (pp. 15–16)

Support services on most contemporary campuses have been extended even beyond the program referred to by Williamson. Now, the active recruitment of students from low socioeconomic strata—especially the recruitment of academically disadvantaged minority youth—has become an accepted obligation of most American higher education institutions. Recruitment alone, however, is not enough. Once admitted, the minority student must be assisted to acquire the requisite academic skills and to overcome success-inhibiting self and social attitudes.

It is not just the failing or the academically disadvantaged student whose potential talents will be wasted. Ewing (1975), after an extensive review of the literature pertaining to college attrition and retention, concluded that approximately one-half of the students who withdraw from college "do so in good academic standing," and that "substantial numbers of the more gifted and creative students" drop out of college (p. 95). The type of evidence cited by Ewing (p. 56) as a basis for his conclusions is shown by the findings reported by Heist (1968).

> Observations in seven quite dissimilar schools indicated that the proportions of identified creatives withdrawing ranged from approximately 50 percent to 80 percent. In five out of seven of the particular institutions included in these analyses, a significantly higher proportion of the creative students on each campus left than did dropout students not identified as creative. The major conclusion to be drawn from the data is that the students who are ranked

> as creative or identified by measured characteristics of creativity either leave some colleges more frequently than or as frequently as all other students not so identified. (p. 54)

The examples given of services provided and the benefits to be derived from them are just a few of the kinds of services provided through student services' programs. The examples pertain to programs that can, when they are effective, produce readily observable, even spectacular, contributions. Yet, student personnel workers also must provide services in much less visible areas. Although the services' aspect is presented in more detail later in this chapter, a brief reference to a few specific services here indicates how essential these services have become. Take, for instance, admissions counseling. Initial college or program placement decisions are of vital importance to many students and to all institutions, but effective admissions counseling requires both expert knowledge of all of the program options available to students and career counseling skills. Consider also financial aids programs. Such programs can take on the characteristics of welfare programs if assistance is provided solely on the basis of economic criteria, or if students think they are looked upon as "welfare" recipients. The value systems, whether appropriately or inappropriately, of many American families may cause these students to reject available help if acceptance of such help seems to imply that they cannot stand on their own economic "feet."

Conversely, families whose incomes are too high to permit them to qualify for federal and state loan programs may become angry with the college representative who has to tell them this, and may even choose a different college because of their anger. Therefore, the personnel staffing financial aids offices must be able to discuss with students and parents in a very sensitive fashion the possible sources of assistance upon which they might draw. More specifically, college financial aids personnel must not only be familiar with a myriad of resources for scholarships, fellowships, and loans, they must also be proficient in the evaluation of applicants by the employment of complex criteria, and be highly skilled in interpersonal relations.

It would appear from the kinds of student needs addressed by admissions and financial aids personnel, that even these seemingly routine administrative areas require staffing by specially prepared individuals. Although some student services are undoubtedly being provided on most campuses today which have become nonfunctional because of changes in student needs or institutional structure, it is difficult to imagine a higher education institution attaining its stated goals without the assistance to students provided by student personnel workers.

To summarize this "foundations of student personnel" section, Fenske's (1980) excellent description of the evolution and current indispensability of student services seems most appropriate.

> Student services emerged and evolved by default, by taking over necessary and sometimes unpopular tasks abandoned by trustees, administrators, and faculty. It has grown into a ubiquitous but somewhat invisible empire in virtually every institution of higher education. During one rather brief period early in this century, it came fairly close to entering the mainstream of the academic program. In general, however, student services as a distinct professional role had never become thoroughly integrated into any of higher education's three principal functions of teaching, research, and service. By assuming, over the years, a multitude of student-related roles and activities yet by remaining estranged from the vital functions of the academic enterprise, student services finds itself in the peculiar situation of being indispensable but peripheral. (p. 3)

Student Personnel Programs

An Overview of Community and Junior Colleges

Community junior colleges were developed in response to postsecondary school educational needs that were not being addressed by four-year institutions. It is not surprising, therefore, that major differences exist between these two types of higher education institutions. Differences are found in student characteristics, and in institutional objectives, philosophies, and programs, for example. These differences may be seen more clearly in the following overview of the two-year college.

Progress in education has long been measured by the extension of educational opportunity and by the numbers of people taking advantage of that opportunity. Universal primary education was the first goal for American education. Once that was achieved, the push began for universal secondary education. Now the opportunity for universal education beyond high school is not far from realization. The junior college is a key to this realization, and its emerging importance was perhaps first signaled in the 1965 enrollment figure: 1,292,753 students—approximately 30 per cent of the eligible age group (Morrisett, 1967, pp. 12–14). In the period following World War II, the United States witnessed this phenomenal "growth of the junior college movement. By 1975, there were 1,230 junior colleges with an enrollment of 4,069,279 (Thompson, 1978, p. 11). The junior college has been labeled by some as the outstanding innovation in American education in the twentieth century. Whether one agrees with this opinion or even accepts the various claims being made for the educational powers of the junior college, one cannot deny its rapid expansion and influence on the changing character of American education.

With the 1968 opening of Nevada Community College at Elko, every state now has at least one junior college. Further, indications are that neither geographic nor population characteristics are limiting factors in junior college development. Such diverse locations as a rural community in New York, metropolitan centers like Cleveland and St. Louis, the desert community of Yuma, a resort area in the Virgin Islands, and a sparsely populated county in the upper reaches of Michigan opened junior colleges in the late 1960s, and none suffered from a lack of students. Educational history continues to prove that once educational opportunities exist, people will take advantage of them.

The Junior College Philosophy. Even though the community junior college is the most rapidly expanding collegiate institution in the United States, it is perhaps also the most misunderstood of all our educational institutions. Nor is this misunderstanding confined to the general public. Indications are that many secondary school counselors, teachers, and administrators still hold popular misconceptions of the educational offerings and characteristics of the junior college, viewing them as providing trade school programs without college credit. It is essential that the junior college staff member not only recognize his or her institutional philosophy but also becomes actively engaged in conveying this awareness to the supporting public.

Although the philosophies of community junior colleges will be understandably different in detail, a review of numerous published statements seem to indicate at least four commonly accepted principles that underlie the junior college philosophy.

The Community Junior College Is Community Oriented

Although community here is used in the broadest sense, the college is designed to serve the advanced educational needs of an identifiable population associated with a specific geographic area. Indeed, in many communities this institution is needed as a logical extension to the community's public school system.

The Community Junior College Provides a Comprehensive Program to Meet a Variety of Educational Needs

Programs typically include the traditional first two years of many collegiate academic programs and also a variety of terminal technical and vocational programs appropriate to the manpower and educational needs of a particular area. With few exceptions, these programs provide college credit.

The Community Junior College Provides Admissions Opportunities for Nearly All High School Graduates

As an institution that seeks to fill the void between high school and the traditional four-year college and which provides further educational opportunities for most youth, admissions requirements of junior colleges are appropriately minimal, requiring only that enrollees be high school graduates or that they provide some evidence of equivalent training.

Student Personnel and Guidance Programs Are Essential Services of the Community Junior College

The need for guidance is highlighted by the fact that the junior college is an open-door college. The two-year college has a responsibility for leading many of its students to face the reality of their situations. They come to college with high ambitions or hopes to enter medicine, teaching, engineering, or law—fields for which they may be unqualified. The junior college has an obligation to help such students achieve a self-understanding on the basis of which they can make realistic educational plans. (Johnson, 1965, pp. 376–380)

Characteristics of the Junior College Student. Although junior college authorities accept guidance as an important phase in the total program of their institutions (as surveys by Starr [1961] and others indicate), the distinguishing characteristics of the community junior college and its students are too significant to simply adopt a scaled-down version of the college guidance program or a souped-up model of the high school guidance program. As noted, the community junior college is a unique educational institution, and its very nature attracts a student body that is also unique. The most obvious of these unique characteristics is the wide diversity of students enrolled. This diversity is ensured by the wide variety of course offerings and programs that attract students of divergent interests, ages, and backgrounds.

Other differences usually noted are a larger portion of part-time students, more employed students, more married students, and a predominantly, if not exclusively, local or commuting student body.

Student Personnel Program Objectives of Community and Junior Colleges

GENERAL OBJECTIVES. Student personnel program objectives of both two- and four-year institutions are derived from institutional objectives, student needs relative to the institution's goals and programs, and the student personnel point of view. The general objectives of community junior colleges, however, will be similar inasmuch as most community colleges have been created for the same basic purposes: to provide additional educational opportunities in keeping with the concept of universal education, and to help meet the employment needs of the nation.

In advocating a student development approach to junior college student personnel work, O'Banion, Thurston, and Gulden (1972) envisioned the outcomes of such an approach to be student increases in

1. Intellectual understanding
2. Skill competencies
3. Socially responsible behavior
4. Flexibility and creativity
5. Awareness of self and others
6. Acceptance of self and others

7. Courage to explore and experiment
8. Openness to experience
9. Efficient and effective ability to learn
10. Ability to respond positively to change
11. A useful value system
12. A satisfying life style. (p. 203)

The statements of envisioned "outcomes" excellently depict the general goals of community junior college student personnel programs. The general goals, restated, would be, "To facilitate the development of intellectual understanding," "to assist students in the development of socially responsible behavior," and so on. Included among the general objectives of community junior college student personnel programs should minimally be added those of facilitating the student's admission and orientation, appropriate program placement, college retention (including financial aspects), and meaningful postcollege placement.

SPECIFIC OBJECTIVES. The specific objectives of a community junior college student personnel program must be formulated for *that* institution. Most student personnel programs, though, will minimally have the following specific objectives

1. To provide information about the institution, its purposes, and its programs to applicants, prospective applicants, and the community at large.
2. To assist the student with the admissions process.
3. To orient the student to the college, its procedures, and its programs.
4. To determine the unique needs, interests, and characteristics of each student.
5. To provide career information and counseling for each student.
6. To assist each student to develop meaningful educational and vocational goals.
7. To provide assistance in overcoming academic skills' deficiencies and academically inhibiting attitudes.
8. To assist each student to obtain—and modify as needed—appropriate course and program replacement.
9. To assist each student to obtain financial aid, including part-time employment, as needed.

10. To assist the faculty to understand, and provide program advisement and instruction in accord with, the student's needs and abilities.
11. To assist the students "to enhance their persons and their lives, enriching them and enabling them to live more fully and effectively." (Vitalo, 1974, p. 34)
12. To provide needed health appraisal and services.
13. To regulate social and other college activities, and assist in the enforcement of all college regulations as dictated by the college structure, policies, and programs.
14. To assist students to utilize services provided by community, state, and federal agencies, such as vocational rehabilitation, drug and alcohol counseling programs, and veterans' affairs.
15. To help students procure appropriate job placements and/or transfer to other colleges and universities.

TYPICAL PROGRAM SERVICES OR FUNCTIONS. To achieve the stated student personnel program objectives a program of student services must be provided. Although the student services' components on community junior college campuses carry the same basic labels as those on four-year campuses, there will be apparent differences in the implementation of the services (Schneider, 1977, p. 465). Typical services and personnel-worker functions are as follows:

Admissions and Orientation. This service would provide for the dissemination of pre-enrollment information, assessment, and advising of potential students, and pre-college or entry educational testing. Both individual and group orientation and entry adjustment activities would be determined. Both the admissions and orientation activities must reflect the fact that many students will not be recent high school graduates or will not be planning to enroll full time. The admissions service will be challenged to create an awareness of and re-educational opportunities among all potential enrollees, youths, and adults in the service area of the college.

Individual Counseling and Advisement. The junior college student must be provided with a planned program of educational and vocational advisement. In addition, the availability of personal counseling for development, adjustment, and decision making is essential. The scope of the counseling service in the junior college will be wide ranging and diverse and may include unique services not usually found in either high school or four-year college programs, such as rehabilitation, retirement, employment, career-reorientation, and marital counseling.

Student Services. Those student services that are appropriately the concern of the junior college student personnel and guidance program include financial assistance, student activities, and occupational-educational placement. In rare instances, housing (and related food services) may also be the legitimate concern of student personnel workers. Whereas the actual operation of the student health service is rightfully the prerogative of professional medical personnel, the student personnel and guidance services program has an interest in seeing that such a service is provided and that a cooperative and complementary relationship exists between the student personnel and the medical staff. In each instance these services must reflect the uniqueness of the individual community junior college and its student population.

Assessment and Placement. Student assessment involves the collection, organization, synthesis, and interpretation of available information for understanding the individual student. Effective placement is dependent on an assessment of the individual's assets and liabilities related to his or her educational-vocational-personal planning and progress. Placement may include part-time or full-time job placement, enrollment in an appropriate curriculum, direction into meaningful activities, and matriculation into advanced educational programs. The community junior college's unique role of providing new educational horizons for many individuals of varied ages and backgrounds while remaining sensitive to employment needs and developments can place a new emphasis on this traditional student personnel service. Effective assessment and placement requires follow-up procedures to investigate and evaluate the results of the program placement practices.

Four-Year Colleges and Universities

Overview. The overall or primary objective of student personnel programs in four-year institutions is to implement the "personnel point of view" philosophy. Obviously an objective that is broad in scope provides little if any help for program planning. To be of planning value the "point of view" must be translated into more visible objectives. From that philosophy, therefore, both general and specific objectives of student personnel programs have been derived by student personnel leaders. Broad, general objectives provide general program direction and are helpful in determining and communicating the purposes of a student personnel program. Specific objectives show needed program services and personnel worker functions.

The kinds of goals and/or objectives that are established for a personnel program will be determined by the role assigned to the program by an institution's president and its student personnel administrators. If the perceived role is "student development," the objectives will be designed to implement, through integration into the instructional program, a "total student" development goal. If a more traditional role is envisioned, the objectives will pertain to services that facilitate but are separate from (complementary to) the instructional program. General objectives (or goals) representing both approaches to student personnel campus roles are presented in the following section. Appendix F contains a statement regarding the role of post secondary school counselors.

Program Objectives. GENERAL OBJECTIVES. Mueller (1961) identified four general objectives of the student personnel worker.

Preserving, Transmitting, and Enriching the Culture. As interpreted by Mueller, higher education's primary goal is "to teach the student his culture, and it is principally the job of the faculty." The student personnel worker's responsibilities are to eliminate insofar as possible such obstacles to learning as financial, emotional, or physical stress, and to "relieve the classroom teacher of much of his responsibility for the students' extraclass behavior, so that the teacher may have time to fulfill his own obligations to scholarship." The major responsibility of the personnel worker, however, is the inculcation of "our cultural heritage by promoting the intellectual approach to all aspects of campus life" (pp. 64–65).

Developing All Aspects of the Personality. Implementation of the personnel point of view, which stresses the wholeness of the individual, necessitates that the student personnel worker undertake "the task of developing and co-ordinating all the other aspects of personality as they are needed to promote the intellectual." The other aspects to which Mueller alluded are "Temperament, character, physical traits, and interests." Mueller envisioned each aspect as having "special involvement in intellectual progress." Moreover, "All these aspects require the practice and experience gained from the extracurricular programs for their proper development and maturity" (pp. 65–66).

Training for Citizenship. "The personnel division will provide practice in (the) techniques and attitudes of good citizenship appropriate to the post-adolescent years and to the higher intellectual and socio-economic levels" (p. 66).

Training for Leadership. If training leaders is an obligation of higher education, student personnel workers must help to identify and motivate potential leaders and assist them to develop the personality traits that will enable them to work effectively. Minimally essential student personnel services will be "full programs of testing, vocational advising and placement" (p. 66).

Mueller's interpretation of the objectives—especially her emphasis on their implementation through the extracurriculum—accurately reflects the traditional "complementary functions" approach to student personnel work. The "complementary functions" approach is based on the belief that the "point of view" philosophy can be effectively implemented through the provision of student services which are separate from, but supportive of, the academic program.

Proponents of the student development approach to student personnel work also utilize the "point of view" philosophy—although an expanded version of it has been recommended (Miller and Prince, 1976, pp. 4–5)—to justify the goals of student personnel programs. They view the *implementation* of the philosophy much differently, however, and therefore the derived goals and/or objectives take on a different character. Actually, as defined by student development proponents, the terms *goals* and *objectives* are *not* interchangeable. In student development literature "goals" are the general or long-range aims whereas "objectives" specify the actions or steps that must be taken to achieve the stipulated goals. "Goal setting is the process of stating the general outcome desired and then defining the more specific results (objectives) that guide the steps in achieving the goals and that provide evidence of accomplishment" (Miller and Prince, 1976, p. 27). In traditional student personnel programs, activities have been emphasized rather than students' learning,

> but in the student development model, program goals are the outcomes expected from students' participation in a given developmental activity. Stating objectives in this way directs attention to the student and to the types of behavior he or she is expected to exhibit as a result of a particular experience. This shift in focus from the student affairs staff to the student and from the activity to the result—should be the intent of developmental programming and should establish a framework for selecting evaluation criteria and procedures. In effect, the student developmental model emphasizes students as developing learners instead of the programs developed to serve them. (Miller and Prince, 1976, p. 27)

Examples of student development goals or general aims—other than the facilitation of the development of the "whole student"—are difficult to find in student development literature. Brown (1980) alluded to the problem when he stated: "For nearly a decade now, the specific content of student development has remained amorphous. Student development *toward* what or *for* what has, in fact, not been considered. If there has been a focus, it has been on interpersonal skills, but most often the focus has been as non-specific as 'self-direction' " (p. 192). As perceived by Brown

> The dimensions of student development include (1) personal identity, which includes having a sense of purpose, a value system, and a vocational (in the broad sense of that term) purpose; (2) interpersonal development, which includes communication skills, ability to understand and empathize with others and to give others emotional support, and group interaction skills; (3) intellectual and academic skills, which permit the individual to engage in life-long learning; (4) aesthetic development, which includes both an awareness of the arts and some sense of personal skill in both appreciation and creation; and (5) physical recreation skills, which, like aesthetic development, include both appreciation and participation (1980, p. 192)

SPECIFIC OBJECTIVES. Examples of specific program objectives are provided here, but as Williamson (1961) pointed out: "Policy making, or the determination of program objectives, must grow out of the local institutional policies, programs, and objectives" (p. 110). Moreover, the determination of objectives is an ongoing process. Williamson emphasized that objectives are not "permanently carved in stone." It is necessary, therefore, that the questions "What are we trying to do? and Why?" be asked almost continually, and that the objectives be modified in accord with the derived purposes (Williamson, 1961, p. 110).

McDavis (1974), in developing and validating an instrument for the evaluation of student personnel programs, compiled an excellent and very comprehensive list of "minimally essential student personnel services' objectives." He constructed a forty-four-item scale that was divided into the following categories and subdivisions

Assistance to Students

1. Assisting students to develop self-understanding and self-identities
2. Assisting students to become self-directed
3. Assisting students to develop values
4. Assisting students to develop interpersonal relations
5. Assisting students to develop educational and career objectives
6. Assisting students to develop leadership and citizenship competencies
7. Assisting students to participate in co-curricula activities

Assistance to University Community

1. Assisting to develop a campus atmosphere
2. Assisting to humanize the university community
3. Assisting to individualize the university community
4. Assisting to interpret student life

Assistance to Faculty

1. Assisting faculty to educate students
2. Assisting faculty to interpret student life

Asssistance to Administration

1. Assisting administration to administer student services
2. Assisting administration to interpret student life

(pp. 103–107)

Typical Program Services or Functions. McDavis (1974) reported that the following services and/or functions typified student personnel programs: counseling and testing services, financial aid programs, health services, orientation programs, placement services, veterans and foreign student services, student housing, student conduct, student government, student activities, student publications, student organizations, and student union (p. 121).

The specific services provided by personnel workers will vary from campus to campus as student and institutional needs dictate. On some campuses only a few of the listed services will be provided, and on other campuses services are provided which are not included in the list. Also, there may be considerable differences among institutions in the functions performed under identically named services. Ayers, Tripp, and Russel (1966), for example, found that "counseling might range from conventional faculty academic advisement to psychotherapy conducted by psychiatrists, and testing definitions could range from the common entrance examinations to the administering of complex psychometric programs by trained professionals. Financial aids and awards practices may denote raising funds for this purpose, administering private loan and scholarship programs, or managing hundreds of thousands of dollars under Federal aid programs" (p. 43).

Because of the great variations among four-year institutions in size, type, purpose, administrative organizational structure, administrative philosophy, identified student needs, definitions of student services' activities, et cetera, the needed services and activities must be individually determined and defined for a specific institution. Excellent assistance in student services' development may be obtained from books such as Delworth, Hanson, and Associates' (1980) *Student Services*, and *College Student Personnel Services*, edited by Packwood (1977).

Student Personnel Program Management

IS STRUCTURE IMPORTANT?

There are differences of opinion about the importance of structure in the implementation of an effective student personnel program. Some student personnel leaders state that structure is *essential,* whereas others believe it to be important, but less important than other functions. Both viewpoints are presented.

Structure, according to Williamson (1961),

> . . . refers to the way in which services are organized and in which they function through the efforts of staff members. . . . an administrative structure consist(s) of the following:
>
> 1. A plan composed of explicit parts or special programs, each of which should be assigned as a responsibility to particular staff
> 2. Formal or readily identifiable directives assigning to a particular member of the staff responsibility and authority for performance of functions included in the general plan of program
> 3. One or more members of the staff who, because of special interest, training, and skills, are judged qualified to perform each function
> 4. Special office location visible to students where the services are to be performed
> 5. Such special equipment and facilities as are necessary in the performance of the functions. (p. 74)

O'Banion and Thurston (1972) believed it to be requisite ". . . that student personnel services be organized in a manner that enables them to permeate the entire campus" (p. 9). O'Banion and Thurston recognized differences of opinion about the issue of structure. They noted that both highly centralized student services programs and decentralized personnel functions have advocates, but whichever structural model is chosen, overall direction of the personnel program is very important. "The parts of the program must be looked upon as a total program with general direction and sufficient administration to insure coverage of the field, implementation of the services, continuous in-service training of workers, and continuing evaluation of the program's effectiveness" (O'Banion and Thurston, 1972, p. 10). Although the O'Banion-Thurston statements were directed at junior college student personnel programs, they apply also to personnel programs in four-year institutions.

Mueller (1961), too, believed that student personnel structure is essential. She wrote that

> on any campus a stable and well-publicized structure for personnel functions is imperative. Some centralization is necessary, and some

> decentralization is equally important in order to distribute the responsibilities and to reach the largest number of students directly. Of primary importance is the proper balance of emphasis to promote the best interests of the total group; for this some degree of centralization under well-trained and experienced administrators is the only answer. (p. 143)

Other student services' leaders, especially student development advocates, see program structure as being of secondary importance to an effective program. Miller and Prince (1976) stated that "the key to a successful student development program is the imaginative and efficient use of available resources, not the organizational structure within which it operates" (p. 156). They added, however, that since "the structure does influence programming," changing a program to a student development approach will probably require modification of the existing structure (pp. 156–157).

Crookston and Atkyns (1974) found, in a survey of institutions throughout the country, that student services' programs were typically structured in one of three ways. Approximately 80 per cent of the institutions surveyed used a centralized line-staff structure (Figure 9–1) in which all service units reported to a chief student services officer.

The second most prevalently used structure was a decentralized approach in which three or more services were clustered into units supervised by a director who reported to a chief student services officer (Figure 9–2). That approach was employed by 11 per cent of the institutions in the sample.

The third administrative structure, used by 1.3 per cent of the institutions surveyed, was a decentralized plan that employed two divisions: programs and structures (Figure 9–3). Each of the

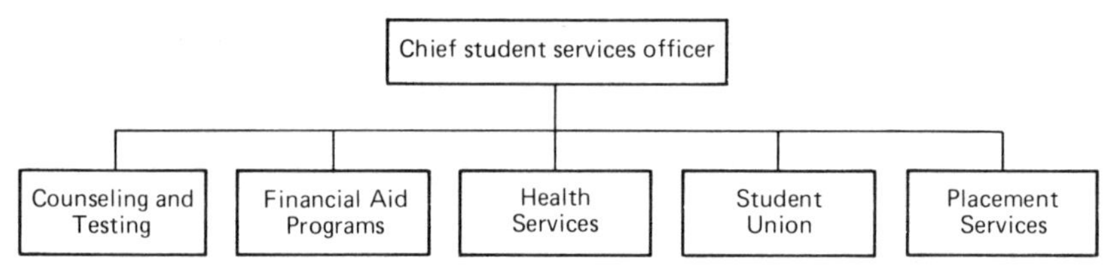

FIGURE 9–1. Centralized Line-Staff Structure of Student Services (Modeled after Miller and Prince, 1976, p. 157).

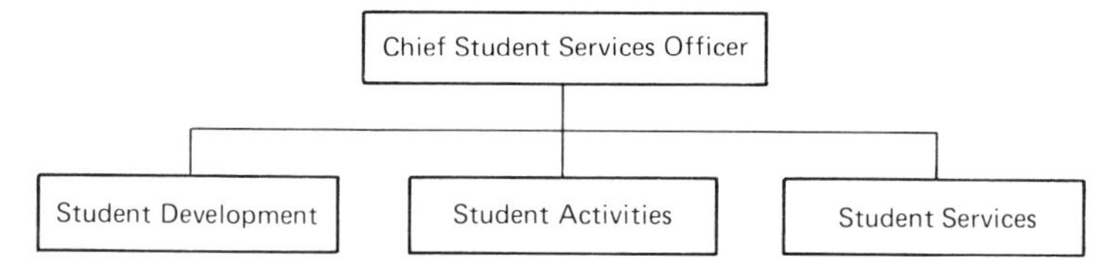

FIGURE 9–2. Decentralized Line-Staff Structure with Three Subdivisions (Modeled after Miller and Prince, 1976, p. 157).

divisions was headed by a director, and the overall program was coordinated by a chief student services officer (Miller and Prince, 1976, p. 157).

Some degree of structure *is* necessary for effective student personnel program management. As indicated by the Crookston-Atkyns findings, the majority of institutions have adopted a centralized line-staff structure. A major difficulty with that administrative structure is that it does not facilitate interservice communication; the staff of each service tend to be concerned almost solely with their own segment of the personnel program. The decentralized approaches represent attempts to improve communication and cooperation among all of the staff, and thus obtain a coordinated team approach to student development. Whether the decentralized approaches to student personnel structure will result in more effective student personnel programs, or will facilitate the integration of academic and student services programs, still remains to be seen. It may be concluded, however, that *some* type of structure must be employed, and that the management responsibilities of each level of that structure must be clearly defined, communicated, and implemented.

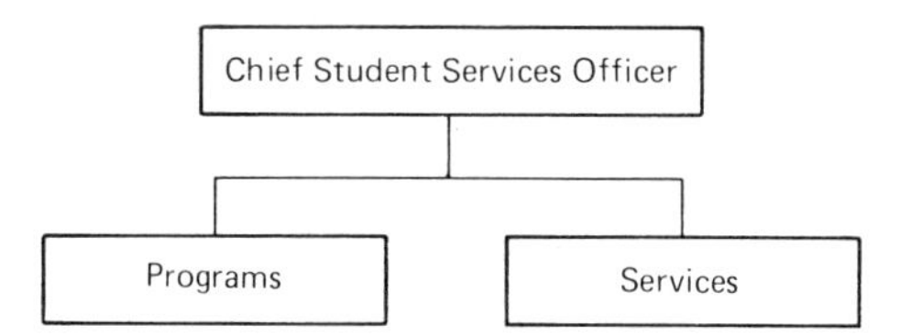

FIGURE 9–3. Decentralized Line-Staff Structure with Two Subdivisions (Modeled after Miller and Prince, 1976, p. 158).

REQUISITE STAFF

The number of staff needed and the qualifications the staff must have to provide an effective program of student services will be determined by such factors as institutional size, institutional mission, institutional administrative structure, identified needs of the institution's students, and the perceived role of student services in the total institutional program. The selection of professional staff members will be greatly influenced if not totally governed by the organizational structure of the student services' program. For example, a centralized line-staff structure will require the placement of specialists in each of the designated service areas, and the "specialist" in one area may have only minimal understandings of the functioning of other student services' areas. Conversely, a decentralized, multiple-program structure will necessitate initial staff specialization in one area, but will ultimately require staff to be enabled to work effectively in all areas of student development.

Regardless of program orientation or structure, the professional personnel staff must have had appropriate professional preparation. As Mueller (1961) pointed out, "To have the confidence of others and the privilege of freedom of action, one must have the knowledge of his field at his command. Popularity, character, and influence are not substitutes for training and experience" (p. 128). Similarly, Packwood (1977) stated that

> College student personnel workers can, as they have throughout the profession's history, make the job bigger and better. To do the job and to do it bigger and better requires commitment of a professional magnitude. Nothing less will see the college student personnel worker through an eighteen-hour day. It requires professional knowledge and skills or a willingness to acquire them. It requires interest in and satisfaction from getting the technical aspects of the job done well. It requires a strong role definition with the ability to articulate it and act according to it. Then, after the job is being performed well, are the professional resources again drawn upon to do the job better: to move, say, admissions or financial aid into a student development framework. Without first being a service specialist, one cannot become a student development specialist or behavioral scientist. . . . Both specialists are professionals, the latter is preferable—and ideal. (p. xxvi)

Characteristics of Effective Programs

Effective student services' programs require "commitment, support, plan, staff, and operational theory" (McDaniel and Lombardi, 1972, p. 89). Essential elements of a student personnel program, according to Schneider (1977), are

1. Coordination to assume that the student personnel program reflects the institution's philosophy and objectives, that all students on the campus are reached, and that the student personnel program is integrated with the instructional programs.
2. A favorable climate for student personnel programs
3. Qualified staff and continuing emphasis on staff development
4. Specifically defined staff roles
5. Meaningful developmental programs
6. Continuous program evaluation and research
7. The provision of sufficient and convenient physical facilities. (pp. 458–462)

Excellent channels for communication among all members of a college community and high levels of trust also characterize effective student personnel programs (Berdie, 1974, p. 182).

From a student development perspective, a set of principles that underlie successful program implementation was formulated by the ACPA Conference on Organizing for Student Development held in 1976. As reported by Miller and Prince (1976) those principles are

1. The self-renewing organization should set goals and make decisions that are congruent with the mission of the college.
2. Since all the components of the system are connected and interdependent, any planned change will touch everyone in some way. Therefore, the planners must make sure that all the members understand what the proposed change is supposed to accomplish and that they share a commitment to it.
3. All available resources—physical, financial and human—should be integrated so that the organization can respond effectively to current needs as well as plan for the future.
4. The decision makers must establish an open communication system in which every participant gives and receives timely and accurate evaluations.

5. The organization should have regular evaluation procedures to assess both its means and its ends.
6. This healthy organization should have a climate that stimulates and supports personal and professional development by its members. (p. 154)

Program Accreditation

An evaluation of an institution's student services program is an integral component of that institution's accreditation review. It is important, therefore, that student personnel workers become familiar with the accreditation process to enable them to assist in the institution's accreditation review and, even more importantly, to enable them to determine if the student services program is fulfilling its intended purposes.

An excellent "working definition" of accreditation has been provided by Kells (1980)

> Accreditation is a voluntary, nongovernmental process conducted by postsecondary institutions to accomplish at least two things—to attempt to hold one another accountable on a periodic basis to live up to stated, appropriate institutional or program goals; and to assess the extent to which the institution or program meets established standards. (p. 9)

According to Dressel (1976), the purposes of accreditation are to

1. certify to the general public, to government, and to other institutions the minimal qualifications of the institutions accredited;
2. provide limited protection against degree mills and disreputable educational practices;
3. provide counsel and assistance to new and developing institutions moving toward accreditation;
4. encourage improvement in institutions by a review of activities, by development of recommendations regarding program quality, and by preparation of guidelines for assessing educational effectiveness;
5. encourage continuous self-study and evaluation;
6. provide a basis for assuring that institutions are worthy of assistance from various federal programs; and

7. provide some protection to institutions against threatened encroachments on their autonomy, which might also destroy educational quality. (p. 405)

Despite the fact that the colleges and universities in the United States which seek accreditation through one of the country's six regional accrediting associations do so voluntarily, accreditation has become so important to higher education institutions that whether or not to seek accreditation may no longer be an option. As Kells (1980) observed, "The (accreditation) process is voluntary only to the extent that an institution is not influenced by the high percentage of institutions that already have been accredited or by the possibility that, without accreditation, eligibility to apply for federal funds might be denied—an aspect added to the process by Congress in the 1960s" (p. 9).

The accreditation process is designed to require, and to suggest procedures for, institutional self-study. Self-study—an approach to evaluating institutional effectiveness—is a requisite first step in obtaining accreditation. The benefits of self-study are such, however, that institutions and programs should not have to be prodded into undertaking internal evaluations of effectiveness just to comply with accreditation requirements. Kells (1980) wrote that "If postsecondary institutions were more like non-educational, profit-seeking, product-oriented businesses, they would conduct useful self-study processes continuously or they would perish" (p. 8).

Accrediting associations both encourage and attempt to facilitate ongoing institutional and program self-evaluation. The North Central Association Handbook on Accreditation (1975), for example, states that "Self-study connotes a special institutional preparation for accreditation which will enable the institution to develop a framework for continued assessment" (p. 61).

Self-study for accreditation review typically includes an analysis or evaluation of the institution's goals and statement of purposes, of educational and learning experiences, of resources for providing educational learning experiences and implementing the goals and objectives, and of the dynamics of the institution—its approaches to decision making and planning (*North Central Association Handbook*, 1975, pp. 62–71).

Kells (1980) believes that if a self-study is to be meaningful, it should not be undertaken just to satisfy accreditation or other external visitation teams. Instead, it should be undertaken as a means to improve thc institution's or program's effectiveness. In other words, a self-study should be internally, not externally, motivated (p. 16). Moreover, "the top leadership must be committed to the process," and "the design of the study must be appropriate to the circumstances of the institution" (p. 16).

For student services evaluation in conjunction with accreditation review, the North Central Association suggests the use of the following "Basic Criteria of Evaluation and Points of Inquiry to Demonstrate Accredidation of the Institution" (p. 14).

Basic Criteria of Evaluation and Points of Inquiry to Demonstrate Accredidation of the Institution

Schedule 4
Student Services

1. Is the management of student personnel services properly exercised and executed to achieve the mission and purposes of the institution?
2. Are student personnel services properly structured to achieve the mission and purpose of the institution?
3. Are there appropriate codification and publication of policies and procedures of student personnel services?
4. Are the student personnel services of sufficient kind and quality to achieve the mission and purpose of the institution? Examples of which may be the following.
5. Are student personnel services adequately staffed?
6. Other

1. Is there evidence that an overall rationale, a statement of goals and objectives, guides the efforts and energies of the professional staff of student services?
2. Are the student services staff appropriately involved in decisions about the institution and its functions?
   a. Does the student personnel staff enjoy access to and have positive relationships with:
      1. teaching faculty
      2. student groups
      3. campus administrators

   b. Does the chief student personnel officer have immediate access to the president and other appropriate officers?
   c. Is there good communication within and among the student affairs offices?
3. Do the program offerings of student services reflect the needs of the institution and its several sub-populations of students; e.g., adult learners, veterans, minority students, handicapped students, individuals with acute problems, or individuals with learning problems, etc.
   a. Do students, faculty and administrators feel that student services is meeting the needs of the intitution?
   b. Does the student affairs unit have mechanisms available for easy communication with faculty committees and is there adequate representation on various institutional committees concerned with student services?
4. Are financial resources sufficient to carry out the goals and objectives of the student services area?
5. Does the work performnce of the staff reflect the training and competency that is needed throughout the institution?
6. Are staff members by virtue of their training and experience competent to perform the tasks assigned?
   a. Is there a systematic evaluation plan for staff members?
   b. Is there a professional development program (which may include sabbaticals, released time, grants, etc.) or in-service training programs to enhance job performance?
7. Are the programs of the office of student affairs explained adequately in appropriate publications?
8. To what extent is there participation in the various programs?
   a. What programs appear to be succeeding or failing?
9. Is the office of financial aid appropriately administered and meeting its objectives and the needs of students?
   a. Are applications for funds, suitably and appropriately processed?
   b. Is the fiscal operations report and the institution's position in agreement with the federal government?
   c. Is the delinquency rate on loans too high?
10. Is the career development and placement office appropriately administered in relation to its objectives and the needs of students?
11. Is the campus or institutional security system appropriately administered and does it meet its objectives and the needs of students?
12. Is the portion of the budget spent on intercollegiate athletics

realistic and appropriate in terms of the mission and purpose of the institution?

13. Does the institution adequately publicize the laws for the protection of student rights?
14. What evidence exists to judge the success of the student affairs programs?
15. Other

Utilization of the NCA evaluational materials for self-study of the student services program should be very beneficial, and it should not take an impending accreditation visit to motivate such program review.

Summary and Implications

Student personnel program management in higher education is a popular role for many counseling professionals. In this role the program manager directs the many student personnel specialists serving students in a variety of higher education settings representing levels from community and technical colleges through universities with advanced graduate programs. In these various settings, counseling program development must, as in other differing environmental settings, reflect the characteristics of the setting and the target population they are designed to serve.

In general, the following services or functions typify student personnel programs in higher education: counseling and testing services; financial aid programs; health services; orientation programs; placement services; student housing; student conduct; student government; student activities; student organizations; student publications; student unions and on many campuses, veterans and foreign student services. A variety of models for delivering these services were identified, but regardless of the model used, some type of structure must be employed and the management responsibilities of each level of that structure must be clearly designed, communicated, and implemented. Further, the professional personnel staff that implements the functioning of a model must, as in all other counseling settings, have appropriate professional preparation. The effectiveness of the program's functioning and the responsibility of program managers to be accountable also implies the importance of evaluation. This evaluation will frequently become a part of the higher education institution's accreditation review and, therefore, program managers must be familiar with this process. Thus, whereas student personnel programs in higher education are more varied in their components than their counseling counterparts in other school and agency settings, we nonetheless conclude that the most effective manager for such programs must, as in other settings, be a trained professional counseling specialist.

CHAPTER 10

Counseling Programs in Noneducational Settings

Introduction and Overview

The history of the counseling profession suggests that counseling programs have been initiated, almost invariably, in response to the needs of major segments of the population for assistance which could not be or was not being provided through traditional institutions. For example,

- higher education counseling was provided in response to student and administrative needs that would no longer be addressed through traditional approaches;
- the importance of providing secondary school counseling oriented toward educational and vocational concerns was recognized during the economic difficulties of the 1930s;
- counseling services were made available by the Veterans Administration to former Armed Forces personnel in virtually every major American city following World War II;
- the steadily increasing proportion of divorces and the reports of crises and breakups led to a great expansion of marriage and family counseling throughout the country.

Thus, it would appear that when a sufficient number of individuals in a given setting are encountering unusual adjustive difficulties, counseling services are initiated in an attempt to assist them. How one tells when a "sufficient number" need help to warrant the provision of counseling has not been made clear. Nor is it clear that the proliferation of counseling services can be attributed to this oversimplified explanation of the development of counseling programs for new target populations. More likely, it is the outgrowth of what we might call a "mental health evolution" that began over 100 years ago with a growing public concern for the humane treatment of the insane, stimulated later by the popularity both in Europe and the United States of Sigmund Freud and his disciples. Later, in this century we can identify specific events and individuals (i.e., Public Law 88-164 [1963]* Parsons, Beers, Rogers) associated with the growing interest in the broad spectrum of mental health, but more subtly and perhaps more significantly has been a gradual but increased interest in the psychological well-being of all age groups from children through the elderly, the development of new professional specialists to serve the needs of unique populations, and the emergence of counseling services in a wide range of institutional and agency settings. In recent generations we might also associate the emergence of community mental health centers with the broader social revolution seeking increased civil rights for all.

It has become obvious, however, that counseling assistance is now being made available in or pertaining to virtually every conceivable type of community agency and/or institution. The envisioned roles and functions of the counselor in several community settings are briefly examined in this chapter, but the counseling settings reviewed provide discussions of only *some* of the many different settings in which counselors are employed.

Underlying Assumptions and Basic Principles

Counseling programs in community and other institutional or agency settings represent a wide range of approaches for delivering the services of this helping profession to the citizenry. The development and implementation of these services is based on

*Public Law 88-164, The Mental Retardation Facilities and Community Mental Health Centers Construction Act of 1963, enacted by U.S. Congress, October 31, 1963.

certain underlying assumptions and basic principles, some of which are specified in the following paragraphs.

Underlying Assumptions

Access to mental health services are a civil right. The Community Mental Health Centers Act clearly indicates that all citizens, regardless of residency, will have access when needed to an agency's services and that these services will be provided regardless of the race, creed, or ethnic origin of the applicant. Provisions for services are also made for those individuals who are limited in their ability to pay. It is a basic assumption that all citizens have the right to receive professional help as needed in the prevention and/or treatment of their mental health disorders—and that such help shall be reasonably accessible.

Public mental health services recognize the broad range of prevention/treatment needs of our citizenry. The broad range of agencies catering to special populations (e.g., aged, youth, unemployed, and hospitalized) and special problems (e.g., substance abuse, marital concerns, and vocational rehabilitation) are in response to a recognition of a broad range of specialized needs. Most community mental health agencies are also capable and do respond to a broad spectrum of needs. Typically, such centers offer in-patient and out-patient services, emergency services, and educational and consultation services. Many centers also provide partial hospitalization services, diagnostic services, and precare/postcare in the community through home visitation programs, "halfway" houses, and foster home placement.

Mental health agencies are primarily staffed by professionals and managed by professionals. It must be assumed that the clients of mental health agencies anticipate a high quality of professional help in coping with their needs that can only come from a qualified helping professional. Although many agencies use paraprofessionals and others in helpful roles, the critical tasks involved in diagnosis and treatment demand the competencies of the trained professional. As with school counseling programs, the management of agency counseling programs must be in the hands of a competent professional whose training background may be in medicine (psychiatry), counseling, clinical or counseling psychology, or social work, but who is at the same time capable of working effectively with an interdisciplinary team. Professional management also increases the likelihood that professional standards will be maintained.

Mental health services are based on client needs, environmental influences, and the agency's capacity and mandate to respond. This assumption is based on the related principles of accountability and relevance. It assumes that services are a response to identified needs and that these services are provided as efficiently and effectively as possible. It also recognizes the uniqueness of the agency's "mission," especially those where ethical and/or legal limitations to services have been established.

Community involvement is important for community mental health agencies. The community mental health center represents a movement toward community recognition of, and responsibility for, the mental well-being of its residents. It is therefore mandatory that community agencies become integrated into the life of the community and have appropriate associations with the communities' agencies and institutions. It is also important that community "input" into the development and operation of a community agency be ensured by a broadly based responsible board of community leaders.

Basic Principles

The basic assumption that community involvement is essential for relevant and accountable community mental health agencies has implications for the basic principles of those agencies that are community-based. Bloom (1977) has suggested seven such principles for the guidance of professional personnel employed in community mental health agencies as follows. (These might be paraphrased slightly for noncommunity based mental health agencies).

Principle 1: Regardless of Where Your Paycheck Comes from, Think of Yourself as Working for the Community
Mental-health programs in the community should be determined by a process of negotiation open to all members of the community. The ultimate power for deciding the nature of the community-based mental-health program should rest with the community, and the mental health professional should work in the community only as long as he or she feels a sense

of congruence between the program desired by the community and his or her own personal and professional value systems.

Principle 2: If You Want to Know About a Community's Mental Health Needs, Ask the Community

It is important that, in the process of determining community-mental-health needs, planners don't limit themselves to asking the opinions of human-service-agency personnel or extrapolating from present mental-health-service statistics. There are at least three other ways to identify community needs. First, public hearings can be held in which members of the community who have something to say abut mental-health needs—their own or those of their family, their friends, or the entire community—can be heard. Second, systematic household surveys can be undertaken in which some sample of persons in the community is identified and interviewed about their impressions of mental-health-related needs in the community. Third, psychiatric patients themselves are an invaluable source of information regarding community-mental-health needs. When a patient is ready to be discharged from psychiatric care, an opportunity presents itself to turn to him or her for help in exchange for the help he or she has received. Ex-patients can be asked what they feel are the needs for mental-health-related services in the community. One question that would be particularly useful to ask former psychiatric patients is how the community (the neighborhood or the larger community) would have had to be structured in order for them not to have developed those kinds of disorganized or disturbing behaviors that resulted in their seeking psychiatric care. A related question would be about what things would have had to have happened differently in their own histories in order for them not to have required psychiatric care.

Principle 3: As You Learn About Community-mental-health-Related Needs, You Have the Responsibility to Tell the Community What You Are Learning

This principle puts the mental-health professional in the role of community educator. The mental-health professional is in an excellent position to learn about situations in the community that need to be corrected and should bring to the community's attention these unmet mental-health needs and the proposals for action designed to meet them.

Principle 4: Help the Community Establish Its Own Priorities
When community-mental-health needs have been identified, it is reasonable to expect that the resources available to the community will not be sufficient to meet all of them. Representatives of the community should play a major role in deciding which needs will be met first and how the limited resources will be divided among the various identified needs. It is theoretically possible, of course, for needs to conflict with each other; that is, in the very act of meeting one need, a program exacerbates the situation with respect to another need. Out of the identification of these kinds of conflicts, programs can emerge that satisfy the entire community.

Principle 5: You Can Help the Community Decide Among Various Courses of Action in Its Efforts to Solve Its Own Problems
This is a special and perhaps unique role for mental-health professionals, who are acquainted not only with needs and with strategies for meeting them used by other communities but also with empirical research results. This knowledge can help them advise the community when it tries to decide among various courses of action. The mental-health professional can identify high-risk groups in the community and discuss alternative ways of dealing with the problems of these groups.

Principle 6: In the Event that the Community Being Served Is So Disorganized That Representatives of Various Facets of the Community Cannot be Found, You Have the Responsibility to Help Find Such Representatives
It is crucial for mental-health professionals to be in good communication with the entire community and its representatives and not merely with selected members of an entrenched power group. Mental-health professionals should be certain that the policy-making board of the mental-health center is organized in such a way that the members of the

board represent all sociocultural groups and socioeconomic levels within the community.

Principle 7: You Should Work Toward the Equitable Distribution of Power in the Community
While it is difficult to make generalizations about optimal distribution of power, the most equitable way of distributing power appears to be in direct proportion to the size of the various identifiable ethnic, linguistic, and economic subgroups within the community. (pp. 260–262)

Bloom then concludes

To the extent that these principles are followed, the community becomes involved in its own mental health and emotional vitality. Its members increase their power over their own lives, which leads to an increase in their competence and self-esteem, which in turn leads to increased emotional robustness and improved mental health. (p. 262)

Organization and Management Strategies

Previous chapters have discussed program organization and management in some detail. The basic principles stated in those chapters are equally applicable to counseling programs in both school and nonschool settings. There are, however, some unique characteristics and organizational factors of community and mental health settings in which counselors function that merit special attention. The following are not suggested as being all inclusive, but rather are examples of distinctive differences that may be found in a community or mental health setting.

Characteristics of Community and Other Mental Health Organizations

- Mental health agencies and institutions are human service organizations designed to enhance the mental well-being of individuals.

- Mental health agencies and institutions are usually tax-supported public service agencies.
- Tax-supported agencies tend to assume certain bureaucratic characteristics associated with large governmental and industrial complexes.
- "Another characteristic of public sector organizations is that persons who need these human care systems have no alternative source for that service; typically there are no competitors. These citizens either accept the services as offered by these institutions or they do without." (Goodstein, 1978)
- Community mental health agencies tend to have interdisciplinary staffs representing minimally such fields as medicine, psychology, and social work.

Implications

- The intended outcomes are different from many other organizations in that a publicly expected service is delivered rather than a product.
- As tax-supported agencies, community mental health agencies have a closeness to the public. They and other similar human service agencies are more vulnerable and susceptible to public pressures.
- "Many organizations in the public sector are ordinarily not task oriented but rather are bureaucratic. . . . This means that doing things properly is more important than getting things done—an approach which can best be maintained in organizations without a profit motive." (Goodstein, 1978)
- "The absence of competition from other service purveyors makes most human service delivery systems quite complacent about themselves and the services they offer. They are guaranteed a potential clientele based upon estimates of the population in their district who need their particular service; they are funded on the basis of these estimates, estimates which they frequently make themselves, and they are left free of many requirements that they demonstrate effectiveness." (Goodstein, 1978)
- Program managers must recognize the necessity and challenge of getting professionals from related but often competing disciplines to work cooperatively and effectively together.

- Program managers obviously want to develop programs which are well organized, efficient, and dependable. The challenge is to do this without destroying the warm, humanistic caring traits that are supposedly characteristic of counseling service organizations.

Organizational Factors

Previous chapters have discussed the functioning of counseling programs within various educational institutions—elementary, middle, and secondary schools and institutions of higher education. In these settings counseling programs represented organizationally service units within institutions that are organized primarily to provide education in the formal sense. Community and other mental health agencies are usually different in that they are organized as a unit to provide counseling services, or may be organized within another human services organization (such as a hospital or employment agency). As such, we may look more broadly at organizational factors.

Organizations are "organized" on the assumption that a collective effort with planned direction and management is the most effective and efficient way to achieve a desired end. Organizations are also often "organized" to assist individuals who have common interests to come together and work toward common goals. However, definitions, in themselves, do not present a clear concept of how organizations function. In this regard, it might prove helpful to operationalize the concept of what an organization is, how it functions, and what it produces.

Steiner (1977) suggests that

> Organizational performance is dependent upon how, in what manner and proportion, it is able to integrate available delivery technology, staff capability and motivation, structure, management styles, communication links, and environmental constraints. Some of these organizational factors are under direct control of the administrator. Other factors can be imported through the influence process. Still others are completely outside the scope and control of the administrator. Diagrammatically, then, as displayed in Figure 10–1, an organization consists of these factors. (p. 15)

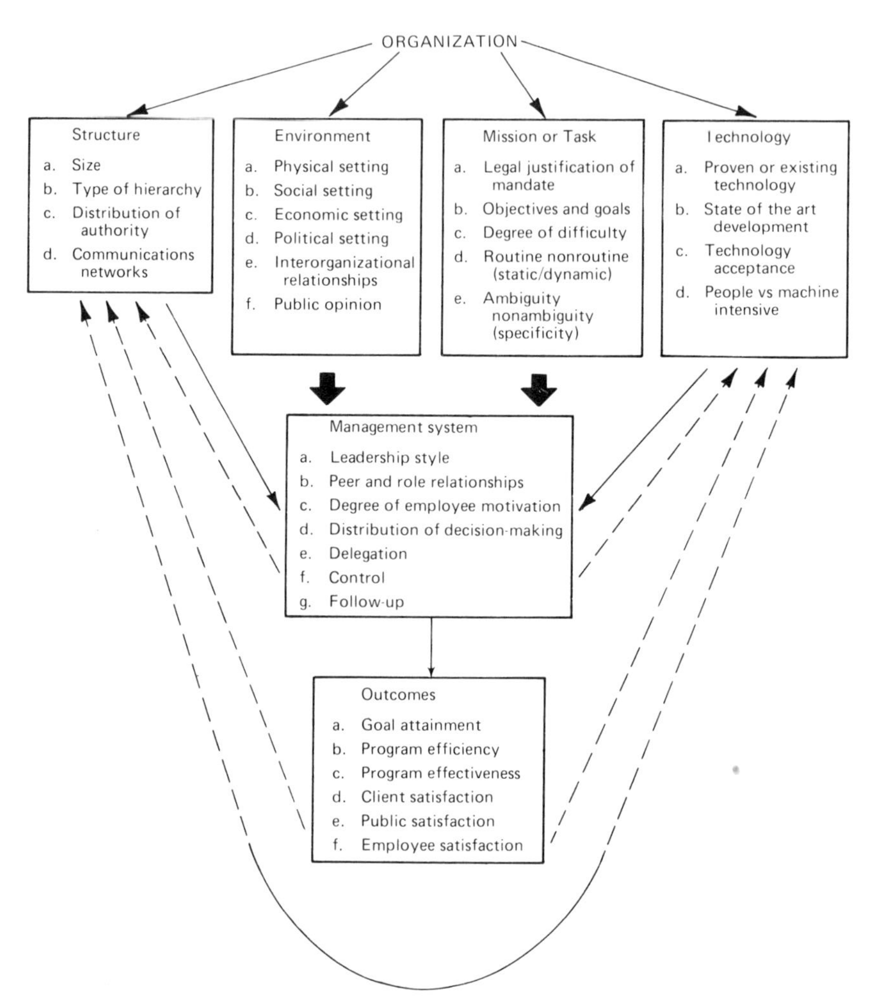

FIGURE 10–1. Organizational Factors. (Source: Richard Steiner. *Managing the Human Service Organization: From Survival to Achievement.* Sage Publications, Beverly Hills, Calif.: 1977, p. 15.)

Steiner (1977) also presents an interesting comparative analysis of public service and private organizations, as depicted in Figure 10–2.

Community Mental Health Programs

Community mental health agencies are one of the most popular sources of employment for counselors. When they are employed

	Private Sector	Public Human Services
INPUT	Assigned Resources: Directly from consumers or investment market	Third-party payment or through taxation
	Time Utilization: Tends to be highly fixed, conforming to engineered work schedules: Organization controls scheduling, with worker bending to time-production constraints	High variability in allocation of time to produce. Professional sets scheduling with client (product), bending to time constraints of work force
	Technology: Utilize sophisticated state of the art technology	Rudimentary technological base
	Nature of Management Work Force: Strength exhibited in analytic and administrative areas	Strengths exhibited in process and interactive dimensions of management
	Nature of Task: High degrees of specialization and routinization	Highly ambiguous and undefined
	Organizational Structure: Tend toward tall bureaucratic organizations with emphasis on production needs	Mixture of bureaucratic and professional modes, with emphasis on client needs
	Social Benefit: Limited concern with potentiality of social benefit—mission to make a profit	High concern for social benefit
PROCESS	Decision-Making: Rapid, based on broad data base—highly technological in nature	Slower, more highly ritualized, emphasizing consensus and compromise, utilizing less well-developed data base
	Administrative Process: Value technique over process—"Get the job done"	Value process over technique—"Do it by the book"
	Organizational Flexibility: High amount of adaptiveness due to limited mandates	Typically inflexible and slow to change due to mandated responsibilities
	Access to Information: Public has limited rights	Public rights protected through "sunshine laws"
	Measurement: Clear and obvious standards of successsful performance possible	More difficult but still possible to measure performance
OUTPUT	Output Benefits: Benefits designed to accrue directly to consumer with secondary economic social impact	Outputs utilized as an instrument of social and economic benefit
	Accountability: Because standards more easily developed, high degree of accountability possible	More difficult to establish standards because of variability of end product
	Type of Output: Tends to be uniform, with high degree of quality control built-in	Tends toward high variability with limited degree of quality control possible

*Source: Richard Steiner. Managing the Human Service Organization: From Survival to Achievement. Sage Publications. Beverly Hills, Ca. 1977. p. 30

FIGURE 10–2. **Summary Comparative Analysis.**

in such settings, counselors can anticipate working and interacting with a professional team representing several of the helping professions. Many community mental health centers are directed by medical personnel (psychiatrists) and thus, many of the admissions criteria and processing, diagnostic and treatment procedures and quality assessment will likely reflect the medical influence.

The specific practices or services frequently provided in community agencies can be classified as follows.

Preventive

Preventive intervention is a service designed to assist groups of individuals identified as high risks for the development of behavior disorders that a program is designed to prevent. Examples might be the provision of a drug-education program for all adolescents in a community or the providing of anticipatory guidance services to workers getting ready to retire. Preventive programs are concerned with identifying, precipitating, and/or perpetuating factors and relationships between these and mental health disorders. Whereas preventive intervention is receiving increased attention in community mental health agencies, Bolman and Westman (1967) identified three major categories for these services over fifteen years ago as person-centered programs, family-centered programs, and society-centered programs.

Crisis Intervention

Crisis intervention is a major service of most community mental health agencies. This service is based on the assumption that mental health services provided during a period of crisis have the prospects of being unusually effective. Bloom (1977) discusses the course of crises as follows.

> Taplin (1971) has recently reviewed the literature on psychological crises and has identified the major assertions commonly made about crises. First, life is a succession of crisis events, or *stresses*, that occur in the normal maturational/developmental/social-learning process. Second, crises have a definite course in time, causing different amounts of personal disruption, or *strain*, at different points in their evolution. (In connection with this second assertion, Caplan

(1963) has identified four phases that are characteristic of crises. First, habitual problem-solving responses are called forth by the situation. Then, failure to resolve the problem results in a rise in tension and a feeling of upset and ineffectuality. Third, emergency and novel methods of problem resolution, which may be successful, are called forth. Finally, if successful resolution has not taken place, distortion of reality, resignation, or unmanageable tension may result, with subsequent disorganization of personality.) Two other assertions are that crises are more accessible to intervention at their peak and may be resolved in adaptive or maladaptive ways. Fifth, a history of successful crisis resolutions increases the probability of successful crisis resolutions in the future. Sixth, assistance in crisis does not have to come from specially trained professionals. Seventh, aspects of the current situation play an important part in sustaining a crisis, and changing the situation the individual faces currently can significantly affect the course of a crisis. Eighth, the onset of a crisis usually involves an identifiable precipitating event, generally of a situational or interpersonal nature. Given these assertions, it is easy to see why the long waiting list, detailed diagnostic study, case conference, and assignment of a client to a therapist for long-term, once-weekly psychotherapy has given way in many community-mental-health centers to efforts to induce people to seek help immediately when they find themselves in a critical period in their lives and to prompt and brief clinical assessment and intervention. (p. 141)

Consultation

Consultation is a major form of indirect service provided by most community mental health agencies. This service may take the form of consulting with other institutions or agencies such as schools, welfare agencies, law-enforcement personnel, substance abuse centers, and hospitals. Case study consultation both within and without the agency can also be anticipated. A recognized leader in the field of mental health and consultation theory, Caplan (1963), suggested four varieties of consultation.

The first he calls *client-centered case consultation*. In this variety of consultation, the primary goal is to help the consultee deal with the presented case. To achieve this goal, the consultant uses his or her specialized skills and knowledge to assist the consultee in making an assessment of the client's problem and to recommend how

> best to deal with the problem. The second variety of consultation Caplan terms *consultee-centered case consultation.* In this type, the consultant attempts to identify the consultee's difficulties in handling the case and to remedy these difficulties, whether they stem from insufficient skill, knowledge, self-confidence, or objectivity. As you can see, this type of consultation offers the promise of increased effectiveness on the part of the consultee in a wide variety of professional encounters in the future. The third variety of consultation Caplan has labeled *program-centered administrative consultation.* In this case, the consultant's primary goal is to suggest some actions the consultee might take in order to effect the development, expansion, or modification of a clinical or agency program. In achieving this goal, the consultant draws not only on general mental-health skills but also on his or her understanding of the functioning of social systems and of the principles of mental-health-program administration. Finally, in *consultee-centered administrative consultation,* the consultant attempts to identify difficulties within the consultee that appear to be limiting his or her effectiveness in instituting program change. (Bloom, 1977, p. 110–111)

Remediation and Rehabilitation Services

A major service of any community mental health center is the diagnosis and treatment of mental disorders. The clients of mental health centers may range in severity from those who require intensive psychiatric-medical treatment to those who need what might be simply labeled routine adjustment counseling. Treatment may take the form of individual and/or group therapy and can involve professionals, paraprofessionals, and peers. Common remediation needs include various personality disorders, substance abuse, spouse and child abuse, and personal relationship adjustments, such as marriage and family or career. Rehabilitation counseling may assist those who must face midlife career change or retirement, loss of spouse as a result of death or divorce, effects of divorce on children, and changes in life-styles created by physical impairment. The goal of remediation and rehabilitation treatment is to enable the client to resume or continue as productive and satisfying a life as possible.

In another view of the activities of community mental health agencies, Lewis and Lewis (1977) depict a multifaceted approach for agencies as noted in Figure 10–3.

Extensive	Intensive
Experiential	
Educational programs concerning the nature of mental health.	Ongoing counseling and rehabilitation programs.
Educational programs encouraging community involvement in planning and evaluating services.	Walk-in assistance with problems of living.
Educational programs to enhance effective mental health development and prevent psychological problems.	Crisis intervention.
Environmental	
Assistance in organizing local community to bring about needed environmental change.	Linkage with support systems and helping network.
Class advocacy in behalf of individuals such as former or present mental patients.	Advocacy in behalf of individual clients.
Organizing and planning for alternatives to hospitalization.	Attempts to secure placements more appropriate than hospitalization.
	Consultation with helping network.

[*Source:* Judith A. Lewis, and Michael D. Lewis, *Community Counseling: A Human Services Approach*, (New York: John Wiley & Sons, 1977), p. 249.]

FIGURE 10–3. Community Counseling in Community Mental Health Agencies

Substance Abuse Centers

In recent years we have witnessed a substantial increase in what we might label nontraditional or specialized counseling centers. Among the more popular of these have been those catering to alcohol and drug abuse. Many drug abuse centers have been organized especially in large metropolitan areas and medium-sized communities. These centers tend to provide three categories of services: (1) educational/prevention, (2) treatment and rehabilitation, and (3) consultation. A fourth activity, research, is also frequently engaged in by the professional personnel of these centers. Some of the programs have residential treatment centers and staffing is frequently comparable to other community mental health agencies.

Most substance abuse centers do an extensive analysis or "work-up" on their clients. This includes the gathering of family, education, and career backgrounds; personal traits; history of substance use/abuse; and other data that may assist the therapist in understanding the background of the client and his or her problems; where the client is currently; and the client's future promise or prognosis. Following this analysis of the client and his or her situation, the therapist may be ready to initiate a treatment program. It is important that program managers and staff be aware of the legal guidelines and implications in the treatment of drug users and of federal regulations governing client records and informational exchange.

Several of the responsibilities of counseling program managers should be emphasized in substance abuse centers. One very obvious responsibility is the accruing of needs assessment data. A second, and related procedure, is an effective public liaison and communications program. Another, sometimes neglected, responsibility is to establish a close working relationship with the counseling staffs of the local schools. This is particularly essential in any program of prevention/education and early detection/treatment of youthful users/abusers. Another often neglected group, the elderly substance abusers, present more difficult problems in both the identification and accessing of them for treatment, but this does not excuse a program's ignoring their needs.

Finally, the program manager must exercise considerable concern in the professional staffing of substance abuse centers. Many counselors, who are excellent in other settings, may not be effective at all in working with substance abuse clients. For example, Forman (1979) noted that

> Even the most experienced counselor can fall prey to the pitfalls inherent in counseling the alcoholic client. The alcoholic population is one of the more difficult with which to cope in the counseling situation. The counselor must be alert to the inherent dynamics of the disease and be willing to use direct, tough, and often radical approaches to break through the client's gamesmanship.
>
> Counselors must recognize that alcoholics, by the time they have become active alcohol addicts, have years of successful manipulation of their environment behind them. Generally, they are much more sophisticated at subliminal manipulation than is the counselor. I have seen many seasoned in-the-field counselors so manipulated by the alcoholic's game that they do not even know when, how, or why they are being manipulated.

This kind of interplay is a dominant characteristic of the helping relationship with alcoholics. It also pervades the alcoholic's relations with all people in their life space and dictates that counselors remain strongly alert to their own feelings. (p. 546)

Counseling Programs for the Elderly

Another population that has received increasing attention in recent years has been those older Americans labeled "the aged." In recent generations this population has increased not only in numbers but as a percentage of the total population as well. (One American in ten is sixty-five years of age or over). As a result, increasing pressures have been placed on societal agencies to expand and improve services to people in this age group. The Older Americans Act of 1965 established the Administration on Aging to administer various federal programs for the elderly and a large network of state and area agencies on aging was established under 1973 amendments to the original 1965 Act. These programs for the elderly include home services, nutrition programs, legal services, housing, nursing homes, and senior centers. Although counselors may qualify for some of the "helping" positions in these programs, the establishment of counseling programs in these settings are still in the developmental stage. Some community agencies, even some college counseling centers, have, however, recognized a need to provide special counseling services for the older American.

An increasing amount of literature is currently emerging in the counseling of the elderly. Counseling program managers serving this population should be familiar with the current research and writing in this field. For example, writings such as Hardy and Cull (1975) suggest

The counselor or psychologist need not modify his approach for the older client. As with other clients counseling should be a sequentially developed or graduated program providing positive concrete feedback relative to progress and should require not only tasks for the older American but should include a program of gradual decision-making responsibility.

There are many indications that the majority of the patients on wards in psychiatric institutions are not in need of psychotherapy as much as they need a redefinition of their role in society. A counseling strategy in working with the older American should be one which reverses the isolationism process of aging and one which is designed to add meaning to the lives of each individual older client as well as activities. A counseling program should also take into consideration the need for remotivation of the older American, the gaining of positive feedback of his capability and adequacy and the introduction of the individual to programs which will facilitate the client's psychological adjustment to aging. (p. 49–50)

O'Brien, Johnson, and Miller (1979) point out that

caring, empathy, and a trusting atmosphere are all qualities that should permeate every helping relationship. But these and the generic counseling skills of listening, promoting client self-understanding, and facilitating constructive behavior change have an added dimension when the client is a senior citizen.

Such persons have specific needs and are at a crucial developmental life stage. Just as youngsters meet new challenges and build defenses against perceived threats from within and outside the self, so the older individual faces concerns associated with changing self-concept and with the grief induced by multiple loss. (p. 288)

O'Brien, Johnson and Miller (1979) go on to say that another

major obstacle to mental health care in life's later years stems from ageism—the attitudes and stereotypes that discriminate against persons on the basis of their longevity (Butler, 1975). Consequently, treating the older person with special respect and sensitivity becomes an issue of basic significance to the gerontological counselor. For example, deciding about the advisability of using a first name or a formal title (Mr., Mrs., Dr., Miss) is an important consideration because of the implied degree of courtesy and deference. Parenthetically, we should note that initially the use of the more formal address is usually preferable because too much informality may connote an additional loss of status, while the counselor's efforts should help assure the elderly persons that they continue to be valuable. (p. 290)

A special adjustment that most of the aging population must deal with is retirement. Here again, counselors are being called on to counsel those individuals experiencing this transition. Johnson and Riker (1981) note that

> As a life-style with new alternatives and increased freedom, retirement may require role modifications that are for some persons quite difficult to make. Our society values work, and personal identity is often heavily drawn from the work role. Therefore individuals approaching retirement must usually reassess these roles. Such reassessment can be highly conscious, organized, and formal or haphazard, casual, and unconscious. The quality of this assessment process depends on personality and perception of environment. As Guttman (1978) points out, the retirement decision results from internal (self-concept and self-esteem) as well as external (life situation) considerations of a highly personal nature. Unraveling these complicated variables can prove a formidable task for the preretirement counselor. (p. 291)

In conclusion, program managers must be aware that only a very small percentage of older Americans are utilizing counseling services. Although older people are remaining outside the counseling environment for several reasons, the setting in which the service is offered plays a significant role in their decision. Kerschner (1979) suggests the employment of two strategies to open the counseling door to older populations as follows:

> 1. to convince the population that a decision to utilize the traditional counseling setting is not something to be hidden, but rather, is a rational and normal response to a pressing concern.
> 2. to institutionalize counseling as one of several preventive health programs and to significantly expand the number and types of settings where counseling might take place. (p. 267)

One of the most promising sites for older adult counseling are the senior centers, which are springing up all over the nation.

> It is important for the reader to be aware of the changes that have taken place in senior centers, changes that have provided an optimal environment for older adult counseling projects. In the early years of these centers, prior to the 1960s, the sites served to provide a haven where the elderly poor could receive some financial and occasional nutritional assistance. Over the next decade, there was a heavy shift toward recreation, and a variety of activities (cards,

> dancing, trips, lectures, etc.) were provided for the elderly in the immediate neighborhood. This recreational and activity focus has prospered and endured into the 1970s, but with one major addition. Today's multipurpose senior center is both a program site and a service site. The older person entering a center such as Baltimore's Waxter Center, San Francisco's Senior Center, or Hollywood's Andrus Older Adult Center can take part in a wide range of activities including exercise physiology programs, legal services, Title VII nutrition programs, memory clinics, and adult counseling programs. Such a major addition to the programs being offered has called for the training and use of individuals capable of delivering quality services. The older adult counseling programs typify this need for trained personnel. (Kerschner, 1979, pp. 270–271)

Marriage and Family Counseling

As noted in Chapter 1, the declining state of the American family as reflected in the high and ever-increasing divorce rate, children living out of wedlock or in single parent households, and various alternatives to traditional family structures has led not unexpectedly to a significant increase in marriage and family counseling. Although much of this increase is reflected in the caseloads of the counseling professionals working out of the traditional community mental health and university counseling centers, the development of both private and tax-supported marriage and family counseling centers in the large metropolitan areas are further indications of the growing demand for this particular service. Moreover, the number of licensed marriage counselors has been rapidly increasing and increased numbers of counselor education programs are seeking to meet the training standards of the American Association of Marriage and Family Therapists.

Managers of counseling programs with significant numbers of clients seeking this type of assistance should be aware of the various approaches that are commonly provided in addition to the traditional individual and couples counseling. These include the following.

Conjoint Marital Therapy

This approach, perhaps the most popular among marital therapists today, is the practice of seeing both spouses together during all of the therapeutic sessions. This approach stresses the importance of working with, and intervening most directly in, the marital relationship and not only with the individuals in the relationship.

Concurrent Marital Therapy

Concurrent therapy is the most traditional theory in marital counseling. In this approach both partners undergo concurrent but separate analysis aimed at each partner developing insights into the neurotic needs that he or she has brought into the marriage leading ultimately to change and a more mature relationship.

("Combined" therapy is the mixing of conjoint and concurrent marital therapy.)

Family Counseling

As an addendum to couples counseling, where children are involved and often a part of the problem, therapy involving the whole family may be planned for. In some instances, co-joint counseling with families is even more effective than one counselor working with a family.

Group Counseling

Increasingly, groups made up of married couples seeking assistance are being established. Therapists report that counseling groups often reach and help resolve emotional conflicts in marriage much faster than working with each couple alone. This approach is labeled as conjoint group therapy.

Male-Female Therapy Teams Working with Couples

This approach has been popularized by such clinics as Masters and Johnson and some proponents suggest that it is the most effective counseling method yet. Although this may be debatable, program managers may want to consider this technique as it offsets the imbalance often felt with a single counselor representing one sex. The therapy team must be extremely sensitive and skilled to utilize this approach effectively. There must also be a high level of trust and respect between the co-therapists, as well as between the co-therapists and their client couple.

Enrichment Groups

The emphasis in enrichment groups is as the title implies—the enrichment or enhancement of the relationship. These enrichment programs may be provided through weekenders or a scheduled series of sessions. The focus may be on such concerns as improving communications skills, the art of compromise, the expanding of leisure/recreational interests, stress management, dual career planning, and decisions regarding parenthood.

Group Family Enrichment

Group family enrichment as described by Weissman and Montgomery (1980) emphasizes educational skill-building techniques using nontherapeutic approaches that enable families to resolve difficulties of family members. The meetings, which employ coaching and videotape feedback, enable parents and children to practice communication, cooperation, and problem-solving skills. Evaluation results indicate that participants become successful in the home environment as a result of their involvement in the multiple-family, group-training sessions.

Sex Therapy

Recent generations have witnessed a significant increase in the public's awareness of the important role of sexual satisfaction in marital adjustment. The large number of popular publications dealing with the topic are indicators that sex is no longer the hush-hush topic that once relegated it to the physician's office (if discussed at all). Sex therapy clinics themselves have become popular (the program manager must be aware of the distinctions between legitimate sex therapy clinics, staffed by professionals, and those that have questionable status as professional counseling enterprises). More importantly, counselors in both agency and school settings are encountering increasing numbers of clients seeking counseling assistance in dealing with their sexuality and sexual concerns.

Career Counseling Programs

Work is the common experience anticipated and participated in by nearly all adults in all societies. (We recognize homemaking as work or a career). Despite this expectancy, despite a recognition of the significant influence of work and careers on the mental well-being of the individual, and despite the increasing complexity of the career world and related career planning, career guidance or counseling until recently was largely left to school counseling programs, government employment offices, and rehabilitation programs.

However, during the 1970s, a series of events combined to sensitize counselors in a variety of settings, as well as the general public to the career needs of our citizenry. These included legislation for women's equality and minority rights, career education acts, persistent unemployment, and career redeployment. As a result, women's centers and minority centers were established, usually with career assistance programs, and career centers themselves were not uncommon. Career oriented counseling is usually available in all of these settings.

Additionally, the Bureau of Occupation and Adult Education, the Office of Career Education, and the National Institute of Education engaged in research and developmental efforts, which led to the development of four operational models for career education, as follows.

1. *The Employer-Based Model* seeks primarily to serve teenage students through an optional out-of-school program of personalized educational experiences in an employer-based setting. The model stresses community participation, particularly by businesses and organizations, in cooperation with the schools, to offer an alternative educational program relevant to the individual's interests and needs.
2. *The Home-Based Model* is designed to introduce a variety of experiences using the home as a center for learning, especially for persons 18 to 25 years of age who have left school. The objectives are to develop educational delivery systems for the home and the community; to provide new career education programs for adults; to establish a guidance and career placement system to assist individuals in occupational and related life-roles; and to develop more competent workers. A Career Education Exten-

sion service will be established to coordinate the use of mass media and career education resource.

3. *The Rural/Residential-Based Model* is a research and demonstration project which will test the hypothesis that entire disadvantaged rural families can experience lasting improvement in their economic and social conditions through an intensive program at a residential center. Families are drawn from a six-state area to the project site in Glasgow, Montana. Programs will provide services to the entire family, including day care, health care, educational programs from kindergarten through adult, welfare, counseling, cultural and recreational opportunities. The objective is to provide rural families with employment capabilities suitable to the area, so that students will be able and ready to find employment in the area after completing the program.
4. *The School-Based Model* is, by far, the most common of the four models, and is the one of greatest interest to us. USOE sponsored the development of six demonstration projects through the Center for Vocational and Technical Education of the Ohio State University. . . . The development and validation effort which was undertaken is quite extensive and includes several school districts. . . . In all, about 115 schools, 4,200 teachers and administrators, and 85,000 students are involved. A single model is being developed for ALL the sites, so that the result will be a model that has been tested for applicability in a variety of settings. Local educational agencies are cooperating in the development of curricular and instructional materials to achieve specific objectives. These "treatments," along with materials located in an ongoing national search, will be classified and catalogued for dissemination to other educational agencies. Extensive in-service teacher education is part of the development program. (Florida Department of Education, Division of Vocational Technical and Adult Education, 1972)

States were also active in model development. As one example, the state of West Virginia (1979) suggested a model program that was intended to serve as a reference and to provide guidelines for the establishment of community-based vocational guidance and counseling programs in West Virginia. Four components of the program developed by the West Virginia State Department of Education in 1979 included self-understanding, decision making, environmental awareness, and job enhancement skill development. Also presented in this program are competencies necessary for a person to function successfully as a community agent. Six organization and management functions and ten provision-of-service functions are also formulated. Interagency cooperation is also presented, noting personnel and responsibilities to public schools, vocational-technical schools, colleges, rehabilitation services, federal programs, social and service organizations, and employer and business groups. Also planned for were expected programs for the respective target populations (elementary, secondary, postsecondary, out-of-school youth, adult education, and other adult programs).

Regardless of the setting in which counselors function or program managers manage, it is evident that many client concerns are going to have a career orientation. These concerns may generally fall into the categories of (1) career decision making, planning, and entry; (2) career related adjustments; (3) career unemployment and/or change; and (4) retirement. Techniques that may be planned for in the development of career counseling programs include (1) individual assessment for career planning or adjustment; (2) career information literature (or access to or liaison with such sources as local libraries, employment offices, and so forth); (3) a career search mechanism or referral process; plus (4) related group guidance and counseling opportunities.

Leisure Counseling

Leisure counseling is not an established specialty or even an area of special need currently responded to in community mental health centers. Rather, leisure counseling is an area of developing interest, research, and theory that we believe will be incorporated into most counseling programs in both community and school settings within this century. Edwards and Bloland (1980) write that

> In the late 1960s, the notion of counseling individuals about their use of leisure time appeared to be an anomaly. That anyone would require professional assistance to decide what to do with one's leisure time seemed at least unnecessary, and at most patently absurd. Yet, as our post-industrial society continued to make more nonwork time available through a reduction in working hours, longer paid vacations, and incentives for early retirement, filling those

> newly available hours became more and more troublesome and unsettling for many people. Today the executives whose success enables them to slow down, the housewives whose children have grown, the young people who wish to develop their potential, the retired workaholics—all are potential candidates for this emerging helping service. (p. 435)

This new counseling specialty is borrowing heavily from the field of recreation and vocational counseling. As noted in the Edwards and Bloland (1980) article:

> The counseling model employed by Edwards, a leisure counselor in private practice, combines two of McDowell's (1977) orientations, "leisure life-style awareness" and "leisure resource guidance" into a nontherapeutic approach that owes much, explicitly and implicitly, to trait-factor vocational guidance. Many of the basic elements of the Parsonian approach are inherent in the model, including the development of self-awareness, awareness of existing opportunities, and counseling assistance to understand the relationship between the two. In addition, referral becomes a significant counselor activity, as clients usually seek to implement the results of this joint approach. (p. 436)

An analysis of leisure counseling models by Tinsley and Tinsley (1981) suggested an emphasis on the following aspects in an optimal approach to leisure counseling:

> 1. Focus on the total individual, not just the individual as a problem in leisure choice.
> 2. Emphasis on the establishment of a counseling relationship embodying the facilitative conditions.
> 3. Conceptualization of the goal of leisure counseling as contributing to the self-actualization of the individual. (p. 45)

Program managers need to be aware, as well as to make their counseling staff sensitive to the possibilities of leisure counseling. Even more precise is an inclusion of a personal-leisure needs component in any needs assessment undertaken by the counseling unit. Finally, programs that do plan to respond to the leisure counseling needs of their target population should examine existing models as reported in professional journals and conferences for possible guidelines in such program development.

Employment Counseling

Another community-based agency that employs counselors are the many local Employment Security offices established by the Department of Labor to provide job placement assistance and attending advising or career counseling for those individuals who are unemployed or seeking a job change. The Department of Labor defines an employment counselor as one who performs counseling duties and who meets the minimum standards for classification as an employment counselor.

Although the focus of employment counselors, as with other employees of the employment security offices, is appropriate job placement of its clientele, the counselors are expected in the process to counsel clients on their personal problems and assist them in developing attitudes, skills, and abilities that will facilitate their employment. Counselors are also involved in data gathering from their clients and in the administration and interpretation of standardized tests. In 1975 the National Employment Counselors Association issued a position paper on the "Role of the Employment Counselor." Portions of this paper are presented in Appendix G.

Counselors in Other Community Settings

Chapter 1 briefly discussed counseling in church or religious affiliated settings and correctional institutions. It is also important that program managers in community agency settings be aware of other helping professionals, especially counselors, and how their efforts may relate to or complement their own agencies' efforts, and vice versa. We include the court system, community youth centers, hospital patient advocate programs, and other social service agencies and centers where appropriate. In all of these relations, program managers are seeking to apply what might be labeled the "c's" of management principles: cooperation, coordination, communications, and consultation. These activities can be influential to those significant and related twins of accountability and survival. When a public image of overlap, duplication of effort, confusion, and/or competition among agencies and waste is created, all agencies suffer. Attention to the "c's" will at least protect the "attending" agency.

Summary and Implications

Counseling programs have developed in a variety of noneducational settings. These programs represent a response to the needs of various populations and the belief that access to mental health services is a civil right. Since most nonschool counseling agencies are community-oriented, community involvement and consciousness on the part of the agency is important.

Community agencies are usually tax-supported public service organizations. As such, they typically have no competition for their services. This may, however, encourage certain bureaucratic tendencies. Staffs are usually interdisciplinary, with the fields of medicine, psychology, social work, and counseling most frequently represented. Programs in these agencies provide services classified as (1) preventive, (2) crisis intervention, (3) consultation, and (4) remediation and rehabilitation.

In addition to community mental health agencies, counselors also function in such community-based agencies as substance abuse centers, programs for the elderly, marriage and family therapy programs, career counseling centers, and leisure and employment programs. It is important that program managers in these various community (and school) settings cooperate, coordinate, communicate, and consult with one another to minimize undesirable impressions that can result from apparent overlapping, duplication, and competition among agencies and services.

CHAPTER 11

Evaluation and Research

Introduction

As previously noted in the introduction to Chapter 3, counseling programs in whatever setting must provide evidence of their accomplishments—their relevancy. They must be accountable. Accountability further suggests that the program's accomplishments are achieved as efficiently and economically as possible. Thus, by its very nature, accountability forms a basis for program change and improvement. Counseling and guidance programs in schools are and should be continuous from elementary through higher education. The school counseling and guidance program should be developmental in nature, should never seek to maintain the status quo, and is most effective when it can develop and change in response to the current needs of its target population. Not all that is old is bad, and change for the sake of change is not in itself a guarantee of program improvement. The continuous development and related change of counseling and guidance programs must be based on objective data that provide direction for such change. These data are most objectively obtained through regular planned needs assessments implemented by evaluation and research.

Evaluation and Accountability

ACCOUNTABILITY

In recent years there have been increasing demands that educators be held accountable for their actions—that some evidence of accomplishments and gains be provided in return for public support and tax investments. This demand for accountability has resulted from unmet expectations—often public—coupled with increased costs to the public. To be accountable means to be responsible—responsible for relevant data-based goals, cost efficient and effective procedures, and measurable outcomes. Measurable outcomes have frequently been a nemesis for counseling programs, and although such evidence may not be as readily obtained as in some enterprises, we must seek this evidence as it is clear that we can no longer expect counseling to be judged "on faith."

This "principle of accountability" also suggests that all phases of the school's educational efforts, including the school's counseling and guidance program, must justify their existence through evidence of their accomplishments. This evidence is best provided through the process of evaluation. Thus, in a sense, evaluation today has a dual role when viewed as a means of providing direction for program development and as a means of indicating to the "paying customers" whether or not they have purchased a "good buy."

Whereas some may view accountability as an additional burden, Krumboltz (1974) has noted that "the potential advantages warrant counselors' efforts to construct a sound accountability system for themselves." Such an accountability system would enable counselors to:

- "Obtain feedback on the results of their work.
- Select counseling methods on the basis of demonstrated success.
- Identify students with unmet needs.
- Devise shortcuts for routine operations.
- Argue for increased staffing to reach attainable goals.
- Request training for problems requiring new competencies." (p. 639)

Krumboltz identified seven criteria to be met if an accountability system is to produce the desired results. These were identified as follows:

a. In order to define the domain of counselor responsibility the general goals of counseling must be agreed to by all concerned parties.
b. Counselor accomplishments must be stated in terms of important observable behavior changes by clients.
c. Activities of the counselor must be stated as costs, not accomplishments.
d. The accountability system must be constructed to promote professional effectiveness and self-improvement, not to cast blame or punish poor performance.
e. In order to promote accurate reporting, reports of failures and unknown outcomes must be permitted and never punished.
f. All users of the accountability system must be represented in designing it.
g. The accountability system itself must be subject to evaluation and modification (p. 640–641)

How would counselors benefit from a sensible accountability system? By learning how to help clients more effectively and efficiently, counselors would obtain:

- More public recognition for their accomplishments.
- Increased financial support.
- Better working relationships with teachers and administrators.
- Acknowledged professional standing.
- The satisfaction of performing a constantly improving and valued service. (p. 640)

Evaluation

Many of the basic textbooks published in the field of counseling and guidance during the 1950s and 1960s referred to "evaluation and research" as a basic service or category for program planning in any comprehensive system of guidance services. These terms were appropriately viewed as interrelated or complementary and sometimes inappropriately as "one and the same." Certainly, evaluative studies can be research studies as well, and vice versa, but conversely, not all evaluations can be viewed as research and many research studies are not designed to collect evaluative data. We now examine evaluation as the distinct activity it is.

The process of evaluation has traditionally sought to provide some appraisal of a program's performance through an assessment of progress toward its stated objectives and/or through comparison with established criteria. "Within-house" evaluations have more frequently utilized the former approach, whereas accrediting associations have usually emphasized the latter. Although local ongoing evaluations are essential to individual program improvement and development, the evaluative criteria of accrediting associations and other external program assessment agencies tend to provide opportunities for comparing individual programs against what is generally acceptable in the field.

Principles of Evaluation. Evaluation is a process for appraising the value or effectiveness of a program or activity. As such, it is most effective when it is conducted within a framework of guiding principles. Seven of these principles are discussed in the following paragraphs.

Effective Evaluation Requires a Recognition of Program Goals. Before any meaningful program of evaluation can be undertaken, it is essential that the goals or objectives of that program be clearly identified. These objectives provide indications of program intent that form the basis for subsequent planning and procedures. The objectives of the program should be stated in clear and measurable terminology. This principle suggests that school guidance programs be evaluated on the basis of "how well it is doing what it set out to do."

Effective Evaluation Requires Valid Measuring Criteria. Once program goals are clearly defined, valid criteria for measuring progress toward these goals must be identified. The development of such criteria is crucial if the evaluation itself is to be both valid and meaningful. For example, if an annual program goal for a junior community college guidance program would be to provide each entering student with a series of three career interviews with a counselor, the measuring criteria could be a simple count indicating the percentage of students who did in fact have such an opportunity. If, on the other hand, the program goal might be to provide each student with "a broadening of his or her career understanding," the measuring criteria is certainly less obvious and may be dependent on a further refinement of what is meant by "career understanding." In other words, vaguely stated goals and vaguely stated criteria lessen the effectiveness of program evaluation.

Effective Program Evaluation Is Dependent on Valid Application of the Measuring Criteria. As discussed in the previous paragraph, valid criteria for measuring progress toward the program's stated goals must be established. It is not sufficient, however, to merely establish criteria; their ultimate validity will depend on their valid application. This implies that effective evaluation of school counseling programs should involve, in each instance, individuals who are professionally competent in both evaluation techniques and understandings of school guidance programs. All too often effective evaluation criteria are dissipated in the hands of evaluators who have at the best only a superficial knowledge of the appropriate roles and functions of school guidance programs.

Program Evaluation Should Involve All Who Are Affected. Evaluation of the school guidance program should first involve those persons who are themselves participants in, or affected by, the program. This would include, in addition to the guidance staff, faculty members and administrators, students and their parents, and, on appropriate occasion, members of the community or supporting agencies. The major contribution to effective evaluation must come from those who have a firsthand knowledge or involvement in the program. External evaluators from governmental agencies, accrediting associations, or other educational institutions can be helpful, but those should not be the sole bases of evaluation.

Meaningful Evaluation Requires Feedback and Follow-through. The evaluation process and even the evaluation report are not in and of themselves of great value. It is only when the results of evaluation are used for program improvement and development that the evaluation process takes on any meaning. This presumes, then, that the results of any program evaluation are made available to those persons who are concerned with program management and development. It also presumes that the program manager and his or her staff will use these results for future program planning, development, and decision making.

Evaluation Is Most Effective As a Planned, Continuous Process. Inasmuch as pupil counseling and guidance is a continuous process, the assessment of such a program is most effective when it is planned as a continuous process. This means that there are specific plans and designated responsibilities for both the ongoing evaluation of a program's progress as well as the more extensive annual or semiannual reviews.

Evaluation Emphasizes the Positive. All too frequently, evaluation is viewed as a threatening process aimed at ferreting out hidden weaknesses and spotlighting outstanding "boo-boos." Although an "accentuate-the-negative" approach will probably continue to be the theme of some evaluators and evaluations, if program evaluation is to produce the most meaningful results possible, it must be conducted in a spirit that is positive and aimed at helping and facilitating program improvement—a spirit that emphasizes strengths as well as weaknesses.

Models of Evaluation. A variety of evaluation models are available for consideration by counseling program managers. Daniels, Mines, and Gressard (1981) note that

> selecting the appropriate evaluation model for any particular evaluation problem may be accomplished by providing answers to six questions. Five of the questions are restatements of the critical dimensions of evaluation as presented in House's (1978) evaluation taxonomy. The sixth question considers the expertise of the would-be evaluator. The questions are:
>
> 1. What is the purpose of the evaluation?
> 2. What question(s) does the evaluation intend to answer?
> 3. What consensual assumptions is the evaluator willing or able to make?
> 4. For whom is the evaluation intended?
> 5. What is (are) the best available method(s) for obtaining answers to the questions asked?

6. Does the counselor/evaluator have the knowledge and technical capability to complete the evaluations? (p. 580)

They further present a taxonomy of major evaluation models (Table 11–1) that was developed by House (1978). p. 579

Daniels, Mines, and Gressard (1981) suggest, however, that practitioners are more concerned with the utility of evaluation models and would likely receive more benefits from a "meta" model or framework that addresses the comparative utility of the various models. This meta model is presented in Figure 11–1. (p. 581)

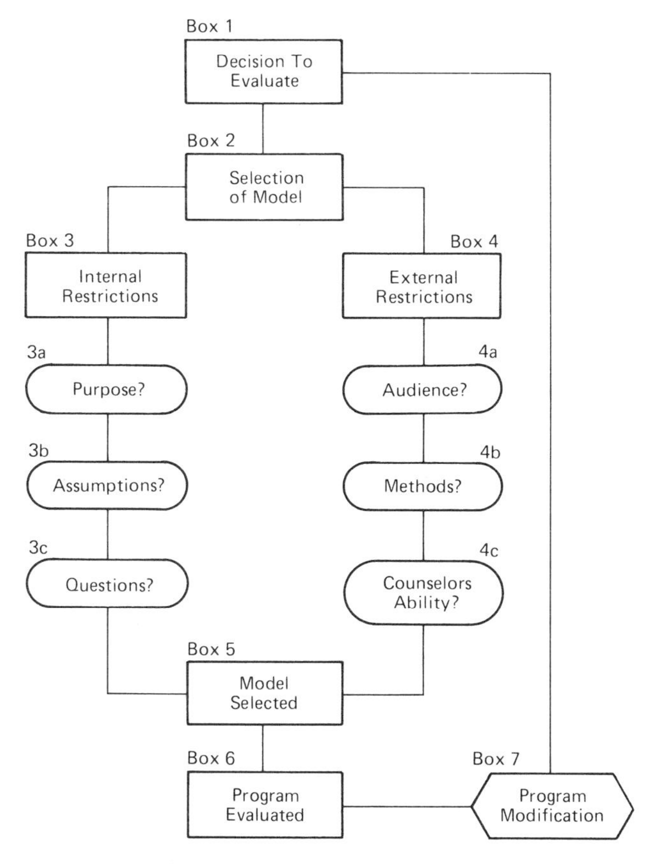

FIGURE 11–1. A Meta-Model Schema of Program Evaluation. (Source: M. Harry Daniels, Robert Mines and Charles Gressard. "A Meta-Model for Evaluating Counseling Programs." *Personnel and Guidance Journal,* 1981. 59(9), p. 581.)

TABLE 11–1. *A Taxonomy of Major Evaluation Models*

Classes of Models	Major Audiences	Outcome	Consensual Assumption(s)
Systems analysis	Economists, managers	Program efficiency	Goals, known cause and effects, quantified variables
Behavioral objectives	Managers, psychologists	Productivity, accountability	Prespecified objectives, quantified variables
Decision-making	Administrators	Effectiveness, quality control	General goals, evaluation criteria
Goal free	Consumers	Consumer choices, social utility	Consequences, evaluation criteria
Art criticism	Connoisseurs, consumers	Improved standards	Critics, standards of criticism
Accreditation	Professional peers, public	Professional acceptance	Panel of peers, procedures & criteria for evaluation
Adversary	Jury, public	Resolution	Procedures, judges
Transaction	Client practitioners	Understanding	Negotiations, activities

Source: Adapted from House (1978).

Instruments for Evaluation. A wide variety of instruments are available or may be constructed to facilitate the process of collecting evaluative data. The more popular of these are rating scales, checklists, and questionnaires. In this process, evaluative criteria are first established followed by the development of instruments that can be used to indicate the degree to which a program measures up. For example, evaluative criteria or checklists utilized by most accrediting associations and many state departments of education reflect this approach. Although this approach to evaluation may locally ignore appropriate objectives and sometimes unique and innovative practices, it does provide guidelines that enable counseling and guidance programs to be compared with generally accepted standards. Table 11–2 provides an example of

Methodology	Typical Questions	Selected References
PPBS, cost benefit analysis	Are the expected effects achieved? What are the most efficient programs?	Bergland & Quatrano, 1973; Rivilin, 1971
Behavioral objectives, achievement tests	Are the students achieving the objectives? Is the teacher producing?	Krumboltz, 1974; Popham, 1975; Thompson & Borsari, 1978
Surveys, questionnaires, interviews, natural variation	Is the program effective? What parts are effective?	Burck & Peterson, 1975; Stufflebeam et al., 1971
Bias control, logical analysis	What are *all* of the effects of the program?	Leviton, 1977; Scriven, 1975, 1976
Critical review	Would a critic approve this program?	Eisner, 1979
Review by panel, self-study	How would professionals rate this program?	Berven & Wright, 1978
Quasi-legal procedures	What are the arguments for and against the program?	Kelly, 1976
Case studies, interviews, observations	What does the program look like to different people?	Schmidt, 1974; Stake, 1975

a simple checklist that could be used to evaluate an elementary or secondary school counseling and guidance program.

Evaluation for Community Mental Health Counseling Programs. As with educational programs, including those of counseling and guidance in schools, community mental health center programs have also felt pressures to conduct systematic program evaluations, partly as the result of the increasing demands of the federal government to verify program efficiency and effectiveness in community mental health centers. In this regard, Public Law 94-63, The Community Mental Health Centers Amendments of 1975, requires community mental health to allocate not less than 2 per cent of their previous year's operating budgets for the con-

TABLE 11–2. ***Checklist to Evaluate a School Counseling and Guidance Program***

Criteria	Yes	No
1. Appropriate data were collected to initiate program planning as evidenced by		
a) community and/or area environmental assessment	_____	_____
b) organizational characteristics assessment	_____	_____
c) target population needs assessment	_____	_____
2. Data collected were organized and interpreted as a basis for determining (in order)		
a) priority needs of student population	_____	_____
b) an ordering of priorities to be served	_____	_____
c) the determination of relevant program goals and objectives	_____	_____
3. The objectives of the school counseling and guidance program are stated and understood by		
a) professional counseling staff	_____	_____
b) other pupil personnel specialists	_____	_____
c) faculty	_____	_____
d) administration	_____	_____
e) parents	_____	_____
f) students	_____	_____
g) other relevant populations	_____	_____
4. These objectives are consistent with the overall educational objectives of the institution	_____	_____
5. There is a planned program for achieving the program's objectives (noted in 1)	_____	_____
6. The planning of this program cooperatively involves		
a) professional counseling staff	_____	_____
b) other pupil personnel specialists	_____	_____
c) faculty	_____	_____
d) administration	_____	_____
e) parents and/or community personnel	_____	_____
7. The program itself involves		
a) professional counseling staff	_____	_____
b) other pupil personnel specialists	_____	_____
c) teaching faculty	_____	_____
d) community resource personnel	_____	_____
8. The school counseling program is under the direction of a trained and certified school counselor	_____	_____
9. The professional staff of the school program is composed of trained and certified school counselors	_____	_____
10. The school counseling and guidance program makes provisions for pupils to		
a) receive regular periodic interpretations of their school records, including standardized test results.	_____	_____
b) identify and practice good study habits	_____	_____

TABLE 11-2 (*continued*)

Criteria	Yes	No
c) understand the relationship between educational preparation and career opportunities	_____	_____
d) integrate career information with subject matter knowledge	_____	_____
e) participate in special career development activities	_____	_____
f) participate in special human relationship development activities	_____	_____
g) participate in small group counseling	_____	_____
h) have individual counseling with a school counselor	_____	_____
11. The program makes provisions for		
a) working cooperatively with faculty in providing appropriate informational and developmental activities for pupils	_____	_____
b) liaison with school-community resource personnel and agencies	_____	_____
c) parental conferences	_____	_____
d) resource materials for teacher, pupil, and parent use	_____	_____
12. The program is evaluated on a regular basis	_____	_____
13. This evaluation involves		
a) professional counseling staff	_____	_____
b) other pupil personnel service specialists	_____	_____
c) school administration	_____	_____
d) faculty	_____	_____
e) pupils	_____	_____
f) others (consultants, parents, community resource people)	_____	_____
14. The results of evaluation are utilized for program accountability, planning, and improvement	_____	_____
15. The achievements and activities of the program are reported regularly to		
a) the school administration	_____	_____
b) faculty	_____	_____
c) other pupil personnel specialists	_____	_____
d) parents	_____	_____
e) interested and involved community personnel	_____	_____

ducting of program evaluation. The law mandates three general types of evaluation, as follows:

- *Quality assurance of clinical services.* Each center is to establish an ongoing quality assurance of its clinical services.
- *Self-evaluation.* Each center will collect data and evaluate its services in relation to program goals and values and to catchment

area needs and resources. "The data shall consist of (a) cost of center operations; (b) patterns of use of services; (c) availability, awareness, acceptability, and accessibility of services; (d) impact of services upon the mental health of residents of the catchment area; (e) effectiveness of consultation and education services; (f) the impact of the Center on reducing inappropriate institutionalization." (National Institute of Mental Health, 1976)

Residents' review: "Each center will at least annually publicize and make available all evaluation data of the type listed above to residents of the catchment area. In addition, it will organize and publicize an opportunity for citizens to review the Center's program of services in order to assure that services are responsive to the needs of residents of the catchment area." (National Institute of Mental Health, 1976)

Research

Defined

As previously noted, research and evaluation are often linked in both discussions and definitions. Wheeler and Loesch (1981) suggest that

> This tendency to consider research and evaluation simultaneously and synonomously is grounded in the common belief that the two activities are actually the same thing. This belief has been confounded and perpetuated through the use of terms which were intended to differentiate research and evaluation, but which in fact had the opposite effect. (p. 573)
>
> Perhaps the only point of substantial agreement in the controversy is that research and program evaluation do differ in purpose. Research is conducted to discover new knowledge, to advance current scientific knowledge, and to build or improve theory. By contrast, program evaluation seeks to provide meaningful information for immediate use in decision making. (p. 574)

Froehle and Fuqua (1981) elaborate that

> Research and evaluation are both classes of inquiry activity, with evaluation denoting a much more applied function. Research has traditionally been used to refer to inquiry performed to produce generalizable knowledge, often without immediate application. We

believe that inquiry in the schools is more likely to become institutionalized when it provides immediate information for problem solving and decision making. In our judgment, it is not a question of whether this or that type of research method is right or better. Both have their place. It's a question of proportions and feasibility (p. 509).

THE RESEARCH PROCESS

Some General Guidelines. We are constantly reminded of the relatively small amount of published research produced by school counselors and other practitioners outside of university settings. As a result, many basic and local questions often go uninvestigated or are responded to by "opinion" only—hardly a basis for accountability. We strongly believe that the practicing on-line counselor must become more active as a researcher in advancing himself or herself professionally as well as his or her profession.

Froehle and Fuqua (1981) believe that some general guidelines warrant consideration.

- The first guideline has already been suggested, namely, that we select inquiry priorities in light of inquiry needs at the local level.

  In comparison with the guidelines that follow, this one should be regarded as the superordinate guideline.
- Encourage inquiry which is centered around current problems and newer modes of practice.

  Like our first guideline, this too is designed to generate information that is more likely to effect appropriate change as a function of its relevance.
- Both qualitative and quantitative approaches may be incorporated into the inquiry system.
- Evaluate the residual effects of intervention in addition to the hoped-for target outcomes.
- Some priority should be given to theoretical (as opposed to empirical) inquiry.
- Practicing counselors assume a greater responsibility for dissemination and that newer modes of dissemination be considered for carrying out that responsibility. (pp. 509–511)

General Procedures. The following overview of research procedures is not presented in the belief that it is sufficiently descriptive to be utilized as a basis for undertaking research. Its purpose is to provide a better understanding of the factors involved in the research process. Hopefully, it will also illustrate that research *can* be undertaken by school counselors who are unsophisticated in research technology.

The first step in undertaking educational research is the recognition of a need for information. In any educational setting, there is a constant and continuing need for information about the adequacy or effectiveness of the approaches being used, the most pressing needs of students, the various characteristics of students, and so forth. Thus, to initiate research, one simply has to determine the kind or kinds of information needed for justifying present practices or with which to develop more effective and more functional practices.

The second step in research is to survey the literature pertaining to the area for which information is needed. The purpose of the literature search is to see if sufficiently adequate answers to the question(s) already exist, to get a better understanding of the specific nature of the desired information, and to get ideas about the approaches that can most effectively be used to obtain the desired information. More on this point is presented in the section entitled "Utilizing Research Reports."

The third step is to identify specifically the nature of the information desired, or stated technically, the formulation of the specific research problem. In this regard, increased familiarity with the problem area acquired through the literature survey will make the task of defining a specific problem much less difficult.

After the problem has been precisely identified the fourth step is to determine the kinds of information needed to permit sound conclusions about the issue(s) in question. This step may simply require a listing of the questions for which answers are needed, or in a more complex study, it may require the development of research hypotheses. In either event, the research tasks must be defined in simple, precise language.

In the fifth step, the procedures for collecting and analyzing the needed information must be determined. In this design stage, the needed sample and the means by which it is to be selected are determined, the instruments and other data-collecting tools or approaches are selected, and the treatments to which the data will be subjected are chosen. The procedures built into the design must include only those that the researcher fully understands and can validly utilize.

The sixth step is the collection of the information demanded by the research questions or hypotheses. This information must be collected with valid procedures or instruments in a predetermined, systematic fashion for a specifically defined group or sample. Again, this may seem complex, but it need not be. When the statement is broken down, it simply says that to be useful for research purposes, observations collected must have been obtained through interviews, tests, questionnaires, and so forth, which are valid for that specific purpose; the observations must have been gathered through specifically stated, ordered procedures which either involved everyone in a given group or were truly representative of that group; and that the groups from which the observations were drawn must have been defined precisely.

In the seventh step, the collected observations are analyzed or, in other words, subjected to the predetermined statistical treatment. The complexity of this step is a function of the design developed in step five of this sequence. It may involve complex statistical treatment, but it need not if the design did not so stipulate.

In the eighth step, the research findings are interpreted and conclusions are drawn. The needed information that led to the study has now been obtained through procedures which satisfy the requirements of scientific inquiry. The questions initially raised can now be answered with valid knowledge.

In the final step the researcher shares the results of his or her research through such dissemination activities as presentations at professional meetings and publications in professional journals.

Utilizing Research Reports. Research results and the research process is important to program managers and other counselors who find it advantageous to have factual data to reinforce or guide their professional judgment. Whether one is an active researcher or not, a counseling professional cannot afford to ignore or gloss over the important research in the field. We must, for example, be aware of both the reservoir of accumulated knowledge dealing with human behavior and the results of current research studies that broaden, deepen, or perhaps alter our understanding of this behavior. Another obvious example is the possible influence of current research on the traditional theories of counseling and career decision making. As research technology continues to improve, we can anticipate an increase in research studies, more sophistication in their methodology and validity in their outcomes, as well as more relevance and application of the findings. Thus, it is important that all practicing counselors not only recognize the importance of research but also be cognizant of what we might label "guidelines" for identifying research of potential significance. These are as follows.

Be Aware of Common Sources of Research Reporting in Your Field

Some common indices and abstracts such as the *Review of Educational Research, The Education Index, Social Science Index, Sociology Index, Index Medicus, Psychological Abstracts* and *Dissertation Abstracts* are good starting points to broadly identify reports of recent research investigations. Publications representing the professional organizations in counseling and related fields such as the *Personnel and Guidance Journal, The Counseling Psychologist, The Counselor Education and Supervision Journal,* the *National Vocational Guidance Association Quarterly, The School Counselor* and the *Elementary School Guidance and Counseling Journal* are rich sources of recent research studies in the field, but their content may also indicate research related to current issues, trends, or problems.

Currently published literature may also report recent research findings. Those rare publications such as the special issues of *The Personnel and Guidance Journal* for April, May, June, 1981 (volume 58, numbers 8, 9, 10) may be "gold mines" of research information for counselors.

Identify Research Studies Which Appear to Be Relevant to Your Own Professional Needs

The abundance of reported research, past and present, is enough to overwhelm the most conscientious researcher. Any user of research findings must learn to be selective lest she or he drown in the ever growing tidal waves of research reporting. Therefore, it is important that we identify as specifically as possible the kind of knowledge we are seeking and focus our search on this topic.

Review the Studies You Have Selected in Terms of the Following:

a. The design of the study: (You may need the assistance of a competent researcher at this point. They are not too difficult to locate if you are close to a large school system, institution of higher education, large mental health agency or state government office). This is important in determining the probable accuracy of the findings, their generalizability to your situation, and the conclusions or implications which can be drawn from them.
b. Readability: Some research reports are technical reports written primarily for other researchers. Both the vocabulary and the statistical methods through which the data are presented may confuse, mislead, or simply confound the reader. Unsophisticated attempts to "figure out" what the report is saying should not be undertaken. If you cannot understand the report you should select a different report to study or you may again seek the help of a competent researcher who can interpret the study to you.
c. Originality of the research: A firsthand report of a study by the researcher(s) who were the principal investigators is more desirable than "second-hand" reporting, summaries, or citations by others. Whereas secondary sources can be useful, they are usually more brief than the original source and may inadvertently misrepresent the findings.
d. Reputation of the author/researcher may also be considered. Established researchers/authors have achieved their preeminence through previous studies that have been endorsed by their peers as sound in design, addressing important needs, and significant in their findings.

Seek Research Studies That Contribute New Knowledge or Understanding

Although studies that verify traditional theories and accepted practices are important, we should also actually seek new ideas and concepts.

Research in Community Mental Health Agencies

Counselors working in community mental health agency settings also have the opportunity to make unique contributions to the field of counseling through their research endeavors. It is important to recognize that different client populations, more diverse and usually more intense client problems, plus greater variation in staff backgrounds and hence, treatment approaches, offer counselor researchers in these settings the opportunity for unique and significant research investigations. It also appears that counselors in these settings are becoming increasingly active researchers. Anderson (1981) suggested several factors that are stimulating research within community mental health centers.

> First, there is the Community Mental Health Center Amendment of 1975 (PL 94-63), which requires community mental health centers to establish ongoing quality assurance programs. This provides an emphasis on research with local application and means that administrators must think in terms of evaluating the techniques and programs used in their centers. (For further discussion see Liptzin, Stockdill, & Brown, 1977.)
>
> Secondly, counselors have become increasingly aware that much of what they were taught in graduate school may not be directly applicable to many of their clients. They see that new approaches are needed. Further, many counselors are dissatisfied with studies now appearing in some journals, because they are too theoretical and the usefulness of the findings is not clear. This dissatisfaction has led to a recognition that counselors may need to provide some of their own solutions to client and agency problems by asking the right research questions.
>
> A third positive factor is the very diversity of the field and, therefore, the wide range of possibilities for acceptable research. There is also the stimulus of considerable cross-fertilization from other fields, such as social work, psychiatry, nursing, law, and others. The possibilities for research in community mental health centers are so wide it is difficult to categorize their limits. (p. 51)

Guidelines for Developing Funded Research Proposals

In recent years, a variety of federal and state legislative acts, plus many philanthropic foundations, have provided funding opportunities for research in areas of concern to professional counselors in both school and nonschool settings. Program managers need to be alert to funding opportunities as well as to guidelines for the developing of proposals for possible funding. Proposals for funded research usually must conform to a format specified by the funding agency. However, since most research proposals follow a similar format, the guidelines that are suggested should be generally applicable.

The purpose of a research proposal is to convey an accurate picture of what is proposed, why it is significant, how it will be accomplished, how it will be evaluated, the competency of those who will undertake it for their specific tasks, how much it will cost, and the adequacy of any required facilities. That purpose is best achieved through simple, clear, and precise language.

Basic to proposal preparation is a clear understanding of the specific information requested by the funding agency and the desired proposal format. It is imperative that the proposal guidelines specified by that agency are carefully read and that all requested information is provided in the order specified.

All specified sections of a proposal format are important, but the four that are briefly explained in the following discussion require special attention.

Statement of the Problem. This section of the proposal should contain a well-defined, specific statement of the problem; the need for such a study (its educational significance); and concisely stated, measurable objectives. Conceptual and research literature should be cited to stress the significance of, or the need for, the study, but the literature cited should be specifically relevant to the proposed study.

Procedures. This section of the proposal must present the design of the study and a fully detailed description of the procedures to be utilized. It should be apparent to a reader that the stipulated procedures will enable the achievement of the project's stated objectives. It should describe the sample to be used and how the sample is to be selected, the instruments and other data-collecting tools or approaches to be utilized, the statistical treatments to be applied, and the evaluational procedures to be employed. If the objectives were definitely stated—as they should be—the evaluational procedures should evolve from them. Although this section must be concise, it must also be complete. A basic criterion for evaluating most proposals is the soundness of the methodology employed.

Personnel and Facilities. This, too, is a most important section, especially in proposals for federal funding. As the purpose of this section is to enable a determination of the research capabilities, care must be taken to identify the personnel involved and to show that by training and experience, these individuals have the research competencies required for the implementation of the proposed study. Similarly, the facilities required for the research endeavor should be described and their availability assured.

Budget. The cost estimates for the proposed project must be accurate, detailed, justifiable, and reasonable. It must be clearly evident how the anticipated expenditures relate to each of the specified procedural steps.

Ethical Issues in Human Research

By its very nature, counseling research, with rare exceptions, must involve human beings. Increased concern for the rights of human subjects in recent generations has resulted in increased efforts on the part of professional organizations and research institutions and agencies, including the U.S. government, to safeguard the rights and dignity of individuals who are involved as subjects of research.

Bigner and Jacobsen (1981) indicate that

> In the past several years, there has been an increased concern among the public as well as investigators about ethical factors of research involving humans. As a consequence, the major professional behavioral science organizations in cooperation with governmental agencies have developed guidelines and standards for human research (American Psychological Association, 1973; Society for Research in Child Development, 1973). These regulations suggest several areas where appropriate concern and attention from researchers should be focused to ensure individuals' rights and protection from potential harm. The principal ethical issues of human behavioral research include: (a) obtaining informed consent of subjects; (b) protecting subjects' right to privacy; (c) assessing potential

> risks from research participation; and (d) initiating peer reviews of proposed research projects. (p. 650)

Summary and Implications

In recent years there has been an increasing demand for accountability by counseling programs in both school and nonschool settings. Accountability suggests a factual data base which suggests program objectives and efficient and effective procedures for accomplishing them. Accountability also requires evaluation and this process is enhanced when certain guiding principles are recognized. These include (1) a recognition of program goals; (2) the use of valid measuring criteria; (3) the valid application of the measuring criteria; (4) the involvement of all who are affected by the counseling program; (5) feedback and follow-through; (6) evaluation as a planned, continuous process; and (7) an emphasis on the positive. A variety of evaluation models and instruments are available to counseling program managers.

Research is also important to program accountability as a means of identifying, validating, or improving effective practices.

The procedural steps that counselors can follow in undertaking research at their level are (1) a recognition of the need for information; (2) a survey of the appropriate literature; (3) a formulation of the specific research problem; (4) a determination of the kinds of information needed to permit sound conclusions; (5) procedures for collecting and analyzing the information; (6) the actual collection of the information; (7) the actual analysis of the data; (8) interpretation of conclusions about the research; and (9) dissemination of the results.

Program managers should also make use of appropriate published research reports and be aware of opportunities and procedures for research funding. In all research involving human subjects, the researchers must be aware of the legal and ethical guidelines for safeguarding the rights and dignity of the individuals involved as subjects.

APPENDIX A

Student Survey

Class rank: ____________ ____________ M_____ F_____

	Yes	No	Not Sure
1. Do you enjoy living in ______________________ ?	____	____	____
2. Do you, for the most part, enjoy school?	____	____	____
3. Do you plan to finish high school:	____	____	____
4. Would you like to continue your education beyond high school?	____	____	____

If yes: vocational/
technical school ____
junior college ____
4-yr. college or
university ____

Any special program?
(Please indicate) ______________________

	Yes	No	Not Sure
5. Is there anything you would like to take in high school that is not offered?	____	____	____

If yes, what? (Please list)

____
____
____
____

	Yes	No	Not Sure
6. Do you feel reasonably sure that you could, at this time, identify any special abilities or aptitudes that you may have?	____	____	____

	Yes	*No*	*Not Sure*
7. Do you feel reasonably sure that you can identify your special interests?	____	____	____
8. Do you feel that you know most of the strong and weak points of your personality?	____	____	____
9. Do you understand yourself to your own satisfaction?	____	____	____
10. Do you feel fairly certain about your career plans at this time?	____	____	____
11. Have you discussed your career plans with any faculty or counselor of this school?	____	____	____
12. Have the programs and/or faculty or counselors of this school helped you in any way in your career planning?	____	____	____
13. Do you feel that there is at least one teacher or counselor in this school who knows you well enough to be of genuine help in working with you on your problems? If yes,	____	____	____

which— teacher ____
counselor ____
both ____

	Yes	*No*	*Not Sure*
14. If your answer to the previous question was yes, do you feel that this teacher or counselor has sufficient time to talk to you?	____	____	____
15. Have you ever had a serious problem that you would have liked to have discussed with some faculty member or counselor immediately?	____	____	____
16. If your answer to the previous question was yes, was it or would it have been possible, regardless of the hour of the school day, to discuss this problem with this person?	____	____	____
17. Have you ever had a problem that you would have liked to talk over with a particular faculty member or counselor but didn't because you were afraid—or just couldn't figure out a way to approach this teacher or counselor with your problem?	____	____	____

18. Would you usually prefer to talk over your personal problems with (Mark in order, with 1 being your first choice; 2, your second choice, etc.)
   a. counselor ____
   b. teacher ____
   c. parents ____
   d. personal friends ____
   e. school principal ____
   f. other (who ?) ____________________

____

19. Check any of the following that are of concern to you and circle those which are your biggest problems.
    a. No jobs on graduation ______
    b. Don't know what I want to be ______
    c. School isn't interesting ______
    d. Relations with the opposite sex ______
    e. No recreational opportunities in community ______
    f. No respect by adults ______
    g. Grades ______
    h. Problems with teachers ______
    i. Problems with parents ______
    j. Problems with my fellow students ______
    k. Continuing my education ______
    l. Smoking ______
    m. Use of drugs ______
    n. Use of alcohol ______
    o. Other (list)
    ____
    ____
    ____
    ____

20. Any other comments that will help your school plan a program to meet your needs?
    ____
    ____
    ____
    ____

APPENDIX B

Parent Survey

M_____ F_____

What grade(s) do you have children in? 9_____ 10_____ 11_____ 12_____
Are they (number each) M_____ F_____

	Yes	*No*	*Not Sure*
1. Do you believe your child (children) enjoys living in ____________________?	_____	_____	_____
2. Does he or she for the most part seem to enjoy school?	_____	_____	_____
3. Do you believe he or she will finish high school?	_____	_____	_____
4. Do you believe your child will continue his or her education after high school?	_____	_____	_____
5. Are there courses or programs that you wish were available which are not currently offered in their school?	_____	_____	_____

If yes, please list:

____

____

____

____

	Yes	*No*	*Not Sure*
6. Do you feel your child (children) understand themselves, their strengths, and their weaknesses?	_____	_____	_____
7. Do you feel the school provides sufficient assistance to your child (children) in terms of:	_____	_____	_____
a. career planning	_____	_____	_____
b. educational planning	_____	_____	_____

	Yes	No	Not Sure
c. personal-social development	______	______	______
d. coping with personal adjustment problems	______	______	______
e. developing healthy living habits	______	______	______
f. understanding self	______	______	______

8. Check √ any of the following that you feel are the problems of students in this school. Circle √ those which you feel are the most pressing.
   a. Lack of career opportunities ______
   b. Lack of career direction ______
   c. Lack of motivation in school ______
   d. Boy-girl relationships ______
   e. Lack of recreational interests or opportunities ______
   f. No respect for adults ______
   g. Poor achievement in school ______
   h. Problems with teachers ______
   i. Family difficulties ______
   j. Problems with peers ______
   k. Poor educational planning ______
   l. Smoking ______
   m. Drugs ______
   n. Alcohol ______
   o. Other (list) ____
   ____
   ____
   ____
   ____

9. Any additional comments?
   ____
   ____
   ____
   ____

APPENDIX C

Teacher Survey

(optional) M_____ F_____
Subject matter area(s) _______________ _______________ _______________
Grade level(s) 9_____ 10_____ 11_____ 12_____
Years in this school; 0–5_____; 6–10_____; 11–15_____; 16+_____
Degrees: BA/BS_____ MA/MS_____ PhD/EdD_____

	Yes	No	Not Sure
1. Do you enjoy living in this community?	_____	_____	_____
2. Do you, for the most part, enjoy teaching in this school?	_____	_____	_____
3. Do you believe most of your students enjoy this school?	_____	_____	_____
4. Are there courses or programs that you feel this school needs to offer which are not presently available to students? If yes, what (please list) ____________ ____________ ____________ ____________	_____	_____	_____
5. Do you feel you understand most of your students?	_____	_____	_____
6. Do you feel most of your students understand themselves, their strengths, and their weaknesses?	_____	_____	_____
7. Do you feel you have sufficient time to assist students regarding their personal and educational concerns?	_____	_____	_____

8. Check √ any of the following that you feel are the problems of students in this school. Circle ⓥ those which you feel are the most pressing.

   a. Lack of career opportunities _____
   b. Lack of career direction _____
   c. Lack of motivation in school _____
   d. Boy-girl relationships _____
   e. Lack of recreational interests or opportunities _____
   f. No respect for adults _____
   g. Poor achievement in school _____
   h. Problems with teachers _____
   i. Family difficulties _____
   j. Problems with peers _____
   k. Poor educational planning _____
   l. Smoking _____
   m. Drugs _____
   n. Alcohol _____
   o. Other (list) ______________________________

9. Any additional comments?

APPENDIX D

Ethical Standards

(Approved by Executive Committee upon referral of the Board of Directors, January 17, 1981).

Preamble

The American Personnel and Guidance Association is an educational, scientific, and professional organization whose members are dedicated to the enhancement of the worth, dignity, potential, and uniqueness of each individual and thus to the service of society.

The Association recognizes that the role definitions and work settings of its members include a wide variety of academic disciplines, levels of academic preparation and agency services. This diversity reflects the breadth of the Association's interest and influence. It also poses challenging complexities in efforts to set standards for the performance of members, desired requisite preparation or practice, and supporting social, legal, and ethical controls.

The specification of ethical standards enables the Association to clarify to present and future members and to those served by members, the nature of ethical responsibilities held in common by its members.

The existence of such standards serves to stimulate greater concern by members for their own professional functioning and for the conduct of fellow professionals such as counselors, guidance and student personnel workers, and others in the helping professions. As the ethical code of the Association, this document establishes principles that define the ethical behavior of Association members.

Section A: General

1. The member influences the development of the profession by continuous efforts to improve professional practices, teaching, services, and research. Professional growth is continuous throughout the member's career and is exemplified by the development of a philosophy that explains why and how a member functions in the helping relationship. Members must gather data on their effectiveness and be guided by the findings.

2. The member has a responsibility both to the individual who is served and to the institution within which the service is performed to maintain high standards of professional conduct. The member strives to maintain the highest levels of professional services offered to the individuals to be served. The member also strives to assist the agency, organization, or institution in providing the highest caliber of professional services. The acceptance of employment in an institution implies that the member is in agreement with the general policies and principles of the instutition. Therefore the professional activities of the member are also in accord with the objectives of the institution. If, despite concerted efforts, the member cannot reach agreement with the employer as to acceptable standards of conduct that allow for changes in institutional policy conducive to the positive growth and development of clients, then terminating the affiliation should be seriously considered.

3. Ethical behavior among professional associates, both members and nonmembers, must be expected at all times. When information is possessed that raises doubt as to the ethical behavior of professional colleagues, whether Association members or not, the member must take action to attempt to rectify such a condition. Such action shall use the institution's channels first and then use procedures established by the state Branch, Division, or Association.

4. The member neither claims nor implies professional qualifications exceeding those possessed and is responsible for correcting any misrepresentations of these qualifications by others.

5. In establishing fees for professional counseling services, members must consider the financial status of clients and locality. In the event that the established fee structure is inappropriate for a client, assistance must be provided in finding comparable services of acceptable cost.

6. When members provide information to the public or to subordinates, peers or supervisors, they have a responsibility to ensure that the content is general, unidentified client information that is accurate, unbiased, and consists of objective, factual data.

7. With regard to the delivery of professional services, members

should accept only those positions for which they are professionally qualified.

8. In the counseling relationship the counselor is aware of the intimacy of the relationship and maintains respect for the client and avoids engaging in activities that seek to meet the counselor's personal needs at the expense of that client. Through awareness of the negative impact of both racial and sexual stereotyping and discrimination, the counselor guards the individual rights and personal dignity of the client in the counseling relationship.

Section B: Counseling Relationship

This section refers to practices and procedures of individual and/or group counseling relationships.

The member must recognize the need for client freedom of choice. Under those circumstances where this is not possible, the member must apprise clients of restrictions that may limit their freedom of choice.

1. The member's *primary* obligation is to respect the integrity and promote the welfare of the client(s), whether the client(s) is (are) assisted individually or in a group relationship. In a group setting, the member is also responsible for taking reasonable precautions to protect individuals from physical and/or psychological trauma resulting from interaction within the group.

2. The counseling relationship and information resulting therefrom be kept confidential, consistent with the obligations of the member as a professional person. In a group counseling setting, the counselor must set a norm of confidentiality regarding all group participants' disclosures.

3. If an individual is already in a counseling relationship with another professional person, the member does not enter into a counseling relationship without first contacting and receiving the approval of that other professional. If the member discovers that the client is in another counseling relationship after the counseling relationship begins, the member must gain the consent of the other professional or terminate the relationship, unless the client elects to terminate the other relationship.

4. When the client's condition indicates that there is clear and imminent danger to the client or others, the member must take reasonable personal action or inform responsible authorities. Consulation with other professionals must be used where possible. The assumption of responsibility for the client(s) behavior must be taken only after careful deliberation. The client must be involved in the assumption of responsibility as quickly as possible.

5. Records of the counseling relationship, including interview notes, test data, correspondence, tape recordings, and other documents, are to be considered professional information for use in counseling and they should not be considered a part of the records of the institution or agency in which the counselor is employed unless specified by state statute or regulation. Revelation to others of counseling material must occur only upon the expressed consent of the client.

6. Use of data derived from a counseling relationship for purposes of counselor training or research shall be confined to content that can be disguised to ensure full protection of the identity of the subject client.

7. The member must inform the client of the purposes, goals, techniques, rules of procedure and limitations that may affect the relationship at or before the time that the counseling relationship is entered.

8. The member must screen prospective group participants, especially when the emphasis is on self-understanding and growth through self-disclosure. The member must maintain an awareness of the group participants' compatibility throughout the life of the group.

9. The member may choose to consult with any other professionally competent person about a client. In choosing a consultant, the member must avoid placing the consultant in a conflict of interest situation that would preclude the consultant's being a proper party to the member's efforts to help the client.

10. If the member determines an inability to be of professional assistance to the client, the member must either avoid initiating the counseling relationship or immediately terminate that relationship. In either event, the member must suggest appropriate alternatives. (The member must be knowledgeable about referral resources so that a satisfactory referral can be initiated). In the event the client declines the suggested referral, the member is not obligated to continue the relationship.

11. When the member has other relationships, particularly of an administrative, supervisory and/or evaluative nature with an individual seeking counseling services, the member must not serve as the counselor but should refer the individual to another professional. Only in instances where such an alternative is unavailable and where the individual's situation warrants counseling intervention should the member enter into and/or maintain a counseling relationship. Dual relationships with clients that might impair the member's objectivity and professional judgment (e.g., as with close friends or relatives, sexual intimacies with any client) must be avoided and/or the counseling relationship terminated through referral to another competent professional.

12. All experimental methods of treatment must be clearly indicated to prospective recipients and safety precautions are to be adhered to by the member.

13. When the member is engaged in short-term group treatment/training programs (e.g., marathons and other encounter-type or growth groups), the member ensures that there is professional assistance available during and following the group experience.

14. Should the member be engaged in a work setting that calls for any variation from the above statements, the member is obligated to consult with other professionals whenever possible to consider justifiable alternatives.

Section C: Measurement and Evaluation

The primary purpose of educational and psychological testing is to provide descriptive measures that are objective and interpretable in either comparative or absolute terms. The member must recognize the need to interpret the statements that follow as applying to the whole range of appraisal techniques including test and nontest data. Test results constitute only one of a variety of pertinent sources of information for personnel, guidance, and counseling decisions.

1. The member must provide specific orientation or information to the examinee(s) prior to and following the test administration so that the results of testing may be placed in proper perspective with other relevant factors. In so doing, the member must recognize the effects of socioeconomic, ethnic and cultural factors on test scores. It is the member's professional responsibility to use additional unvalidated information carefully in modifying interpretation of the test results.

2. In selecting tests for use in a given situation or with a particular client, the member must consider carefully the specific validity, reliability, and appropriateness of the test(s). *General* validity, reliability and the like may be questioned legally as well as ethically when tests are used for vocational and educational selection, placement, or counseling.

3. When making any statements to the public about tests and testing, the member must give accurate information and avoid false claims or misconceptions. Special efforts are often required to avoid unwarranted connotations of such terms as *IQ* and *grade equivalent scores*.

4. Different tests demand different levels of competence for administration, scoring, and interpretation. Members must recognize the limits of their competence and perform only those functions for which they are prepared.

5. Tests must be administered under the same conditions that were established in their standardization. When tests are not administered under standard conditions or when unusual behavior or irregularities

occur during the testing session, those conditions must be noted and the results designated as invalid or of questionable validity. Unsupervised or inadequately supervised test-taking, such as the use of tests through the mails, is considered unethical. On the other hand, the use of instruments that are so designed or standardized to be self-administered and self-scored, such as interest inventories, is to be encouraged.

6. The meaningfulness of test results used in personnel, guidance, and counseling functions generally depends on the examinee's unfamiliarity with the specific items on the test. Any prior coaching or dissemination of the test materials can invalidate test results. Therefore, test security is one of the professional obligations of the member. Conditions that produce most favorable test results must be made known to the examinee.

7. The purpose of testing and the explicit use of the results must be made known to the examinee prior to testing. The counselor must ensure that instrument limitations are not exceeded and that periodic review and/or retesting are made to prevent client stereotyping.

8. The examinee's welfare and explicit prior understanding must be the criteria for determining the recipients of the test results. The member must see that specific interpretation accompanies any release of individual or group test data. The interpretation of test data must be related to the examinee's particular concerns.

9. The member must be cautious when interpreting the results of research instruments possessing insufficient technical data. The specific purposes for the use of such instruments must be stated explicitly to examinees.

10. The member must proceed with caution when attempting to evaluate and interpret the performance of minority group members or other persons who are not represented in the norm group on which the instrument was standardized.

11. The member must guard against the appropriation, reproduction, or modifications of published tests or parts thereof without acknowledgment and permission from the previous publisher.

12. Regarding the preparation, publication and distribution of tests, reference should be made to:

a. *Standards for Educational and Psychological Tests and Manuals*, revised edition, 1974, published by the American Psychological Association on behalf of itself, the American Educational Research Association and the National Council on Measurement in Education.

b. The responsible use of tests: A position paper of AMEG, APGA, and NCME. *Measurement and Evaluation in Guidance*, 1972, 5, 385–388.

c. "Responsibilities of Users of Standardized Tests," APGA, *Guidepost*, October 5, 1978, pp. 5–8.

Section D: Research and Publication

1. Guidelines on research with human subjects shall be adhered to, such as:

a. *Ethical Principles in the Conduct of Research with Human Participants*, Washington, D.C.: American Psychological Association, Inc., 1973.

b. Code of Federal Regulations, Title 45, Subtitle A, Part 46, as currently issued.

2. In planning any research activity dealing with human subjects, the member must be aware of and responsive to all pertinent ethical principles and ensure that the research problem, design, and execution are in full compliance with them.

3. Responsibility for ethical research practice lies with the principal researcher, while others involved in the research activities share ethical obligation and full responsibility for their own actions.

4. In research with human subjects, researchers are responsible for the subjects' welfare throughout the experiment and they must take all reasonable precautions to avoid causing injurious psychological, physical, or social effects on their subjects.

5. All research subjects must be informed of the purpose of the study except when withholding information or providing misinformation to them is essential to the investigation. In such research the member must be responsible for corrective action as soon as possible following completion of the research.

6. Participation in research must be voluntary. Involuntary participation is appropriate only when it can be demonstrated that participation will have no harmful effects on subjects and is essential to the investigation.

7. When reporting research results, explicit mention must be made of all variables and conditions known to the investigator that might affect the outcome of the investigation or the interpretation of the data.

8. The member must be responsible for conducting and reporting investigations in a manner that minimizes the possibility that results will be misleading.

9. The member has an obligation to make available sufficient original research data to qualified others who may wish to replicate the study.

10. When supplying data, aiding in the research of another person, reporting research results, or in making original data available, due care must be taken to disguise the identity of the subjects in the absence of specific authorization from such subjects to do otherwise.

11. When conducting and reporting research, the member must be familiar with, and give recognition to, previous work on the topic, as well as to observe all copyright laws and follow the principles of giving full credit to all to whom credit is due.

12. The member must give due credit through joint authorship, acknowledgment, footnote statements, or other appropriate means to those who have contributed significantly to the research and/or publication, in accordance with such contributions.

13. The member must communicate to other members the results of any research judged to be of professional or scientific value. Results reflecting unfavorably on institutions, programs, services, or vested interests must not be withheld for such reasons.

14. If members agree to cooperate with another individual in research and/or publication, they incur an obligation to cooperate as promised in terms of punctuality of performance and with full regard to the completeness and accuracy of the information required.

15. Ethical practice requires that authors not submit the same manuscript or one essentially similar in content, for simultaneous publication consideration by two or more journals. In addition, manuscripts published in whole or in substantial part, in another journal or published work should not be submitted for publication without acknowledgment and permission from the previous publication.

Section E: Consulting

Consultation refers to a voluntary relationship between a professional helper and help-needing individual, group or social unit in which the consultant is providing help to the client(s) in defining and solving a work-related problem or potential problem with a client or client system. (This definition is adapted from Kurpius, DeWayne. Consultation theory and process: An integrated model. *Personnel and Guidance Journal,* 1978, 56.

1. The member acting as consultant must have a high degree of self-awareness of his-her own values, knowledge, skills, limitations, and needs in entering a helping relationship that involves human and-or organizational change and that the focus of the relationship be on the issues to be resolved and not on the person(s) presenting the problem.

2. There must be understanding and agreement between member

and client for the problem definition, change goals, and predicated consequences of interventions selected.

3. The member must be reasonably certain that she/he or the organization represented has the necessary competencies and resources for giving the kind of help that is needed now or may develop later and that appropriate referral resources are available to the consultant.

4. The consulting relationship must be one in which client adaptability and growth toward self-direction are encouraged and cultivated. The member must maintain this role consistently and not become a decision maker for the client or create a future dependency on the consultant.

5. When announcing consultant availability for services, the member conscientiously adheres to the Association's *Ethical Standards*.

6. The member must refuse a private fee or other remuneration for consultation with persons who are entitled to these services through the member's employing institution or agency. The policies of a particular agency may make explicit provisions for private practice with agency clients by members of its staff. In such instances, the clients must be apprised of other options open to them should they seek private counseling services.

Section F: Private Practice

1. The member should assist the profession by facilitating the availability of counseling services in private as well as public settings.

2. In advertising services as a private practitioner, the member must advertise the services in such a manner so as to accurately inform the public as to services, expertise, profession, and techniques of counseling in a professional manner. A member who assumes an executive leadership role in the organization shall not permit his/her name to be used in professional notices during periods when not actively engaged in the private practice of counseling.

The member may list the following: highest revelant degree, type and level of certification or license, type and/or description of services, and other relevant information. Such information must not contain false, inaccurate, misleading, partial, out-of-context, or deceptive material or statements.

3. Members may join in partnership/corporation with other members and-or other professionals provided that each member of the partnership or corporation makes clear the separate specialties by name in compliance with the regulations of the locality.

4. A member has an obligation to withdraw from a counseling relationship if it is believed that employment will result in violation of the *Ethical Standards*. If the mental or physical condition of the member renders it difficult to carry out an effective professional relationship or if the member is discharged by the client because the counseling relationship is no longer productive for the client, then the member is obligated to terminate the counseling relationship.

5. A member must adhere to the regulations for private practice of the locality where the services are offered.

6. It is unethical to use one's institutional affiliation to recruit clients for one's private practice.

Section G: Personnel Administration

It is recognized that most members are employed in public or quasi-public institutions. The functioning of a member within an institution must contribute to the goals of the institution and vice versa if either is to accomplish their respective goals or objectives. It is therefore essential that the member and the institution function in ways to (a) make the institution's goals explicit and public; (b) make the member's contribution to institutional goals specific; and (c) foster mutual accountability for goal achievement.

To accomplish these objectives, it is recognized that the member and the employer must share responsibilities in the formulation and implementation of personnel policies.

1. Members must define and describe the parameters and levels of their professional competency.

2. Members must establish interpersonal relations and working agreements with supervisors and subordinates regarding counseling or clinical relationships, confidentiality, distinction between public and private material, maintenance, and dissemination of recorded information, work load and accountability. Working agreements in each instance must be specified and made known to those concerned.

3. Members must alert their employers to conditions that may be potentially disruptive or damaging.

4. Members must inform employers of conditions that may limit their effectiveness.

5. Members must submit regularly to professional review and evaluation.

6. Members must be responsible for inservice development of self and-or staff.

7. Members must inform their staff of goals and programs.

8. Members must provide personnel practices that guarantee and enhance the rights and welfare of each recipient of their service.

9. Members must select competent persons and assign responsibilities compatible with their skills and experiences.

Section H: Preparation Standards

Members who are responsible for training others must be guided by the preparation standards of the Association and relevant Division(s). The member who functions in the capacity of trainer assumes unique ethical responsibilities that frequently go beyond that of the member who does not function in a training capacity. These ethical responsibilities are outlined as follows:

1. Members must orient students to program expectations, basic skills development, and employment prospects prior to admission to the program.

2. Members in charge of learning experiences must establish programs that integrate academic study and supervised practice.

3. Members must establish a program directed toward developing students' skills, knowledge, and self-understanding, stated whenever possible in competency or performance terms.

4. Members must identify the levels of competencies of their students in compliance with relevant Division standards. These competencies must accommodate the para-professional as well as the professional.

5. Members, through continual student evaluation and appraisal, must be aware of the personal limitations of the learner that might impede future performance. The instructor must not only assist the learner in securing remedial assistance but also screen from the program those individuals who are unable to provide competent services.

6. Members must provide a program that includes training in research commensurate with levels of role functioning. Para-professional and technician-level personnel must be trained as consumers of research. In addition, these personnel must learn how to evaluate their own and their program's effectiveness. Graduate training, especially at the doctoral level, would include preparation for original research by the member.

7. Members must make students aware of the ethical responsibilities and standards of the profession.

8. Preparatory programs must encourage students to value the ideals of service to individuals and to society. In this regard, direct financial remuneration or lack thereof must not influence the quality of service

rendered. Monetary considerations must not be allowed to overshadow professional and humanitarian needs.

9. Members responsible for educational programs must be skilled as teachers and practitioners.

10. Members must present thoroughly varied theoretical positions so that students may make comparisons and have the opportunity to select a position.

11. Members must develop clear policies within their educational institutions regarding field placement and the roles of the student and the instructor in such placements.

12. Members must ensure that forms of learning focusing on self-understanding or growth are voluntary, or if required as part of the education program, are made known to prospective students prior to entering the program. When the education program offers a growth experience with an emphasis on self-disclosure or other relatively intimate or personal involvement, the member must have no administrative, supervisory, or evaluating authority regarding the participant.

13. Members must conduct an educational program in keeping with the current relevant guidelines of the American Personnel and Guidance Association and its Divisions.

APPENDIX E

Ethical Principles of Psychologists

Preamble

Psychologists respect the dignity and worth of the individual and strive for the preservation and protection of fundamental human rights. They are committed to increasing knowledge of human behavior and of people's understanding of themselves and others and to the utilization of such knowledge for the promotion of human welfare. While pursuing

This version of the Ethical Principles of Psychologists (formerly entitled Ethical Standards of Psychologists) was adopted by the American Psychological Association's Council of Representatives on January 24, 1981. The revised Ethical Principles contain both substantive and grammatical changes in each of the nine ethical principles constituting the Ethical Standards of Psychologists previously adopted by the Council of Representatives in 1979, plus a new tenth principle entitled Care and Use of Animals. Inquiries concerning the Ethical Principles of Psychologists should be addressed to the Administrative Officer for Ethics, American Psychological Association, 1200 Seventeenth Street, N.W., Washington, D.C. 20036.

These revised Ethical Principles apply to psychologists, to students of psychology, and to others who do work of a psychological nature under the supervision of a psychologist. They are also intended for the guidance of nonmembers of the Association who are engaged in psychological research or practice.

Any complaints of unethical conduct filed after January 24, 1981, shall be governed by this 1981 revision. However, conduct (a) complained about after January 24, 1981, but which occurred prior to that date, and (b) not considered unethical under prior versions of the principles but considered unethical under the 1981 revision, shall not be deemed a violation of ethical principles. Any complaints pending as of January 24, 1981, shall be governed either by the 1979 or by the 1981 version of the Ethical Principles, at the sound discretion of the Committee on Scientific and Professional Ethics and Conduct.

these objectives, they make every effort to protect the welfare of those who seek their services and of the research participants that may be the object of study. They use their skills only for purposes consistent with these values and do not knowingly permit their misuse by others. While demanding for themselves freedom of inquiry and communication, psychologists accept the responsibility this freedom requires: competence, objectivity in the application of skills, and concern for the best interests of clients, colleagues, students, research participants, and society. In the pursuit of these ideals, psychologists subscribe to principles in the following areas: 1. Responsibility, 2. Competence, 3. Moral and Legal Standards, 4. Public Statements, 5. Confidentiality, 6. Welfare of the Consumer, 7. Professional Relationships, 8. Assessment Techniques, 9. Research With Human Participants, and 10. Care and Use of Animals.

Acceptance of membership in the American Psychological Association commits the member to adherence to these principles.

Psychologists cooperate with duly constituted committees of the American Psychological Association, in particular, the Committee on Scientific and Professional Ethics and Conduct, by responding to inquiries promptly and completely. Members also respond promptly and completely to inquiries from duly constituted state association ethics committees and professional standards review committees.

Principle 1: Responsibility

In providing services, psychologists maintain the highest standards of their profession. They accept responsibility for the consequences of their acts and make every effort to ensure that their services are used appropriately.

a. As scientists, psychologists accept responsibility for the selection of their research topics and the methods used in investigation, analysis, and reporting. They plan their research in ways to minimize the possibility that their findings will be misleading. They provide thorough discussion of the limitations of their data, especially where their work touches on social policy or might be construed to the detriment of persons in specific age, sex, ethnic, socioeconomic, or other social groups. In publishing reports of their work, they never suppress disconfirming data, and they acknowledge the existence of alternative hypotheses and explanations of their findings. Psychologists take credit only for work they have actually done.

b. Psychologists clarify in advance with all appropriate persons and agencies the expectations for sharing and utilizing research data. They avoid relationships that may limit their objectivity or create a conflict of interest. Interference with the milieu in which data are collected is kept to a minimum.

c. Psychologists have the responsibility to attempt to prevent distortion, misuse, or suppression of psychological findings by the institution or agency of which they are employees.

d. As members of governmental or other organizational bodies, psychologists remain accountable as individuals to the highest standards of their profession.

e. As teachers, psychologists recognize their primary obligation to help others acquire knowledge and skill. They maintain high standards of scholarship by presenting psychological information objectively, fully, and accurately.

f. As practitioners, psychologists know that they bear a heavy social responsibility because their recommendations and professional actions may alter the lives of others. They are alert to personal, social, organizational, financial, or political situations and pressures that might lead to misuse of their influence.

Principle 2: Competence

The maintenance of high standards of competence is a responsibility shared by all psychologists in the interest of the public and the profession as a whole. Psychologists recognize the boundaries of their competence and the limitations of their techniques. They only provide services and only use techniques for which they are qualified by training and experience. In those areas in which recognized standards do not yet exist, psychologists take whatever precautions are necessary to protect the welfare of their clients. They maintain knowledge of current scientific and professional information related to the services they render.

a. Psychologists accurately represent their competence, education, training, and experience. They claim as evidence of educational qualifications only those degrees obtained from institutions acceptable under the Bylaws and Rules of Council of the American Psychological Association.

b. As teachers, psychologists perform their duties on the basis of careful preparation so that their instruction is accurate, current, and scholarly.

c. Psychologists recognize the need for continuing education and are open to new procedures and changes in expectations and values over time.

d. Psychologists recognize differences among people, such as those that may be associated with age, sex, socioeconomic, and ethnic backgrounds. When necessary, they obtain training, experience, or counsel to assure competent service or research relating to such persons.

e. Psychologists responsible for decisions involving individuals or policies based on test results have an understanding of psychological or educational measurement, validation problems, and test research.

f. Psychologists recognize that personal problems and conflicts may interfere with professional effectiveness. Accordingly, they refrain from undertaking any activity in which their personal problems are likely to lead to inadequate performance or harm to a client, colleague, student, or research participant. If engaged in such activity when they become aware of their personal problems, they seek competent professional assistance to determine whether they should suspend, terminate, or limit the scope of their professional and/or scientific activities.

Principle 3: Moral and Legal Standards

Psychologists' moral and ethical standards of behavior are a personal matter to the same degree as they are for any other citizen, except as these may compromise the fulfillment of their professional responsibilities or reduce the public trust in psychology and psychologists. Regarding their own behavior, psychologists are sensitive to prevailing community standards and to the possible impact that conformity to or deviation from these standards may have upon the quality of their performance as psychologists. Psychologists are also aware of the possible impact of their public behavior upon the ability of colleagues to perform their professional duties.

a. As teachers, psychologists are aware of the fact that their personal values may affect the selection and presentation of instructional materials. When dealing with topics that may give offense, they recognize and respect the diverse attitudes that students may have toward such materials.

b. As employees or employers, psychologists do not engage in or condone practices that are inhumane or that result in illegal or unjustifiable actions. Such practices include, but are not limited to, those based on considerations of race, handicap, age, gender, sexual preference, religion, or national origin in hiring, promotion, or training.

c. In their professional roles, psychologists avoid any action that will violate or diminish the legal and civil rights of clients or of others who may be affected by their actions.

d. As practitioners and researchers, psychologists act in accord with Association standards and guidelines related to practice and to the conduct of research with human beings and animals. In the ordinary course of events, psychologists adhere to relevant governmental laws and institutional regulations. When federal, state, provincial, organizational, or institutional laws, regulations, or practices are in conflict with Association standards and guidelines, psychologists make known their commitment to Association standards and guidelines and, wherever possible, work toward a resolution of the conflict. Both practitioners and researchers are concerned with the development of such legal and quasi-legal regulations as best serve the public interest, and they work toward changing existing regulations that are not beneficial to the public interest.

Principle 4: Public Statements

Public statements, announcements of services, advertising, and promotional activities of psychologists serve the purpose of helping the public make informed judgments and choices. Psychologists represent accurately and objectively their professional qualifications, affiliations, and functions, as well as those of the institutions or organizations with which they or the statements may be associated. In public statements providing psychological information or professional opinions or providing information about the availability of psychological products, publications, and services, psychologists base their statements on scientifically acceptable psychological findings and techniques with full recognition of the limits and uncertainties of such evidence.

a. When announcing or advertising professional services, psychologists may list the following information to describe the provider and services provided: name, highest relevant academic degree earned from a regionally accredited institution, date, type, and level of certification or licensure, diplomate status, APA membership status, address, telephone number, office hours, a brief listing of the type of psychological services offered, an appropriate presentation of fee information, foreign languages spoken, and policy with regard to third-party payments. Additional relevant or important consumer information may be included if not prohibited by other sections of these Ethical Principles.

b. In announcing or advertising the availability of psychological products, publications, or services, psychologists do not present their affiliation with any organization in a manner that falsely implies sponsorship or certification by that organization. In particular and for example, psychologists do not state APA membership or fellow status in a way to suggest that such status implies specialized professional competence or qualifications. Public statements include, but are not limited to, communication by means of periodical, book, list, directory, television, radio, or motion picture. They do not contain (i) a false, fraudulent, misleading, deceptive, or unfair statement; (ii) a misinterpretation of fact or a statement likely to mislead or deceive because in context it makes only a partial disclosure of relevant facts; (iii) a testimonial from a patient regarding the quality of a psychologist's services or products; (iv) a statement intended or likely to create false or unjustified expectations of favorable results;(v) a statement implying unusual, unique, or one-of-a-kind abilities; (vi) a statement intended or likely to appeal to a client's fears, anxieties, or emotions concerning the possible results of failure to obtain the offered services; (vii) a statement concerning the comparative desirability of offered services; (viii) a statement of direct solicitation of individual clients.

c. Psychologists do not compensate or give anything of value to a representative of the press, radio, television, or other communication medium in anticipation of or in return for professional publicity in a news item. A paid advertisement must be identified as such, unless it is apparent from the context that it is a paid advertisement. If communicated to the public by use of radio or television, an advertisement is prerecorded and approved for broadcast by the psychologist, and a recording of the actual transmission is retained by the psychologist.

d. Announcements or advertisements of "personal growth groups," clinics, and agencies give a clear statement of purpose and a clear description of the experiences to be provided. The education, training, and experience of the staff members are appropriately specified.

e. Psychologists associated with the development or promotion of psychological devices, books, or other products offered for commerical sale make reasonable efforts to ensure that announcements and advertisements are presented in a professional, scientifically acceptable, and factually informative manner.

f. Psychologists do not participate for personal gain in commercial announcements or advertisements recommending to the public the purchase or use of proprietary or single-source products or services when that participation is based solely upon their identification as psychologists.

g. Psychologists present the science of psychology and offer their services, products, and publications fairly and accurately, avoiding misrepresentation through sensationalism, exaggeration, or superficiality. Psychologists are guided by the primary obligation to aid the public in developing informed judgments, opinions, and choices.

h. As teachers, psychologists ensure that statements in catalogs and course outlines are accurate and not misleading, particularly in terms of subject matter to be covered, bases for evaluating progress, and the nature of course experiences. Announcements, brochures, or advertisements describing workshops, seminars, or other educational programs accurately describe the audience for which the program is intended as well as eligibility requirements, educational objectives, and nature of the materials to be covered. These announcements also accurately represent the education, training, and experience of the psychologists presenting the programs and any fees involved.

i. Public announcements or advertisements soliciting research participants in which clinical services or other professional services are offered as an inducement make clear the nature of the services as well as the costs and other obligations to be accepted by participants in the research.

j. A psychologist accepts the obligation to correct others who represent the psychologist's professional qualifications, or associations with products or services, in a manner incompatible with these guidelines.

k. Individual diagnostic and therapeutic services are provided only in the context of a professional psychological relationship. When personal advice is given by means of public lectures or demonstrations, newspaper or magazine articles, radio or television programs, mail, or similar media, the psychologist utilizes the most current relevant data and exercises the highest level of professional judgment.

l. Products that are described or presented by means of public lectures or demonstrations, newspaper or magazine articles, radio or television programs, or similar media meet the same recognized standards as exist for products used in the context of a professional relationship.

Principle 5: Confidentiality

Psychologists have a primary obligation to respect the confidentiality of information obtained from persons in the course of their work as psychologists. They reveal such information to others only with the consent of the person or the person's legal representative, except in those unusual circumstances in which not to do so would result in clear danger to the person or to others. Where appropriate, psychologists inform their clients of the legal limits of confidentiality.

a. Information obtained in clinical or consulting relationships, or evaluative data concerning children, students, employees, and others, is discussed only for professional purposes and only with persons clearly concerned with the case. Written and oral reports present only data germane to the purposes of the evaluation, and every effort is made to avoid undue invasion of privacy.

b. Psychologists who present personal information obtained during the course of professional work in writings, lectures or other public forums either obtain adequate prior consent to do so or adequately disguise all identifying information.

c. Psychologists make provisions for maintaining confidentiality in the storage and disposal of records.

d. When working with minors or other persons who are unable to give voluntary, informed consent, psychologists take special care to protect these persons' best interests.

Principle 6: Welfare of the Consumer

Psychologists respect the integrity and protect the welfare of the people and groups with whom they work. When conflicts of interest arise between clients and psychologists' employing institutions, psychologists clarify the nature and direction of their loyalties and responsibilities and keep all parties informed of their commitments. Psychologists fully inform consumers as to the purpose and nature of an evaluative, treatment, educational, or training procedure, and they freely acknowledge that clients, students, or participants in research have freedom of choice with regard to participation.

a. Psychologists are continually cognizant of their own needs and of their potentially influential position vis-à-vis persons such as clients, students, and subordinates. They avoid exploiting the trust and dependency of such persons. Psychologists make every effort to avoid dual relationships that could impair their professional judgment or increase the risk of exploitation. Examples of such dual relationships include, but are not limited to, research with and treatment of employees, students, supervisees, close friends, or relatives. Sexual intimacies with clients are unethical.

b. When a psychologist agrees to provide services to a client at the request of a third party, the psychologist assumes the responsibility of clarifying the nature of the relationships to all parties concerned.

c. Where the demands of an organization require psychologists to violate these Ethical Principles, psychologists clarify the nature of the conflict between the demands and these principles. They inform all parties of psychologists' ethical responsibilities and take appropriate action.

d. Psychologists make advance financial arrangements that safeguard the best interests of and are clearly understood by their clients. They neither give nor receive any remuneration for referring clients for professional services. They contribute a portion of their services to work for which they receive little or no financial return.

e. Psychologists terminate a clinical or consulting relationship when it is reasonably clear that the consumer is not benefiting from it. They offer to help the consumer locate alternative sources of assistance.

Principle 7: Professional Relationships

Psychologists act with due regard for the needs, special competencies, and obligations of their colleagues in psychology and other professions. They respect the prerogatives and obligations of the institutions or organizations with which these other colleagues are associated.

a. Psychologists understand the areas of competence of related professions. They make full use of all the professional, technical, and administrative resources that serve the best interests of consumers. The absence of formal relationships with other professional workers does not relieve psychologists of the responsibility of securing for their clients the best possible professional service, nor does it relieve them of the obligation to exercise foresight, diligence, and tact in obtaining the complementary or alternative assistance needed by clients.

b. Psychologists know and take into account the traditions and practices of other professional groups with whom they work and cooperate fully with such groups. If a person is receiving similar services from another professional, psychologists do not offer their own services directly to such a person. If a psychologist is contacted by a person who is already receiving similar services from another professional, the psychologist carefully considers that professional relationship and proceeds with caution and sensitivity to the therapeutic issues as well as the client's welfare. The psychologist discusses these issues with the client so as to minimize the risk of confusion and conflict.

c. Psychologists who employ or supervise other professionals or professionals in training accept the obligation to facilitate the further professional development of these individuals. They provide appropriate working conditions, timely evaluations, constructive consultation, and experience opportunities.

d. Psychologists do not exploit their professional relationships with clients, supervisees, students, employees, or research participants sexually or otherwise. Psychologists do not condone or engage in sexual harassment. Sexual harassment is defined as deliberate or repeated comments, gestures, or physical contacts of a sexual nature that are unwanted by the recipient.

e. In conducting research in institutions or organizations, psychologists secure appropriate authorization to conduct such research. They are aware of their obligations to future research workers and ensure that host institutions receive adequate information about the research and proper acknowledgment of their contributions.

f. Publication credit is assigned to those who have contributed to a publication in proportion to their professional contributions. Major contributions of a professional character made by several persons to a common project are recognized by joint authorship, with the individual who made the principal contribution listed first. Minor contributions of a professional character and extensive clerical or similar nonprofessional assistance may be acknowledged in footnotes or in an introductory statement. Acknowledgment through specific citations is made for unpublished as well as published material that has directly influenced the research or writing. Psychologists who compile and edit material of others for publication publish the material in the name of the originating group, if appropriate, with their own name appearing as chairperson or editor. All contributors are to be acknowledged and named.

g. When psychologists know of an ethical violation by another psychologist, and it seems appropriate, they informally attempt to resolve the issue by bringing the behavior to the attention of the psychologist. If the misconduct is of a minor nature and/or appears to be due to lack of sensitivity, knowledge, or experience, such an informal solution is usually appropriate. Such informal corrective efforts are made with sensitivity to any rights to confidentiality involved. If the violation does not seem amenable to an informal solution, or is of a more serious nature, psychologists bring it to the attention of the appropriate local, state, and/or national committee on professional ethics and conduct.

Principle 8: Assessment Techniques

In the development, publication, and utilization of psychological assessment techniques, psychologists make every effort to promote the welfare and best interests of the client. They guard against the misuse of assessment results. They respect the client's right to know the results, the interpretations made, and the bases for their conclusions and recommendations. Psychologists make every effort to maintain the security of tests and other assessment techniques within limits of legal mandates. They strive to ensure the appropriate use of assessment techniques by others.

a. In using assessment techniques, psychologists respect the right of clients to have full explanations of the nature and purpose of the techniques in language the clients can understand, unless an explicit exception to this right has been agreed upon in advance. When the explanations are to be provided by others, psychologists establish procedures for ensuring the adequacy of these explanations.

b. Psychologists responsible for the development and standardization of psychological tests and other assessment techniques utilize established scientific procedures and observe the relevant APA standards.

c. In reporting assessment results, psychologists indicate any reservations that exist regarding validity or reliability because of the circumstances of the assessment or the inappropriateness of the norms for the person tested. Psychologists strive to ensure that the results of assessments and their interpretations are not misused by others.

d. Psychologists recognize that assessment results may become obsolete. They make every effort to avoid and prevent the misuse of obsolete measures.

e. Psychologists offering scoring and interpretation services are able to produce appropriate evidence for the validity of the programs and procedures used in arriving at interpretations. The public offering of an automated interpretation service is considered a professional-to-professional consultation. Psychologists make every effort to avoid misuse of assessment reports.

f. Psychologists do not encourage or promote the use of psychological assessment techniques by inappropriately trained or otherwise unqualified persons through teaching, sponsorship, or supervision.

Principle 9: Research with Human Participants

The decision to undertake research rests upon a considered judgment by the individual psychologist about how best to contribute to psychological science and human welfare. Having made the decision to conduct research, the psychologist considers alternative directions in which research energies and resources might be invested. On the basis of this consideration, the psychologist carries out the investigation with respect and concern for the dignity and welfare of the people who participate and with cognizance of federal and state regulations and professional standards governing the conduct of research with human participants.

a. In planning a study, the investigator has the responsibility to make a careful evaluation of its ethical acceptability. To the extent that the weighing of scientific and human values suggests a compromise of any principle, the investigator incurs a correspondingly serious obligation to seek ethical advice and to observe stringent safeguards to protect the rights of human participants.

b. Considering whether a participant in a planned study will be a "subject at risk" or a "subject at minimal risk," according to recognized standards, is of primary ethical concern to the investigator.

c. The investigator always retains the responsibility for ensuring ethical practice in research. The investigator is also responsible for the ethical treatment of research participants by collaborators, assistants, students, and employees, all of whom, however, incur similar obligations.

d. Except in minimal-risk research, the investigator establishes a clear and fair agreement with research participants, prior to their participation, that clarifies the obligations and responsibilities of each. The investigator has the obligation to honor all promises and commitments included in that agreement. The investigator informs the participants of all aspects of the research that might reasonably be expected to influence willingness to participate and explains all other aspects of the research about which the participants inquire. Failure to make full disclosure prior to obtaining informed consent requires additional safeguards to protect the welfare and dignity of the research participants. Research with children or with participants who have impairments that would limit understanding and/or communication requires special safeguarding procedures.

e. Methodological requirements of a study may make the use of concealment or deception necessary. Before conducting such a study, the investigator has a special responsibility to (i) determine whether the use of such techniques is justified by the study's prospective scientific, educational, or applied value; (ii) determine whether alternative procedures are available that do not use concealment or deception; and (iii) ensure that the participants are provided with sufficient explanation as soon as possible.

f. The investigator respects the individual's freedom to decline to participate in or to withdraw from the research at any time. The obligation to protect this freedom requires careful thought and consideration when the investigator is in a position of authority or influence over the participant. Such positions of authority include, but are not limited to, situations in which research participation is required as part of employment or in which the participant is a student, client, or employee of the investigator.

g. The investigator protects the participant from physical and mental discomfort, harm, and danger that may arise from research procedures. If risks of such consequences exist, the investigator informs the participant of that fact. Research procedures likely to cause serious or lasting harm to a participant are not used unless the failure to use these procedures might expose the participant to risk of greater harm, or unless the research has great potential benefit and fully informed and voluntary consent is obtained from each participant. The participant should be informed of procedures for contacting the investigator within a reasonable time period following participation should stress, potential harm, or related questions or concerns arise.

h. After the data are collected, the investigator provides the participant with information about the nature of the study and attempts to remove any misconceptions that may have arisen. Where scientific or humane values justify delaying or withholding this information, the investigator incurs a special responsibility to monitor the research and to ensure that there are no damaging consequences for the participant.

i. Where research procedures result in undesirable consequences for the individual participant, the investigator has the responsibility to detect and remove or correct these consequences, including long-term effects.

j. Information obtained about a research participant during the course of an investigation is confidential unless otherwise agreed upon in advance. When the possibility exists that others may obtain access to such information, this possibility, together with the plans for protecting confidentiality, is explained to the participant as part of the procedure for obtaining informed consent.

Principle 10: Care and Use of Animals

An investigator of animal behavior strives to advance understanding of basic behavioral principles and/or to contribute to the improvement of human health and welfare. In seeking these ends, the investigator ensures the welfare of animals and treats them humanely. Laws and regulations notwithstanding, an animal's immediate protection depends upon the scientist's own conscience.

a. The acquisition, care, use, and disposal of all animals are in compliance with current federal, state or provincial, and local laws and regulations.

b. A psychologist trained in research methods and experienced in the care of laboratory animals closely supervises all procedures involving animals and is responsible for ensuring appropriate consideration of their comfort, health, and humane treatment.

c. Psychologists ensure that all individuals using animals under their supervision have received explicit instruction in experimental methods and in the care, maintenance, and handling of the species being used. Responsibilities and activities of individuals participating in a research project are consistent with their respective competencies.

d. Psychologists make every effort to minimize discomfort, illness, and pain of animals. A procedure subjecting animals to pain, stress, or privation is used only when an alternative procedure is unavailable and the goal is justified by its prospective scientific, educational, or applied value. Surgical procedures are performed under appropriate anesthesia; techniques to avoid infection and minimize pain are followed during and after surgery.

e. When it is appropriate that the animal's life be terminated, it is done rapidly and painlessly.

APPENDIX F

ASCA Role Statement

The Practice of Guidance and Counseling by School Counselors

The following role statement is an incorporation and revision of four role statements prepared separately in the 70s. "The Unique Role of the Elementary School Counselor" was originally published in Elementary School Guidance and Counseling, *Volume 8, No. 3, March 1974. It was revised and the revision, approved in August 1977 by the ASCA Governing Board, was printed in* Elementary School Guidance and Counseling, *Volume 12, No. 3, February 1978. "The Role of the Middle/Junior High School Counselor" was circulated separately in photocopy form by ASCA. "The Role of the Secondary School Counselor" first appeared in* School Counselor, *Volume 21, No. 5, May 1974; the revision, formulated by the 1976–77 ASCA Governing Board, was printed in the March 1977* School Counselor *(Volume 24, No. 4). "The Role and Function of Postsecondary Counseling" first appeared in* School Counselor, *Volume 21, No. 5, May 1974.*

The present version, incorporating all four role statements, was prepared in October 1980 by G. Dean Miller upon invitation from ASCA officers J. Thompson, H. Washburn, and J. Terrill. The role statement as it appears below was approved by the 1980–81 ASCA Governing Board in January 1981.

Professional Rationale

The national association believes that the professional identity of the school counselor is derived from a unique preparation, grounded in the behavioral sciences, with training in clinical skills adapted to the school setting. This statement attempts to identify and clarify the role of the school counselor who functions at various educational levels in United States society. The different educational levels (elementary, middle or junior high, secondary, and postsecondary) approximates the different steps of developmental growth from childhood through adolescence to adulthood. Therefore, the focus of school counselors serving different school levels is differentiated by the developmental tasks necessary for the different stages of growth the students confront going through school. This statement also commits to public record certain professional responsibilities of school counselors and identifies a set of philosophic assumptions about the conditions under which important psychological growth occurs in the practice of guidance and counseling.

It is understood that schools in all societies are concerned with transmission of cultural heritage and socialization of the youth. Career socialization is recognized as a very important aspect of this process. In the United States, schools are concerned about the individual student, and it is through the concept of guidance that efforts are directed toward personalizing the school experience in a developmental way.

Counselors as developmental facilitators function as school-based members of student support-services teams that include staff members from other helping professions such as school psychology, social work, and nursing. These staff, depending upon their student-staff ratios and service orientation, may also function in a specialized remedial way to assist with problem areas and—beginning with the very young—join counselors to intervene in a developmental way to foster psychological growth and thereby attempt collectively to prevent the costly, hard-to-change negative behavior characteristics that often begin to take form and retard growth by the middle elementary school grades.

Counselors believe that students achieve and grow in positive ways when competencies develop and the home and school strive both separately and together to establish supportive interpersonal relationships and maintain healthy environments. Counseling and guidance is an integral function in the school that is maximized when counselors provide consultation and in-service programs for staff regarding the incorporation of developmental psychology into the curriculum. They also provide parents with additional understanding of child and adolescent development in order to strengthen the role of parents in the promotion of growth in children. Individual and small group counseling is provided to complement indirect helping through parents and teachers. Important direct interaction with students, however, is provided through a developmentally oriented guidance curriculum. Counselor interventions, regardless of their conceptual origin, aim to serve the needs of students who are expected to function in school settings in the various educational, vocational, and personal-social domains. As the student progresses through the different school levels, assistance with processing information, problem solving, and decision making is increased in proportion to the developmental demands made upon students and their ability to conceptualize and assume responsibility for the consequences of their behavior.

The validation of new knowledge from the behavioral sciences along with social and economic changes in society impact the role of the counselor and other members of the school staff. Through study and retraining, the effective practicing counselor—regardless of the educational level of the students serviced—continues to be informed and competently skilled throughout the professional career.

The Nature of the Helping Process

To accommodate students at different educational levels, the organizing and specifying of various guidance programs across the life span calls for an awareness of developmental needs identified in the psychology of children, adolescents, and adults. The clinical skills and knowledge base of the counselor is most effectively used if effort is directed in an organized way toward making the school, the teachers, and the curriculum sensitive to those aspects of personal development most associated with life success. Because of its association with life success the cognitive-developmental stages of psychological maturity deserve highest recognition in conceptualizing the major thrust of guidance interventions for the different educational levels. Such interventions aim to do more than inform students about problems they will face: The purpose is to promote through education important life success qualities (development of competencies, ego maturity, moral reasoning, and so forth). Counselors performing under this theoretical orientation will tend to emphasize certain interventions, no matter what the level of the educational setting—elementary, middle or junior high, secondary, or postsecondary. Major functions performed by such school counselors include the following:

- Structured developmental guidance experiences presented systematically through groups (including classrooms) to promote growth of psychological aspects of human development (e.g., ego, career, emotional, moral, and social development). Such interventions can logically become an integral part of such curriculum areas as social studies, language arts, health, or home economics. Individual or small group counseling is provided when the needs deserve more attention or privacy.

- Consultation with and in-service training for teachers to increase their communication skills, improve the quality of their interaction with all students, and make them more sensitive to the need for matching the curriculum to developmental needs of students.
- Consultation and life-skills education for parents to assist them to understand developmental psychology, to improve family communication skills, and to develop strategies for encouraging learning in their children.

As noted above, counselors serving different school populations function differently, due primarily to the variations in the developmental stages of the students and the organization of the school. Some of the major level differences in functions include the following.

Elementary School Counselors

- Provide in-service training to teachers to assist them with planning and implementing guidance interventions for young children (preschool to 3rd grade) in order to maximize developmental benefits (self-esteem, personal relationships, positive school attitude, sex-fair choices, and so forth) in the hope of preventing serious problems or minimizing the size of such problems, if and when they do occur.
- Provide consultations for teachers who need understanding and assistance with incorporating developmental concepts in teaching content as well as support for building a healthy classroom environment.
- Accommodate parents who need assistance with understanding normal child growth and development; improving family communication skills; or understanding their role in encouraging their child to learn.
- Cooperate with other school staff in the early identification, remediation, or referral of children with developmental deficiencies or handicaps.
- As children reach the upper elementary grades, effort is directed through the curriculum toward increasing student awareness of the relationship between school and work, especially the impact of educational choices on one's life-style and career development.

Middle or Junior High Counselors

- Concentrate efforts (through group guidance, peer facilitators, and teacher in-service training) to smooth the transition for students from the more confining environment of the lower school to the middle or junior high school where students are expected to assume greater responsibility for their own learning and personal development.
- Identify, encourage, and support teachers (through in-service training, consultation, and co-teaching) who are interested in incorporating developmental units in such curriculum areas as English, Social Studies, Health, and Home Economics.
- Organize and implement a career guidance program for students that includes an assessment of their career maturity and career-planning status; easy access to relevant career information; and assistance with processing data for personal use in school-work related decision making.

Secondary Counselors

- Organize and implement through interested teachers guidance curricula interventions that focus upon important developmental concerns of adolescents (identity, career choice and planning, social relationships, and so forth).
- Organize and make available comprehensive information systems (print, computer-based, audio-visual) necessary for educational-vocational planning and decision making.
- Assist students with assessment of personal characteristics (e.g., competencies, interests, aptitudes, needs, career maturity) for personal use in such areas as course selection, post-high-school planning, and career choices.
- Provide remedial interventions or alternative programs for those students showing in-school adjustment problems, vocational immaturity, or general negative attitudes toward personal growth.

Postsecondary Counselors

- Participate in a comprehensive program of student support services to facilitate the meeting of transitional needs throughout adulthood (orientation activities; academic, personal, and career counseling; financial aids; independent living; job placement, career development; geriatric concerns; and so forth).
- Through individual and cooperative efforts with other staff, offer

students the opportunity to participate in deliberate psychological education that fosters maturity in such areas as ego development, moral reasoning, career development, and emotional aspects of personal relationships.
- To accommodate students with varying maturity and ability levels, provide differential assistance to help students identify and use school and community-based opportunities (internships, independent study, and travel) in order to crystalize vocational choice and career plans (e.g., choice of major, choice of vocation, lifestyle, and work values).

Professional Commitment of School Counselors

The counselor, as a school-based practitioner, is bound in relationship with others to certain practices. These counseling and guidance relationships are based on the following principles:

- It is the counselor's obligation to respect the integrity of the individual and promote the growth and development (or adjustment) of the student receiving assistance.
- Before entering any counseling relationship, the individual should be informed of the conditions under which assistance may be provided.
- The counseling relationship and information resulting from it must be kept confidential in accordance with the rights of the individual and the obligations of the counselor as a professional.
- Counselors reserve the right to consult with other competent professionals about the individual. Should the individual's condition endanger the health, welfare, or safety of self or others, the counselor is expected, in such instances, to refer the counselee to another appropriate professional person.
- Counselors shall decline to initiate or shall terminate a counseling relationship when other services could best meet the client's needs. Counselors shall refer the client to such services.

Commitment to Students

- The counselor recognizes that each student has basic human rights and is entitled to just treatment regardless of race, sex, religious preference, handicapping condition, or cultural differences.
- The counselor is available to all to provide assistance with per-

sonal understanding and use of opportunities, especially those available in the school setting.

- The counselor assumes that both cognition and perception influence behavior and the valuation process.
- The counselor in the helping relationship creates an atmosphere in which mutual respect, understanding, and confidence prevails in the hope that growth occurs and concerns are resolved.

Commitment to Parents

- The counselor recognizes that parents are the first teachers of their children and in this regard have a profound influence upon human development.
- Parents are entitled to basic human rights and their facilitative-supportive relationship to learning is recognized in the educational partnership that embraces the home and school.
- To capitalize upon the influence of parents in the educational process, the counselor involves them at strategic periods and events in order to maximize the student's response to opportunities provided by the school.

Commitment to Teachers

- The counselor acknowledges that teachers, in creating positive, interactive relationships with students, provide the primary basis for intellectual, emotional, and social growth in the school.
- The counselor, in the consulting relationship, endeavors to acquaint teachers with applications of various theories of learning and human growth in order that a good match occurs between curriculum interventions and student developmental needs.
- The counselor recognizes that teachers need support and assistance in dealing with the normal problems of student growth and adjustment, especially during the period of adolescence.

Commitment to Administrators

- The counselor acknowledges that the school administrator plays the major role in providing the support necessary for implementing and maintaining an organized team approach to guidance in the school. The counselor depends upon the school administration to support the elimination of unnecessary clerical work and other activities that detract from program delivery and counseling.

- The counselor, in recognizing the importance of the administrator's contribution, develops a close working relationship with the administrator and provides technical assistance so that appropriate assessment, planning, implementation, and evaluation occur relative to the guidance needs of the students.
- In identifying the counselor's responsibility in implementing an organized guidance program, legislative mandates and professional ethics must be taken into consideration in matters dealing with confidentiality and privileged communication as well as what duties constitute good professional practice.

Commitment to Others in the Community

- The counselor is aware that others in the community play a significant role in the overall development of children and youth.
- To capitalize upon the above contributions, the counselor maintains an ongoing set of liaison relationships with various individuals and agencies in an effort to coordinate programs and services on behalf of students in the school and those in transition status between school and some other institution.
- Ongoing relationships are formed on the premise that cooperative efforts are in the best interest of the individuals concerned when personal information is treated in an ethical manner.

The Counselor's Responsibility to the Profession

To assure good practice and continued growth in knowledge and skills for the benefit of students, parents, and teachers, as well as the profession, the counselor:

- Has an understanding of his or her own personal characteristics and their effect on counseling-consulting relationships.
- Is aware of his or her level of professional competence and represents it accurately to others.
- Is well informed on current theories and research that have impact-potential upon professional practice.
- Uses time and skills in an organized systematic way to help students and resists any effort aimed at unreasonable use of time for nonguidance activities.
- Continues to develop professional competence and maintains an awareness of contemporary trends in the field as well as influences from the world at large.

- Fosters the development and improvement of the profession by assisting with appropriate research and participating in professional association activities at local, state, and national levels.
- Discusses with professional associates (teachers, administrators, and other support staff) practices that may be implemented to strengthen and improve standards or the conditions for helping.
- Maintains constant efforts to adhere to strict confidentiality of information concerning individuals and releases such information only with the signature of the student, parent, or guardian.
- Is guided by sound ethical practices for professional counselors as embodied in the *Ethical Standards* of the American Personnel and Guidance Association—American School Counselor Association.
- Becomes an active member of American School Counselor Association and state and local counselor associations in order to enhance personal and professional growth.

APPENDIX G

Role of the Employment Counselor

An association consisting of and representing professional counselors must address itself to basic issues within the profession. The issue of counselor roles in a given setting depends on a mutual interpretation between the employer and the counselor. In the past, counseling in the employment service has been subject to varied interpretation by federal, state, and local officials.

President Odell of NECA appointed a committee to write a position paper on the role of the employment counselor. The committee members were Anthony Fantaci (Chairman), Robert Philbrick, Dean Call, and David Meyer. The committee has completed its work and the following position paper has been officially adopted by action of the NECA Board of Trustees.—Alan Horwitz

Rationale for Employment Counseling

As with counselors in other work settings, the employment counselor is a member of the counseling profession, differing from other members only in terms of the work setting and the nature of the problems presented by the clientele served. The employment counselor generally assists persons who are faced with an immediate problem related to employment, usually involving job choice, job change, or job adjustment. Since counselees come to the employment counselor's attention as a result of applying for a job, they are often referred to as "applicants." In providing the needed assistance the employment counselor considers factors both within and outside the counselee, such as psychological, physical, and socioeconomic factors that bear on the counselee's current status and that may have some effect on his or her future. Thus the employment counselor is concerned with the individual's potential and actual strengths and weaknesses, and with helping the counselee to understand the physical, mental, and emotional growth processes of individuals, but he or she must also understand these processes to use human service facilities and job opportunities for the benefit of the counselee.

The employment counselor believes that each person should have equal opportunity to develop and use individual talents for the betterment of self and the community, and that this is a developmental, lifelong process in which any number of institutions and other individuals, including the employment counselor, may play significant roles.

The employment counselor believes that work represents a meaningful expression of the individual's self-concept and values, and that individuals have the capacity to change, to grow, and to make intelligent decisions. However, the increasing complexity of the industrialized work world, constantly evolving through technological change, makes it increasingly difficult for the individual, without assistance, to make decisions regarding the choice of an occupation and preparation for it. Through the counseling process, the counselee is helped to achieve better understanding of self and of the occupational world, and to relate individual interests and talents to the demands of various occupational outlets. Thus employment counseling is an important element of the total spectrum of manpower services. For those in need of this service, it becomes an integral component of the placement process and a prerequisite to suitable job placement. Throughout the employment counseling process, the belief in freedom of choice is basic.

The employment counselor believes that there are situations in which active intervention by the counselor, or client advocacy, is an essential additional component of effective counseling. When successful individual adjustment is obstructed by environmental factors, and when the counselee is unable to effect needed change, the counselor has an obligation to act on the counselee's behalf within the limits of applicable law, regulation, and policy.

Definition of Employment Counseling

Employment counseling is the process whereby an employment counselor and counselee work together in order that the latter may gain better self-understanding and knowledge of the world of work and more realistically choose, change, or adjust to a vocation. The employment counselor will usually:

1. Assist an inexperienced person who has not made a satisfactory vocational choice to review and evaluate present and potential qualifications and relate them to occupational requirements so that the counselee may select an appropriate occupation, education, or training, and develop a realistic vocational plan;
2. Provide or help obtain needed employability services to prepare counselees for entry into the world of work. This employability service may include in-depth counseling; referral to further education, training, or medical assistance; and, often, simple orientation to the world of work;
3. Assist an experienced worker who wishes to or must make an occupational change to explore possible alternative fields of work, choose a more suitable occupation, and develop a plan to make the change to appropriate employment;
4. Assist a worker who has encountered barriers to entering, holding, or progressing on a job to discover, analyze, and understand the vocational and personal problems involved and make and carry out the necessary plans for adjustment.

This assistance is provided so that the counselee is helped to (a) recognize the problems involved, (b) make effective, satisfying decisions, and (c) select an appropriate kind of work or developmental task. In helping a counselee gain better understanding of self in relation to the world of work, the counselor may use both individual and group counseling methods and techniques.

The Counselor's Responsibility to the Applicant

In a counseling relationship, the employment counselor:

- Demonstrates respect for the worth, individuality, and dignity of the counselee, creating a climate that is conducive to counseling.
- Attempts to reach a common understanding with the counselee regarding the nature of the employment counseling problem.
- Clearly indicates the conditions under which counseling is provided, including the confidential nature of information received during the counseling interview.
- Adopts a flexible approach to assessment, using only those measures that are valid for the counselee.

- Interprets test results in a way that does not impair the counselee's freedom of choice.
- Helps the counselee in self-evaluation, self-understanding, and self-direction, thus developing the counselee's decision-making ability regarding appropriate occupational goals and plans.
- Informs the counselee concerning occupations, including traits and abilities needed, training requirements, and occupational trends.
- Assists the counselee in understanding the economic changes that have taken place and are taking place and their relevance to choosing, preparing for, or finding employment in a suitable occupational field.
- Assists the counselee to develop an employment plan that reflects the counselee's own judgement concerning potentialities, interests, values, and other pertinent factors as related to the demands and rewards of appropriate career fields and occupations.
- Treats vocational choice not as a terminal point but as a developmental process that may require change in the future.
- Assumes the role of advocate as necessary and intervenes on the counselee's behalf with individuals and/or community agencies or institutions, as appropriate.
- Helps the counselee understand the environment and social structure of an office, plant, or other employment setting in which he or she is placed.
- Follows through on the agreed-on occupational plan, providing referral and placement assistance as necessary until job adjustment is achieved.
- Provides assistance within the bounds of professional expertise; refers the counselee to other professionals when other assistance is required.
- Accepts the responsibility for analyzing the effects of counseling on the counselee and working to achieve more positive effects when needed.

The Counselor's Responsibility to the Employing Agency

Among organizations or agencies in which the employment counselor may operate are public employment services, other government agencies, private profit or nonprofit agencies, industry, vocational and technical schools, colleges, and universities. Each of these organizations or agencies has basic objectives and policies and procedures to meet these objectives that may affect or modify the role or operation of the employment counselor. To ensure maximal professional effectiveness, the employment counselor should do the following things.

- Promote a clear understanding among fellow employees of the role of employment counseling in achieving the objectives of the organization.
- Work with fellow employees to accomplish the goals of the organization.
- Work cooperatively with fellow employees in assisting applicants requiring agency services in addition to counseling.
- Attempt to resolve conflicts, if any, between organization policy and the counseling program.
- Participate in the planning, development, and evaluation of the counseling program.
- Promote and implement a continuing inservice and outservice training program for counselors.
- Promote training in interpersonal and communication skills among other staff members and maximum participation in services such as identifying counseling need, obtaining information, and so forth.

The Counselor's Responsibility to the Community

The employment counselor has a professional responsibility to see that other agencies whose clients may need employment counseling are aware of the services the employing agency provides. The employment counselor has an equal responsibility for knowing what services (under what conditions) other agencies can provide for those counselees who might possibly need such services. Where adequate directories of community agencies do not exist, the employment counselor has a responsibility to promote or facilitate the development of such directories. When the needed services themselves are not available, the employment counselor is responsible for bringing this lack to the attention of those individuals or organizations that are in a position to do something about it.

The Counselor's Responsibility to the Counseling Profession

The employment counselor has a responsibility to the profession as well as to counselees, the employing organization, and the community. Included in this overall responsibility are specific responsibilities for:

- Understanding of self and of the effects of the counselor's personal qualities and actions on counseling relationships.

- Awareness of personal competencies and limitations, and willingness to refer a counselee to another agency or individual who can provide those services that the employment counselor cannot provide.
- Continuing self-development in areas related to employment counseling.
- Participation in professional association activities at the local, state, and national levels.
- Participation in appropriate operations research.
- Promotion of improved standards and conditions of employment within the employment counseling profession.
- Provision of meaningful and helpful information to other professional personnel who are assisting the counselee.
- Respect for the confidential nature of information received in the counseling interview, revealing only that to which the counselee has consented, within the limits of applicable law, regulation, and policy.
- Adherence to the APGA code of ethics and the code of ethics for counseling within the employing agency.

Employment Counselor Competencies

In order to carry out employment counseling responsibilities effectively, the employment counselor must develop the following basic competencies.

Relationship skills. The ability to establish a trusting, open, and useful relationship with each counselee, accurately interpreting feelings as well as verbal and nonverbal expressions, and conveying to the applicant this understanding and whatever pertinent information and assistance is needed.

Individual and group assessment skills. The ability to provide ongoing assessment in individual and group settings involving the appraisal and measurement of the counselee's needs, characteristics, potentialities, individual differences, and self-appraisal.

Group counseling. The ability to apply basic principles of group dynamics and leadership roles in a continuous and meaningful manner to assist group members to understand their problems and take positive steps toward resolving them.

Development and use of career-related information. The ability to develop and use educational, occupational, and labor market information to assist counselees in making decisions and formulating occupational plans.

Occupational plan development and implementation. The ability to assist the counselee in developing and implementing a suitable employability plan that helps move the jobseeker from current status through any needed employability-improvement services, including training and related supportive services, into a suitable job.

Placement skills. The ability to ascertain and to communicate understanding of employers' personnel needs, to make effective job development contacts, and to assist the counselee in presentation of qualifications in relation to the employer's needs.

Community relations skills. The ability, based on extensive knowledge of the important service delivery systems in the community, to assist counselees in obtaining the services needed.

Workload management and intra-office relationships skills. The ability to coordinate the various aspects of the total counseling program in the employing agency, resulting in a continuous and meaningful sequence of services to counselees, agency staff, and the community.

Professional development skills. The ability, based on interest in furthering professional development, to engage in activities that promote such development individually and within the profession, and to demonstrate by example the standards and performance expected of a professional employment counselor.

Bibliography

Abbe, A. E. Consultation to a school guidance program. *Elementary School Journal,* 1961, *61*(6), 331–337.

Abelson, H. I., Fishburn, P. M., & Cisin, I. *National survey on drug abuse,* 1977. Rockville, MD.: National Institute on Drug Abuse, 1977.

Alcohol and health report: New knowledge. Second Special Report to the U.S. Congress. Washington, D.C.: U.S. Government Printing Office, June, 1974.

Alexander, W. M. Introduction: How fares the middle school? *The National Elementary Principal,* 1971, *51*(3), 8–11.

Alexander, W. M., & George, P. S. *The exemplary middle school.* New York: Holt, Rinehart & Winston, 1981.

Alschuler, A. S. (Ed.) with Carl, J., Leslie, R., Schweiger, I., & Uustal, D. *Teacher burnout.* Washington, D.C.: National Education Association, 1980.

American Nurses Association, Division on Psychiatric and Mental Health Nursing, *Statement on psychiatric and mental health nursing practice.* Kansas City: 1976.

American Psychological Association, Ad Hoc Committee on Ethical Standards in Psychological Research. *Conduct of research with human participants.* Washington, D.C., 1973.

Anastasi, A. *Psychological testing* (4th ed.). New York: Macmillan, 1976.

Anderson, W. How to do research in community mental health agencies. *Personnel & Guidance Journal* 1981, 59(8), 517.

Argeropoulos, J. Burnout, stress management & wellness. *Chronicle Guidance Professional Subscription.* Moravia, N.Y.: 1981.

Asher, J. W. *Educational research and evaluation methods.* Boston: Little, Brown, 1976.

Aubrey, R. Power bases: The consultant's vehicle for change. *Elementary School Guidance & Counseling,* 1972, *7*(2), 90–97.

Aubrey, R. F. Relationship of guidance and counseling to the established and emerging school curriculum. *The School Counselor,* 1979, *26*(3), 150–162.

Ayers, A. R., Tripp, P. A., & Russel, J. H. *Student services administration in higher education.* Washington, D.C.: U.S. Department of Health, Education and Welfare, 1966.

Beers, Clifford. *A mind that found itself.* New York: Longmans, Green, 1908 (republished by Doubleday, 1953).

Belkin, G. S. *Practical counseling in schools* (2nd ed.). Dubuque, IA.: W. C. Brown, 1981.

Berdie, R. Planning student personnel services in higher education. In T. F. Harrington, *Student personnel work in urban colleges.* New York: Intext Educational Publishers, 1974.

Best, J. W. *Research in education* (4th ed.). Englewood Cliffs, N.J.: Prentice-Hall, 1981.

Bigner, J. J., & Jacobsen, R. B. Models of developmental research: Individual and families. *Personnel & Guidance Journal,* 1981, *59*(10), 650.

Blackham, G. J. *Counseling: Theory, process & practice.* Belmont, CA.: Wadsworth, 1977.

Blocher, D. H. *Developmental counseling* (2nd ed.). New York: Ronald Press, 1974.

Blocher, D. H. Toward an ecology of student development. *Personnel & Guidance Journal,* 1974, *52,* 360–365.

Bloom, B. L. *Community mental health: A general introduction.* Monterey, CA.: Brooks/Cole, 1977.

Bockus, F. *Couple therapy.* New York: Jason Aronson, 1980.

Bolman, W. M., & Westman, J. C. Prevention of mental disorder. An overview of current programs. *American Journal of Psychiatry,* 1967, *123,* 1058–1068.

Bombeck, E. Aunt Erma's cope book. New York: McGraw-Hill, 1979.

Boy, A., & Pine, G. Avoid counselor burnout through role renewal. *Personnel & Guidance Journal,* 1980, *59,* 161–163.

Brown, R. D. *Student development in tomorrow's higher education: A return to the academy.* Washington, D.C.: Student Personnel Series No. 16, American College Personnel Association, American Personnel & Guidance Association, 1972.

Brown, R. D. The student development educator role. In U. Delworth & G. Hanson & Associates, *Student services—A handbook for the profession:* San Francisco: Jossey-Bass, 1980.

Brubacher, J. S., & Rudy, W. *Higher education in transition.* New York: Harper & Row, 1968.

Burack, E. H., & Torda, F. *The manager's guide to change.* Belmont, CA.: Lifetime Learning, 1979.

Bureau of Census. U.S. Department of Commerce. *Consumer Income.* No. 120, 1979.

Burgess, J. H. *System design approaches to public services.* Cranbury, N.J.: Associated University Press, 1978.

Butler, R. *Why survive? Being old in America.* New York: Harper & Row, 1975.

Caplan, G. Types of mental health consultation. *American Journal of Orthopsychiatry,* 1963, *33,* 470–481.

Caplan, G. *The theory and practice of mental health consultation.* New York: Basic Books, 1970.

Carlson, R. O. Succession and performance among school superintendents. *Administrative Science Quarterly,* 1961, *6,* 210–227.

Christensen, V. R. Bringing about change. In U. Delworth, G. Hanson & Associates, *Student services: A handbook for the profession.* San Francisco: Jossey-Bass, 1980.

Clark, D. L. et al. *New perspectives on planning in educational organizations.* San Francisco: Far West Laboratory on Educational Research and Development, 1980.

Cleve, J. Combatting occupational burn out in the helping professions. *Chronical Guidance.* Moravia, N.Y.: 1980.

Clifton, R., & Dahms, A. *Grassroots administration: A handbook for staff and directors of small community-based social-service agencies.* Monterey, CA.: Brooks/Cole, 1980.

Cohen, S. *Therapeutic potential of marijuana.* New York: Plenum, 1976.

Cohen, S. Marijuana: A new ball game. *Drug Abuse and Alcoholism Newsletter,* 1979, *8*(4), 1–3(a).

Cowley, W. H. Reflections of a troublesome but hopeful Rip Van Winkle. *Journal of College Student Personnel,* 1964, *6,* 66–73.

Crocker, E. C. Depth consultation with parents. *Young Children,* 1964, *20*(2), 91–99.

Crookston, B. Student personnel—All hail and farewell! *Personnel & Guidance Journal,* 1976, *55,* 26–29.

Crookston, B. B., & Atkyns, G. C. A study of student affairs: The principal student affairs officer, the functions, the organization of American colleges and universities 1967–1972 (a preliminary summary report). *National Association of Student Personnel Administrators,* 1974.

Daniels, M. H., Mines, R., & Gressard, C. A meta-model for evaluating counseling programs. *Personnel & Guidance Journal,* 1981, 59(9), 578–582.

Delworth, U., Hanson, G., & Associates. *Student services—A handbook for the profession.* San Francisco: Jossey-Bass, 1980.

Dewey, J. *Democracy and education.* New York: Macmillan, 1916.

Dinkmeyer, D. C., & Caldwell, C. E. *Developmental counseling and guidance: A comprehensive school approach.* New York: McGraw Hill, 1970.

Dinkmeyer, D. C., & Dinkmeyer, D. C., Jr. Consultation: One answer to the counselor role. *Elementary School Guidance & Counseling,* 1978, *13*(2), 99–103.

DiSilvestro, F. R. The school counselor & political activity: Influencing school boards. *The School Counselor,* May, 1980, 351–356.

Dressel, P. L. *Handbook of academic evaluation.* San Francisco: Jossey-Bass, 1976.

Dusek, J. B. *Adolescent development and behavior.* Chicago: Science Research Associates, 1977.

Eckerson, L., & Smith, H. *Elementary school guidance: the consultant* (reprint of three articles in *School Life*), U.S. Department of Health, Education and Welfare, Office of Education, 1962.

Edelwich, J., & Brodsky, A. *Burn-out.* New York: Human Sciences Press, 1980.

Editorial Research Reports, Vol. 11. Washington, D.C.: Congressional Quarterly, Inc., 1973.

Edwards, P. B., & Bloland, P. A. Leisure counseling and consultation. *Personnel and Guidance Journal,* 1980, *58*(6), 436.

Eichborn, D. H. *New knowledge of 10 through 13 year olds.* (Paper presented at the conference on "The Middle School Idea," November 11, 1967, at the College of Education, University of Toledo, Toledo, OH.)

Euclid City Schools. *Final Report: Elementary Guidance Program.* Euclid, OH.: 1967–1968.

Ewalt, J. R. Staff review. In M. Jahoda, *Current concepts of positive mental health.* New York: Basic Books, 1958.

Ewing, P. E., Jr. Increasing college freshman persistence through outreach counseling strategy. Unpublished doctoral dissertation, The University of Toledo, 1975.

Faust, V. The counselor as a consultant to teachers. *Elementary School Guidance & Counseling,* 1967, *1*(2).

Faust, V. *The counselor-consultant in the elementary school.* Boston: Houghton Mifflin, 1968.

Fenske, R. H. Historical foundations. In U. Delworth, G. Hanson & Associates. *Student services—A handbook for the profession.* San Francisco: Jossey-Bass, 1980.

Florida Department of Education. Division of Vocational Technical & Adult Education. *Career education: An introduction.* Tallahassee, FL., 1974.

Forehand, G. A., & Gilmer, B. V. H. Environmental variations in studies of organizational behavior. *Psychological Bulletin,* 1963, *62,* 361–382.

Forman, S. I. Pitfalls in counseling alcoholic clients. *Personnel & Guidance Journal,* 1979, *57*(10), 546.

Francis, D., & Woodcock, M. *People at work: A practical guide to organizational change.* La Jolla, CA.: University Associates, 1975.

Fresno City Unified School District, California. Survey of burglary and vandalism occurrent and preventive measures in 25 large California school districts. (Summary report.) Fresno, CA.: Office of Planning and Research Services. 1978.

Froehle, T. C. & Fuqua, D. R. Systematic inquiry in the school context. *Personnel & Guidance Journal,* 1981, *59*(8), 509–510.

Gallup Opinion Index. Marijuana in America: Percentage who have tried marijuana. (Report 143). Princeton, N.J.: June, 1977.

Gazda, G., Asbury, F. R., Balzer, F. J., Childers, W. C., & Walters, R. P. *Human relations development: A manual for educators* (2nd ed.). Boston: Allyn & Bacon, 1977.

Geoffroy, K., & Mulliken, R. The school psychologist—school counselor team. *Journal of Counseling Services,* 1980, *3*(3), 27.

George, R. L., & Cristiani, T. S. *Theory, methods and processes of counseling & psychotherapy.* Englewood Cliffs, N.J.: Prentice-Hall, 1981.

Gibson, R. L. *Career development in the elementary school.* Columbus, OH.: Charles E. Merrill, 1972.

Gibson, R. L. Adolescent behavior—the normal and the not so normal. In D. R. Eyde, F. J. Menolascino, A. H. Fink (Eds.), *Education of the Early Adolescent with Behavioral Disorders.* Omaha, NE: Nebraska Psychiatric Institute, University of Nebraska Medical Center. (Symposium) 1979.

Gibson, R. L., & Higgins, R. E. *Techniques of guidance: An approach to pupil analysis.* Chicago: Science Research Associates, 1966.

Gibson, R. L., & Mitchell, M. H. *Introduction to Guidance.* New York: Macmillan, 1981.

Gibson, R. L., & Mitchell, M. H. Theirs and ours: Educational-vocational problems in Britain and the United States. *Vocational Guidance Quarterly*, 1970, 108–112.

Gibson, R. L., & Mitchell, M. H. Identification of effective concepts in placement and follow-up. (A technical report.) State of Indiana and Indiana University, 1976.

Globetti, G. Teenage drinking. In N. J. Estes & M. E. Henineman (Eds.), *Alcoholism: Development, consequences and interventions.* St. Louis, MO.: C. V. Mosby, 1977.

Goodstein, L. D. *Consulting with human service systems.* Reading, MA.: Addison-Wesley, 1978.

Goodyear, R. K. Counselors as community psychologists. *Personnel & Guidance Journal*, 1976, *54*, 512–516.

Goslin, D. A. *The school in contemporary society.* Glenview, IL.: Scott, Foresman, 1965.

Gove, P. B. (Editor-in-chief). *Webster's third new international dictionary (unabridged) of the English language.* Springfield, MA.: G & C Merriam Company Publishers, 1976.

Granowsky, L., & Davis, L. Three alternative roles for the school psychologists. *Psychology in the schools*, 1974, *11*, 415–421.

Griffiths, D. E. Administrative theory and change in organizations. In M. B. Miles, *Innovations in Education.* New York: Teacher's College Press, 1964.

Griffiths, D. E., Hemphill, J., & Frederiksen, N. *Administrative performance and personality.* New York: Bureau of Publications, Teachers College, Columbia University, 1962.

Guidance services for Ohio schools. Division of Guidance and Testing, Ohio Department of Education. Columbus: 1976.

Guttmann, D. Life events and decision making by older adults. *The Gerontologist*, 1978, *18*(5), 462–467.

Hagedorn, H. J., Beck, K. J., Nuebert, S. F., & Werlin, S. H. *A working manual of simple program evaluation techniques for community mental health centers.* Rockville, MD.: National Institute of Mental Health, prepared by Arthur D. Little, Inc., 1976.

Halpui, A. W. How leaders behave. Theory and research in administration. New York: Macmillan, 1966.

Hansen, J. C., Stevic, R. K., & Warner, R. W. *Counseling: Theory and Process* (3rd ed.). Boston: Allyn & Bacon, 1982.

Hardy, R. E., & Cull, J. G. *Organization & administration of service programs for the older American.* Springfield, IL.: Charles C. Thomas, 1975.

Havighurst, R. J. The middle school child in contemporary society. *Theory and Practice*, 1968, *7*, 120–122.

Heist, P. Creative students: College transients. In P. Heist (Ed.), *The creative college student.* San Francisco: Jossey-Bass, 1968, 35–55.

Hosford, R. E., & Ryan, T. A. Systems design in the development of counseling and guidance programs. *Personnel & Guidance Journal,* 1970, *49*(10), 222.

House, E. R. Assumptions underlying evaluation models. *Educational Researcher,* 1978, *7*(8), 4–12.

Hoyt, K. B. A primer for career education. In D. J. Srebalus, R. P. Marinelli, & J. K. Messing, *Career development: Concepts and procedures.* Monterey, CA.: Brooks/Cole, 1982.

Hurst, J. C., Weigel, R. C., Morrill, W. H., & Richardson, F. C. Reorganizing for human development in higher education: Obstacles to change. *Journal of College Student Personnel,* 1973, *14,* 10–15.

Jahoda, M. *Current concepts of positive mental health.* New York: Basic Books, 1958.

Johnson, B. L. Footnotes on the junior college. *Phi Delta Kappan,* 1965, *46,* 376–80.

Johnson, R. P., & Riker, H. C. Retirement maturity: A valuable concept for preretirement counselors. *Personnel & Guidance Journal,* 1981, *59*(5), 291.

Johnston, L. D., Bachman, G. G., & O'Malley, P. M. Drugs and the class of 1978: Behaviors, attitudes, and recent national trends (1975–1978). Ann Arbor: Institute for Social Research, University of Michigan, 1979.

Julian, A. III, & Kilmann, P. R. Group treatment of juvenile delinquents: A review of the outcome literature. *International Journal of Group Psychotherapy.* (Federal Bureau of Investigation, U.S. Department of Justice, Uniform Crime Reports for the U.S., 1973.)

Kaufman, R. A., & Harsh, J. R. Determining educational needs: An overview. In D. G. Hays & J. K. Linn, *Needs assessment! Who needs it?* Eric Counseling & Personnel Services Clearinghouse in collaboration with the American School Counselors Association, 1977.

Kellogg, M. S., & Burstiner, I. *Putting management theories to work.* Englewood Cliffs, N.J.: Prentice-Hall, 1979.

Kells, H. R. *Self-study processes: A guide for postsecondary institutions.* Washington, D.C.: American Council on Education, 1980.

Kerschner, P. A. Programs and environments for counseling adults: An overview. In M. L. Ganikos (Ed.), *Special Training Project on Counseling the Aged.* Leesburg, VA.: American Personnel & Guidance Association, 1979.

Klagsbrun, F. *Youth and suicide.* Boston: Houghton Mifflin, 1976.

Kovar, M. G. Adolescent Americans: What of their medical and health problems? *Current*, 1979, *212*, 29.

Krumboltz, J. D. An accountability model for counselors. *Personnel & Guidance Journal*, 1974, 52, 639–646.

Kuhn, A. *Unified social science*. Homewood, IL.: Dorsey Press, 1975.

Kurpius, D. J. Consultation theory and process: An integrated model. *Personnel & Guidance Journal*, 1978, 56(6).

Lee, E. Suicide and youth. *Personnel & Guidance Journal*, 1979, 57, 201–202.

Lefton, R. E., Buzzotta, V. R., Sherberg, M., & Karraker, D. L. *Effective motivation through performance appraisal*. New York: John Wiley, 1977.

Lenning, O. T. Assessment and evaluation. In U. Delworth, G. Hanson, & Associates. *Student services—A handbook for the profession*. San Francisco: Jossey-Bass, 1980.

Lewis, J. A., & Lewis, M. D. *Community counseling: A human services approach*. New York: John Wiley, 1977.

Lewis, M. D., & Lewis, J. A. The counselor's impact on community environments. *Personnel & Guidance Journal*, 1977, 55, 356–358.

Liptzin, B., Stockdill, J. W., & Brown, B. S. A federal view of mental health program evaluations. *Professional Psychology*, 1977, *8*, 543–552.

Loughary, J. W. The computer is in. *Personnel & Guidance Journal*, 1970, *49*(3), 185–186.

Maddox, G. L., & McCall, B. C. *Drinking among teenagers: A sociological interpretation of alcohol use by high school students*. New Brunswick, N.J.: Rutgers Center of Alcohol Studies, 1964.

Margolis, R., & Popkin, N. Marijuana: A review of medical research with implications for adolescents. *Personnel & Guidance Journal*, 1980, 59(1), 7.

Meeks, A. R. Guidance in the elementary school. *Journal of the National Education Association*, 1962, *51*, 30.

Miller, G. D. *ASCA role statement*. American School Counselors Association. Leesburg, VA., 1981.

Miller, G. M., & Pappas, J. G. Middle school counselors view their priorities. *Elementary School Guidance and Counseling*, 1978, *4*, 291.

Miller, T. K., & Prince, J. S. *The future of student affairs*. San Francisco: Jossey-Bass, 1976.

Miringoff, M. L. *Management in human service organizations*, New York: Macmillan, 1980.

Moorefield, S. North, south, east and west side story. *American Education*, 1977, *XIII*, 12–16.

Morrisett, L. Educational assessment and the junior college. *The Junior College Journal*, 1967, *37*, 12–14.

Moos, R. Evaluating treatment environments: A social-ecological approach. In R. H. Moos, *Evaluating Correctional & Community Settings*. New York: John Wiley, 1975.

Morgan, L. B. The counselor's role in suicide prevention. *Personnel & Guidance Journal,* 1981, 59(5), 284–286.

Mueller, K. H. *Student personnel work in higher education.* Boston: Houghton Mifflin, 1961.

Myrick, R. D. The practice of counseling in the elementary school. *The Status of Guidance and Counseling in the Nation's Schools.* Washington, D.C.: American Personnel & Guidance Association, 1977.

McCully, C. H. *Works of C. Harold McCully* (compiled by L. L. Miller) *Challenge for change in counselor education.* Minneapolis, MN.: Burgess, 1969.

McDaniel, J. W., & Lombardi, R. Organization and administration of student personnel work in the community college. In T. O'Banion & A. Thurston (Eds.), *Student Development Programs in the Community Junior College.* Englewood Cliffs, N.J.: Prentice-Hall, 1972.

McDavis, R. J. The development and validation of an instrument to evaluate student personnel services in colleges and universities. Unpublished doctoral dissertation, The University of Toledo, 1974.

McDowell, C. F. An analysis of leisure counseling orientations and models and their integrative possibilities. In D. M. Compton & J. E. Goldstein (Eds.), *Perspectives of Leisure Counseling.* Arlington, VA.: National Recreation & Park Association, 1977, 59–75.

McGuire, W. Teacher Burnout. *Today's Education.* 1979, *68*(4), 5–7.

National Education Association and the American Medical Association. *Joint Committee on Health Problems in Education.* Prepared by the National Committee on School Health Policies, Washington, D.C., 1966.

National Employment Counselors Association. Role of the employment counselor. *Journal of Employment Counseling,* 1975, *12,* 148–149.

National Institute of Education. *Safe schools—Violent schools.* Washington, D.C.: Government Printing Office, 1977.

National Institute of Mental Health. *A working manual of simple program evaluation techniques for community mental health centers.* Rockville, MD.: U.S. Department of Health, Educatioin & Welfare, 1976.

North Central Association of Colleges and Schools. Commission on Institutions of Higher Education. *Handbook on accreditation.* Boulder, CO., 1975.

North Central Association of Colleges and Secondary Schools (Guidance Committee). Paraprofessionals in school counseling programs, 1972. R. L. Gibson, chairperson.

North Central Association. Commission on Institutions of Higher Education. Draft: Guide for the evaluation and accreditation of postsecondary and higher education institutions, 1981.

O'Banion, T., & Thurston, A. (Eds.). *Student development programs in the community junior college.* Englewood Cliffs, N.J.: Prentice-Hall, 1972.

O'Banion, T., Thurston, A., & Gulden, J. Junior college student personnel work: An emerging model. In T. O'Banion & A. Thurston (Eds.), *Student development programs in the community junior college.* Englewood Cliffs, N.J.: Prentice-Hall, 1972.

O'Brien, C. R., Johnson, J. L., & Miller, B. Counseling the aging: Some practical considerations. *Personnel & Guidance Journal,* 1979, 57(6), 288–290.

Packwood, W. T. (Ed.). *College student personnel services.* Springfield, IL.: Charles C. Thomas, 1977.

Pate, R. H., Jr. The counselor in a psychological society. *Personnel & Guidance Journal,* 1980, 58(8), 521.

Patouillet, R. A., & Marin, R. L. Guidance: Agent of the counterculture. *Elementary School Guidance and Counseling,* 1979, *13*(4), 244–247.

Patterson, C. H. *The counselor in the school.* New York: McGraw-Hill, 1967.

Personnel and Guidance Journal, 1970, *49*(3).

Personnel and Guidance Journal. A brief look at computers. Adapted with permission from material published by the American Federation of Information Processing Societies. 1970, *49*(3), 1973.

Peter, L. J., & Hull, R. *The peter principle.* New York: William Morrow, 1959.

Peterson, W. D., Eddy, J., & Pitts, G. D. Historical perspectives of college student personnel work. In J. Eddy, J. Dameron & D. Borland, *College student personnel development, administration and counseling.* Lanham, MD.: University Press of America, 1980.

Pine, A., & Masluch, C. Characteristics of staff burnout in mental health settings. *Hospital & Community Psychiatry.* 1978, *29,* 233–237.

Podemski, R. S., & Childers, J. H., Jr. The counselor as change agent: An organizational analysis. *The School Counselor,* 1980, 27(3), 1973.

Prediger, D. J., Roth, J. D., & Noeth, R. J. *Nationwide study of student career development: Summary of results.* The American College Testing Program, Research and Development Division, No. 61, 1973.

President's Commission on Mental Health. *Report to the President.* Washington, D.C.: U.S. Government Printing Office, 1978.

Purkey, W. W. *Self concept and school achievement.* Englewood Cliffs, N.J.: Prentice-Hall, 1970.

Rachal, J. V., Williams, J. R., Brehm, M. L., Cavanaugh, B., Moore, R. P., & Eckerman, W. C. *A national study of adolescent drinking behavior, attitudes, correlates.* Rockville, MD.: National Institute of Alcoholism & Alcohol Abuse, 1975.

Robertson, I. *Sociology.* New York: Worth Publishing Company, 1977.

Ryan, C. W., & Sutton, J. M., Jr. Perceptions of career education: Implications for school counselors. *The School Counselor,* 1978, *25*(4), 265–269.

Rudolph, F. *The American college and university—A history.* New York: Vintage Books, 1962.

Sanders, I. T. *The community: An introduction to a social system* (2nd ed.). New York: Ronald Press, 1966.

Schmidt, L. D. Why has the professional practice of psychological counseling developed in the United States? *The Counseling Psychologists,* 1977, *7*(2), 19–21.

Schneider, A. A. *Counseling and the Adolescent.* San Francisco: Chandler, 1967.

Schneider, L. D. Junior college services. In W. T. Packwood (Ed.), *College student personnel services.* Springwood, IL.: Charles C. Thomas, 1977.

Shane, J. G., Shane, H. G., Gibson, R. L., & Munger, P. F. *Guiding human development.* Belmont, CA.: Wadsworth, 1971.

Shaw, M. C. The development of counseling programs: Priorities, progress and professionalism. *Personnel & Guidance Journal,* 1977, *55*(6), 339.

Shertzer, B., & Stone, S. *Fundamentals of Guidance* (4th ed.). Boston: Houghton-Mifflin, 1981.

Slater, A. D. A study of use of alcoholic beverages among high school students in Utah. *Quarterly Journal of Studies on Alcoholism,* 1952. *13,* 78–86.

Solzhenitsyn, A. *One Day in the Life of Ivan Deriesovich.* New York: Dalton, 1963.

Spergel, I. Community problem solving. Chicago: University of Chicago Press, 1969.

Spiegel, J. *Transactions.* New York: Science House, 1971.

Spoth, R., & Rosenthal, D. Wanted: A developmentally oriented alcohol prevention program. *Personnel & Guidance Journal,* 1980, *59*(4), 212.

Springer, C. H. The systems approach. *Saturday Review,* 1967, *50*(2), 56.

Srebalus, D. J., Marinelli, R. P., & Messing, J. K. *Career development: Concepts and procedures.* Monterey, CA.: Brooks/Cole, 1982.

Stamm, M. L., & Nissman, B. S. *Improving middle school guidance: Practical procedures for counselors, teachers, and administrators.* Boston: Allyn & Bacon, 1979.

Starr, J. M. Guidance practices in selected junior colleges in the Northwest. *Junior College Journal,* 1961, *31,* 442–445.

Steiner, R. *Managing the human service organization: From survival to achievement.* Beverly Hills, CA.: Sage, 1977.

Stiltner, B. Needs assessment: A first step. *Elementary School Guidance and Counseling,* 1978, *12*(4), 239–240.

Strang, R. *The role of the teacher in personnel work.* New York: Teachers College, Columbia University, 1935.

Super, D. *Computer assisted counseling.* New York: Teachers College Press, 1969.

Sylwester, R. Stress. *Instructor,* March, 1977, 72–76.

Tannebaum, R., & Schmidt, W. H. How to choose a leadership pattern. *Harvard Business Review,* 1973, *51,* 162–180.

Taplin, J. R. Crisis theory: Critique and reformulation. *Community Mental Health Journal,* 1971, *7,* 13–23.

Tegtmeyer, V. The role of the school counselor in facilitating sexual development. *Personnel & Guidance Journal,* 1980, *58*(6), 433.

Terreberry, S. The evolution of organizational environments. *Administrative Science Quarterly,* 1967, *12,* 490–613.

Thompson, J. W. The growing role of community colleges. *Journal of College Student Personnel,* 1978, *19,* 11–15.

Thurston, A. The decade ahead. In T. O'Banion and A. Thurston, *Student development programs in the community junior college.* Englewood Cliffs, N.J.: Prentice-Hall, 1972.

Tindall, Judy (Column Editor). Middle/Junior high school counselors' corner. *Elementary School Guidance and Counseling Journal,* 1978, *12*(4), 291.

Tinsley, H. E. A. & Tinsley, D. J. An analysis of leisure counseling models. *The Counseling Psychologist,* 9(3), 45.

Tondow, M., & Betts, M. L. Computer-based course selection & counseling. *Journal of Educational Data Processing,* 1967, *4,* 216–241.

Townsend, R. *Up the organization.* New York: Knopf, 1970.

U.S. Bureau of the Census. *Statistical Abstract of the U.S.: 1976* (95th ed.). Washington, D.C.

U.S. Bureau of the Census. *Statistical Abstract of the U.S.: 1980* (100 1st ed.). Washington, D.C. 1980: Government Printing Office.

Van Hoose, W. H., Pietrofesa, J. J., & Carlson, J. *Elementary school guidance and counseling: A composite view.* Boston: Houghton Mifflin, 1973.

Vitalo, R. L. A course in life skills. *Journal of College Student Personnel,* 1974, *15,* 34–38.
Wall, W. D. *Education and mental health.* Paris, France: UNESCO, 1955.
Walsh, D. Classroom stress and teacher burnout. *Phi Delta Kappan,* 1979, *61*(4), 253.
Walz, G. Technology in guidance: A conceptual overview. *Personnel & Guidance Journal,* 1970, *49*(3), 175.
Walz, G., & Benjamin, L. A change agent strategy for counselors functioning as consultants. *Personnel & Guidance Journal,* 1978, *56,* 331–334.
Warheit, G. J., Bell, R. A., & Schwab, J. J. *Planning for change: Needs assessment approaches.* Gainesville, FL.: J. Hillis Miller Health Center, University of Florida, 1974.
Warnath, C., & Shelton, J. The ultimate disappointment: The burned-out counselor. *Personnel & Guidance Journal,* 1976, *55,* 172–195.
Warner, R. W., Jr. Individual counseling. Atlanta, GA.: Georgia Department of Education, 1980. In J. C. Hansen, R. K. Stevic & R. W. Warner, Jr., *Counseling: Theory and process* (3rd ed.). Boston: Allyn & Bacon, 1982.
Warren, R. L. *The community in America* (2nd ed.). Chicago: Rand McNally, 1972.
Weissman, S., & Montgomery, G. Techniques for group family enrichment. *Personnel & Guidance Journal,* 1980, *59*(2), 113.
West Virginia State Department of Education. Bureau of Vocational-Technical and Adult Education. *The comprehensive community-career and vocational guidance and counseling model.* Charleston, WV.: 1979.
Wheeler, P. T., & Loesch, L. Program evaluation and counseling: Yesterday, today and tomorrow. *Personnel & Guidance Journal,* 1981, *59*(9), 573.
Williamson, E. G. *Student personnel services in colleges and universities.* New York: McGraw-Hill, 1961.
Woodcock, M., & Francis, D. *Unblocking your organization.* La Jolla, CA.: University Associates, 1979.
Worzbyt, J. C. *Elementary school guidance: Program planning, organization and implementation.* Harrisburg, PA.: Pennsylvania State Department of Education, 1978.
Young, N. K. Secondary school counselors and family systems. *The School Counselor,* 1979, *26*(4), 247–253.
Zimpfer, D. G. *Selection & Training of paraprofessionals for counseling & personnel work in education.* Kent, OH.: Bureau of Educational Research & Services, Monograph Series, Kent State University, 1979.

Name Index

Subject Index